GROWING BERRIES AND GRAPES AT HOME

BY J. HAROLD CLARKE

With a New Foreword by the Author

DOVER PUBLICATIONS, INC., *New York*

Published in Canada by General Publishing
Company, Ltd., 30 Lesmill Road, Don Mills,
Toronto, Ontario.
Published in the United Kingdom by Constable
and Company, Ltd., 10 Orange Street, London WC 2.

This Dover edition, first published in 1976, is
an unabridged republication of the work originally
published in 1958 with the title *Small Fruits for
Your Home Garden* by Doubleday & Company, Inc.,
Garden City, N.Y., to which has been added a new
Foreword specially written by the author for the
present edition.

International Standard Book Number: 0-486-23274-3
Library of Congress Catalog Card Number: 75-32365

Manufactured in the United States of America
Dover Publications, Inc.
180 Varick Street
New York, N.Y. 10014

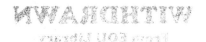

Foreword to the Dover Edition

It might seem that a horticultural book printed in 1958 and reprinted less than twenty years later should require little or no revision. However, there have been developments which require a change in certain items of information valid only twenty years ago. These revisions are in the field of pest control and variety recommendations.

THE USE OF PESTICIDES. At the time this book was written, home gardeners were using many of the spray materials then recommended for commercial growers. As new and more effective pesticides were developed, the organic gardening movement became more aggressive and, with the aid of groups which have become known as "the environmentalists," Congress was induced to pass legislation which effectively prohibited home gardeners from using a great many of the more valuable pesticides. These restrictions now apply almost as harshly against commercial fruit growers. Pesticides cannot be used except for the particular crops and at the rates and the times of applications indicated on the labels. Registration of pesticides requires such careful testing that it is extremely expensive, and under present law registrations must be obtained for each crop and pest. There are a very few chemicals which can be used for the control of insects, diseases or weeds in the home garden but in general the home gardener is the forgotten man in this particular field.

Registered pesticides may have their registration withdrawn by the Environmental Protection Agency, and so specific recommendations made in this book might be outdated at any time.

It is true that a number of pesticides may be found on the shelves at the garden center, but many of the most effective materials are absent. As a general rule the home gardener may safely purchase and use, according to the labels on the packages, any materials displayed for use by legitimate dealers, since retailers must be quite conscious of the regulations with which they are bound to conform.

Home gardeners coping with pests they find difficult to control should check with their County Agricultural Agent or write to the State Extension Service asking for current recommendations.

CHEMICALS MAY NOT BE NEEDED. It should be remembered that very often no sprays are required to control insects or diseases of small fruits. Certainly no sprays should be applied unless there is an evident and important need for them. Every gardener has weed problems but weeds can usually be controlled by cultivation or by mulching, so that chemical herbicides will probably not be needed in most cases.

Much has been said about biological control of pests but it has probably been oversold. The most important biological control is undoubtedly the use of varieties which have genetic resistance to important diseases and, in some cases, even to serious insect pests. Many of the new berry varieties being introduced by experiment stations are considered important additions to our gardens for the very reason that they are resistant or immune to serious diseases caused by fungi or viruses. Other biological methods of control, such as the use of predator insects and the growing of certain companion plants to repel insects or nematodes, are still largely experimental. The idea that plants will be more disease-free and insect-free if grown without chemical fertilizers appears to have no basis in scientific fact.

THE NEWER VARIETIES. In Chapter 19 of the first edition I told something of the work of plant breeders in producing better varieties of berries and other fruits. Some of the promise indicated there has been fulfilled to the benefit of both commercial growers and home gardeners. Much of this breeding was directed at resistance to pests and to unfavorable local conditions such as low temperature, heat, drought, and lack of dormancy-inducing day length and chilling. For best results the home gardener should, as far as possible, choose varieties bred for, and adapted to, his own particular area.

A description of all the newer varieties of berries, including their specific virtues, would take more than our available space. The following lists are offered with the suggestion that supplemental information be secured from local sources such as county agricultural agents and state experiment stations. All have been named in recent lists of recommended varieties from one or more states.

And what about the older varieties included in this book? A few are undoubtedly inferior to the newer sorts but most are still good. Combined with the newer introductions, they present to the home gardener a wealth of material to choose from, material on the average of better quality and more satisfactory than ever before available.

No listing of the newer wine grapes is included although a great deal of progress has been made in this field. However, to produce acceptable wines, in most parts of the country, the grape varieties should be carefully matched with soil, climate and general culture required by those specific varieties. This indicates the necessity of securing local information.

The following tables include some of the promising varieties introduced, or recommended, for certain states since the first edition of this book. With few exceptions, they are presented as additions to the previous lists rather than as substitutes. Varieties marked with an asterisk (*) are considered to be everbearers.

ADDITIONS TO TABLE XII (see page 178)
Strawberries

New England	*New York*	*Other Middle Atlantic States*	*Great Lakes Area*
Earlibelle	Fletcher	Darrow	Fletcher
Garnet	Garnet	Earliglow	Marlate
Guardian	Holiday	Marlate	Midway
Midway		Midway	Redchief
Ozark Beauty*	*Gulf States*	Raritan	Redglow
Redglow	Dabreak	Redchief	Sunrise
Sunrise	Headliner	Redstar	
Suwanee	Tangi	Vesper	*Great Plains*
Vesper			Fort Laramie*
	Central Missis-sippi Valley	*Northern Missis-sippi Valley*	
Southeastern States	Atlas	Badgerbelle	*California*
Apollo	Cyclone	Ogallala*	Fresno
Atlas	Delite	Ozark Beauty*	Sequoia
Earlibelle	Guardian	Redcoat	Tioga
Sunrise	Marlate	Stoplight	Tufts
Titan	Midway	Trumpeter	(these replace
	Redchief		Lassen and
	Sunrise		Shasta)
			Northwest
			Benton
			Hood
			Olympus
			Quinalt*
			Rainier
			Shuksan

ADDITIONS TO TABLE XIII (see page 214)
Raspberries

New England
Black Hawk—black
Clyde—purple
Earlired—red
Fallred*—red
Success—purple

Other Middle Atlantic States
Allegany—black
Allen—black
Citadel—red
Heritage*—red
Reveille—red
Scepter*—red
Sentry—red
Southland*—red

Lower Mississippi Valley
Allen—black
Fallred*—red
Scepter*—red

New York
Allen—black
Citadel—red
Clyde—purple
Jewel—black
Heritage*—red
Hilton—red

Southeastern States
Cherokee*—red
Dormanred—red
Heritage*—red
Pocahontas—red
Southland*—red

Upper Mississippi Valley
Amethyst—purple
Black Hawk—black
Boyne—red
Fallred*—red
Itasca—red

Northwest
Fairview—red
Meeker—red

ADDITIONS TO TABLE XIV (see page 238)
Blackberries

REGION	BUSH	TRAILING
New York and New England	Darrow	Smoothstem
Middle Atlantic	Darrow Cherokee Comanche Ranger Raven	Black Satin Dirksen Thornless Smoothstem Thornfree (all the above are thornless)
Southeast	Ebony King	Caroline Early June Flint Gem Georgia Thornless
Gulf States	Brazos	Flordagrand Oklawaha
Lower Mississippi Valley	Cherokee Comanche	
Southwest	Early Wonder	
Central Mississippi Valley		Black Satin Dirksen Thornless

ADDITIONS TO TABLE XV (see page 269)
Blueberries

REGION	HIGHBUSH	RABBITEYE
Middle Atlantic	Collins	
	Lateblue	
Southeast	Harrison	Bluebelle
	Morrow	Climax
		Garden Blue
		Menditoo
		Woodard
Gulf States		Bluebelle
		Bluegem
		Briteblue
		Climax
		Coastal
		Delite
		Menditoo
		Southland
Great Lakes	Bluehaven	
	Elliott	
Northern Missis-sippi Valley	Northland	

ADDITIONS TO TABLE XVI (see page 302)
Table Grapes

REGION	BUNCH	MUSCADINE
New England	Romulus	
New York	Alden Buffalo Himrod Romulus Suffolk Red	
Middle Atlantic	Himrod Lakemont Price Rosebelle Steuben	
Southeast	Blue Lake	Albermarle Carlos Cowart Magnolia Noble Southland
Gulf States		Burgaw Carlos Chief Dearing Magoon Southland
Central States	Himrod	
Northwest	Island Belle Schuyler	

ACKNOWLEDGMENTS

In attempting to make my recommendations coincide with those of authorities who know local conditions best, I have contacted experiment station or extension horticulturists in nearly all the states for information. Their helpful co-operation is gratefully acknowledged. This information has been arranged to apply to districts larger than single states which required, inevitably, some close decisions. I hope that any apparent digressions from local recommendations will be minor and cause no confusion.

My gratitude extends to all horticulturists, and other scientists, past and present, who have helped to build up that great mass of research results which we now accept so casually as "basic information."

Especial thanks are expressed at this time to Dr. George M. Darrow, recently retired from the United States Department of Agriculture, where he was, for many years, in charge of small fruits research. He not only added many superior selections to our list of berry varieties, through his plant breeding efforts, but has written numerous bulletins on small fruits for both commercial growers and home gardeners. This appreciation is expressed, not only for suggestions regarding certain parts of this book, but especially for advice and co-operation over a period of many years.

My wife and my son, Paul E. Clarke, have valiantly carried on while I have neglected other things to get this written and are deserving of my sincerest gratitude.

J. H. C.

Contents

ACKNOWLEDGMENTS   xiii
LIST OF ILLUSTRATIONS   xix
INTRODUCTION   xxi

PART ONE: THINGS TO CONSIDER BEFORE ATTEMPTING TO GROW SMALL FRUITS

1. REASONS FOR GROWING SMALL FRUITS AT HOME   2
Small space required; reliability; freshness; for freezing or preserving; landscape use; what are small fruits?

2. SUITABLE CLIMATE FOR THE VARIOUS SMALL FRUITS   10
Where small fruits are grown commercially; where they can be grown; the best areas and possible areas; effect of summer heat, winter cold, spring frosts; water requirements; methods of offsetting unfavorable climate.

3. SOIL CONDITIONS ARE VERY IMPORTANT   26
What is a good soil for berries; special requirements for special fruits; unfavorable soils may be improved.

PART TWO: METHODS OF CULTURE, FERTILIZING, AND PEST CONTROL

4. MODERN CULTURAL METHODS   40
Why cultivate; erosion problems; cover crops; soil conditioners; mulching and its problems.

5. FEEDING THE PLANTS   61
How plants grow; elements supplied by the soil; the major and minor elements; deficiency symptoms; soil acidity; organic vs. inorganic; dry and liquid fertilizers; foliar feeding; effects of overfeeding.

6. PROBLEMS OF TOO LITTLE OR TOO MUCH WATER   86
How plants use water; too little—irrigation methods; too much—drainage problems.

7. MODERN METHODS OF WEED CONTROL   96
How weeds cause damage; harmless weeds; bad weeds; cultivation as a means of control; mulching; chemical weed control.

8. PREVENTION OF PLANT DISEASES   111
What causes plant diseases; how they injure the plant; types of diseases—virus, bacterial, fungus; resistant varieties; sanitary measures; spraying; the newer fungicides; spray equipment.

9. INSECTS AND THEIR CONTROL   135
Chewing and sucking insects; how they injure plants; control, sanitary measures, sprays; the new insecticides.

10. OTHER PESTS AND NUISANCES   147
Nematodes; birds; moles; rabbits.

11. DESIGNING AND PLANTING A SMALL FRUITS GARDEN   156
Kinds of small fruits to include; how many of each; planting as part of the vegetable garden, with tree fruits, as part of the landscape; grapes for shade; planting plans.

PART THREE: SPECIAL REQUIREMENTS FOR, AND INFORMATION ABOUT, THE VARIOUS FRUITS

12. START WITH STRAWBERRIES   174
Why strawberries are so generally grown; soil and climate; varieties; culture; pest control.

13. FRESH RASPBERRIES, HOW TO GROW THEM   211
Perishable, hard to get in the market, easy to grow; red, black, and purple types; varieties; where to plant; culture, insect and disease pests.

14. BLACKBERRIES AND DEWBERRIES   234
The various types; some rather aggressive; where to plant; varieties; culture; control of pests.

15. CURRANTS AND GOOSEBERRIES   249
Personal preferences; use in the landscape; varieties; culture; pest control.

16. THE CULTIVATED BLUEBERRY, OUR NEWEST FRUIT   263
The various types, Gulf to Canada; special soil requirements; landscape use; varieties; cultural requirements; disease and insect control.

17. SOME OTHER BERRY CROPS   289
The cranberry; highbush cranberry; elderberry; wonderberry.

18. GRAPES ARE FINE FOR THE HOME GARDEN   297
Go well with small fruits; types of grapes and their adaptability; how to use in the landscape; varieties; culture; pest control.

**19. WHAT THE PLANT BREEDERS ARE ACCOMPLISHING WITH SMALL
       FRUITS**   324
Many breeders working in this field; what has been accomplished; problems still unsolved; how the plant breeder works; amateur plant breeding.

20. YEAR-ROUND ENJOYMENT   341
Quick freezing methods; canning vs. freezing; preserves; jellies; juices.

21. COULD I MAKE A FEW DOLLARS FROM BERRIES?   354
Selling plants, fruit, jams, and jellies; how large a planting; the picker problem; a good 4-H project.

INDEX   365

List of Illustrations

PHOTOGRAPHS

To get berries that are really fresh—pick 'em yourself 3
Blueberries are beautiful 5
Sheridan grapes are excellent for the home garden 8
Covering strawberry rows with mulch after the first freeze 14
An unusually good crop on a single strawberry plant 22
Latham raspberries on soil that is almost pure sand 30
Puyallup raspberries in the Northwest 32
A stony soil which produces fine strawberries 35
A mulch keeps the weeds down and conserves moisture 48
These long clusters of blueberries will not size up well 57
Coville blueberry bush pruned to give fruit of good size 58
A homemade liquid fertilizer applicator 66
Well-fed Rubel blueberries 78
Contour planting will help distribute irrigation water evenly 87
Soaker hose irrigating strawberries 92
Too much water but soil ridged so roots are out of water 94
Weeds kept under control by frequent shallow cultivation 101
Pine needle mulch in newly set blueberry field 103
Blueberries mulched with sawdust in the row 106
Red raspberry shoot infected with mosaic 117
Old fruiting raspberry canes cut out to be burned 124
Clean foliage and fruit indicate freedom from pests 136
Spraying for pest control 141
A sure way to keep birds from stealing blueberries 151
Cheesecloth cover is effective in excluding birds 153
Home garden with blackberries, raspberries, strawberries 159
The Delaware grape, delicious to eat out of hand 162
A cool and attractive spot under a simple grape arbor 163
A rather formal grape arbor during the dormant season 165
Blueberries in tubs may be moved where desired 170
A posthole digger used to lift out a strawberry plant 183
Setting plant dug with a posthole digger 185
A sawdust mulch has kept weeds down and berries clean 196
A fruiting lateral of the Puyallup red raspberry 212

Red raspberries trained to a trellis of poles   219
Red raspberry canes may be made to support themselves   224
Two quarts of luscious bush blackberries   235
Jerseyblack, Brainerd, and Evergreen blackberries   240
Lucretia dewberries growing on a two-wire trellis   244
Chautauqua gooseberries, a very large, green fruited variety   250
A well-pruned red currant bush   255
A well-branched two-year-old blueberry plant   273
This bush of Atlantic blueberry has been well pruned   278
Blueberry picker with small pail attached to her waist   279
Home garden strawberry patch adjacent to cranberry bog   291
Two varieties of elderberry growing in New Jersey   292
Ripe fruit of Adams elderberry   294
Vinifera grapes to cover a small arbor   299
Delaware grapes ripening uniformly   311
A grape vine, American type, on a Kniffin trellis   314
Vine pictured on page 314 after pruning   315
Plant breeders C. D. Schwartze and George M. Darrow   326
Strawberry crosses can easily be made on potted plants   329
Paper bags cover flower clusters ready for pollination   335
The Atlantic blueberry, a product of plant breeding   338
Garden-fresh berries dipped in confectioners' sugar   342
A "gift package" of strawberries in an egg carton   347
Single layer field trays for local sales   357
Latham raspberries packed with the cavities turned down   361

The above photographs are by the author.

DRAWINGS
Small fruits combined with a vegetable garden   161
Strawberry planting depths and planting systems   182
Novel methods of planting strawberries   188
Methods of pruning and training brambles   222

Introduction

The increase in knowledge of small fruits problems has been rapid the past few years, keeping pace with the advancement of the science of agriculture and of science in general. For example, the study of virus diseases in the strawberry has led to methods of producing virus-free plants which can practically revolutionize strawberry growing. The breeders of small fruits have learned how to "breed in" resistance or immunity to some of the previously incurable diseases. At the same time they have developed new qualities of flavor and adaptability to adverse soil and climatic conditions. The development of new chemicals has permitted the control of certain insects, diseases, and weeds which had been discouraging to both commercial growers and home gardeners.

SCIENCE AND AGRICULTURE. That this is an age of unprecedented scientific progress is being constantly impressed upon us by radio, television, movies, the daily press, and hundreds of magazines and technical journals. But we may not have realized that almost every new development in the general field of science affects agriculture in some way. In like manner new facts and principles worked out in the agricultural laboratory, or even in field plots, may be of unexpected value in other phases of science such as medicine or human nutrition. For example, radioactive isotopes, by-products of wartime atomic studies, are used to "tag" certain elements so the passage of nutrients from soil or fertilizer into and throughout the plant can be traced and studied. Much of the early work on antibiotics was based on soil researches in agricultural laboratories, and now it has been found that certain important plant diseases can be controlled by antibiotic sprays.

I do not mean to imply that every phase of berry growing has been solved, or even studied, by the scientists. Neither should it be assumed that berry growing is more complex than other forms of gardening, or that the person completely ignorant of scientific horticulture may not occasionally be very successful in this field. After all, many of the berries thrive in the wild with no help from man. It is simply my feeling that this book, giving the essentials of the art of growing small fruits in the home garden, as developed over many decades, should also include pertinent basic information supplied by modern research.

This is the age of the "how to" book, the "do it yourself" publicity, with "instructions a child can follow." I hope I will be forgiven if I try to word my instructions so they will convey something of the basic principles involved. Thus the gardener may solve for himself problems, when they arise, as they inevitably will, which are not specifically covered by "instructions." There may be a few like the fruitgrower whom I once heard say to an experiment station staff member, "We don't care about the reasons, just tell us what to spray with and we'll spray." However, in most meetings of fruitgrowers and home gardeners which I have attended, the desire was for basic background information as well as for the immediate recommendations.

This is not an encyclopedia, nor is it a "cookbook" presentation with recipes to be followed to the letter. Local conditions of weather, soils, and presence or absence of pests preclude the giving of such exact directions. It is to be hoped it will encourage additional reading and stimulate thought about growing things, and why they behave as they do.

For most of my life I have been connected in one way or another with scientific horticulture, as student, teacher, research worker and commercial grower. During that time I have published both technical articles and the simplest of popular stories for newspaper and magazine. These latter often seemed to me to be too "elementary" but this was difficult to determine. Perhaps the methods of the chemical laboratory have been developed to a higher degree than the methods of evaluating the effectiveness of the printed word presented in various ways. However, I am a believer in stressing the causes and reasons back of recommended horticultural practice, provided the reasons are not too vague or entirely too technical. And so in the following pages I hope to give as much of the scientific background as will serve a useful purpose.

THE COMMERCIAL GROWER. While this is being written primarily for the home gardener it should be of value to the small commercial grower. In the case of berry crops it is hard to draw the line between the home garden and commercial production. Many commercial enterprises have developed from a home berry patch, and many gardens bring in a few extra dollars from the sale of berries beyond the family's needs. Much of my work over the years has been with the commercial industry. Perhaps this book should have been directed toward them. But it seemed that the need was greater for something that might appeal particularly to the home gardener. Since the principles of plant growth, nutrition, and pest control are the same in the hundred-acre strawberry field as in the one-row "patch," the fundamental facts to be conveyed are the same. And, judging from my experience with garden clubs and various other groups of amateur gardeners, many of them are as far advanced scientifically as the commercial growers. Is it wishful thinking, therefore, to assume that a book written for the home gardener with an inquiring mind may find some readers among commercial growers, especially those who are just starting, or about to start, with a berry crop?

It might be noted that the principles of plant growth, and to a large extent the methods of culture, are essentially universal. Therefore, what is said in the following pages, although written primarily for the gardener in the United States, would apply also to gardeners in other lands, especially those with climatic conditions similar to ours. Of course there would be some differences in varieties, in the specific pests to be controlled, and in the terminology used. Plants do not recognize boundary lines and so methods recommended for our northern states should apply equally as well to those parts of Canada just across the border. For various reasons, including personal preferences, there are some differences in the varieties commonly grown, and so the Canadian reader might want to check with local sources of information on this particular subject.

There are various reasons for writing this book at the present time, besides the increase in actual total knowledge about small fruits. For many years, in experiment station work and out of it, I have been trying to answer questions about small fruits. Frequently there has been a request for the name of a book on small fruits which would answer the home gardener's questions. Many books have been written on this subject, it is true, some primarily for the student, others for the commercial grower only, some are out-of-date, some so general as to be of little help in answering any but the simplest questions. Some of the old books, written a hundred years ago, were excellent for their time and were written by gifted and devoted horticulturists. But fruitgrowing, even back-yard berry growing, is a science, whether we like it or not, and the science of a hundred years ago, or fifty, or even twenty-five, is not the science of today in any field.

Although there are magazines for almost every conceivable subject, there is no national magazine devoted to any of the berry crops. There is one exception, *Cranberries,* devoted to that fruit, which is the one that will probably never be adapted to home garden culture, except under a very rare set of conditions. Several national agricultural journals give some sporadic attention to small fruits, but they are not seen by most home gardeners.

MIGRATION TO AND FROM THE CITIES. Years ago, as the migration from country to city was just getting into full swing, it seemed as if home fruitgrowing might be doomed. There was a tendency, even on the part of those staying on the farm, to rely on the commercial fruitgrower and to specialize on wheat, cotton, or hogs, just as the fruitgrower might be strictly an apple or peach grower. Perhaps that trend, from an economic standpoint, was sound, but many quality-conscious farmers still grow their own berries, and with new varieties and new methods the number may well increase. Significantly, the recent trend among city dwellers has been toward the suburbs, the increased lawn and garden space being one of the impelling motives. Actually, this reverse migration has overflowed the suburbs, and around some of the larger cities the zone of "farms" occupied, if not always farmed, by commuters has extended for as much as fifty miles or more.

Anyone with garden space can grow a few berries. Potentially, this includes a major part of our population.

Part One

THINGS TO CONSIDER
BEFORE ATTEMPTING
TO GROW SMALL FRUITS

CHAPTER 1

Reasons for Growing Small Fruits at Home

The small fruits offer many advantages in minimum space requirements, earliness of bearing, and reliability of productiveness to those who definitely want to grow fruit of some kind for their own use. Tree fruits are fine, for the person who is in a position to give them the space and the care they require. But small fruits are the real home-garden fruits, and there are many good reasons for including some or all of the various types in the family garden. Pest control has always been less of a problem with small fruits than with the tree fruits. New developments in insect and disease control and the introduction of disease-resistant varieties, particularly of strawberries, make small fruits even more attractive.

THE MATTER OF SPACE. There are a few places where soil or climate are somewhat unfavorable, although in any locality where a lawn and ornamental plants will do reasonably well some of the small fruits can be expected to do at least as well. Of course there are some tiny yards where space just isn't available for anything larger than a geranium, and in the slightly larger garden there may still be more plants on the gardener's want list than there is usable space. If the gardener is mostly interested in lawn, shrubs, and flowers, but at least casually in fruit, then he might well consider how the small fruits could be integrated with the other garden elements without sacrificing the ornamental features.

On most farms, of course, there is ample space for a family small fruits plot. Such a planting is very commonly at one side of the vegetable garden. It is true that some farmers are too busy with the main farm business, involving very long hours, to grow any garden at all, but a relatively high percentage of farms do have gardens which contain one or more berry crops.

We are not particularly trying to "sell" the idea of small fruits for the home garden, but rather to help people make their decisions by presenting the pertinent facts; and, for those who are already planning to set out small fruit plants of some kind, to help them find solutions for their problems in so far as possible.

The best way to get berries that are really fresh—pick 'em yourself.

We shall stress, from time to time, that local advice may be needed in connection with problems closely tied to soil conditions, climate, and other factors. For the person interested in planting a berry crop but doubtful of the wisdom of doing so because of local conditions, a call to the county agricultural agent will bring advice on this, and also help in selecting the best varieties, and other useful information.

FRESHNESS IS DIFFICULT TO BUY. One of the most impelling reasons for wanting fresh berries is their unique flavor and generally excellent edible quality. This edible quality is closely associated with freshness, so that the best berries will come from one's own garden or from some other nearby source. Since certain berries, as for instance blackberries, must be fully ripe to have the highest quality, it is obvious that commercial handling of a real quality product is very difficult, if not impossible. It follows that with these particular fruits about the only way to have them at their peak flavor is to grow them.

Berries in the garden lend themselves admirably to "impulse" use. What could be better than a serving of fresh berries when mealtime creeps up with no dessert planned? Or what better as something special for the unexpected guest? For berries are almost universally liked.

Only those who have had intimate personal experience with berries can appreciate the joys of eating the fruit "out of hand," just as it is picked from the bush or vine. Personally, I consider that to be the ultimate in fruit-eating pleasure, and particularly toward the end of the season, when the scattering fruits remaining scarcely warrant a regular picking but their fully ripe sweetness is likely to compel a search for every last one, once we have started to sample them.

FOR HOME PROCESSING. While stressing the appeal of fresh fruit I do not want to belittle the importance and desirability of canned, preserved, and frozen berries. There are many fine products the homemaker can prepare from any home-grown berries not consumed fresh, but many of those products can be purchased and so may not constitute so potent an argument for home production. However, some homemade preserves, and other products, are not so easy to duplicate from the grocery shelf.

It would be somewhat difficult to determine accurately how consumption of berries in the average home compares with that of twenty-five, fifty, or a hundred years ago but I would guess it to be considerably less. This does not mean that people have lost their liking for fruit but simply reflects the changing face of modern agriculture as affected by higher costs. In the early days nearly every town and village had one or more nearby market gardeners who produced berries in season, often in conjunction with vegetables or tree fruits. Berries, picked early the same morning, were often peddled from house to house before noon. But in the commercial production of small fruits, either extensive or small scale, there is a great deal of hand labor, especially in harvesting the crop, and so far it has not been possible to replace much of it with machinery, although some progress has been made.

BERRIES DIFFICULT TO BUY. It is not only on the farm that high labor costs have worked against small fruits. In the grocery store, or supermarket, the trend is toward products which can be stacked on the counter, or in the freezing cabinet, and left there until the shopper picks them up. Berries are rather highly perishable and must be kept cool, looked over frequently for mold, and put in a

Cultivated blueberries are beautiful to look at as well as to eat.

cooler overnight. If the humidity is high, or if the berries have been picked wet, the problems are increased. And with the best of care losses may be high unless the grocer has stocked a minimum supply, or unless he works directly with some local and progressive grower who is especially careful about quality. As fresh berries have become less easy to obtain, prepared desserts, ice cream, canned fruits, and other products have become more readily available.

Time was when people looked forward eagerly for the first fresh berries, the first dessert of the early summer, and then placed their order for preserving berries toward the end of the season, when the price had come down. We no longer watch for that first fruit, nor recognize it when it appears. We have been having frozen berries the year round, and fresh fruits of various kinds, possibly including some berries, from distant producing sections, so "out of season" that we tend to forget just when the strawberry or raspberry season occurs. And so we find homemakers innocently asking for fresh currants in October, or for local strawberries when nearby plantings are just coming into bloom.

Some might say that we are getting along pretty well with our prepared desserts and puddings (possibly with box tops to be turned in for kitchen gadgets) and with our frozen berries always available. And I quite agree that frozen berries have been a boon to the industry, and to the consumer. But it just emphasizes the fact that, with supplies as they are, the family which wants a fair quantity of fresh berries during the season must live near a particularly good fruit stand or market, or near a commercial grower who sells at the farm, or must be prepared to grow its own supply.

VITAMINS AND OTHER NUTRITIVE VALUES. Although fresh berries have been getting scarcer on many tables there are good reasons, besides the pleasure of eating a delicious product, why most families might like to reverse that trend. The importance of fresh fruit in the diet of the average family has been emphasized by the researches into the value of vitamins, minerals, and other constituents, so that a fruit, or a fruit juice, has become the usual thing at breakfast.

Most of the berries are reasonably high in vitamin C, and in the minerals, acids, and flavor constituents which tend to give that sense of gustatory satisfaction so important to good digestion. It is difficult to present tables of nutrient values for small fruits because of the many kinds and varieties available. That varieties differ is abundantly evident. As a matter of fact the breeders are now working to increase nutrient values as well as size, appearance, and quality. Experiment station workers in New York reported vitamin C content of strawberry varieties studied varied from 40 to 104 milligrams of vitamin C per 100 grams of fruit. Workers in North Carolina found a rather wide range of vitamin C content in varieties of raspberries, dewberries, and blackberries. It is still not possible to buy berries with a guaranteed vitamin content, but it will probably be possible, one of these days, to purchase plants of varieties known to be relatively high with respect to vitamin-producing ability.

ADAPTED TO LANDSCAPE USE. There are many ways small fruit plantings may be worked into the landscape plan as definite decorative elements. Perhaps most gardeners who have ample space for vegetable and fruit production will prefer to design their plantings from a strictly utilitarian standpoint. Even in the larger garden, however, the small fruits may be located for efficiency in management and still fit harmoniously into the over-all landscape design. From the standpoint of efficiency, of course, we would like to have the plants in one or more rather long rows, especially if they are to be cultivated, although if there is to be a permanent mulch the long rows are not so important.

It is only a matter of common sense to put the bush fruits along the side of the garden where they will look the best, with relation to the other garden features. Often they can serve as a screen to hide an undesirable view, or as a fence to keep the neighborhood children from wandering too freely into the vegetable area. Very commonly a row or two of berries is used to separate the lawn and the flower area from the vegetable garden, a hedge serving as both screen and fence. In the smaller garden, or where no vegetables are raised, the bush fruits may be planted in groups in the shrub border, taking care, of course, that those brambles which send up suckers are so located that they do not make a nuisance of themselves.

In the very small garden individual bush fruit plants, such as blueberries, may be included in the perennial border very satisfactorily. But these are problems of design and are covered at greater length in the chapter on "Designing and Planting a Small Fruits Garden." At this stage we are concerned with the question of whether or not to plant any of the small fruits, and are just pointing out that the small size of the plants, their varied shapes and textures, do make possible their use in the landscape plan of the small home.

What has been said about the bush fruits applies equally well to grapes. In fact there are situations where a grapevine or two can be worked in to advantage even though there may be too little space for the other fruits. Certainly the pleasure of eating grapes plucked dead ripe from an overhead trellis is something to be remembered. Types of grapes are available for practically every climate and soil, except, unfortunately, for the area in which the author now lives, where the low summer temperature results in exuberant growth but the grapes do not ripen. In this same climate the berry crops ripen normally, although relatively late in the season.

THIS DISCUSSION INCLUDES GRAPES. The term "small fruits" usually includes those crops marketed under names which include the word "berries," as strawberries, raspberries, blackberries, dewberries, gooseberries, elderberries, blueberries, and cranberries. In addition currants are always included in the small fruits list. Although the combination is probably more often referred to as "small fruits and

Sheridan grapes, which are late ripening and keep longer than most of the "slip skin" varieties, are excellent for the home garden where there is a fairly long growing season.

grapes," grapes are sometimes considered as small fruits, and are included in this book because of their adaptability to home growing.

WHAT IS A BERRY? Botanically a berry consists of a fleshy ovary wall enclosing one or more seeds, and so a grape is a berry, as is a gooseberry, currant, blueberry, or cranberry. But so, for that matter, is a tomato. And the strawberry consists of a fleshy, edible receptacle, covered with akenes, which are dry, one-seeded fruits, similar to the seeds of the sunflower. The bramble fruits, including the raspberry, blackberry, and dewberry, are aggregate fruits, made up of a number of small individual fruits adhering to each other and to the receptacle. These small individual fruits with their single hard seed are known as drupes or drupelets, and technically are similar to the larger drupes such as the peach, plum, and apricot.

From the above it is evident that the "berries" are grouped together, horticulturally, for convenience, and that, aside from their low-growing habits, they have few points of resemblance. Each particular kind of berry, of course, does represent a definite botanical group. The brambles all belong to the genus *Rubus,* including a number of species, and are in the Rose family (Rosaceae), as is the strawberry, which is in the genus *Fragaria.* The currant and gooseberry both belong to the genus *Ribes,* of the Saxifrage family (Saxifragaceae). The cranberry and blueberry belong to the genus *Vaccinium* of the Heath family (Ericaceae). The grape belongs to the genus *Vitis,* Vine family (Vitaceae).

All of these fruits, of diverse botanical groups, are alike in producing edible fruits on rather small plants which are well adapted to growing in the home garden. Which are the best for a particular garden will depend greatly on local conditions, and the information developed in the following pages is designed to help each home gardener decide for himself which one to grow, or if he will try them all.

CHAPTER 2

Suitable Climate for the Various Small Fruits

Some small fruits are found in every state in the Union. It is true that in the desert states only a few people grow them and then, necessarily, under irrigation. On a small scale it would be possible to grow certain ones, especially strawberries, under what might seem almost impossible conditions by making up a soil mixture, possibly in some sort of a container or planter, and furnishing sufficient water. Partial shade might have to be provided also. This is an extreme case, but people who have homes in very desolate areas sometimes go to great lengths to have a little green around the house, a shrub or two, some flowers, and if desired a few strawberry plants in an artificially constructed bed. Such extreme methods are unnecessary, of course, in most of the states, as there are places in practically all of them where some of the small fruits will grow without extraordinary soil preparation. It is true that in many cases they will have to be given additional water, but that is more or less commonplace with commercial agriculture, as well as home gardening, in those drier climates.

COMMERCIAL BERRY-GROWING AREAS. It might be thought that the best conditions for small fruits would be found in those states where they are grown on an extensive commercial scale. This may indicate that conditions are relatively favorable, but not necessarily that they are the best. The fact that no berries are grown commercially nearby is no particular reason for avoiding small fruits. As a matter of fact there is usually more incentive in the noncommercial areas, as one of the prime reasons for growing berries in the home garden is that they are best when fresh, and do not stand long-distance shipments too well.

Very frequently, commercial production depends on concentration of population, hence a market for the product. Other factors which are important are the matter of transportation and precedent. Where berries have gotten started as a commercial crop, usually on a very small scale to begin with, the production often builds up for a number of reasons. Growers swap experiences, and may begin to buy or sell co-operatively. Buyers from distant cities begin to come in, and the more buyers there are the more profitable the berries may be and so more are produced, which in turn attracts more buyers. Processing plants are built where there is an ample supply of fruit, which in turn encourages additional planting. The soil and climatic conditions in the first place may have been no better than they are in an adjacent county or state, but the crop just got started in one district and not in the other.

TABLE I

Some of the States Where Small Fruits and Grapes Are Important Commercial Crops, Arranged Approximately in Order of Acreage.

Strawberries[1]	Raspberries	Blackberries and Dewberries
Oregon	Michigan	Oregon
California	Oregon	Texas
Tennessee	New York	California
Michigan	Washington	Washington
Louisiana	Ohio	Michigan
Washington	Pennsylvania	Arkansas
Arkansas	Minnesota	Oklahoma
Kentucky		Alabama
New York		North Carolina

Currants and Gooseberries	Cultivated Blueberries	Grapes
New York	New Jersey	California
Oregon	Michigan	New York
Washington	North Carolina	Michigan
Michigan	Washington	Pennsylvania
		Washington
		Ohio

[1] Acreage, especially of strawberries, varies from year to year, and so the order of listing the states might also vary somewhat, depending on whether the figures are for a particular year or an average of several years.

A knowledge of which are the more important states in the production of small fruits and grapes may be helpful, as it indicates, at least, that satisfactory soil and climatic conditions are to be found within their borders. A list of those states is given in Table I. However, just as satisfactory growing conditions may be found in a number of other states. It is also true that in some of the important commercial states good growing conditions are to be found in rather small areas. In the West there is heavy concentration of berry and grape production in certain favored valleys and there are relatively large areas where these crops could be grown commercially only with considerable difficulty.

HOME GARDEN BERRIES POSSIBLE ALMOST ANYWHERE. In many sections where the land is hilly or mountainous there will be small patches in valleys, or on gentle slopes, where home garden plantings of some of the berry crops would grow very well. In the very dry areas, of course, water may be a limiting factor, but, after all, a home in a particular spot must have sufficient water for household purposes. It takes very little more water to irrigate a small patch of strawberries, or other berries, or a small vegetable garden. It might be said that generally small fruits will grow well in all agricultural crop areas where there is sufficient water available either from natural rainfall or irrigation.

Most cities have been started where there is a fair supply of water, and where soil conditions are sufficiently satisfactory to produce lawns and gardens about the houses. This may not be true about some mining towns, but in the suburbs of any of the larger towns and cities conditions reasonably favorable to small fruits are usually to be found. Of course it is true with berries, as it is with growing any other plants, that the more extreme the environmental conditions the more extreme will need to be the measures to modify or overcome them.

SUMMER HEAT. Those who live in the northern part of the country may seldom think of summer heat as a limiting factor in the production of crops, but it is often so. Several types of berries, and particularly certain varieties, do not do well where there are many days of temperatures close to 100 degrees. Of course it is difficult to separate the effects of summer heat, length of day, drouth, and unfavorable soil conditions, as all of them may be factors in producing unsatisfactory growth.

Some crops, such as certain varieties of European grapes, seem to thrive on what many people would consider to be excessively high summer temperatures. However, most of the small fruits do not do as well where the summers are very hot as where they are more moderate. This simply means that those who live in regions of very high summer temperatures must be especially careful in selecting the varieties they attempt to grow. The harmful effects of heat may be direct or they may be indirect, resulting from too rapid drying out of the soil and the encouragement of red spider and certain diseases.

SPRINKLING TO PREVENT HEAT DAMAGE. High temperatures may be offset to some extent by partial shading or by judicious sprinkling. By the latter we mean not only sprinkling to provide sufficient soil moisture, but sprinkling during the hottest part of the day to lower the temperature and cut down on water loss from the leaves. Such sprinkling to lower the temperature might not be practical in those areas where there are a great many days of excessively high temperatures during the summer. In such areas the problem will have to be met mostly by the proper selection of varieties.

A steady high temperature is sometimes not as damaging as one or two days which are much warmer than the preceding period. This is well illustrated by what happens to cranberries in this general area, southwestern Washington. The summer temperatures are relatively low, seldom going above 70 degrees. This results in rather succulent growth, especially when there are several days of cloudy weather. Under these conditions a single day of a temperature around 85 degrees, during early or midsummer, may cause serious damage, burning the growing tips and scalding the developing berries. Cranberry growers, in order to combat this hazard and also to combat frost, which will be mentioned later, installed sprinklers in most of their commercial producing fields. These sprinklers are turned on when the temperature gets to about 80 degrees, and the water evaporating from the surface of the berries and leaves lowers the temperature sufficiently so that damage is avoided. This practice is something to think about when you hear people caution against the use of water on plants during a hot sunny day. Perhaps it would be best to continue sprinkling, once it has started during such a day, as there is a possibility that some scalding or burning might result if there is a light sprinkling and then it is stopped while the sun is extremely hot.

It is true that, under certain conditions, very frequent sprinkling may be conducive to the development of diseases such as mildew. But then one would have to decide whether the mildew or the possible heat damage is more important, and there is the possibility of minimizing the damage caused by the disease by the use of the proper fungicides.

Temporary shading during periods of extreme heat would be effective in reducing temperature, but seldom would one attempt to shade an entire berry planting. However, such measures might be worth considering for a small planting under extreme climate conditions. It is sometimes possible to plant berry crops where they will be partially shaded during the middle of the day or early in the afternoon when the heat damage is most likely to occur, although in most of the country these crops should have full sun. Under the chapters on the various fruits, mention will be made of some varieties that would be especially suitable for very hot conditions.

WINTER COLD. In the northern part of the country, winter cold may be a limiting factor. There are parts of the upper Mississippi Valley and the Great Plains states where only extremely hardy,

Covering strawberry rows with a mulch of salt hay after the first freeze has killed the cover crop of oats. They will be left covered until danger of freezing weather is past.

cold-resisting varieties should be attempted. Even here, cultural methods, especially the use of mulch on strawberries, and the proper care and possible winter protection of some of the brambles, will help to offset the likelihood of freezing injury. Resistance to cold will vary with different fruits and different varieties but, in general, if a temperature of minus 10 degrees, or colder, is to be expected most winters, then the gardener should be rather careful in selecting the varieties he expects to grow. Information as to hardiness of varieties may be available from the local county agent or other sources.

Some years ago a map was developed at the Arnold Arboretum, from Weather Bureau data, in which the United States was divided into nine zones based on the average annual minimum temperatures for each zone. Some nurseries indicate the zones in which a particular variety of plant will probably be hardy. One can look at the map and determine his zone number and thus be able to decide if the variety is one he would be justified in trying. This hardiness map has been further refined by Dr. Henry Skinner of the National Arboretum under the auspices of the American Horticultural Council.

Although the general concept of these zones is excellent, such maps can hardly be printed on a scale large enough for a person living in hilly country to determine exactly what his zone number is. In fact in an average-sized town, in rolling or mountainous country, the average minimum temperatures in different parts of the town might range through two zones, depending on altitude, exposure, and air drainage. You might reside in Zone 6 as indicated by the map, but your home might be in an unusually cold, or unusually favored, place, and by temperature be classified in Zone 5 or 7.

HARDINESS RATINGS. A few years ago I helped work out, for the American Rhododendron Society, a hardiness rating scale which has proven useful. This scale is based on *the minimum temperature during midwinter, which a well-matured and unprotected plant of a particular variety might be expected to withstand without any visible injury to leaf, stem, or flower.* The various classes are as follows:

H–1 hardy to −25°F (and possibly lower)
H–2 hardy to −15°F
H–3 hardy to −5°F   *H–5* hardy to +15°F
H–4 hardy to +5°F   *H–6* hardy to +25°F
                                       H–7 hardy to +32°F

Suggested ratings for a number of varieties of small fruits were submitted to several experiment station workers who are well qualified to criticize them. Naturally they did not all agree on every variety, as they have been observing berry crops under quite different growing conditions, but the area of agreement was sufficient to encourage the inclusion of a rating table which should be qualified as tentative or preliminary. The ratings as suggested are based on personal experience and a summary of the suggestions from other horticulturists. It is hoped they will be useful to gardeners who might like to try some variety from another part of the country.

TABLE II

Tentative Hardiness Ratings for Small Fruits and Grapes

Strawberries (unmulched; if well mulched at least one class lower)

Hardiest of all, Cheyenne varieties	*H–1*
Arrowhead, Dunlap, Evermore	*H–2*
Most varieties	*H–3*
Albritton	*H–4*

Red Raspberries

Chief, Durham, Latham, Sunrise	*H–1*
Newburgh, New Hampshire, Taylor	*H–2*
Canby, Sumner	*H–3*
Puyallup, Washington, Willamette	*H–4*
Mandarin	*H–5*
Rubus albescens	*H–7*

Black Raspberries   *H–2*

Purple Raspberries

Sodus, Success	*H–2*

Blackberries and Dewberries

Alfred, Snyder	*H–1*
Bailey, Eldorado, Hedrick	*H–2*
Blowers, Lawton, Lucretia	*H–3*
Boysen, Cascade, Chehalem	*H–4*
Austin, Evergreen, Himalaya, Logan, Olallie[2]	*H–4*
Regalness	*H–5*

Currants

Red Lake and most others	*H–1*

Gooseberries

Chautauqua, Como, Pixwell, Poorman, Welcome	*H–1*

[2] These five varieties are placed in the same class as the three directly above but are probably not quite so hardy.

Blueberries	
Bluecrop, Blueray, Concord, Earliblue	*H–1*
Other cultivated varieties	*H–2*
Rabbiteye varieties, *V. ovatum*	*H–4*
Cranberry, flooded	*H–1*
Cranberry, not flooded	*H–3*
Lingonberry	*H–1*
Elderberry, eastern	*H–1*
Elderberry, western	*H–2 and 3*
Highbush Cranberry	*H–1*
Grapes	
Beta	*H–1*
Concord, Fredonia, Red Amber	*H–2*
Other eastern varieties	*H–2 and 3*
Hardiest viniferas	*H–3*
Most viniferas	*H–4 and 5*
Muscadines	*H–4*

It must be realized that, while we may consider hardiness as an inherent or genetic characteristic, it can be greatly modified by growing conditions, maturity of the plant, and by temperature fluctuations as will be brought out later.

Most gardeners have a pretty good idea as to how cold it gets in their garden, and even in different places in the garden. It might pay those who do not to purchase a maximum-minimum thermometer and do some checking during the coldest winter weather and in the coldest part of the garden. Ten degrees may seem to be a large range for one hardiness rating step, but it is doubtful if a smaller range would be more satisfactory as growing conditions affect hardiness so much.

SPRING FROSTS. Spring frosts are a hazard in many areas, although they could hardly be considered as a limiting factor. It may be that, in a few frost pockets, the frequency of killing spring frosts would be sufficient to make home garden berries in those particular spots rather questionable. By the same token, however, the frosts would also play havoc with ornamental plants, particularly the shrubs, perennials, and bulbs. They would also be a hazard to the vegetable garden. In other words, if a person is interested in any form of gardening he will avoid such frost pockets if at all possible.

It is a well-known fact that cold air is heavier than warm air and tends to sink to the lowest level. If there are usually strong winds, especially at night, then the likelihood of frost damage is much less. During cold quiet nights, however, there is a very definite stratification of air with cold air next to the ground and progressively warmer strata above. Commercial growers take advantage of this when they use wind machines, with propellers of some type, to mix the warm air with cold, or to pull down the warm air and cause it to displace the heavier cold air.

The commercial orchardist and berry grower has learned to look over his available sites rather critically before actually planting. He likes to be up on a little slope if possible, with lower ground at one side so that there is an opportunity for cold air to drain off. This, of course, is impossible in very flat country and the average home garden is too small to have very much slope, and most building areas are likely to be on fairly low level ground. However, it is well to be conscious of the possibility of cold air draining into one's garden or, on the other hand, the possibility of air drainage out toward a lower area. The movement of air based only on differences in temperature is very easily interfered with by trees and shrubs. A hedge, for instance, will almost completely stop the flow of air on a frosty night. This means that any opening through such a barrier, to be effective in permitting cold air to drain out, will have to be at least several feet wide and not obstructed by shrubbery.

CHECK YOUR TEMPERATURES. If a gardener has any reason to suspect the possibility of such frost pockets, it would be well worth his time to borrow some of the neighbors' thermometers, first check them to see that they are all in agreement, and then place them at various spots in his garden during a cool or frosty night. The ideal way is to suspend them a few inches from the ground, all at the same height of course, and put a board a few inches above to prevent rain or dew from hitting them directly. By checking the temperatures a few nights, around midnight, or the wee small hours of the morning, if he wants to measure the coldest period, he will be able to tell whether there is any appreciable difference in the likelihood of frost in the various locations.

It would then seem to be wise to put the coldest areas in lawn, or some hardy ornamentals, or in the vegetable garden where plantings could be made late in the spring. It is true, of course, that in frost pockets early fall frosts are just as likely to be present as late spring frosts. However, with berry crops the early fall frosts are usually not important. In fact they may be desirable in tending to mature and "harden up" the tissues so that they will be more able to withstand low temperatures later in the winter.

RATE OF TEMPERATURE FALL IS IMPORTANT. In discussing temperatures it should be brought out that the actual minimum temperature is not the only factor affecting winter injury, but that the temperature during several days previous is also important. In other words, a warm spell in winter will make the plants more susceptible to winter injury. This has been worked out in some detail with peaches, but there is no reason to think that it is not also true with small fruits. By the same token, gradually increasing cold will cause the plants to harden up so that they will survive a temperature which would seriously injure them if preceded by relatively warm weather. It is interesting to know that after warm spells in the winter the plants are somewhat more tender, but that a following period of cold weather may again cause them to harden up and become more resistant. So if you have had plants winter injured one year at a given temperature but they survived the same temperature with no damage during another winter, you will probably find that the temperatures during the days and nights immediately previous to the cold spell were responsible. Another important factor, of course, is the condition, or growth status, of the plants, as in one case they may have been more highly fertilized too late in the summer and thus made more succulent and cold susceptible.

Where the planting has to be made on a spot known to be subject to frosts, then the question arises as to whether any protection may be provided. We are all familiar with the fact that orchards, especially in California, may be heated with oil heaters to prevent frost damage effectively, unless the temperature drops extremely low. In other orchards airplane propellers are placed on high towers, where they mix the warm air from above with the cold air near the ground. These are effective, within certain limits, and would give protection in the home garden, but probably are more or less out of reason in small suburban gardens because of expense, and because of possible trouble with the neighbors if oil heaters discharge soot over their homes.

SPRINKLING TO PREVENT FROST. The use of sprinklers to prevent frost is becoming more general. This idea was first developed on the cranberry farms of the Northwest, where practically all commercial bogs are now under sprinklers. When there is likelihood of frost the sprinklers are started and allowed to run until the temperature is definitely above 32 degrees, and apparently going to stay there. On very cold nights this may mean that there will be a coating of ice over the field by morning, although it does no particular harm as the cranberry vines are lying on, or close to, the ground, anyway. The use of sprinklers on nursery stock and tree fruits is just as effective in preventing frost damage, but may result in the accumulation of so much ice that the plants will be broken down. However, with strawberries, which are close to the ground, sprinkling is coming to be an accepted means of frost prevention in some areas. In the home garden, sprinkling could be used for strawberries, but one would need to be sure that adjacent shrubs or trees would not be covered enough to accumulate such a coating of ice that they might break down. With strawberries, and most other fruits also, the danger of frost damage usually is greatest from the time the flower buds begin to push until after the young fruits have started to develop.

The protection offered by sprinkling does not necessarily depend on the temperature of the water as it is applied, but rather on the heat of fusion which develops when water turns to the solid, or ice crystal, form. As long as there is free water on the outside of the leaf or flower, even though the plant may be encased in ice, the temperature of the plant tissues will stay around 32 degrees and there will ordinarily be no injury. Each gardener would have to consider the conditions in his own garden and the length of time he would have to let the sprinklers operate. If the soil is rather low and wet the excess water might be a problem. A rather fine mist is desirable, although, if it is too fine, light air currents may carry it away from the plants to be protected. Any type of sprinkler can be used but it should be one which will not clog easily, for if the sprinkler stops it may be burst by the pressure of ice and of course the plants would then be left unprotected.

The amount of protection which can practically be achieved by sprinkling has not been definitely determined, and would vary with conditions. It would amount to several degrees at least, possibly as much as 8 or 10. The flowers would not freeze at 32 degrees, but would at 29 or 30, so if there is 8-degree protection no appreciable damage should occur down to about 22 degrees. If sprinklers are to be used they should be started at about 32 or 33 degrees so they will be in operation when the temperature reaches the danger point.

STUDY WEATHER CONDITIONS. Any attempts to prevent frost damage will require close attention to weather forecasts and a careful study of local weather conditions. When checking temperatures to determine whether or not some form of frost protection for strawberries will be needed, one should keep in mind that the temperature at the level of the blossoms, on a cold, quiet night, will be 5 or 6 degrees lower than at eye level (5 feet) where most thermometers are mounted.

Occasionally it might be desirable to protect a small strawberry bed by covering it with some sort of blanket, a tarp, old bags, or what not. Where a straw mulch is used it is practical to fluff up the mulching material and put enough of it over the plants to cut down the possibility of frost damage very appreciably.

Fortunately, the larger growing berry plants, such as the brambles, are not so susceptible to frost; they bloom later and the flowers are at a considerable distance from the ground and thus avoid that very cold layer within a few inches of the soil surface. Late-ripening varieties of strawberries bloom later and so are less likely to be caught. In some cases the fact that the blossoms are normally borne on rather short stems, and so are under a protecting canopy of leaves, may be a factor. As a general rule, it is nice to have the berries growing on fairly long stems, so that they are out where one can find them at picking time, rather than nestled down in the crown of the plant. But in very cold spots the resistance to frost is more important.

Considerable emphasis has been laid on frost protection, but this applies specifically to "frosty" areas. Throughout most of the United States small fruits are grown quite satisfactorily with no protection against frost, and so the prospective home garden berry grower should not be unduly alarmed about this problem.

LENGTH OF DAY. Another climatic factor to be considered is the length of day or photoperiod. It is well known that certain varieties of strawberries grow along the Gulf Coast, others in the middle states, and still others in the northern states. It is not always easy to tell the reason why varieties seem to be thus limited to their particular areas. They are affected by many things—soil conditions, summer and winter temperatures, and rainfall. However, it was recently shown by Dr. George Darrow of the U. S. D. A. that strawberries are also very definitely affected by length of day. Some northern varieties do not do well when they are grown in Florida, for instance, where day length during the winter months is longer than it is further north. Northern varieties tend to become ever-bearing in habit when grown in the extreme South. With other plants, such as blueberries, length of day is possibly a factor, but resistance to low winter temperatures, or to summer heat, is probably more important in determining how far north or south varieties will grow and produce normally.

WATER REQUIREMENTS. If one were to rely entirely on natural rainfall, the amount of rain and its distribution during the season would be very important in determining where small fruits may be grown satisfactorily. However, irrigation is so common a practice now that it is more or less taken for granted, especially with crops of high acre value such as the small fruits. The irrigation required may vary from one or two applications a summer, in the fairly humid sections, to situations where all of the water must be applied. In general, the amount of water required would be about the same as

An unusually good crop on a single strawberry plant. The straw mulch prevented the splashing of sand or mud, so the berries can display all their natural beauty.

for a vegetable garden, or as needed to maintain a lawn and the ordinary garden flowers and shrubs in good condition. On deep soils, the grapes and brambles particularly will root quite deeply and be able to take advantage of all the moisture there is in the soil better than some other, more shallow rooted, plants. Grape and raspberry roots will go down as much as four to six feet if the subsoil is reasonably favorable for their penetration. Strawberries seldom root below sixteen or twenty inches and often less.

VARIETAL ADAPTABILITY. Small fruits are usually grown, not just as a "kind" of fruit, but as a horticultural variety of that fruit. Varieties originate rarely as bud mutations, usually as seedlings, either chance seedlings or from controlled crosses made by some plant breeder. The breeder selects those seedlings which appear to be promising and propagates them asexually. This means by taking off runners in the case of strawberries, by making cuttings of grapes, currants, and gooseberries, by taking tip layers from black raspberries and dewberries, and by making root cuttings or digging up suckers of red raspberries and the bush blackberries. The plants of a variety propagated in this way are all actually a part of the original seedling plant, and are identical with it and with each other, in so far as all their hereditary characteristics are concerned. It occasionally happens that one lot of plants of a given variety will appear to be quite different, and will grow quite differently from another lot of the same variety. This difference may be due to virus infection which will be discussed later.

The horticultural variety is the basis of all horticultural crop production. One variety may be very successful under certain conditions, whereas another variety might be an absolute failure under the same conditions. It is very important, therefore, to secure, not only a good variety, but one which is adapted to your particular soil and climatic conditions. Some varieties have a great deal more resistance to low temperatures than others. Some are late in starting and late in blooming and less likely to be caught by spring frosts. Some are adapted to a relatively long day during the winter and early spring and others to a relatively short day. Some are inclined to remain dormant for a long time in the early summer if they did not experience the amount of cold weather that they needed during the winter. Some are much more susceptible to diseases than are others. All this points up the importance of ordering plants of varieties which are known to be suitable for your particular area.

WHERE TO BUY PLANTS. In general it is possibly safest to buy from a nearby nursery, as they will likely have varieties which are suitable for local growing and the plants will be in transit a relatively short time. However, if you know the variety you want, and that it is adapted to your locality, then actually it may be grown in any reasonably satisfactory climate and, if moved to your garden, will do just as well as if the plants had been grown locally. In other words, the fact that the plants have been grown under a different set of conditions does not mean that they have become "acclimated" to those conditions and hence undesirable for your own use. The reaction of the plant is dependent on its genetic make-up and the environmental conditions which are found in your garden.

BUY FOR EDIBLE QUALITY. In choosing varieties for the home garden, attention should be given primarily to edible quality, flavor, and possibly size of berry, rather than to shipping quality. In other words, the best commercial variety in your neighborhood might not be the one which would give you the most pleasure in your own garden. Some varieties are like the Lupton strawberry, which for many years was a very important commercial variety in the East, although the berry was rather punky and dry and generally inferior in edible quality, but it was an excellent shipper. New varieties are being developed all the time, many of them very desirable. However, one should be careful about such new varieties, as, unfortunately, a few nurserymen have the habit of introducing new things frequently to obtain the publicity value of putting out something new, even though the variety may not be worth very much. It would be best, for your main planting at least, to stick to the list of varieties recommended for your area by your county agent or your agricultural experiment station.

Every gardener, whether he grows berries or not, should be able to read a nursery catalog with a critical eye. Statements of finest quality, jumbo size, and resistance to all kinds of pests are frequently overdrawn. If you will just think seriously and a bit critically, while reading a description of a new variety, you will probably be able to decide for yourself whether the claims made are overdrawn advertising claims or actually are the truth. A nurseryman advertising a variety for the first time may use all of the superlative adjectives, but if he is advertising an old variety he knows that many people are acquainted with it and that his description would immediately be spotted as a phony. The new variety may prove to be unreliable, but by that time he has another new one to describe and introduce. The reading of a nursery catalog is really an art and a science which should be studied by any gardener.

Much of the recent breeding work with small fruits has been done by various experiment stations and the U. S. Department of Agriculture. New varieties introduced by these agencies are thoroughly tested, especially in the states in which they originate, and the descriptions as given are as reliable and accurate as they can be made.

OFFSETTING UNFAVORABLE CONDITIONS. Varieties can sometimes be grown out of their optimum environment by certain cultural methods, which may often be beneficial in other ways, besides making it possible to grow the particular variety wanted. Irrigation has already been mentioned. Mulching, especially with strawberries, which is almost universal in the home garden to keep the berries clean, will also serve to prevent winter injury if properly applied in the right amount. These and other methods of offsetting unfavorable growing conditions will be discussed in connection with the individual fruits in later chapters.

CHAPTER 3

Soil Conditions Are Very Important

Berries are grown, both commercially and in the home garden, on a very wide range of soils, and for several reasons. In the first place, most of the small fruits are far from "fussy" about the kind of soil in which they are grown. Then the different kinds of fruits vary somewhat in their requirements, and one can usually find some one kind which will "do" on a particular soil. Furthermore, varieties of one kind of fruit may be quite different, one preferring a rather light soil, others soils which have more clay in them and so are called heavier. But probably the most important factor working in favor of the home gardener, who wants to grow berries, is the multitude of ways in which any given soil may be improved for a particular crop. If the soil is too heavy or too light, too moist or too dry, too acid or too alkaline, too poor or too rich, there are things which can be done to make it more nearly ideal for the crop in mind. Some of these things are strictly the result of modern agricultural research, others come simply from the accumulated wisdom of practical farmers and gardeners who have learned the hard way, but whose lessons have been passed on to son and daughter, and neighbor, until they have become a most important part of garden "know-how."

The ideal soil would be one which would grow a berry crop to perfection with the least amount of conditioning. Berries in general, like many vegetable, flower, and even grain, crops, prefer a deep, medium to light sandy loam, naturally fertile, relatively high in organic matter, with a water table at least two feet down in winter and not too low in summer. It should not be deficient in any important element, and relative freedom from noxious weeds and serious disease or insect pests is desirable. This is the ideal, but it is well to remember that if you can grow other crops you can grow at least some kinds of berries.

HEAVY AND LIGHT SOILS. In describing soils, the terms "light" and "heavy" are commonly used and perhaps should be defined. The term "heavy" refers to soils that are made up of very small particles.

Such soils are called clays, or if they are somewhat mixed with larger particles may be called clay loams. The soil scientists have definite descriptive terms, which they associate with certain particle sizes, as indicated in the following table.

TABLE III

NAME	DIAMETER OF PARTICLES IN MILLIMETERS
Gravel	2.0 and larger
Coarse sand	2.0 to 0.2
Fine sand	0.2 to 0.02
Silt	0.02 to 0.002
Clay	0.002 and smaller

A loam soil contains 20 to 50 per cent sand, 20 to 50 per cent silt, and 30 per cent or less clay. A sandy loam contains more sand, a clay loam more clay.

The clays, with their very small particle size, will have a very large number of particles in a given volume and a very large particle surface area. Such a soil will absorb and hold a large quantity of water and will dry out much slower than a coarser soil. This is a good trait in dry weather but in winter and spring may result in a soggy condition, poor drainage, and the death of many of the roots which had grown down the previous summer when the water table was low but are below the water level when it rises, as it usually does, during the winter or the rainy season. Under extreme conditions this may result in very shallow root systems and consequently more drouth injury on such wet soils than occurs on dryer areas.

The light soils are made up of coarse particles, called gravel or sand, and as more fine material is found the soil may be called a loamy sand, or a sandy loam. The sandy soils are, of course, well drained but tend to dry out quickly and to lose their available nutrients (plant foods) relatively rapidly by leaching during rainy weather.

So we see that each kind of soil has certain advantages and certain disadvantages. The commercial grower may weigh all these, decide on the type he wants for a particular crop, and then select the field most nearly meeting his specifications, or perhaps he may try to purchase land more suitable for his purpose. The home gardener, especially if he lives on a farm, may range as widely as his holdings permit in search of the best soil. He has probably already settled that question by selecting a site for a vegetable garden, considering not only soil but also convenience—accessibility to water and buildings where tools and supplies may be stored.

Actually, unless soil conditions are very unusual, other factors may be more important in locating the berry-growing area. This results in the soil problem being one of amelioration rather than selection. However, it is very helpful to have a good idea of what your soil conditions are so that you can choose kinds and varieties of berries which are reasonably well suited to those conditions. A complicating factor, as will be discussed later, is that certain diseases and insects may be much more of a problem in one soil than in another, and so we have sometimes to consider, not only the soil that will be best for the berry crop, but also the soil conditions which will be least favorable for the insect or the disease.

SOILS FOR DIFFERENT KINDS OF BERRIES. Varieties of each kind of fruit will vary somewhat in their requirements as to soil texture, but, in general, strawberries seem to do best on a sandy loam. If we grade the whole range of agricultural soils as very light to very heavy, then strawberries would do well on a medium light soil. Red raspberries seem to prefer a medium soil, with the black raspberries doing well on slightly heavier, possibly medium to medium heavy. Dewberries of the Lucretia or Austin type do very well on a light soil, with the Boysen type preferring slightly heavier, or medium light to medium. The upright blackberries vary considerably, but a medium to medium heavy soil would suit most. The trailing types, such as Evergreen, do well on medium to medium heavy soils. Currants and gooseberries grow well on medium heavy soils. Some varieties of grapes seem to prefer a medium light, others medium or even medium heavy, soils. Blueberries are at their best on a light, or even a very light, soil, provided it has a good supply of organic matter and the water table is relatively close to the surface.

No doubt exceptions to the above recommendations as to soil types will occur to anyone who has had wide experience with berries, but if one is to specify a particular soil for a kind of fruit, then my own experience leads me to these conclusions. What is more important is the methods which may be used to improve a soil, or to make it more nearly ideal for a particular fruit. And few are the garden plots which cannot be improved; no soil is really perfect. Without restricting ourselves to any one fruit, let us consider how soils may be improved.

SOILS THAT ARE TOO LIGHT. There are extensive areas in the coastal regions, around the Great Lakes, and in other parts of the country where the soil ranges from almost pure sand to very light sandy loam. The Long Beach Peninsula, where my own home (Heathcote) is located, is a long, narrow sand spit cast up by the Pacific, just north of the mouth of the Columbia River. As far as any one has gone down, when putting in a well, there is nothing but sand, with now and then a log to interfere with the pumping down of the sand point.

Along the beach there are dunes of blow sand, which, at some little distance from the water, have become anchored by certain dune grasses. Once the sand was anchored the dune grasses and a few other plants became more abundant, putting their roots down far enough to find moisture. From there on it was a matter of centuries, with decaying leaves and other plant material accumulating in the low spots, and with each increment of accumulation the plant-growing conditions were better, so there was more debris. Growth of many species finally became luxuriant and so abundant that in many of the lower areas great amounts of moss and other plant materials accumulated. This, being covered with water during the winter months, finally became peat, and now supports an extensive cranberry industry. The plant cover gradually spread out of the low spots to cover the entire peninsula, except right along the beach, so that the sand in the uncleared areas now has a layer of 3 to 6 inches of leaf mold. When this is turned under by the plow it results in a "soil" of sand and organic matter, which maintains good stands of pasture grasses, the usual home garden vegetables, ornamental plants, berry crops, and some tree fruits.

This amelioration of beach sand to form a usable soil has been materially aided by a high rainfall and a water table which is close to the surface at all times and above the surface in some places to form extensive marshes during the rainy winter months. And so nature has shown that even beach sand, given ample water, can be made productive. Without the water this peninsula would be desert sands, as is shown in certain real desert areas where sand dunes move so continuously that even cactus fails to become established. This little description of our growing conditions here at Heathcote

Latham raspberries on the East Coast on soil that is almost pure sand. Yields are better than the size of the plants might lead one to expect.

was given, partly to show what can be done on sand, and partly so that I can refer, understandably, from time to time to our own growing conditions.

And so from an impersonal standpoint—sand can be used successfully for most of the small fruits if properly conditioned. The first requisite is water, and this means irrigation water of some kind, even where there is a good annual rainfall, for sand lets the water leach through very quickly. In certain parts of New Jersey, in which state I spent many years, it was sometimes said facetiously of some of the light soils that a drop of water travels faster after hitting the soil than it did before. If the soil is almost pure sand it will require sprinkling at least every three days in hot dry weather. Surface irrigation just won't work, of course.

SANDY SOILS LEACH RAPIDLY. As the water passes through sandy soil so quickly it tends to leach out, rather rapidly, the soluble salts which, in the main, provide the nutrients required by all plants. And the sand particles do not easily give up any essential elements which may be a part of their own chemical constituents, as do the very fine particles in a clay or, to a lesser extent, in a loam. The gardener must be constantly on guard to provide additional nutrients, particularly nitrogen, as they become exhausted. Sometimes plants will show in a very few days, after heavy rains or after growth starts in the spring, that they are being starved, and applications of fertilizer must be made promptly to maintain continuous good growth. The incorporation into the soil of rather large quantities of organic matter in the form of manure, mulching material, compost, or even wood chips will increase the ability of the soil to hold both moisture and plant foods, with the exception of nitrogen. Large amounts of organic matter will necessitate the use of additional nitrogen as indicated in Chapter 5.

It is hardly necessary to say that the addition of clay to sand will make it more retentive of moisture and nutrients, although such treatment might be of interest to some who are growing berries on a very limited space or in a specially made bed. However, in places where a very sandy soil is found clay is probably hard to come by in any quantity.

SHIFTING SANDS. It is amazing to see sand blowing across the dunes at the beach only minutes after a hard shower, but in windy weather sand at the surface will dry out very quickly and start to blow. The blowing sand may not only cover the garden fence but plants as well, and those which are not covered will be scarified or even cut off. Sprinklers operating during the blow will hold the sand, but in some places bad sand blowing occurs during freezing weather, so sprinklers would have to be used with great caution to prevent bursting of pipes. Windbreaks will help a great deal, as will having the soil in ridges, so that the moving sand will be trapped in the furrows. A cover crop or mulch of any kind will be effective if it provides a good soil cover. Many readers may think this is a hypothetical situation, but I have seen extensive agricultural areas in several states where blowing sand was a serious problem.

Probably few soils are as nearly pure sand as our own, but what has been said about sand applies, only in lesser degree, to the large areas where the prevailing soil type is loamy sand to sandy loam. These light soils are found in extensive use where many, if not most, of our horticultural crops are grown commercially. They all require careful attention from the standpoint of water and nutrient supply and the building up of, or even maintaining, a desirable organic-matter content.

Puyallup raspberries in the Northwest. Heavier, more fertile soil encourages taller growth and higher yields than on the very light soil illustrated on page 30.

While this section is designed primarily to indicate how soils may be improved, after saying so many things about the problems involved in handling very light soils, it is only fair to say that these soils also have some very desirable characteristics. They usually respond well and quickly to use of water and fertilizers, they are "early," easily prepared even during the winter if not frozen, and certainly more pleasant to work on during wet weather than the clays. Weed control is likely to be less difficult, and certain diseases, as red stele of strawberry, may be less damaging. So, if your soil is mostly sand, make the most of it.

SOILS TOO HEAVY. Soils that have a high proportion of clay are usually too heavy for ideal growth of berry crops. They are likely to be poorly aerated, that is, they do not contain enough air, and especially oxygen. This lack of good aeration is caused partly by the fineness of the soil particles, and also indirectly by the fact that these small particles hold so much water that, during the winter, the soil is likely to be waterlogged, which rather effectively excludes air. The ability of certain plants to thrive on heavy soils is probably associated with their ability to grow with a minimum supply of soil oxygen. There is no gainsaying that the heavier soils are generally more fertile than lighter types and hold moisture better. Unfortunately certain soil organisms which cause root rot diseases, such as red stele of strawberry, are more likely to spread and to survive over a long period on the heavier soils.

By and large it is easier to modify a soil that is too light than one that is too heavy, since the soil that is too light may do a pretty good job if simply given enough water. Conversely a too heavy soil should only be watered when it is really necessary, as it is very easy to overwater. Unfortunately it is impossible to shut off the rain like a sprinkler, and also somewhat difficult to remove excess water. Drainage, surface or tile, will help, provided there is a place for the water to go. Surface drainage is often associated with undesirable erosion, and it may be desirable to contour sloping ground to slow down surface runoff. Under certain conditions tile, usually 4-inch clay tile, may be very helpful. The heavier the soil, the slower water will move laterally and the closer together the tile drains will have to be. Local advice may be needed on this point, but in very heavy soil a drain every 20 feet would not be too close. In general, the shallower the drains have to be to reach a usable outlet, the closer together they must be. (See Chapter 6.)

SOIL TOO DRY: See Chapter 6.

SOIL TOO POOR: See Chapter 5.

SOIL TOO RICH. Soils that are too rich for berry crops are not common, to say the least. I have seen gardens where berry crops were growing too luxuriantly, making wonderful cane and foliage growth but not so much fruit, and with accentuated problems of control of weeds and such diseases as mildew and fruit rots. Actually these soils were usually not too fertile naturally but had been quite fertile, and then had received large quantities of manure, or commercial fertilizer, or both, so that the result was the same. Such conditions, if man-made, are no particular problem, as a simple cessation of plant food applications will usually correct the condition within a reasonable time. This process can be speeded up by the growing of a cover crop, such as rye or some other fast-growing nonlegume, during the winter, late fall, early spring, or whenever a portion of the area is available. It is well to remember that such a cover crop will require large amounts of water, and the gardener will have to be careful, in dry weather, that the berry crop is not injured by this competition for moisture.

In greenhouses it sometimes happens that excessive fertilization results in the accumulation of toxic quantities of certain elements. Leaching with large quantities of water will help to reduce such a dangerous concentration, a practice which could be used on a small area in the garden to counteract the effect of too much fertilizer, possibly applied accidentally. To be effective, such a radical treatment would involve a fairly light soil that would permit ready passage of water, an ample supply of water, and care to avoid waterlogging soil in which there are plants which might be injured. Natural leaching the following winter will probably be much more effective. One is wise to avoid excessive applications.

SOIL TOO WET. The excess-water problem in heavy soils has already been discussed, but light soils also may be too wet if there is some obstruction to drainage or if the water table is naturally very high. From where I am writing I can see a row of raspberries and some strawberries which are growing very satisfactorily, and yet a hole 3 feet deep would soon have water standing in the bottom, and during the winter such a hole would fill up to within 18 inches or 2 feet of the top. With as much as 12 to 15 inches of rain in a single month not uncommon during the winter months, it is obvious that drains must be kept in good working order. But in such a light soil, if the water table can be kept a foot or more below the surface at all times, most of the small fruits will grow very well.

There are parts of our country where there is a great deal of flat land, so flat that it is almost impossible to prevent water from standing on top of the ground, in every little depression, during fairly long periods. Such conditions may not seriously affect annual vegetable or flowering plants, but woody plants do not like to have their roots under water for several days at a time. Some berries, strawberries and blueberries at least, will do reasonably well if the soil is ridged up a few inches and the plants set on top of the ridges, so that at least a portion of the root system will be above the water at all times. The exception to this dislike for a waterlogged soil is the cranberry, which is often kept under water most of the winter, but this is a commercial crop which does not adapt itself well to the home garden, except under very special conditions.

The only feasible way, other than putting in drains, to remove water from a heavy soil is by the use of lush-growing cover crops, such as rye, which by transpiration can pump out large quantities of water as described in Chapter 6. Unfortunately this may not be very effective during the winter when the soil has its largest water content, but it will help to dry out the soil in the spring as the cover crop begins to grow rapidly.

Incorporation of sand or organic matter will benefit a heavy soil in proportion to the amount of the material added. Organic matter, to be effective for such a purpose, should be rather coarse and woody, such as sawdust or wood chips or coarse straw or corncobs. Such additives will help the surface soil, but if the subsoil is excessively heavy, inclined to be sticky and relatively impervious to water, the adding of enough sand or organic matter to materially improve the soil, from the standpoint of drainage and aeration, is a very large task.

SOIL TOO STONY. The presence of stones in the garden, provided they do not indicate solid rock so close to the surface that the soil is

A stony soil in New Jersey which produces fine strawberries. This picture was taken in early spring before the plants had made much leaf growth.

very shallow, are more of a nuisance to the gardener than to the berry plants which he might set out. In other words, the rocks would not unfavorably affect the growing conditions, provided a way can be devised to control weeds other than by cultivation. I have seen orchards in New England thriving under a "mulch" of stones so close together that very little of the soil could be seen. But for ease of planting, weed control, and general moving about in the area, it will probably be advisable to remove the largest and most obnoxious of the rocks. The old New Englanders built stone fences out of them, and the modern gardener can usually find a use for as many as he wants to pick up. But the main thing to remember is that the plants will grow very happily among stones.

SOIL TOO SHALLOW. The term "shallow soil" is usually used to designate a condition where there is a shallow layer of surface soil, underlain by a subsoil which may be stony, sandy, or too dense and of poor fertility. Such a soil may be "deepened" by plowing under quantities of organic matter, commercial fertilizer, and lime if needed. Many times, on sloping land, erosion has removed all of what at one time was surface soil, leaving an almost sterile condition. The improvement of such a soil may be quite a job but it can usually be done, even to approaching the quality of a similar uneroded soil. Of course, where erosion has been so severe it must be expected to continue in the future if not controlled. Berry crops, which lend themselves so well to mulch culture, may be just the thing to try on a problem slope. Not ideal for the crop, of course, but possibly the best use of the land.

Shallow may also describe a soil which has solid rock or shale close to the surface. I once lived on such a soil in New Jersey, a Penn loam, with brown shale within a foot of the surface; at least it was that shallow, or worse, at Raribank, the rather badly eroded farm on which we lived. It was a dry soil, but reasonably fertile and responsive to good treatment when water was applied, or even when the natural rainfall was caught and conserved by mulch.

SOIL TOO ACID. This problem will be discussed in some detail in Chapter 5. Actually most of the berry crops prefer an acid soil, and the blueberry does best on soil that would be too acid for many garden crops.

SOIL TOO ALKALINE. The average agricultural or garden soil over most of the United States is not likely to be too alkaline, except for the blueberry, unless excessive applications of lime have been made. Berries are not commonly grown in the real alkaline parts of the country, but in those places where commercially produced berries are not available locally fresh fruit is more of a luxury, and so home-grown berries would justify more effort. Soil acidity is a rather complicated problem, and the injurious effects of too much acidity, or too much alkalinity, may not be due primarily to acidity, or lack of it, as such, but to the effect of acidity or alkalinity on certain soil constituents which in turn may affect the plants by their absence or presence in excess. Hence the effect of a given degree of acidity may be different in one soil from what it is in another soil of the same acidity but different chemical composition. (See Chapter 5.)

SOIL DEFICIENT IN ORGANIC MATTER. Organic matter in soils has so many useful and beneficial effects that its addition to nearly any mineral soil is helpful. (For more details see Chapter 5.)

SOIL WITH TOO MUCH ORGANIC MATTER. Actually this condition probably does not occur except in peat or muck soils, or where an old strawstack is in the process of rotting down. In the peat soils there may be problems of drainage, acidity, and nutrition, which, if solved, will usually result in the soil's being satisfactory for cranberries, blueberries, strawberries, and possibly some of the other berries. When I was a boy in the Middle West it used to be the custom in our neighborhood to thresh the wheat and rye so the strawstack would be quite close to the farm center, often in one of two or three small lots used for hogs, calves, chickens, or possibly for garden or potato patch. After the strawstacks were used for bedding, consumed directly by the farm animals, and weathered away so that only a foot or so of fine, almost dustlike material remained, the lot might be plowed for potatoes, melons, or some other similar crop. The results were very good if this was done the right year, when decay had reached the proper stage. But if it was done a year or two too soon the results were poor. However, water for irrigation was not usually available, and nothing was known then about the great demands for nitrogen made by the soil organisms, which build up to great numbers in the process of decay of dry organic matter such as straw. With water and readily available nitrogen, such a condition could result in a very fine garden, just as actually happened when the soil was naturally low and moist, and when farm animals had worked over the straw pile in sufficient numbers and for sufficient time to provide a good supply of manure.

Part Two

METHODS OF CULTURE,
FERTILIZING, AND PEST CONTROL

CHAPTER 4

Modern Cultural Methods

There was a time when "culture" was more or less synonymous with cultivation or tillage. At the present time, and as used here, the term covers most of the practices involved in raising a crop. In this chapter we propose to cover various methods of handling the soil, cover crops, soil conditioners, and mulching. Mulching has come of age and is used extensively in many branches of agriculture but nowhere to better purpose than with small fruits. However, cultivation cannot yet be relegated to the realm of tradition, in spite of various harmful effects resulting from uncontrolled, or unlimited, cultivation.

In recent years we have seen books and numerous magazine articles, dealing with soil conservation, which have condemned, in no uncertain terms, practically all cultivation. It is true that, taking the country as a whole, some, and often serious, erosion and loss of valuable topsoil into the streams has usually occurred where the soil was taken out of the original grass, weeds, or underbrush and plowed and cultivated enough to prevent a good cover of plants from reinstating itself. As usual the best answer probably lies somewhere between the old uncontrolled cultivating of the early farmers and the "no cultivation" dogma of some modern journalistic soil savers.

CULTIVATION AND WEED CONTROL. The modern farmer has learned how to control his cultivation, get benefit from it, and still keep erosion within reasonable limits. Let us see, therefore, what cultivation actually accomplishes in the way of making conditions more suitable for growing plants. In the first place, if the soil is covered with grass or weeds it is almost essential that it be plowed or rototilled before trying to plant any kind of a crop, whether it be garden seeds or berry plants. If the soil is not properly prepared, then the new plants will have to compete with established weed plants and will be at a great disadvantage. The weeds will take the plant food and the water which the crop plants need and will shade them at a time when they need full sun. In limited areas the same thing could be accomplished by spreading mulching material on the soil heavily enough to completely kill out the weeds, a little difficult if they happen to be strong growing perennial weeds. Cultivation is undoubtedly an effective method of controlling most common weeds. That is, they can be controlled if cultivation is frequent enough, and if the cultivating tools are such as to either stir the soil very thoroughly or shave the roots off just below the soil surface.

CULTIVATE FOR AERATION. Another effect of cultivation is aeration, important on some soils of fine texture which are inclined to be sticky in the spring. Such soil cannot be cultivated very early as it is difficult to do a good job until it is dry enough so that the cultivator teeth will scour brightly. We do not know all the things aeration may accomplish in such soils, but probably it is a factor in the rapidity with which certain plant nutrients in the soil change into a form that is available to the plant. It also probably affects the growth and functioning of various soil micro-organisms, which are important in making the soil fertile and well adapted to plant growth. We know that various operations, such as cultivation, have certain end effects, but just what the intermediate steps may be is sometimes rather difficult to say.

TOO MUCH AERATION. The effect of cultivation on the development of organisms which normally cause decay of organic matter is sometimes startling and may be quite harmful. I have seen light, sandy soils on the East Coast brought under cultivation for the first time. In the wild brushland there was a layer of 2 to 4 inches of leaf mold, so when the soil was first plowed it had a large amount of organic matter in the surface 6 inches and was an excellent soil for many berry crops. However, it was the custom, at one time, for this soil to be cultivated quite frequently and this provided exceptionally good aeration, so that during hot summer weather the organic matter was "burned out" very rapidly. Usually within four or five years after such soil had been put under the plow it had faded to dirty white in color, and casual examination would lead one to call it almost pure sand. Five years before it had been quite dark in color and well intermixed with decaying vegetation. On such soils it should be understood that every cultivation increases the oxidation, or the burning out, of organic matter, and the omission of as many cultivations as possible, unless actually necessary, would seem to be desirable.

The same situation occurs in peat soils. When a swamp is drained there is a practically level surface of peat or muck, from several inches to several feet in depth. Such soil, if properly handled and fertilized, can be very productive for certain truck crops and even for strawberries. However, there is usually a rank weed growth, and frequent cultivation may be practiced to control the weeds. The result is that the organic matter gradually oxidizes and disappears. The cultivation, plus the use of commercial fertilizers, stimulates such growth of micro-organisms that more peat will disappear in one year than was formed over a great many years when the bog material was accumulating.

Actually, peat material may be used up without the cultivation, simply by lowering the water table to increase aeration, and by applying fertilizers, which help to increase the growth of micro-organisms. This is evident in cranberry bogs in various parts of the country. Cranberry growers sometimes say that old stumps down in the peat seem to work up through it and emerge on top of the soil. Examination will show that these stumps were resting on firmly compacted sand or even hardpan. What has happened is that the peat is oxidizing and disappearing into the air, in the form of carbon dioxide and water, and the surface of the bog has been lowered, while firm objects such as stumps seem to be pushing up through it.

CULTIVATING FERTILIZERS INTO THE SOIL. Certain fertilizers can be placed on top of the soil and they will dissolve in the first rain, or irrigation water, and percolate down to the roots. There are other fertilizers, however, which will penetrate the soil very, very slowly. Cultivation is about the only means there is of getting such fertilizers, as well as lime and crop residues, well down into the soil where they will do the most good. Fortunately, some of these elements, such as phosphorus, may normally be present in the soil in sufficient quantities so they will not need to be added. They may also be applied in rather large quantities, before planting, for instance, and will become available over a period of three or four years. This makes it possible to mulch for some years or until deficiency of these particular elements may be expected to occur again. Even then it may not be necessary to plow the ground, if it is mulched, as the roots tend to come to the surface, or rather the intersurface between soil and mulch, or even up into the mulch material. There they can more readily secure fertilizer elements than they could if all the feeding rootlets were several inches below the surface.

CULTIVATION AND PEST CONTROL. There are other reasons for cultivation. For instance, under certain conditions, insecticides for soil insects, such as wireworms, may need to be cultivated in. Sterilization for nematodes, or plant diseases, usually requires that the material be applied a few inches under the surface, practically impossible without cultivation. Another cultivation may be necessary to aerate the soil after sterilization so that there will be no danger of plant injury from the chemical used. Cultivation may also be effective in destroying overwintering forms of certain insects and disease organisms.

DUST MULCH. One thing that has been pretty definitely proven, during the last several years, is that the old idea of cultivating to provide a dust mulch to conserve moisture is an erroneous idea. At several experiment stations plots were set up on which weeds were controlled by chemical means, or by shaving the soil surface with a sharp tool, as compared to conventional cultivation. In most cases the cultivation resulted in more rapid evaporation of moisture. Most gardeners have noticed how moist the soil can be, under the surface, after several dry days, and how quickly it will dry out, once it is stirred up or turned over. The trend now is to do as little cultivating for weed control as possible and to use shallow, sharp blades which will cut off the weeds without stirring the soil to any great depth.

PREPARATION FOR PLANTING. It should not be assumed that very shallow cultivation before planting is better than deep plowing. Usually before a perennial crop, such as one of the berries, is planted it is desirable to work in fertilizers such as phosphorus, lime, magnesium, and other materials if they are needed, and to get them thoroughly mixed with the soil as deeply as can be conveniently done. Manure or crop residues may need to be plowed under to increase the organic matter and deepen the surface soil, that part which contains most of the plant nutrients. By deep plowing I am thinking of about 10 inches and not 2 feet, which might be considered deep tillage by some gardeners from the old country where gardens were often spaded two spits deep.

As the soil is being prepared for planting we must decide whether to leave it loose or compact it. This will depend on the nature of the soil and the season. If the soil is heavy and wet then it may be best to leave it as rough and loose as possible to promote drying out. If, on the other hand, the soil is sandy, one which drys out rapidly, and particularly if the planting is rather late in the spring, then it would be desirable to leave it relatively well packed. On a farm scale this might be done by using a Culti-packer or roller. In the garden it might be accomplished by a small lawn roller or, if irrigation is available, by simply turning the sprinklers on and watering down. Even if the water does not actually make the soil very compact it will fill the pores with moisture and prevent further drying out, which is what we are trying to do anyway.

SOIL-WORKING IMPLEMENTS. The type of implement used to work up the soil before planting may be any one of several with which most gardeners are familiar. There is the old-fashioned plow, which actually turns the soil over and which will place a surface accumulation of trash or mulching material down into the bottom of the furrow. For certain types of soils and under certain conditions it is obvious that this is a good method. On the other hand, many gardeners now use Rototillers or Rotavaters, having revolving teeth of some kind, which tear up the whole soil mass and leave it very loose. This type of implement does essentially the same job as the plow plus the disc and harrow, which were the standard farm implements for so many years. From my own experience I would rate the small Rotavator type of implement quite highly for the small gardener. This will mix any material on the surface throughout the depth of the cultivated area rather than placing it on the bottom of the furrow.

It may be desirable to plow or rotavate in the fall or in the spring, depending on whether the soil will dry out rapidly and whether weeds are likely to grow during the winter. If the berry plot is plowed in the fall, unless planting is to be done then, it probably would be best to leave it rather rough over winter, then harrow, rotavate, or rake it down in the spring for planting.

SUMMER CULTIVATION. After planting, some people find it satisfactory to continue cultivating throughout the summer and during following years, whereas others may switch over to mulch as soon as the plants are set, or after the first year of cultivation. More will be said about mulching later in this chapter, but the decision will probably hinge on the availability of mulching material. Cultivation from time to time during the summer can be effective in controlling weeds, if supplemented by hand hoeing close to the plants. Fertilizers will be worked into the soil closer to the root area. Driving rains will usually soak in better where the soil is loose than where it has not been stirred, although a mulch will hold the water and reduce surface runoff just as well as, or better than, cultivation. It should be pointed out that the actual stirring of the soil is bound to kill many of the roots in the stirred zone. It seems a little hopeless, therefore, to speak of "loosening up the soil" so the roots can grow through it, because each time it is loosened the roots are injured and dragged around, if not completely broken off.

When I was a boy on the farm the man who cultivated his corn three times was considered a rather poor farmer but the one who cultivated five, or even six, times was considered to be a good farmer. Certainly he could be credited with being the hardest working and making the greatest effort. However, I often recall the great masses of corn roots which streamed back from the cultivator teeth when I pulled up at the end of the row. There was a feeling that the root system of the plant could be "forced down" by this surface cultivation which took off the upper layer of roots, but the roots broken off were not really compensated for by any deeper penetration of the root system as a whole. It is much better as a general practice, therefore, to do the deep plowing when the soil is being prepared for planting and, after that, to cultivate as shallowly as possible, consistent with effective control of weeds, if that is the method being used.

The idea has often been expressed that one should cultivate after each rain to re-establish the dust mulch. Sometimes that may be the logical time for cultivation, but primarily because that is when weed seeds start to germinate and when they can be most easily killed.

EFFECT OF COVER CROPS. Cover crops are those grown between the berry, or grape, rows, not for harvesting, but to improve the soil or in some way benefit the berry crop. For instance, rye may be sown in late summer between rows of raspberries to help prevent soil erosion during the winter, prevent injury from blowing sand, add organic matter to the soil, and help to dry it out in the spring. The rye will be plowed, disked, or rotavated under in the spring after it has grown a few inches high and before the soil has become dry enough so that the cover crop might harmfully compete with the berry crop for water. Cover crops have certain other minor uses such as holding nutrients which become available during the winter, when they are more likely to leach away, and releasing them to the berry plants after the cover crop has been plowed under and started to decay. Those who are growing berries under cultivation, on sticky, wet soils, will appreciate some kind of a cover during the winter. One doesn't wander around in the berry patch much at that time of year, but there are certain necessary operations, such as pruning, and it is much pleasanter to walk on the cover crop than on bare, sticky soil.

In certain areas the cane fruits are likely to be injured by freezes during the fall or early winter. This injury may occur at temperatures which would not be injurious later in the winter, but in the fall and early winter the canes are still rather succulent, and possibly in a semigrowing condition, at which time they are much more susceptible to injury by cold. It is possible to slow down late summer growth materially by seeding a cover crop, perhaps in mid-July, so that it will be up and beginning to compete for soil moisture and fertility by late August. Of course, if the soil is rather poor, and there happens to be a very dry fall, the competition may be injurious to the berry plants. That is something that one has to consider, then use his best judgment.

USEFUL COVER CROPS. There are quite a few things which may be used as cover crops. Some, such as soybeans, will not live over winter. They may be used, under certain conditions, to add organic matter and, as they are legumes, to add nitrogen to the soil. As a general rule, a crop which lives over winter is desirable, as it will grow a little while in the spring to provide more organic matter to turn under and to dry out the soil more rapidly. Rye is sometimes used, but this is a rather aggressive crop and one has to turn it under at the right stage or it may "get away" and make so much growth that it will be injuriously competitive. Crimson clover is a good crop where it will grow well.

Oats may be used as a fall-sown crop in the warmer areas where it will winter over. In northern districts it may be used as a fall cover crop, specifically because it will not stand the winters and so there will be no problem of eliminating it in the spring. I have used it in that way for strawberries. We wanted a crop which would help prevent erosion and soil blowing in late summer but which would die down during the winter, so that a straw mulch could be put over the berries and also over the cover crop, which would not have to be plowed down in the spring. Some varieties of oats are quite hardy, however; occasionally during a mild winter we had some survival and had to hand pull the oat plants which were growing vigorously through the mulch.

It goes against the grain to say a good word for weeds, but pound for pound they may be as useful and actually worth as much as a seeded cover crop. Some commercial growers stop cultivating in July and let the weeds grow, actually hoping for a good crop, as that will mean more organic matter to turn under. This isn't exactly a practice to be recommended but is better than no cover at all during the winter. The principal objection to weeds as cover crops is that the practice may encourage noxious species such as Canada thistle and quack grass. Natural weed growth may be spotty and uneven, with poorest growth where it is most needed. A good cover crop, properly seeded, and fertilized if needed, should give better results than weeds, and you'll not have to answer so many embarrassing questions.

SOIL CONDITIONERS. A great deal has been written recently about soil conditioners so that we have come to think of them as being certain chemicals which will cause the soil to flocculate and have a better texture or better physical make-up for plant growth. Krilium is one which has been given considerable publicity. It will undoubtedly work under certain soil conditions, primarily on the heavy clays which tend to be sticky in wet weather and to bake in dry weather.

There are many other "soil conditioners," however, such as cinders, sand, and organic matter to lighten a heavy soil, clay to make a light soil heavier, lime or gypsum to cause flocculation in certain poorly drained clay soils. Once one has determined that his soil is not in ideal condition then he can undoubtedly find some material to apply which will improve its condition. Whether the cost and effort will be worth while or not will depend on just how much conditioning is needed. Certainly if we intend to raise berries primarily under mulch then the use of a chemical soil conditioner to improve the tilth of the soil would be less important than it would be with annual vegetable crops, for instance. The soil texture seems to improve under mulch and it is not compacted by heavy tractors pulling the cultivating implements.

MULCHING. Mulching has long been a common practice with some of the berry crops and is becoming more widely used as a method of management. The term refers, not to the so-called

A mulch of salt hay keeps the weeds down and conserves moisture for use of the grapevines.

dust mulch, but to the covering of soil with any kind of material to keep down the weeds, conserve moisture, and eliminate the need for cultivation. Depending on the material, it may also help prevent erosion and keep the fruit clean. If the material is organic in nature it will eventually add to the organic content of the soil, as sooner or later the mulch, or what is left of it, will be turned under or worked into the soil.

There are other effects of mulching which are probably less well known. There is a very definite effect on soil temperature. In some experiments I ran many years ago in New Jersey we found that the soil in a raspberry patch, 3 inches under the surface, was about 20 degrees cooler under mulch, during a fairly hot day, than at the same depth under cultivation or "dust mulch." The material used in this case was salt hay, and at the time the test was run it had matted down so that it was about 2 inches in thickness. It is true that we do not know too much about the effect of soil temperatures on the well-being of the roots, but there is no doubt in my mind that a temperature of 90 degees, 3 inches under the surface, was definitely unfavorable to the raspberry roots.

Experiments in apple orchards, particularly in Ohio, have indicated that the soil under a grass mulch, where the grass had been mown and raked around the trees, was higher in available potassium than where no mulch was used. This seemed to be a definite effect of the mulch, due to factors other than the leaching of potassium out of the mulch into the soil. In other words, biological, or chemical, processes in the soil were affected in such a way that more of the potassium became available for plant use.

EFFECT OF SAWDUST ON ACIDITY. There was a widespread belief for many years that a sawdust mulch would make the soil more acid, hence less favorable for most plants. This is apparently not true. I recall what was probably the first large blueberry patch mulched with sawdust which I visited in Massachusetts in 1929. This field, about a quarter acre in extent, was heavily mulched and the plants were doing very well. They were being given a considerable amount of commercial fertilizer, which is significant. Mindful of the current idea that sawdust increases acidity we took samples under the mulch and in a grassy fence row immediately adjacent. The mulched samples turned out to be a little less acid than the unmulched. Wondering if by any chance the samples had been switched, I wrote to friends who got additional samples, and the original results were verified.

LACK OF NITROGEN UNDER SAWDUST. Some years ago when little was known about actual soil acidity any soil which did not seem to grow plants normally was said to be "sour." Possibly this was because under certain conditions the application of lime might give good results. Research work done a number of years ago, however, showed that the yellowing of the foliage of plants grown under a sawdust mulch was due to lack of nitrogen. When readily soluble nitrogen was applied, the plants took it in and soon became a normal green in color and made a perfectly normal growth. Other dry organic matter, such as crop residues, had the same effect as sawdust. Farmers used to burn straw because they felt that plowing it under would hurt the soil in some way. Actually it did cause the following crop to be somewhat deficient in nitrogen and possibly less valuable to the farmer. The reason for the nitrogen deficiency in such cases is that soil micro-organisms, which cause the organic matter to decay, build up in numbers very rapidly. They require nitrogen for their own protoplasm and compete for it with the plants which have been mulched, or with the crop plants which are being grown in an area where dry organic matter has been turned under. If extra nitrogen can be made available at the time the plants need it, then both micro-organisms and crop plants will have enough.

Eventually the micro-organisms will die and decay and the nitrogen of their bodies will become available to the plants. Just how long this will take is a question. Usually one should figure on adding extra nitrogen for at least two or three years after starting to use a mulch, or after sawdust or other dry organic matter has been worked into the soil. One researcher found that grapes responded to extra nitrogen for six years after mulching was started. On poor soils nitrogen may be needed every year on mulched areas, as it is on cultivated areas, but after two to five years no more should be needed under mulch than under cultivation.

The exact amount of nitrogen needed in any case will depend on the natural fertility of the soil and a number of other factors. On soils of average or low fertility it will probably be advisable to double the amount of nitrogen the first year after a sawdust mulch is applied to counteract the effect of the increased numbers of micro-organisms. What has been said about mulched plants requiring extra nitrogen would not apply if the material used were legume hay—clover, soybeans, sweet clover, alfalfa. As a matter of fact a heavy legume mulch might provide too much nitrogen on some soils.

HOW A MULCH CONSERVES MOISTURE. A mulch conserves moisture by preventing it from evaporating into the air. This is accomplished by preventing the direct rays of the sun from hitting the soil and air currents from being in direct contact with the soil surface. It is a common experience to pick up a board lying on the soil, during dry weather, and to find it quite moist underneath, even though the surrounding area is very dry. That board is acting as a mulch. Actually a layer of boards over the soil would provide a very good mulch, aside from the matter of expense and possible convenience.

STONES AS A MULCH. Many things have been reported as mulches, from tin cans to cull apples. There are, however, a number of materials which are more or less satisfactory. One which comes to mind first is gravel, or small stones, particularly flat stones. In some New England orchards a stone mulch has been quite satisfactory so far as control of moisture is concerned. The same thing applies in the rock garden where certain types of plants grow better if they can get their roots in under a stone where the soil is more likely to be cool and moist. One advantage of the stone mulch is that there would be no nitrogen tied up because of it, and there would be no decay with consequent necessity of replenishing the mulch. The main objection, as I would see it, is that weeds and grass will grow up between the stones fairly readily and the stones make weed control rather difficult by any means except chemicals.

PAPER AND POLYETHYLENE. Another type of mulch which has been used in some localities is paper, or other low-cost sheet material, which can be laid down to make a practically airtight cover over the soil. Other materials which have been studied, and used commercially to some extent, are aluminum foil and polyethylene sheeting. The black type of polyethylene is made specifically for mulching and is superior to the translucent type for that purpose. Paper mulch first became common in Hawaii where it was used between rows of pineapples. On the extensive farms there machines were used to lay the paper in long rolls, and to hold it by throwing a little ridge of soil on each edge of the strip. This system was brought back by visitors to the islands and tried in various parts of the United States.

Several experiment stations conducted practical research on the value of paper mulch in the garden. From the results of others and from experiments I have conducted myself, I gather that paper mulch, in this country, does not have too many advantages. In the first place it tends to disintegrate in rainy weather, and then it will blow off if there is much wind. It is difficult to walk over it without punching holes, and the wind will catch under these holes and lift or tear strips of paper. Weeds begin to grow through the holes, and along the edge of the paper, and if they are controlled by cultivating then the paper is damaged or destroyed. They may be pulled by hand or destroyed by a chemical weed killer. A combination paper-mulch and strawberry-plant offer was made for many years by certain nurseries and I presume a rather large number of home gardeners tried the paper. Possibly some found it useful and are continuing, but in general it is not widely used.

Black polyethylene has its advantages over paper and will probably be somewhat more satisfactory under humid conditions. It is supposed to be usable for at least two seasons and possibly more. Paper could not be taken up and relaid and, where it was kept in one place over winter, in my experience, it was not satisfactory the next spring and summer.

One disadvantage of both paper and polyethylene is that they are impervious to water, or we may say almost so in the case of paper. That means that if natural rainfall is to get through to the root zone, rather than evaporate on the paper surface, holes must be punched at certain intervals. These holes permit weeds to get started and become bigger if the weeds are pulled out. Another material which does permit water to go through, but which will prevent the growth of weeds, is glass wool. Some experimenting has been done with it but it is not in common use.

MULCHES OF ORGANIC MATERIAL. Most of the mulching material which has been used in this country in the past, and which is now being used, both commercially and in the home garden, is organic in nature, that is, it is plant material of some kind. Most of these materials are quite satisfactory in so far as the mulching effect is concerned, choice depending on availability and price. They are mostly fairly easy to spread and eventually will be turned under and be beneficial to the soil in addition to their direct effects as a mulch.

STRAW AND HAY. One of the most frequently used materials, especially in the Middle West, is straw, wheat straw, rye, or oats. This makes a good mulch but has some disadvantages. Usually some grain is left in the straw and it will germinate in the spring and create a weed problem, in addition to the various types of weed seeds which occasionally come in with the straw. Some straw is rather long and difficult to handle. I knew one strawberry grower who chopped his straw into lengths of 3 or 4 inches and blew it onto the plants where it made a better mulch in some ways than the longer straw. Any straw, before it gets wet and matted down, is likely to blow off the planted area.

Spoiled hay is occasionally used. This is all right in most respects but occasionally brings in an undesirable amount of weed seeds.

SALT HAY. Along the East Coast salt hay, made from a rather fine-textured grass growing on tideland meadows, is used extensively for strawberries. This is short and easy to spread, very tough, long lasting, wind resistant, relatively free of weed seeds, and in general a very desirable type of mulching material.

CORNSTALKS. Cornstalks seem rather coarse for mulching material but I have seen them used both whole and chopped, the latter being more satisfactory in many ways. However, in raspberry fields I have seen corn cut in bundles, the bundles laid end to end between the rows and parallel to them, and the strings cut to provide a coarse but effective mulch.

GROW YOUR OWN. For commercial plantings, of strawberries for instance, the securing of a sufficient amount of mulch is such a problem that the grower frequently has to work out some method of producing his own. One combination which I have used to some extent has been Sudan grass sown in early summer and cut before it goes to seed. The stubble was then disced and seeded to rye, which was cut the following spring just before the seeds matured. This permitted the production of two crops of good mulching material a year from the same land. However, it caused a serious drain on soil fertility, and so an adequate amount of fertilizer has to be included in such a program.

MULCHES AVAILABLE IN LIMITED AREAS. In the Northeast, buckwheat hulls are sometimes used. They make an excellent mulch but are in demand by home gardeners for mulching shrub borders and flower beds because the material is nice appearing, in addition to being effective and long lasting. Where buckwheat hulls could be secured for a reasonable price they would be fine for any of the small fruits. Another material, peanut hulls, is more or less a local product and probably best consumed locally. Such materials although essentially waste products, or so considered in the past, are usually difficult to obtain from any distance because of the cost of bagging and transportation.

Ground-up corncobs make a good porous mulch where available. In my boyhood days corncobs were available for fifty cents for a large wagonload, but I presume that is no longer true because, as is the case with almost all waste products, various means of utilizing the material have been found and prices established accordingly.

LEAVES. A novel mulching material, used to some extent in our own locality, is cranberry leaves which are cleaned out from the berries when they are brought in at harvest time. The berries are harvested in the water by a machine which strips them from the vines and at the same time knocks off a good many leaves which float with the berries and are taken into the packing house. Cranberry leaves make very good mulch as they are easily spread, rather long lasting, and do not blow away in our rather high winds. On the East Coast the prunings from cranberry marshes are occasionally baled and sold for mulch.

In some towns shade-tree leaves are raked up and taken to the city dump. Sometimes arrangements can be made to secure truck-loads of these leaves for very little cost. Leaves make a good mulch, but after they mat down they are pretty tight and in some cases they may interfere with proper aeration. Before they get wet and mat down, however, the leaves of many species of trees are very light and tend to blow around rather freely. Home gardeners who use leaves around ornamental shrubs often throw a few evergreen boughs over them to hold them down.

PINE NEEDLES. Pine needles, or pine shatters, as they are some-times called, make a very good mulch. In some places they can be raked up on the forest floor, obtainable for the going after them. Pine needles have been a rather commonly used mulch for many years along the southern Atlantic Coast, and along the Gulf. I recall seeing fairly large acreages of strawberries in Louisiana mulched with needles of the long-leafed pine. These plants were grown in hills and the needles worked under the leaves by hand in order to keep the berries clean from spattering mud. At that time it was thought that the pine needles would "poison the soil," so after the crop was picked they were carefully raked up and taken off the land. This was justified, perhaps, from the standpoint of economy, as I presume they were used again. However, the poisoning effect was presumably the old problem of the tying up of nitrogen by dry organic matter.

SAWDUST. In recent years one of the most satisfactory and widely used mulches, in a number of fields of horticulture, has been sawdust. This is a material which will prevent growth of most weeds. Some things, like quack grass, will grow through it but tend to become very shallow rooted and can easily be pulled by hand. It will not blow easily and is relatively fire-resistant, especially if kept moist below the surface by occasional sprinkling during very dry weather. Sawdust is probably the longest lasting of any of the or-ganic mulching materials; it spreads easily and, with care, may even be thrown on top of the plants to filter down through the foliage and cover the soil beneath.

For many years there was a feeling that certain types of sawdust might be satisfactory but other types would not. Modern research seems to indicate that sawdust of any of the common woods may be used for mulching. Some may tie up nitrogen more rapidly than others because they decay more rapidly and thus give rise to a larger population of micro-organisms. Cedar and redwood sawdust would probably last longer than most others and, according to recent experiments, seem to have no undesirable effect on the soil. Redwood bark and fir bark have both been ground up to sawdust fineness and marketed as mulching materials. They are long lasting and satisfactory, provided they are available at a usable price.

CAN ONE AFFORD TO MULCH? Perhaps more should be said about the cost of mulching, but it depends so directly on the availability and local cost of material that any general figures which I could give would be of little value. I do feel that mulch is ideal for most small fruits in the home garden, and it would certainly be desirable to investigate local materials and at least estimate what it would cost to mulch the area you devote to those crops. In figuring the cost one should not lose sight of the eventual value to the soil of adding the organic matter. When one puts on a given amount of dry straw, or peanut hulls, or sawdust he is adding almost that many pounds of organic matter, as the water content is relatively small. On the other hand one can plow under a green cover crop, and only a small portion of the plant material is dry organic matter and of value in improving the soil.

A FEW DISADVANTAGES. In considering the disadvantages of mulching, the cost, which is the first thing that comes to mind, presumably is a disadvantage of almost every operation in the garden, or in the home, or in business. However, we would consider it a real disadvantage here only if the cost outweighs the possible benefits to be secured. Another disadvantage is the possibility of fire, which may be a real hazard where straw, or hay, or other dry material is used and the area is not covered by sprinklers. It would certainly be desirable to have a fire lane around such a mulched plot. By that I mean a strip, a few feet wide, of cultivated land or mown lawn. Actually, even a straw mulch is usually a serious fire problem only until the first rain, after which it will be dry at the surface but moist underneath. Of course, if there is a long dry period and water for sprinkling is not available, then the fire hazard may build up. Sawdust, buckwheat hulls, peanut hulls, and cranberry leaves which mat down and tend to hold moisture are much less a hazard than the more strawy materials.

Under certain conditions mice may be a nuisance in a mulched garden. This has been true in apple orchards also, although programs of poison baiting and, more recently, sprays with certain chemicals have been reasonably effective. Fortunately, most of the small fruits and grapes do not seem to be particularly attractive to mice. I have seen mulched areas in several localities where mice were obviously present but did not gnaw the bark, as they so often do with apple trees. In the home garden which is near the house the more or less continuous traffic in and around the area will tend to discourage mice, and it should not be too difficult to control them, especially with the aid of the family cat.

MULCH AS IT AFFECTS COLD INJURY. There is one further objection to mulching and that is that there is sometimes more frost injury to mulched than to unmulched plants. The reason is that the mulch acts as an insulating blanket, and prevents the radiation of heat from the soil, and so on a quiet, frosty night the air temperature may be 3 or 4 degrees higher just above cultivated soil than over the mulch. On the other hand, mulching material may be used to help prevent actual winter injury. In the colder parts of the country it is very desirable to cover strawberry beds with mulching material as soon as they have frozen solid. The object is to protect against still lower temperatures, and also to prevent periodic thawing and refreezing which, in some soils, will cause the plants to heave completely out of the ground. Where the mulch is to be used for winter protection, that will affect the choice of material, the time of application, and the amount used. This will be discussed further in the chapter on strawberries.

PRUNING. Pruning will be considered in more detail under the individual fruit headings, but there are certain general observations which will apply to all plants. By pruning, of course, is meant the removal of any branches or shoots, during winter or summer, for whatever purpose. There are several reasons for pruning. For instance, the fruiting canes of raspberries and blackberries die after the crop is produced and should be cut out immediately, or certainly in fall or early spring, in order to avoid the nuisance of having to work around the dead canes the next harvest season. The removal, and burning, of these dead canes also eliminates the disease spots or lesions which occur on them and, by that much, reduces the likelihood of disease spread the following season.

Pruning may be effective in shaping the plant, in causing it to branch, or to keep it within bounds where it can be easily reached by the picker, or to train it onto a particular type of trellis. Furthermore, if it removes fruit buds, pruning reduces the potential fruit set which may be useful from the standpoint of thinning to

These long clusters of blueberries look promising, but the berries will not size up as well, or have as good flavor, as if the shoots had been pruned back. See picture on page 58 for proper balance between fruit and foliage.

give the fruits remaining a better chance to develop. With certain plants, such as grapes, if the crop is not reduced by pruning, the plant will overbear very heavily and the fruit produced will be of poor quality.

BOTH STIMULATING AND DWARFING. Pruning in general is both a stimulating and a dwarfing process. Actually, the plant is dwarfed immediately by the amount that is cut off. Pruning is also a stimulating process, however, as it will usually cause the plant to grow more rapidly, depending on the time of year and the type of pruning done. However, this increased growth, or stimulating effect, will usually not equal the amount cut off. The effect of pruning has been studied for many years, especially with peaches and apples, and it has been found that the pruned trees, although they make more rapid growth, at the end of a given period are usually smaller than the unpruned trees. The stimulating effect probably has several causes, but we might simply say the pruning reduces the number of growing points above ground but does not reduce the root surface. We may surmise therefore, that each growing point has a larger supply of water, mineral plant foods, and possibly hormones, which cause it to make a more rapid growth.

The trend with apples and most other tree fruits has been toward less pruning, but these principals cannot be applied to small fruits and grapes without many qualifications. They tend to bear so heavily that pruning of considerable severity to reduce the crop is essential for proper fruit development and quality.

TIME TO PRUNE. Pruning is usually done during late fall, winter, or early spring. Some of the blackberries and raspberries, if pruned early in the fall, may tend to make growth early in the spring, early enough to run some risk of frost damage. In the berry regions with which I have been familiar it was usually felt that a relatively late pruning of dewberries was advisable because of the possibility of a late freeze. The canes lying on the ground are less likely to be injured by cold than they are after being tied up on the trellis. With

Coville blueberry, grown in Oregon. This bush was well pruned to give fruit of good size and also good shoot growth.

any kind of plant which is likely to suffer from winter injury, pruning rather late in the spring is worth considering, because at that time the dead or injured wood can be seen, pruned out, and the plant developed out of what is left. If the same plant was pruned in the fall it is possible that the hardier shoots might have been removed and some of those which were left might have been winter injured, thus necessitating additional pruning to remove the injured branches.

Generally speaking, there seems to be very little difference, which can be measured by plant growth or production, between pruning in the fall or spring, aside from the matter of winter injury. Even pruning during the growing season in most cases is not harmful, although it may result in the breaking off of blossoms, or fruits, or fruit spurs, which would be undesirable. However, pruning in late summer at a time when succulent new shoot growth, susceptible to cold injury, might be stimulated would be undesirable. It should be understood, of course, that the cutting out of canes of raspberries and blackberries after fruiting would not have a stimulating effect, as they are dead or practically dead at that time.

Pruning may be a help in various phases of pest control, as will be brought out under certain specific fruits. This applies both to insects and diseases.

TRAINING. Closely associated with pruning is the matter of training—that is, cutting, bending, and tying the plants so that they will grow in a form most suitable for efficient management. This is almost universally practiced with grapes, and there are a number of different methods of training the vines, depending on the locality and variety. We speak of training raspberries and blackberries to trellises, which are erected to hold them up and keep them from breaking off, or allowing their fruit to rest on the ground. In some cases, this training may involve cutting or it may simply mean tying up. Types of trellises for the various fruits will be discussed later.

AND NOW HORMONES. During recent years an entirely new chapter has been added to the science of fruit culture, namely the use of hormones of various types. Some of these will be considered under weed control, but others are used directly on the plants. Certain hormones are sprayed on tree fruits in the spring, to thin the fruits, and the same, or similar, materials, at different concentrations, used in late summer to make the fruits stick on the tree rather than drop before they are fully mature and ready to be picked. So far as I know, hormones for thinning have not been used on small fruits. However, a gibberellin spray has been reported as eliminating the need for berry thinning of certain grape varieties. It did this, apparently, by stimulating growth of the cluster stem so the grapes were not crowded too tightly as they would be without the hormone treatment.

Hormones have also been used to cause an increase in fruit size. Results, especially at the Oregon Experiment Station, indicated that spraying with certain hormones resulted in a definite increase in size of strawberries and some of the bramble fruits. The way the hormones work has not been completely solved, and some other investigators have failed to get the same results. This means, presumably, that the materials will work with certain varieties or certain environmental conditions, but may not work under other conditions. It would seem, at this time, that these materials, if used by the home gardener, should be tried experimentally, leaving some untreated plants as checks. This is a fascinating field and more discoveries may be expected.

Fertilizing, irrigating, and controlling weeds are just as much a part of "culture" as are mulching and pruning, but the discussion of these subjects is necessarily extensive enough to warrant the separate chapters which follow.

CHAPTER 5

Feeding the Plants

The feeding of plants is a problem complicated by the many variables. In the first place different kinds of plants may require slightly different feeding technics, although this idea has been much overworked in the past. With one or two striking exceptions, which will be brought out later, the berry plants and grapes all require about the same kinds and quantities of plant food so that, in most cases, the whole berry area can be handled as one unit from the standpoint of fertilization.

SOILS MAY DIFFER GREATLY. The one most important variable is the variability of soils and their nutritive levels. In the small garden, especially an area that has been in garden crops for some time, the soil is usually fairly uniform, although if the ground slopes there may be very definite poor spots, as compared to other good spots. However, the soils in different communities may differ greatly, so that field fertilizer experiments in one place really tell the whole story only for that particular place. They may be quite valuable for a whole valley, or section of a state, and somewhat less valuable for other sections where the soil conditions are not comparable to those where the experiment was conducted. But to tell whether the conditions are comparable some additional local experiments may have to be conducted. This is not to belittle the field fertilizer experiments, or "trials," as they are more properly called, but to point out that one cannot simply read that Professor So-and-So found best production of strawberries came from using a heavy application of superphosphate, and then use the results as an infallible guide to the production of strawberries in a garden at some distance from the location of the experiment. Of course, there are some places where the soil may be quite level and uniform, and a definite fertilizer program may be suitable for a fairly large area. It will be very helpful, however, for the gardener to know something about the feeding habits of plants, what are the symptoms of too little, or too much, of various elements, and what to do to correct them.

61

YOUR RESULTS SATISFACTORY? THEN CARRY ON. If you have been grow-ing vegetables, or garden flowers, on a particular area with good success, then most of the small fruits, possibly excepting blueberries, should do reasonably well with the same fertilizer program. If you are new in the neighborhood some of the neighbors will be glad to tell what they use. In most counties an agent of the Agricultural Extension Service will know local conditions and can give you a program of fertilizer use that will get you off to a good start. If the results are satisfactory then your problems in this field are likely to be very simple. Sometimes, however, the plants may just not re-spond as you think they should, and then is the time when a knowl-edge of how plants grow and function, and how they indicate various nutrient deficiencies, will help you do the right thing to im-prove conditions, not only for the berry crops, but for other vege-table or ornamental plants as well.

PLANT CELLS AND THEIR FUNCTIONS. All kinds of woody plants are made up of groups of cells which have been differentiated to per-form certain functions. First there are the meristematic cells which go to make up tissues called meristem. These are the small, divid-ing, or growing cells which divide to reproduce more meristem, and also to produce other cells which gradually differentiate, or change into other kinds of tissue, such as conducting tissue. This latter tissue is made up of relatively long, more or less tubelike, cells through which water and mineral nutrients from the soil are conducted to the leaves, blossoms, and fruits. Other conducting cells carry to the stems and roots the sugars which have been manu-factured in the leaves. In the typical woody stem the meristematic cells make up the thin cambium layer, which splits when the bark is peeled off, and from which xylem cells are formed inside and phloem cells are formed outside. Xylem and phloem, respectively, are the conducting tissues which carry water and dissolved mate-rials up the stem and down the stem. When a tree trunk is girdled the phloem is cut and the food materials manufactured in the leaves cannot be carried to the roots, so that they eventually starve and die and then the whole plant dies. The orchardist uses his knowl-edge of these facts to repair trees that have been girdled by mice, or cold injury, by bridge grafting, or on the other hand to affect the nutrient status of the tree by partial girdling, to hasten fruit bearing.

Other kinds of cells become storage tissues, usually large, irregular, thin-walled cells such as found inside the potato. Some tissues function primarily as strengthening tissues so that the plant becomes woody, and stands erect, instead of being soft and spreading like some weeds.

In the leaves, and sometimes in stems, there are cells whose function is to produce and contain the green coloring matter, chlorophyll, which is the real food-manufacturing part of the plant. These cells are usually somewhat variable in shape but not elongated like the conducting tissues. They are somewhat loosely joined together so that there are air spaces scattered through the tissue. These intercellular spaces in turn are connected with the extremities of the conducting tissues, or vessels, so there can be direct passage from the chlorophyll-bearing, food-manufacturing cells in the leaf to growing or storage cells in stems and roots.

There are other specialized cells, of course, such as the reproductive cells. The epidermal cells provide a barrier to hold moisture in and may be modified to form prickles, as in raspberries, which probably function as protective devices. However, the plant has to give off moisture into the air, and take in certain gases, in its life processes, so the epidermis has other modified cells which make up the stomata, minute openings from the outside to the intercellular spaces in the leaf.

Knowledge of the different types of cells won't, in itself, enable one to grow any better berries, but it will help one to understand the functions of the different organs, which should be of value in several ways.

THE ALL-IMPORTANT GREEN LEAVES. The primary function of the leaves is photosynthesis, a vital but complicated process whereby the leaves take in, through their stomata, carbon dioxide from the air and combine it with water, which comes up from the roots, to form sugar, through several chemical steps. The energy necessary to accomplish this change, or synthesis, is sunlight operating through the green coloring matter in the leaves. The green material is known as chlorophyll, and acts as a catalyst in that it is necessary for the synthesis but is not used up or combined in the process. The general effects of photosynthesis have been known for many years, but there are still many things we do not know about the intermediate steps. But this is not a textbook of plant physiology, just enough of an explanation, we hope, of the functioning of leaf, root, and stem so the gardener will know what to expect, and possibly what to do, when that functioning is interfered with.

Most of a living plant is water, possibly 50 to 90 per cent. If a plant is pulled up, or cut off, and exposed to the sun, or just dry atmosphere, the water will evaporate, leaving only a small part of its original weight. The dry matter consists partly of nitrogen and minerals which have come in from the soil, through the roots, comprising a very small fraction of the original weight. The other part of the dry matter is mostly what we know as wood, plus sugars and starches. These latter compounds were manufactured in the leaves. They constitute organic, as contrasted to inorganic, matter—the carbon dioxide, nitrogen, minerals, and water which were the raw materials from which the organic matter was made. Photosynthesis might well be considered the most important chemical reaction in the world, since it is the one which makes life on the earth possible. It is directly responsible for plant growth, and indirectly animal growth also, as all animals are directly, or indirectly, nourished by green plants.

FACTORS AFFECTING PHOTOSYNTHESIS. We are not so interested at this point in a philosophical discussion of survival, but in learning what happens to an individual plant when its photosynthetic activities are interfered with. The removal of any leaf surface, by insect or disease attack, by pruning, spray injury, or by burning with too much fertilizer, will reduce the photosynthetic activities of the plant by that much, which in turn will result in proportionate reduction in stored foods or growth of flower and fruit, of additional leaves, stems, and roots. We can realize then that picking leaves off a grapevine, so the sun can get to the fruit, will reduce the amount of sugar which can be manufactured by the leaves of that vine to go into the fruit, hence a slower ripening fruit with lower sugar content, just the opposite of what the gardener is trying to accomplish.

At this point some may begin to wonder if this means that all pruning is undesirable. Not at all, although pruning does bring about a reduction in leaf surface and hence in photosynthetic activity. But if the pruning is done during the dormant season the leaves have already ceased to function and have fallen or are ready to fall. Pruning in the dormant season does reduce potential leaf surface by removing leaf buds, but it also has a stimulating action, so that the various benefits from pruning may more than offset the harmful effect of photosynthetic reduction.

WATER IS TRANSPIRED. Another function of the leaves is transpiration. This is the giving off into the atmosphere of water, from the intercellular spaces, which was not used up in the process of photosynthesis. Certain elements from the soil, such as nitrogen, potassium, phosphorus, and other minerals, are required in the building up of plant tissues, and particularly protoplasm, the stuff of life in the living cells. These nutrients can get to the leaves only in solution and, as they are in very dilute form in the soil water, it takes a great deal more water to carry enough of them than would be required for photosynthesis. Through the process of transpiration these materials are transported up through the stem to the leaves, coming in contact with various types of cells which may use or store the materials dissolved in the water, and the excess water itself is then evaporated out through the stomata. It has been estimated that a stalk of corn will transpire, during its lifetime, as much as a barrel of water, and that a fair-sized apple tree may give off as much as a ton of water during the season. This will explain why plants tend to dry out the soil about them, and why weeds may be quite harmful by transpiring as much as, or more than, the planted crop.

STEMS. The functions of stem tissues, comprising branches and twigs, as well as the main stem or trunk of the plant, are primarily support and conduction; support to get the leaves up in the air and arranged so they will have sufficient light; conduction to carry water and dissolved materials from the soil up to the leaves, and sugars and other soluble organic materials from the leaves to stems, roots, or wherever growth is being made. Obviously if the stem is cut off there can be no conduction through it, but the effect of partial plugging of conducting tissues is not so easily seen. This seems to occur when certain diseases attack a plant.

The effect of complete girdling has already been mentioned, but partial girdling occurs whenever the bark is torn off or injured inadvertently by tools, or by insects or diseases. Complete girdling of the main stem usually results eventually in the death of the plant and is a method often used to kill unwanted trees. If the girdle is very narrow, it may heal over in time for the necessary elaborated food materials to be translocated to the roots and save the plant. This is sometimes done for a purpose with grapes, just as it is with apple trees. So far as I know there is no place for girdling as a horticultural practice with the berry crops.

ROOTS. The function of the roots is to anchor and support the plant and to take in water and certain essential elements in solution form. The water comes in through the walls of single-celled

A homemade liquid fertilizer applicator. A hose, controlled by a clamp, discharges liquid back of a tooth on this wheel hoe. It is sure to reach the root zone.

epidermal structures known as root hairs, by the process of osmosis. In this process materials pass through a cell wall which has no visible openings, so only very simple forms, ions rather than the larger molecules, can go through. For instance, nitrogen from nitrate of soda enters the plant as the nitrate ion, nitrogen and oxygen, and not as the sodium nitrate molecule. Nitrogen from green manures, compost, or other organic matter cannot enter the plant until decomposed to a point where nitrate, or ammonium, ions are present in the soil solution. Such nitrogen then is taken in, in exactly the same form as from nitrate of soda or ammonium sulphate, hence has the same physiological effect. Of course the residues from the organic matter may have certain beneficial effects on soil structure or soil physics. The fact that plants absorb from the soil the same simple compounds from commercial fertilizers as from organic residues is sometimes not considered by the people who condemn all commercial fertilizers as being contrary to nature.

Because of the physical nature of the membrane of the root hairs there is certain selectivity in absorption of materials from the soil solution. However, the plant has no conscious control, and poisonous materials will be freely taken in if present in solution in a form in which they can be absorbed. This is the principle behind the use of certain weed killers, as well as the reason for unsatisfactory results when certain elements may be present in excess, as in some alkali soils.

FLOWER AND FRUIT. The other important organs of a plant are flower and fruit, whose functions in general are well known. At least the berry grower has little occasion to use his knowledge of the functioning of these organs in any horticultural practice, except to be sure conditions are right for pollination and fertilization. The tree fruit grower may thin flowers or fruit to prevent overbearing, but this is not so frequently needed with the berry crops. Occasionally thinning of blueberry blossoms, or developing fruit, may be desirable, although proper pruning usually eliminates the need for this operation. Grape berry thinning, for certain varieties is a commercial practice.

THE CARBOHYDRATE-NITROGEN RELATIONSHIP. It is evident from what has been said that a plant gets part of its food materials, or nutrients, from the air, primarily carbon dioxide, and part from the soil, nitrogen and minerals. It is only reasonable to think that there should be some sort of an optimum balance between the materials from these two sources. And there is, since the amount of solution coming into the plant is regulated to some extent by the leaf area for transpiring purposes, and the leaf area also regulates roughly the amount of carbon dioxide taken in. Some years ago two plant physiologists, Kraus and Kraybill, studied this relationship, especially between the carbohydrate materials, such as sugars and starches, resulting from photosynthesis, and the various nitrogen compounds, resulting from the intake and assimilation of nitrate and ammonium ions, the two common forms in which nitrogen is absorbed. This was simplified to some extent and came to be known as the carbohydrate-nitrogen relationship, less accurately as carbohydrate-nitrogen ratio, or sometimes just C/N. This subject may seem too technical for the home gardener but, once understood, it is a very useful concept and can be of considerable help in solving nutritional problems.

First let us remember that carbohydrates, starting with simple sugars, are manufactured in the leaves, and that nitrogen is taken in through the roots. There is nitrogen in the air, of course, but plants can't make use of atmospheric nitrogen unless it is converted to usable form by symbiotic micro-organisms, as is true in legumes —and none of the berry crops are legumes. So for the plant to build up a large amount of carbohydrates it would have to have a large, healthy leaf surface, and anything which curtails that leaf surface will curtail the amount of carbohydrate materials the plant can manufacture. Likewise, to take in a large supply of nitrogen, the plant would have to have an extensive, healthy root system, and there would have to be a good supply of nitrogen in the soil in a form the plant can absorb and utilize.

THE FOUR CLASSES. Kraus and Kraybill analyzed their tomato plants, grown with varying amounts of nitrogen but an ample supply of the other mineral nutrients, and concluded that they could be divided into four groups which might be summarized as follows:

Group I, high carbohydrate, low nitrogen; characterized by weak growth and nonfruiting.

Group II, moderately high carbohydrate, moderately high nitrogen; characterized by good strong growth and fruitfulness.

Group III, low carbohydrate, moderately high nitrogen; characterized by very vigorous growth and nonfruitfulness.

Group IV, low carbohydrate, very high nitrogen; characterized by weak growth and nonfruitfulness.

It is obvious that plants in Group II would be desired for fruit production, and in Group III for certain leafy vegetables. Furthermore it is the *relationship* between carbohydrate and nitrogen that is important; essentially the same growth reaction will be obtained if nitrogen is increased, or if carbohydrates are reduced. Hence a plant could be changed from Group II into Group III, or at least in that direction, by heavy nitrogen fertilization, by heavy pruning which reduces the leaf surface, or potential surface, by shading, by controlling weeds, thus allowing more of the available nitrogen to go to the fruit plant. It is not an uncommon experience for a home gardener to have an old apple tree which is too weak to bear a good crop because of lack of nitrogen. He may decide to fix it up right, so he applies a nitrogen fertilizer, prunes rather heavily, and possibly spades under a sod which has been competing with the tree. All three operations have the same effect on the plant, and it may be thrown from Group I entirely past II to Group III, so becomes very vigorous but still unproductive.

AS APPLIED TO BERRIES. Fortunately most of the small-fruits plants have a rather wide range of carbohydrate nitrogen "ratio" within which they will be productive. However it is usually easy to find berry plants which are "high carbohydrate" or "low nitrogen" plants, that is, they tend toward Group I and are rather slow growing, the leaves are yellowish, and the crop small, or if the number of fruits is large they will be of small size and inclined to mature unevenly. Such a condition may possibly be due to a disease, or to the lack of some nutrient other than nitrogen, but in a large proportion of such cases the addition of nitrogen will solve the problem.

Likewise it is not unusual to find berry plants of various kinds which are making a rampant growth, have large dark green leaves, but are producing a small crop. Such plants are "low carbohydrate," or "high nitrogen," tending toward Group III. (Small-fruits plants seldom reach Group IV unless greatly overfed with some high nitrogen fertilizer such as chicken manure, or almost completely defoliated by insects or disease.) The obvious treatment for such overvegetative, high nitrogen plants is to refrain from adding more nitrogen, prune as lightly as possible, control pests to maintain a good leaf surface, and possibly seed down to some cover crop, such as rye or oats, which will help to exhaust the excess nitrogen in the soil.

A little study of these carbohydrate-nitrogen situations should help you apply your nitrogen fertilizers much more scientifically than you might otherwise, and get your plants in a condition so that you can say they look "happy" and "like it here."

OVERFERTILIZING WITH NITROGEN. As can be seen from the above, one could start with a soil that is deficient in nitrogen, but not in other nutrients, and by adding successive increments of nitrogen could bring the plants from Group I, weak, yellowing, non-productive, through the well-balanced condition of Group II, to the over-vegetative condition of Group III. That is, one must avoid using too much nitrogen.

The other elements do not behave in the same way as nitrogen. If they are deficient in the soil the plant will not make a normal growth; it may be yellowish (chlorotic), weak, unproductive. If the deficiency is sufficient to reduce the crop it will usually cause some symptoms on leaf or stem which will make it possible to identify the element which is lacking—not lacking completely, but present in very small quantities, or in a form which the plant cannot use. In such a deficient soil the addition of certain increments of the element in question, in a suitable form, will gradually eliminate the deficiency symptoms, and if the other elements are present in sufficient quantity will bring the plant into normal good growth and production. After that point is reached, however, additional increments will not, as was the case with nitrogen, cause additional, overvegetative growth. And so we find sometimes that very large amounts of an element, such as phosphorus, may be added without visible result. It is true that too much of certain materials, particularly some of the minor elements, will cause injury to the plant, but it will not be characterized by overvigorous growth.

RESPONSE TO VARIOUS ELEMENTS. It is possible, of course, for the physiologists to show that certain vital processes are interfered with when there is a shortage of some essential element, but it is hardly correct to think of that element as being specific for that particular process. Best growth and production, and best quality of fruit, will be obtained by a proper carbohydrate-nitrogen balance, and by a sufficient quantity and proper balance of the other nutrient elements. If that is reasonably well attained then it seems to me that the idea of applying any one element to cause fruit buds to form, or to make the fruit firmer, or of better color just won't hold water. At least most fertilizer experiments with berries have failed to indicate that any element, except perhaps an oversupply of nitrogen, after serious deficiencies have been corrected, affects fruit quality or firmness to any extent.

So let us say that phosphorous and potassium are necessary for growth and should be added if the soil does not have an adequate supply. The same might be said for calcium and magnesium, two other essential elements, although lime may be needed for its effect on acidity, and on the availability of other elements, even though there may be enough calcium available in the soil. Apply these elements, if needed, to get good over-all growth and not to "produce wood," "mature the wood," "make the berries firm," or any other supposedly specific effect.

DEFICIENCY SYMPTOMS. A good question now is, what are the symptoms by which the gardener can determine if his plants need any one of the important elements? This is not simple, because more than one element may be lacking and so the symptoms are complicated. The symptoms of deficiency of one element sometimes closely resemble the symptoms indicating the lack of another element. Therefore the attempt to identify specific deficiency symptoms, except in the case of nitrogen, might well be made only when it seems the only way to solve a problem.

In the first place if the plants are growing and producing well with whatever fertilizer, or lack of fertilizer, you are using it is a good idea to continue, as nothing succeeds like success. If you are new at gardening in your neighborhood ask a local gardener who seems to get results. In most localities now the agricultural agent is just as much interested in the home gardener as he is in the commercial grower. He can probably suggest a good fertilizer program just by looking at your garden, because of his knowledge of what others have done in similar circumstances. He may even be able to have some soil tests made for you, which should be helpful, although it is not nearly as simple as having your battery tested, or the water in your radiator, to tell you just how much antifreeze to use for zero temperature. It's true you may get a report that says to use so many pounds of superphosphate per acre, but there are many modifying factors, and such a report should be considered as a guide in establishing a program and not a specific set of directions to be followed exactly. Your county agent can tell you if any particular elements are generally deficient in your part of the county. If soils in the area generally are low in potassium, for instance, it would be the better part of wisdom to include potash in your fertilizer, as it will be if you use a complete formula.

Another thing which may complicate the picture is insect and disease injury. For instance, certain virus diseases (see Chapter 8) may cause the plants to be dwarfish, slow growing, pale in color, and they may easily give the impression of being starved. If you suspect virus trouble you might use weeds as indicators, one of the good things to be said for weeds. If the weeds are vigorous, dark green, and growing rapidly, but your raspberry plants (or other berries) are stunted and yellowish, then it would seem that something besides lack of fertility is to blame. Such retarded, poor growth and pale, dull leaves may be caused by red spider in hot, dry weather, but this pest may also work on most species of weeds.

NITROGEN. Usually the first thing to check, if you suspect that your soil is deficient in nutrients, is nitrogen, as it is probably more often necessary to add this element than any other. Slow growth, and an over-all yellowish green, rather than a good deep green, are the usual symptoms, fortunately rather easy to check. Nitrogen from the soluble salts such as nitrate of soda, or sulfate of ammonia, is quickly available. By making an application and working it into the soil, or watering it in if the area is mulched, you should be able to see the plants green up within a couple of weeks if lack of nitrogen was the problem. If they do not respond, then something else is at fault. Of course it is possible that nitrogen is lacking, but that some other elements also are so deficient that the plant cannot respond when nitrogen is applied.

PHOSPHORUS. If the soil is lacking in phosphorus the plant growth will be somewhat less than optimum, twigs slender, and often with some red pigment evident, leaves pale and dull, but not as yellowish as where nitrogen is short. Unfortunately some soils have the ability to "fix" phosphorus in an insoluble form, unavailable to the plant, and rather rapidly too. If you are on such a soil it may be best to consult your county agent. Two methods may be used to help counteract this tendency. The phosphorus fertilizer may be placed in concentrated bands so there will be more than the soil, immediately in contact with the material, can fix. Massive, or "dynamite," applications are sometimes recommended, in which case some of the phosphorus may remain available for more than one year.

POTASSIUM. Lack of potassium, commonly spoken of as lack of potash, will cause chlorotic spots especially at the margins of the leaves, which later turn brown and die.

CALCIUM. Lack of calcium may cause weak, slightly chlorotic growth and short stubby roots. In most soils lack of calcium will be no problem unless the soil is acid enough to need lime to correct the acidity, but there are cases, I understand, in certain alkali soils where calcium may be lacking. That would be a specialized problem calling for help from local soils specialists.

MAGNESIUM. Magnesium deficiency is characterized by creamy yellow areas between the veins while the veins remain green.

MINOR ELEMENTS. Much has been written in recent years about the so-called minor elements, iron, sulfur, boron, zinc, manganese, copper, molybdenum, all essential for plant growth but in very minute amounts. Most home gardeners will not need to worry about providing these materials in the fertilizer program. There are areas of course, where lack of one or more of the minors may be an important factor in growing various kinds of plants. If there is a real deficiency of boron, for instance, your area will probably be known as "boron deficient" and fertilizer sold by your local dealers may already be fortified with borax. In fact modern fertilizer mixers frequently include a "shotgun" mixture of the minor elements in their regular grades. Of course individual salts of single minor elements can be obtained, but it is better to get them already incorporated in a complete fertilizer mixture, as the amounts per acre are so small, a few ounces to a few pounds, that it would be difficult to apply them by themselves.

In most cases minor element deficiencies are not easy to diagnose. If the plants are growing and producing normally there is nothing to worry about. Usually in such cases the addition of any of the minor elements will be of no value so far as the crop is concerned, and we have not progressed enough, scientifically, to be sure that they would be of appreciable value, nutritionally, to the consumer. Of course there is a possibility that, under certain conditions, there may be a deficiency of some element, either major or minor, that is sufficient to reduce growth and production, perhaps only slightly, but still not severe enough to produce leaf symptoms.

The two minor elements which have been found lacking more frequently than the others are iron and boron. Fortunately there are fairly easy means of spotting deficiencies of these two. Where boron is thought to be deficient it can be determined fairly easily by planting turnips in the soil in question, and if there is a lack of boron large portions inside the root will be brownish, the so-called "brown-heart" symptom. Conversely if turnips grow normally there is little likelihood that the berry plants need more boron, and since there is relatively little margin between the amount needed to correct deficiency and the amount which will cause injury, it would be wise not to use it unless there is some evidence it is needed.

Iron deficiency usually shows up in alkaline soils, not because there is no iron in the soil, but because, under alkaline conditions, it is in insoluble form. The usual symptom is a chlorosis, or yellowing, of the foliage which cannot be corrected by the addition of nitrogen.

When iron, in a readily soluble form, such as iron sulfate, is applied to a soil where iron deficiency symptoms are evident on growing plants, it may give temporary relief but will probably be "fixed" by the soil almost immediately. Very large, or very frequent, applications therefore would be necessary to prevent the recurrence of the deficiency symptoms. In Hawaii the iron salt solution has been sprayed on pineapple foliage to provide the plants with sufficient iron to prevent chlorosis. In this country foliar treatments of fruit crops have not been entirely satisfactory, and so research workers have tried many different methods of getting the necessary amount of iron into the plants.

Two forms of iron (and certain other minor elements) have been developed for soils where iron chlorosis has been difficult to correct. One is agricultural frits, in which several of the minor elements are incorporated into a glasslike material which is then exploded or ground to a coarse powder. Plant roots seem to have the ability to extract the elements from the glass, over a long period, but in the meanwhile they are not fixed by the soil. The other form, iron chelate, has been used successfully in several states. These chelates are organic compounds in which the iron is held in such a way that it can be taken in by the plant, but is not "fixed" to an unavailable form by the soil. Chelates for alkaline and for acid soils are available under different trade names. They would be worth trying if your berries are persistently yellowish in foliage and the condition is not corrected by reasonably heavy application of ammonium sulfate.

SOIL ACIDITY. The pH, or hydrogen ion concentration, scale of soil acidity has become fairly well known to gardeners. In this scale pH 7 is the neutral point, pH 6 is 10 times more acid, pH 5 is 10 times more acid than pH 6. The importance of pH, of course, is that plants grow well within a limited range, some in the alkaline range, some in a very acid range.

Soil may be made more acid by applying sulfur or sulfuric acid, or ammonium sulfate. Aluminum sulfate is sometimes recommended but I do not like it because aluminum is toxic to plants under some conditions. Ammonium sulfate is about as effective as aluminum sulfate in acidification, and, in addition, instead of leaving a toxic residue, the ammonium ions provide a good source of nitrogen, in fact the preferred source for blueberries, and probably the best for the other berries in those soils alkaline enough to require some acidification. My preference would be to try ammonium sulfate for acidification before using sulfur or sulfuric acid.

The soil is a very complex mass of various chemical compounds constantly interacting with each other and with myriad forms of life, bacteria, fungi, insects, and nematodes. Many of the chemical reactions are influenced by the pH. It is quite logical, therefore, that a particular berry crop, as strawberries, growing in one soil at pH 4.5 might benefit from the addition of lime to make the soil more nearly alkaline, but another soil, at the same pH, might show no such benefit from lime. It is impossible, therefore, to set up a table giving an absolute optimum pH for all soils. For most of the small fruits and grapes good growth will occur over a rather wide range with the optimum usually between pH 5 and pH 6.5. The optimum for blueberries would lie somewhere between pH 4 and pH 5.5. The pH test is easy to make with the small testing outfits available from several sources. Some county agricultural agents will make pH tests on request.

In general regions of high rainfall have rather acid soils as the salts, which might accumulate to form alkaline soil, are leached out and some are carried away in the runoff. Conversely the very dry regions are likely to be alkaline. In the regions of moderate rainfall soils may vary considerably, and it is here that soil tests will be of the greatest value. Here again it is well to reason that, if the plants are growing and producing well, the pH must be reasonably satisfactory, and any attempts at acidification or liming should be made on a small experimental scale. If growth is not satisfactory, even with what should be adequate fertilization, then adjusting of the pH is one of the things to consider.

LIME. The standard method for raising the pH value is by adding lime, preferably before planting so it can be worked into the soil. On established plantings, which are under mulch, it can be applied on the mulch and will eventually be washed down and become effective in correcting a too acid condition. Cultivating it into the soil before planting, or between the rows of plants, is better, because it will give much quicker results. The amount to use will be governed by the kind of lime, the acidity of the soil, any other soil condition that needs to be corrected by lime, and the texture of the soil. The following table gives suggested amounts to use.

TABLE IV

Approximate Amount of Ground Limestone Per Acre
Needed to Change the Reaction from pH 4.5 to pH 5.5

TYPE OF SOIL	POUNDS OF LIMESTONE
Sandy Loam	1200
Fine Sandy Loam	1600
Loam	1900
Silt Loam	2100
Clay Loam	2300

Many gardeners will pick up a bag or two of lime at the lumberyard and it will probably be hydrated lime. They will need to use only about three fourths as many pounds of this material as of ground limestone for a given area. Rates of application are given in pounds per acre although few home garden berry plantings will be of the acre size. The results of most soil experiments are reported on the acre basis, and it is easy to compute for a plot of any size by multiplying the number of pounds recommended per acre by the number of square feet in the plot and dividing by 43,560, the number of square feet in an acre. In the rather rare soils where there is a high pH value, but low calcium, it may be desirable to add calcium in some form other than lime; the commonly used material is gypsum, or calcium sulfate.

ORGANIC VS. INORGANIC FERTILIZERS. Much has been written in recent years about the relative merits of organic as compared with inorganic fertilizers. The former are of plant or animal origin, as dried blood, ground bone, cottonseed meal, and others, whereas the inorganics are mined or made chemically, frequently as a by-product from some industrial process. Which of these are "natural" fertilizers is a moot question, as plants cannot take in the plant or animal materials as such, but only after they are broken down to simple form, identical with that formed by the inorganic fertilizer. The effect on the plant, and on animals or humans who eat the plant products, is the same. It is true that organic materials break down slowly, thus releasing their essential elements for the use of the plants over a long period. With some materials this may be a distinct disadvantage because of the very long period required for decay; with others it may be an advantage, making the nutrient elements available throughout the growing period. But inorganics also vary in their rate of solution and the effects of some of them may be visible over a comparatively long time.

Unfortunately the term "organic," as used for certain fertilizers, is confused by some people with the term "organic matter," which covers such soil amendments and conditioners as cover crop and cash crop residues, straw, hay, sawdust, and peat moss, which will be of benefit to any mineral soil. Such organic matter is useful largely because of the woody material, which lasts for some time before fully decaying, and, in proportion as it remains, it results in increasing water holding capacity of dry soils, and causing better aeration of heavy soils. The organic fertilizers usually available decay rather quickly and, having a minimum of woody content, do not have much effect on the physical nature of the soil.

The best basis for comparison between organics and inorganics is price, and that is usually in favor of the latter. True, the organics release their nutrient elements over a long period, but the same effect may be secured from repeated applications of a chemical fertilizer, and that may be more desirable because more controllable. On my own sand patch I use a complete fertilizer before planting, and then mostly ammonium sulfate, whenever the plants show by becoming slightly yellow that they need more nitrogen.

The reader may gather from the foregoing that I am not an "organic gardener." I use all the organic matter I can find the time and energy to put into the soil, natural farm manures when available, and would be glad to have more. But if I did not use chemical fertilizers, especially nitrogen, my berry plants would be slow growing and yellow, or else I would be spending considerably more money than I am at present for organic fertilizers. As for the idea that there would be less trouble with insects or diseases if commercial fertilizers were not used, that is hard to see when we consider that the plant takes in the same simple chemical compounds from organic fertilizers as from inorganic materials. The good effects of organic matter are acknowledged by everyone, but the argument that nonorganics are harmful isn't borne out by scientific experiments.

COMPLETE FERTILIZERS. As a matter of convenience fertilizing materials are mixed in various proportions to produce "complete" fertilizers. To be considered complete they must contain nitrogen (N), phosphorus (P), and potassium (K) and may, or may not, contain other essential elements. These elements, N, P, and K are always written in that order and mixed fertilizers are usually known by a formula, as 5-10-5, which means that it contains 5 per cent nitrogen, 10 per cent phosphorus pentoxide, and 5 per cent potassium oxide. Formulas of the so-called mixed goods vary, depending on what is demanded by the growers for specific crops,

Well-fed Rubel blueberries. This variety is seldom planted now because of relatively small size, but proper pruning and fertilizing will cause a variety to perform to the maximum of its capabilities.

and more especially for specific soils which may be deficient in one essential element and not in another.

As a general rule a home garden berry grower will probably do well to use a good mixed fertilizer that has been found suitable for his general soil type. He may be using a little more of one or two elements than he actually needs, but it would be difficult to determine exactly how much of each element the soil needs. That will even vary from year to year, depending on weather and soil microorganisms. Even with the use of a complete fertilizer in early spring, most commercial growers find that they may need to supplement with single element material, especially nitrogen, during the growing season. It would be well for the home gardener to be acquainted with some of these individual materials, as he may find it distinctly advantageous to use one or more of them. Pertinent information is arranged in the table on the following page.

It is difficult to rate the materials in Table 5 on the basis of desirability, as one might be desirable under one set of conditions and not on a different soil or in a different climate. There are additional materials, less commonly used, which may also be quite satisfactory, but there are good reasons, such as price and availability, why they are not more often used.

"NAME" FERTILIZERS. How about the highly advertised mixed materials sold under a trade name? Usually it is safe to buy on the basis of guaranteed analysis which should appear on the bag or on an attached tag. The fertilizer industry is fairly closely regulated and, in most states at least, the analysis is checked by state inspectors. Most manufacturers use essentially the same raw materials, and so one brand is likely to be just about as good as another. Some manufacturers include the more important minor elements and that might be useful, if your soil needs them, and the price is commensurate with the amounts added. I would be suspicious of any brand which states that minor elements, and possibly vitamins and hormones, are added but does not specify what or how much.

There are complete fertilizers, of high analysis, in which the essential elements are provided in the form of completely soluble salts. These are quite expensive, but are especially good for quick results. They may be put on in liquid form, with a sprinkling can, or a special dispenser, which attaches to a garden hose, and are almost immediately available to the plants. Certain brands are being used quite generally by florists and nurserymen. The cost of

TABLE V

Some Common Fertilizer Materials

MATERIAL	ESSENTIAL ELEMENT	PER CENT	REMARKS
Nitrate of Soda	Nitrogen	16	Leaves alkaline residue
Ammonium Sulfate	Nitrogen	21	Leaves acid residue
Ammonium Nitrate	Nitrogen	35	Takes up moisture rapidly
Urea	Nitrogen	46	Used for both soil and foliar feeding
Calcium Cyanamide	Nitrogen	22	Leaves alkaline residue, may cause injury unless used in moderate amounts during dormant season
Ammonium Phosphate	Nitrogen Phosphorus	16 or 11 (P_2O_5) 20 or 48 (P_2O_5)	A good combination of two important elements
Superphosphate	Phosphorus	14 to 20 (P_2O_5)	Becomes available over a long period
Treble Superphosphate	Phosphorus	45 (P_2O_5)	
Bone Meal	Nitrogen Phosphorus	Under 1 About 12	Good but expensive
Muriate of Potash	Potassium	48 (K_2O)	Readily soluble
Potassium Sulfate	Potassium	48 (K_2O)	Readily soluble, possibly less likely to cause injury to plants than muriate

packaging and distributing these materials in small units is necessarily high. If you live in an agricultural area you will probably find the standard fertilizer mixtures in 80-pound bags will provide the most, in the way of essential elements, for the money.

BARNYARD MANURE. Barnyard manure, of any kind, is hard to beat for any of the small fruits, either worked into the soil before planting or applied as a surface dressing during the winter. Besides their considerable content of N, P, and K the manures provide organic matter, some of the minor elements, and possibly other compounds favorable to plant growth. However, manure is not too easy to obtain, except for the farm gardener, and many farms are now operated entirely by truck and tractor. It has one serious drawback in that it may be, and usually is, a source of weed seeds. There are several dried manure products on the market, at least some of which have been steam sterilized to kill the weed seeds. These materials are understandably rather expensive.

POULTRY MANURE. Poultry manure is also quite satisfactory, but is very high in nitrogen and, unless mixed with a considerable amount of litter, will have to be applied carefully to avoid over-stimulation of the plants, and even possible burning of the new shoots. It is usually applied during the early winter so it will be leached down by spring. In areas near large poultry producers this may well be one of the cheapest sources of nitrogen.

WHEN TO FERTILIZE. The time of application of fertilizer is governed by several factors. Unless a soil is known to contain sufficient of one or more of the principal essential elements it will be desirable to apply a complete fertilizer before planting. Certain elements, particularly phosphorus, tend to remain where they are applied and do not move through the soil to any extent, either vertically or horizontally. Hence the importance of turning under a good application of phosphorus, either in a complete mix or as superphosphate, before the plants are set. In some soils it is best to apply a band of phosphorus containing material some 3 to 6 inches to one side of the newly set, or to be set, plants. It should be close enough so the roots will quickly reach the band, but not close enough to cause burning of the roots. With this high concentration in a limited space the soil will not fix all of the phosphorus as fast as it becomes available, and so the roots will be able to obtain their requirements. In soils that are very deficient in phosphorus this preplanting application may be quite heavy, to carry as nearly as possible through the life of the planting. Local advice, as to amounts, should probably be sought if your soil is one which fixes phosphorus rapidly.

SPRING APPLICATIONS. On established plantings, on all soils that are not well supplied with the major elements, it is usually advisable to put on a complete fertilizer during late winter or early spring. If the soil is one which leaches badly it might not be desirable to put on a readily soluble nitrogen carrier during early winter, as much of the nitrogen might be lost by the time growth starts in the spring. However, plants can absorb and hold a certain amount of nitrogen, even while dormant, so if there is not too much readily soluble nitrogen, and it is where the roots can reach it, winter application may work satisfactorily.

Usually whatever phosphorus and potassium the plants will need is put on in this winter or early spring application. Nitrogen is frequently added later in the spring and even into the summer, especially on very light soils. These later applications could be avoided by applying enough in early spring to carry through the growing season, provided some material, such as an organic source, is used, which will release the nitrogen throughout the season. However, this would have its disadvantages as the season may be rainier than usual, or dryer, and the nitrogen may be used up too soon, or may last too late into the fall and encourage late, soft growth which is susceptible to winter injury.

SIDE DRESSINGS. Many commercial growers like to apply side dressings, from one to two or three, when, and if, they think the plants need it, as indicated by the rapidity of growth and color of foliage. Side dressing with a readily available form of nitrogen such as nitrate of soda, or sulfate of ammonia, then cultivating or watering it in, will usually cause the plants to respond within a few days. In the small garden a really quick response can be gotten by putting on a soluble material, such as urea, through one of the gadgets which attach to the garden hose. It is possible to get too much soluble material on the leaves, and cause burning, so it is a good precaution to continue sprinkling for a few minutes after the material in the container is used up.

AVOID LATE SOFT GROWTH. In all except the states where winter freezes are no problem it would be best not to apply nitrogen after midsummer as it may stimulate late, cold-susceptible growth. If the soil is very light, and it is realized, after midsummer, that the plants are very deficient in nitrogen, it might be possible to make a very light application which would green up the leaves, and possibly stimulate a little root growth, without causing dangerously soft, late growth of shoots. On the richer soils it will be necessary to stop nitrogen fertilization earlier in the summer than on soils quite deficient in nitrogen.

LIQUID AMMONIA. There have been two comparatively recent developments in the use of nutrients in solution. One is the use of liquid ammonia, which is a relatively cheap source of nitrogen where it can be used on a large scale. It comes in tank cars, or trucks, and is put on from tanks mounted on a tractor, through hose and pipe connections, so that it is ejected back of a cultivator tooth and covered immediately. At present this method does not seem adapted to the home garden unless it is rather large and unless commercial application equipment is at hand.

FOLIAR APPLICATIONS. Another development has followed the discovery that certain plants, apparently not all, absorb nitrogen, and to a limited extent certain other elements, through the leaves. Hence the interest in "foliar feeding." Under certain conditions it has been found practical to include a small amount of urea with a summer spray on apples to quickly "tone up" trees which are beginning to show nitrogen deficiency. Whether such sprays would work on all of the small fruits I cannot say. However, I have used urea in solution, with good results, for a number of kinds of plants, because it is a cheap source of nitrogen, very quickly available, and it dissolves in water as readily as sugar. I was not particularly concerned as to whether the nitrogen entered the plants through their leaves or through the soil, which would have been practically as quick, if it was well watered in.

There are other materials which lend themselves to fertilizing with a hose. Sulfate of ammonia, for instance, may be used in this way if the foliage is promptly flushed off. There are also highly concentrated complete formulas, that is, with a high percentage of the various nutrients, which are made from soluble salts in such a way that they will dissolve readily in water. These are usually rather expensive because made in limited quantity from salts which cost more than the ones commonly used in the fertilizer industry. The question may well be raised as to the possibility of dissolving in water an ordinary complete fertilizer, such as a 5-10-5, and applying it in the same way. Some of the ingredients would dissolve readily but others, especially the phosphates, would remain as a sludge in the bottom of the container.

As a general rule fertilizers applied before planting are broadcast and worked into the soil because the roots of the berry plants will soon spread throughout the soil. Deep placement of the phosphorus and lime, if the soil especially needs the latter, is desirable because of the relatively slow rate of movement of these elements. The nitrogen and potash move more readily through the soil, but if they are combined to make a "complete" then the placement will be determined by the component which requires most careful placement.

METHODS OF APPLYING FERTILIZERS TO THE SOIL. Various kinds of mechanical spreaders have been used for berry crops in commercial fields, some being drills, such as used for grain crops, and others built on the principle of the old-fashioned clover seeder, to throw the material over the whole area, including under the bushes where the drill could not reach. The latter type of spreader leaves the fertilizer on top of the ground, fine for mulched plantings, or for soluble materials. For the small berry planting there is probably no spreader equal to a pail and a pair of willing hands. By hand application individual attention can be given to plants that are a little below average, or to the poorer spots in soil that is not uniform. None of the common fertilizers will damage the hands, although they might cause some smarting if there are any fresh cuts. Gloves, or a tin can, or scoop of some kind will protect the hands but make spreading a bit more awkward.

For an application during the dormant season it is not necessary to spread the material so that it forms an absolutely uniform coating. It is usually easiest to spread among the canes of the brambles, and over the top of the strawberry row. Actually there would be some point to applying the fertilizer to bush berries in a band around the plant or just outside the cane row. It would make the phosphorus more concentrated, and not so likely to be fixed by the soil before the plants can get it, and it would encourage growth of weeds in a strip where they could be reached with the cultivator or other implements. Strawberries are sometimes injured by application directly on the row, especially if the fertilizer is not uniformly spread. If strawberries in the home garden are grown in the hill system it would be easy to hand spread fertilizer between the plants. For later applications, on any of the berry crops, it would be desirable to keep the fertilizer away from direct contact with the plants, especially new shoots or other leafy growth near the soil surface, as it will likely stick and cause burning.

OVERFEEDING. There is a possibility of overfeeding on the small plot where the gardener is trying to give the plants just all the nutrients they will take. Overfeeding with nitrogen will cause excessive growth and the fruit will rot very readily, if not promptly picked, or if there is rainy weather. Overfeeding with phosphorus will usually not cause injury. However, an oversupply of either potash or magnesium seems to make the other nutrient less available to the plant, so if there is very heavy use of potash it may be necessary to bring up the magnesium, and if magnesium is very high to watch out for potash deficiency symptoms.

What we have not yet found is a fertilizer that will grow a fine crop of berries but not stimulate the growth of weeds.

CHAPTER 6

Problems of Too Little or Too Much Water

Probably everyone of us has experienced extreme thirst and shuddered at the thought of what would happen if we could not get water. We have also seen pets, or farm animals, left by accident or thoughtlessness until they suffered from thirst, and observed their panicky scramble to drink, and drink again, finally to lie down with obvious relief. For plant lovers, the sight of plants, drooping and wasting away during a drouth, arouses a feeling of compassion, as if the plants were conscious of their plight. But whether we have a feeling of sympathy for the plants, or only a feeling for our own economic situation, we are well aware, or should be, that an adequate supply of water is a must for satisfactory plant growth and berry production.

MORE GROWERS USING IRRIGATION. Fortunately some gardeners are located in regions of abundant rainfall and can grow these crops without supplementary water. However, commercial fruit growers are finding that there is hardly a locality where the plants would not benefit, at some time during the year, from additional water, and so the use of irrigation is spreading to regions formerly considered as having abundant rainfall. This does not mean that annual precipitation is becoming less, or that the weather is "changing," but that the plants in these areas were at times receiving less than their optimum amount of water, even though they did not wilt or show obvious signs of distress. It does mean, perhaps, that the growers had not been quite sensitive enough to their plants' needs to see the symptoms, or, seeing, they thought that, though the plants were showing signs of distress, they would suffer no real crop loss.

Water has a most important place in plant growth and functioning. In the first place it makes up the largest part, by weight, of a growing plant, and when that water is permitted to evaporate to a certain point without replacement the plant dies. We pull weeds from the soil and lay them on the surface, in the sun. Within a short time they have become limp, a little later stiff and brittle, and are soon dead unless some of the roots were accidentally covered with soil. But if we pull the same weeds, lay them on the surface just as a rain starts to fall, or under a sprinkler, they will remain turgid for several days and in the meanwhile send out roots and re-establish themselves.

WATER ESSENTIAL TO LIFE. Water, then, is an essential component of living plant tissue, and even of protoplasm itself, the ultimate living material. All the nitrogen and mineral nutrients from the soil come into the plant in solution, and are conducted from roots to leaves in the transpirational stream. Likewise, the sugars manufactured in the leaves are translocated to the other parts of the plant in solution, to be used in the formation of woody tissues, or stored as starch, or other carbohydrate compounds. And water, of course, combined with the carbon dioxide of the air, in the leaves, to form those sugars in the first place. There are other less well understood functions of water in the plant, such as the cooling effect, during extremely high temperatures, of the evaporation of the water vapor from the leaves.

Where there is considerable slope, contour planting will help greatly in preventing erosion. In this California planting it was necessary in order to distribute irrigation water evenly.

EXTRACTION OF WATER FROM THE SOIL. The ability of a plant to extract water from the soil depends on the extent of the plant's root system, the amount of water in the soil, the concentration of the soil solution, and the texture of the soil. Other factors, such as air and soil temperature, doubtless play a part. Obviously the deeper the roots the better they can obtain water, as the water table falls, the surface soil dries out in the spring, and the dry season approaches. Here is where deep soil preparation before planting will help, especially where the subsoil is deficient in some nutrients, or too porous, or too dense and poorly aerated. Deep plowing, working in coarse organic matter, getting lime and phosphorus down deep in soils, where they are needed, will help materially in encouraging deep root growth. Sometimes there is a hardpan which needs to be broken up by a subsoiler, or pan breaker, or even by dynamite in extreme cases.

Water and the materials dissolved in it are taken into the root hairs by the process of osmosis, by which water goes through a semipermeable membrane, from the more dilute to the more concentrated solution. As the soil becomes dryer the soil solution becomes more concentrated, hence intake slows down at the same time the total amount of moisture in the root area is at a very low level. If fertilizer is applied at such a time it will cause the soil solution to become more concentrated, and in extreme cases it may be so concentrated that it will actually draw water from the roots and then injury, or fertilizer "burn," occurs. This is much more likely to happen if the material is applied unevenly with large amounts falling in one spot.

SOIL TEXTURE AND WATER AVAILABILITY. Very fine-textured soils, clays and clay loams, hold a larger amount of water than sandy soils which "dry out" quickly. But the very fine particles have a tendency to hold on to the water so that plants in clay may reach a wilting condition while there is still a considerable amount of water present. Such water is "bound" water, and not "free" or available to the plant. A clay loam would reach such a "wilting percentage" at about 20 per cent by volume, whereas a sandy loam could reach about 9 per cent water before wilting occurs. Hence in determining total soil moisture, by drying in an oven for instance, one must take into account the texture of the soil when interpreting the results in terms of adequacy for plants.

RAINFALL AND IRRIGATION. In attempting to determine whether or not total water in the soil is sufficient, or likely to be sufficient, if you are in doubt it would be helpful to consult local weather records. In relatively level country such records, even from a weather station at some little distance, will be useful. In hilly, mountainous land such records are not so dependable unless the station is nearby. For instance, not so far from here, on the Olympic Peninsula, there are places where the average annual rainfall varies over 100 inches within a relatively few miles.

Total annual rainfall may not be so important as its distribution. An excess of rain during the winter may be a liability instead of an asset. In our own locality we are likely to have five to fifteen times as much rain during a month of midwinter as during midsummer. By contrast, where I previously lived in New Jersey the rain averaged about 3½ inches per month winter and summer. Furthermore it did not vary greatly from year to year.

During hot summer weather berry crops should have about an inch of water a week for optimum growth, and there are very few places where that can be counted on from natural sources. So in almost any section of the country there will be times when the addition of water will be of real benefit to the plants. In some places this may take the form of one or two waterings a year, during short drouth periods. In others it may not be possible to count on any rainfall during the summer, and all water must be supplied by irrigation.

WHEN TO WATER. The experienced gardener can do a pretty good job of deciding whether, or when, to water by observing the turgidity of his plants, possible wilting of tips during the heat of the day, the wilting of surface rooted weeds, even when the deeper rooted berry plants show no sign of needing water, and by digging into the soil to examine its appearance and "feel." Reliance should be on all these signs, rather than on any one alone. Plants will sometimes wilt, temporarily, on a very drying (hot and windy) day, even when the soil is full of moisture. Such wilting probably doesn't hurt anything, except on days of excessive heat, but could be eliminated by sprinkling during the hot part of the day.

Scientists have long been considering, and with some success, the problem of a gauge which would show, on a scale, the moisture situation beneath the surface. There are now available instruments, known as tensiometers, which measure the "pull" of the drying soil in extracting water from a porous clay cup buried in the soil.

Another method is measurement of conductance, across a given distance of soil, between two electrodes. These measuring instruments are becoming more refined and useful and may eventually reach the point where the gardener will buy one as naturally as buying a hoe and a rake. So far they have been used for experimental purposes and on large commercial farms, where the determining of the proper time to irrigate is most important.

Before taking up the details of supplying water by irrigation it might be worth while to say again that mulching will help greatly to retard loss of moisture by surface evaporation. In favorable climates it will be possible to grow any of the small fruits reasonably well with mulch, and without irrigation. During a dry season a good mulch might be equivalent to adding several inches of irrigation water, although it would depend on the weather, nature of the mulch, and adequate control of weeds.

IRRIGATION METHODS. There are many methods of getting irrigation water where you want it, into the soil in which your plants are growing. In some areas surface irrigation, either in basins around a tree, or in rills between rows of berries, or across a field to be seeded, is the standard method. If you live in such an area and have an available irrigation ditch adjacent, or handy, to your berry patch, then that is probably the system to use and there will be "know-how" in your neighborhood as to methods and timing.

The great majority of home gardeners, however, will have water under pressure in pipes, rather than in an open ditch, and if such is the case some sort of a sprinkler system will probably be easier to manage, more convenient, and it will be easier to get uniform application, especially on uneven land. The small garden can usually be watered from the household system with the aid of the garden hose. The larger planting should have pipes of appropriate size laid permanently, or at least semipermanently, so that sprinkling equipment can be turned on by simply opening a valve.

PORTABLE SYSTEMS. A popular development of recent years is the portable system of lightweight aluminum pipe, 2, 3, or 4 inches in diameter usually, with rapid couplers so the system can be moved readily after a strip has been thoroughly watered. Revolving nozzles about 40 feet apart are located on short risers which fit into the couplings. These nozzles may be obtained with openings of various sizes, depending on the amount of water available, and other factors. The small nozzles give a fine spray, easily blown in the wind, but do not thrash the plants around or splash the soil as do the larger ones. If you have a garden large enough to warrant a system of this kind the salesmen will be glad to give you data on nozzle performance. There is even a nozzle purported to throw the water in a square pattern, but most have a circular pattern so that you have to figure enough overlap to get sufficient moisture on all parts of your garden. Moving the system will not be a long or difficult job but you will have to have a way to move, and not across a field with wire trellises.

FIXED PIPES PROBABLY BEST. For my part, in the small or medium-sized garden, I would prefer fixed pipes, to avoid the chore of moving. The system we have in our own garden, and which has been quite satisfactory, consists of galvanized steel pipes, carried on the tops of posts high enough so one can walk or use a tractor or other implement under them. The posts are about 12 feet apart in rows 40 feet apart. We try to lay out our plantings so the posts will cause little, if any, interference with the ordinary garden operations. In the overhead pipes very small nozzles are inserted at 3-foot intervals. The water comes out in tiny solid streams, but soon breaks up in the air to provide good coverage.

The entire line can be rotated to throw the sheet of water to either side. We do this manually, but automatic turners may easily be secured—for a price. We have a great deal of wind and feel that hand turning is more satisfactory in fighting the wind and getting the water where we want it. Most of these pipes are connected permanently to underground mains, so all that is necessary is to open the valve and occasionally rotate the pipe.

We have one 90-foot length of this kind of equipment, with aluminum pipe, which we use to water a garden 180 feet long. After one end is watered we drag the whole 90 feet along the tops of the posts to the other end. By uncoupling this pipe, shorter lengths can easily be obtained to carry to other places for temporary use, where they may be laid on the ground, or on boxes, short posts, or movable horses. There is a hose coupling at one end, so the garden hose is attached, water turned on, and the system is in operation. One advantage of this system, over one with revolving nozzles, is the rectangular pattern.

FOR SMALL PLOTS. There are perforated plastic hoses, which can be used in much the same way as the above, and some at least are quite satisfactory for small plots. When fruit is ripening there

would be some advantages if the water could be applied directly
to the soil, as by surface irrigation. There are various types of
soaker hoses which can be laid along the row and which will distribute water directly on the soil surface. One length will cover
only a narrow strip, so there may have to be frequent moves, a somewhat messy job.

For a very small berry planting, the old garden hose with a good
sprinkler nozzle will do a good job, provided you hold it in one
place long enough. There are various types of lawn sprinklers too
numerous to mention. Most of them will do a good job if you will
let them. Judge them by cost, simplicity, size of area covered, and
uniformity of coverage over the whole pattern.

HOW TO WATER. The tendency, too often, is to get everything wet
—above ground. Dig in occasionally and be sure the water is soak-

Soaker hose irrigating strawberries in Maryland. Note salt hay mulch
between the rows.

ing down to where it can do some good. If the plants need water, but are bearing ripe fruit, give them a thorough soaking, right after picking, then let them dry off for at least a week, unless the demand for water is too terrific. In this way you may get a little more berry rotting than with no watering at all, but not nearly as much as if you sprinkled more lightly every day or two.

I like to water in the morning or the middle of the day, rather than during the evening, so the plants, and particularly ripening fruit, can dry off before night—less disease problem that way. I can almost hear someone say, "But you wouldn't water while the sun is shining on the plants, would you?" I surely would, usually do, and have never witnessed any damage to the plants.

SOURCE OF WATER. The source of water may be a well, pond, stream, or city main, the principal difference being cost and convenience. City water is usually good, even though fairly heavily chlorinated, but it is inconvenient to be served notice that no sprinkling of lawn, or garden, may be done during the worst dry spell of the season. Having one's own supply is fine, but out of reach of most city dwellers. In some small-town or suburban areas, wells already in existence might be retained, strictly for irrigation, after city water mains have been installed. For the farm garden the water is likely to come from the household supply, or if it is an irrigated farm, from the regular irrigation supply. In alkaline regions some thought may have to be given to the quality of the water, but otherwise any sanitary source is satisfacto.y. Sanitary source is emphasized because one would hardly want his ripening strawberries sprinkled with contaminated water.

Books could be written, and have been, about the various kinds of pumps, power units, and other equipment for irrigation, but the berry garden will probably be watered from an established source. I might just suggest the possibility of an additional well for this particular job. I have a very small electric pump, of the type commonly used for domestic purposes, which is used only for sprinkling. In times of drouth, when the household water may become a bit short, it is comforting to let the sprinklers run continuously if need be, knowing that the water for the house will not be affected. This small system will handle 75 to 100 feet of the semipermanent pipe sprinklers already described.

TOO MUCH WATER. The problem of too much water may be serious in winter, just as lack of water is in summer. It is hard to say

Too much water in this blueberry field. However, the soil has been ridged so plants have a good part of their root systems out of water and they have made fairly good growth. The men are taking cuttings.

just when there is too much. On our sandy soil it can rain contin- uously for days, but the plants do not seem to mind, except in the low spots where water actually stands on the surface, or where the water table is almost at the surface. Even then, if it drains off within a day or two, no damage may be done. But if the soil is covered with water for a week, there is likely to be trouble; the roots suffer and, if it is summer, the leaves will turn yellow and many plants will die. A little more standing water will be tolerated in winter than during the growing season, but standing water at any time should call for remedial measures, namely drainage.

It is to be hoped that the berry planting is on a site that can be drained; some aren't and that is too bad. If one must grow berries under such conditions ridging might be tried. If a portion of the roots can be kept above the water the plants may come through all right. There is danger that roots below the water level will be killed off, then when the soil dries out in the summer these shallow-rooted specimens may be killed by drouth unless watered.

DRAINAGE METHODS. Drainage may be by open ditch or tile, preferably the latter if there is a choice and if there is a convenient outlet for the tile. Occasionally a soil is found with a hardpan so shallow that it will hold both roots and water undesirably near the surface. Puncturing this hardpan by drilling through with a posthole augur, or by dynamite or subsoiler, may not only solve the drainage problem but permit the plants to root much more deeply, and so be more drouth resistant in the summer. Cover crops will help to dry off the soil in the spring, but if the water actually stands on the surface the cover crop will not be very effective in eliminating the excess, and may itself be killed out in such a soggy situation.

Good drainage is quite important with respect to certain soil-borne diseases, in addition to its direct effect on the berry plants. These diseases will be discussed in the chapters on strawberries and bramble fruits.

CHAPTER 7

Modern Methods of Weed Control

Weeds have been a symbol of undesirable elements since biblical times, and probably earlier. We usually think of such things as thistles, smartweed, quack grass, and chickweed when we hear the word, but actually it has a somewhat wider meaning. For it may include any unwanted plant. A "plant out of place" is one definition for a weed. So in a strawberry bed a good stand of clover, which would be wanted in a pasture, is a weed.

In this part of the country there are two strong-growing, trailing blackberries, the Evergreen and the Himalaya, which have escaped from cultivation and are probably the worst weeds in large areas of pasture land. We have wild strawberries, most of which are infected with virus diseases, near our fruiting rows, and we would surely like to be rid of them. Commercial strawberry growers, as well as home gardeners, occasionally want to destroy all of an old planting that is virus infected and start again with virus-free plants. It is important then that every one of the old plants be destroyed, lest aphids migrate to the new planting and bring the dreaded virus principle. A neglected vineyard may be a breeding place for numerous grape pests, endangering well-cared-for vines in the neighborhood, and we might then look upon the abandoned plants as weeds. So while the home gardener might, on the one hand, desire a material which would kill everything but blackberries, the dairyman may be looking for a weed killer specifically to eradicate blackberries in his pasture. There is actually one such combination sold as a "blackberry killer."

HOW WEEDS CAUSE TROUBLE. Weeds may cause damage in a great variety of ways, including damage to aesthetic values, which is of real importance in the home garden. But there is actual harm to the plants where weeds grow rampant, the amount varying in more or less direct proportion to the number and size of the weeds. Weeds require the same growing conditions as the berry plants, that is, they must have water, soil nutrients, and light, so in proportion as they have these things the berry plants are deprived of them. In a fairly dry season a weedy strawberry patch may suffer from drouth; another on the same soil, but free of weeds, may have enough water for normal growth. Water used by the weeds is lost, but nutrients the weeds use may eventually be returned to the soil, if they are turned under or composted. But in the meanwhile they have robbed the berry plants at a time when they needed feeding. Competition for light is less often considered, but it is real nevertheless. We have probably all seen plants, in a thick growth of weeds, grow up slender and willowy, with lower leaves turned yellowish, or dropped altogether.

Another hidden hazard is their effect on insect and disease control. Some diseases develop most rapidly in dense, shaded, poorly aerated places, and of course any kind of spraying, or dusting, is greatly hindered by any weeds which grow up high enough to interfere with spray which should go onto the berry plants. Cost of harvesting, at least in time, if we do it ourselves, is one of the greatest costs involved in berry production, and weed growth can slow that operation by at least a half. So all in all weeds are a problem, in many places the only real cultural problem which the home garden berry grower will face.

KNOW YOUR WEEDS. The first step in satisfactory control of any pest is to know all you can about it, be it disease, insect, or weed, not necessarily its Latin name but whatever you can learn about its habits. For weeds this would include the answers to: When it is likely to appear in the spring? Will it grow all winter? Does it spread by underground stems or only by seed? Will it be killed by the first frost? What soils does it prefer? and Is it a serious pest or relatively harmless? Most gardeners already have such a nodding acquaintance with the weeds prevalent in their own garden. It will help to go a step further and learn the scientific name, or at least the usually accepted common name, so that one can read reports of new weed killers, or new methods, and know when these reports concern weeds of immediate interest. So "know your weeds" is good advice.

Your state experiment station may have some good bulletins on weed control, and possibly a manual for weed identification; several states do. This book cannot be a complete weed manual so I will not try to give descriptions of even the worst ones, but will mention some by common names, names so familiar that most gardeners will undoubtedly recognize them.

Each locality has its bad weeds, and those that can be considered almost harmless, although some may question whether there is a harmless weed. Perhaps if a plant doesn't do any harm it isn't a weed, or it may be a weed at one time of the year, and a harmless plant at another time. Some commercial berry growers, for instance, cultivate and hoe to keep a berry field clean of things such as pigweed and lamb's-quarters, during spring and early summer, and then let them grow to form a cover crop during late summer and fall. I can't quarrel with their reasoning, but in the home garden I would prefer some other cover crop, or better still, mulch. Still some of the less aggressive annual weeds are not nearly as harmful in late summer as they were during the early spring, unless late-summer water supply is critically short.

BAD WEEDS. I won't mention any specific weeds as being harmless, or even unimportant, as some gardener, somewhere, would undoubtedly be able to contradict me from the standpoint of his own conditions. It will be a little safer, perhaps, to name a few general classes of weeds for which the gardener should be on the lookout. Some of these would be: (a) poisonous plants, such as poison ivy, a persistent weed under some conditions; (b) climbers, such as morning-glory, honeysuckle, and others, which, once started, may entirely overrun bush fruits in a short while; (c) those with underground, perennial stems, possibly the worst weeds of all, such as quack grass, Canada thistle, sorrel, and nettles; (d) the rank growing annuals, such as smartweed, which reseed themselves so prodigiously and grow so fast that one can leave for vacation and come back a month later to find the strawberry patch completely inundated. There might be other classes or groupings which gardeners in various parts of the country could think of.

WEED CONTROL AND THE SCIENCE OF AGRICULTURE. From time immemorial the gardener has pulled weeds by hand, and will probably be doing so for many years to come. As a matter of speculation we may think of the very first attempts at plant "culture," by some "above the average" or "desperate for food" cave man, consisting of pulling weeds away from a wild berry bush or grapevine, probably to better reach and examine the green fruit. Then through the dim recesses of his half-human intelligence there gradually took form the idea that what he had done was good. And thus was born the science of agriculture.

Science has given us implements of iron, horses and oxen to pull the implements, and, much, much later, little purring monsters of steel which do not tire, and most recently chemicals which will kill the weeds, sometimes even among the crop plants and without injuring them. What will be next? Will the scientists provide us with pollen carrying a sterility factor, to be dropped over an area from a plane, to insure seeds which will not grow, much as has been done with certain insect pests? Or will they find radiations so specific that they can be used, over a wide area, to affect only one species of plant, causing lethal mutations? Or will the breeders produce such strong and aggressive berry plants that they will grow right through a weed cover and eventually choke out the weeds? Or, as has actually been done in certain cases, specific insects and diseases, or nematodes, to attack and destroy one species of weed? Some of these ideas may be a bit fantastic, of course, but not more so than some of our selective weed-killing chemicals seemed forty years ago.

We hope the above paragraph will be read some hot evening, after a tough afternoon fighting weeds, when we don't really know whether we have accomplished anything significant or not. It may give one a little lift, a dream for the future, and take one's mind off the terrible thought that we are only half done, and should spend the next afternoon doing the same thing.

HAND PULLING. As of now, and for the foreseeable future, there are places where hand pulling is the only practical way to remove weeds, such as those which are growing up among the strawberry runners or tight against the tender shoot of a young grapevine. There are often spots where it would be difficult to use chemical weed killers without endangering the berry plants. As a matter of fact, where berry plants are worked into the landscape planting, and mulched, pulling is the most satisfactory way of controlling most weeds. Under such circumstances it will help a great deal to eradicate weeds, by any means, as completely as possible, before planting. If that is done, and young weeds are pulled out before they develop very far, the job will become progressively easier.

It is no great trick to pull many annual weeds before they ripen their seed. However, if you are trying to eradicate annuals, such as smartweed, you will have to be especially vigilant in the autumn. As the days shorten, late-germinating seeds will produce tiny plants, only an inch or so high, that will bloom almost as soon as they come through the soil, and set seed too. Earlier starting plants, of the same species, will not bloom until they are several inches high, so are much less likely to be overlooked.

Eradication of perennials with underground stems, by hand pulling, is next to impossible because the stems break and leave roots and underground stems to start new top growth. However, under a fairly deep mulch some of the perennials, such as quack grass, tend to produce their underground stems on top of the soil where they can be "peeled" out much more easily than in cultivated areas. With a number of the really tough perennials, however, pulling will have to be supplemented with chemical weed killers if there is to be much hope of eradication.

USE OF THE HOE. Hand hoeing and pulling might be considered as supplementary methods. With small seedlings of annual weeds, hoeing is effective, but not very speedy, satisfactory for small plantings, and as a supplement to cultivation on plantings of commercial size. When I was a small boy on the farm it would have seemed an insult to the intelligence of the American people to write directions for hoeing. Nearly everyone had learned the hard way. During the years I have broken in a good many boys, and adults, and not all from the city, to garden work, and I can say that a knowledge of hoeing is not universal, nor inborn.

Directions are simple. First, keep the hoe sharp, filed with a bevel on the side away from the operator. Use the instrument as a scraper, just under or at the surface of the soil. Weeds are more likely to die if cut off cleanly at this point than if dug out with part of their root system intact and ready to start growth again if covered ever so slightly. The weeds cut off, if fairly large, should be raked together and either dumped on the compost pile or stacked in fairly large piles, where any that start growth can be easily stirred up so they will dry out and die. Where the weeds are quite small, and a good job of shaving is done, the cuttings can be left thinly scattered on the soil, not bunched up, and most will die rather promptly unless there is rain immediately after. Occasionally some big weeds may have to be "chopped," but for ordinary weeds the hoe should not be used as a chopper, which is the way the novice, and sometimes the "experienced" garden man, is prone to use it. Chopping doesn't kill as many weeds, leaves the surface uneven, and harder to hoe next time, and stirs up the soil so that it drys out more than if just scalped.

WEED CONTROL BY MEANS OF CULTIVATION. Cultivation has already been discussed in Chapter 4, and although it has other functions, weed control is usually the most important. Hence the cultivator teeth, or shovels, should be designed to work as shallow as possible, cutting off the weeds and doing a minimum of damage to the berry plant roots. There are many types of cutter shovels or blades for the various sizes of cultivators, from wheel hoe to tractor mounted. What has been said about shallow cultivation, of course, does not apply to soil preparation before planting, when usually it is "the deeper the better." Many of the small, modern, rotary tillage implements can be used for weed control, although the larger, heavier machines are better for soil preparation. We have one of the lighter types, with L-shaped blades, which can be used rather satisfactorily for weed control by keeping it moving and not letting it dig in too deeply.

Weeds in this New Jersey blueberry field are kept under perfect control by frequent very shallow cultivation plus hand hoeing and raking. This also helps control certain insects and diseases, especially mummy berry.

The frequency of cultivation, to obtain satisfactory weed control, will vary with conditions. In some gardens it will be necessary after each rain. But do not cultivate by time schedule, every week, or every two weeks. The fewer the cultivations the better, so cultivate only when you need to, to kill weeds, or for some special purpose, as working in a side dressing of fertilizer which you can't conveniently or satisfactorily (superphosphate for instance) water in.

MULCH FOR WEED CONTROL. A mulch material which completely excludes light will effectively control weeds, and may be used for eradication of difficult perennial species, preferably before the berries are planted. After they are planted there will have to be space for the berry plants to grow up between strips of mulching material, and weeds will surely find those spaces, sufficiently at least so there will be some survival. Asphalt roofing paper will give such complete coverage and regular mulch paper is almost as good. Black polyethylene is a recent development in this field—for covering the entire area, for eradication, or just between the rows for the usual mulching effect.

These materials will prevent moisture loss from the soil surface by evaporation, but will also prevent rain from reaching the soil, except between strips or through holes. Heavy rains will probably drain down through the interspaces; light showers may simply evaporate from the surface of the sheet. The gardener should keep a rather close watch on moisture conditions under any of the sheet mulches. Paper, or polyethylene, mulch will have to be firmly fastened to the soil by wires bent into staple form, with 3 to 6 inches to be pushed into the ground, or by soil pulled over the edge to weight it down, or a combination of both in windy country. Soil over the edges of the sheets is a place for weeds to grow, although it may soon dry out so few weeds will survive.

There are other mulch materials, which I consider better than the sheet materials, in many respects, where obtainable. They will help control some weeds but may possibly make harder to control, except with the assistance of chemicals, some of the deep-rooted perennials, as Canada thistle, once they are established. The obvious is to eradicate before planting and then prevent such weeds from getting established. Sawdust, buckwheat hulls, and salt hay are some of the better fine-textured materials which are rather effective in control of most weed species if applied to a depth of 3 or 4 inches after settling.

CONSIDER WEED GROWTH WHEN FERTILIZING AND IRRIGATING. As weeds respond to water and plant nutrients in the same way as the berry plants it is difficult to obtain any effective control by manipulating these factors. However, it will usually be best to refrain from applying fertilizers, or more water than is absolutely necessary, in late summer, in order to harden up the berry canes for winter. Restraint in watering and fertilizing at this time will help with the weed problem, as well as make the berry plants better able to withstand low temperatures. This will apply as well to plants grown in the landscape, as any shrubby ornamental plants will be more susceptible to cold injury if they go into the winter in a soft, vegetative condition.

A hard frost will effectively cut down soft annual plants, such as chickweed, smartweed, and pigweed, although some species will survive more frosts than others. By the time they are cut down they

Pine needles were used to mulch this newly set blueberry field in Maryland. Cultivation between the rows controls weeds. Such deep cultivation, if near the plants, would destroy much of the very shallow root system.

will probably have ripened their seed, so the gain will be aesthetic and temporary.

CHEMICAL WEED CONTROL. Effective chemical weed control is a modern development, although some compounds, such as common salt, kerosene, lubricating oil, and others, have long been used sporadically. However none of these earlier used chemicals were very satisfactory. Great progress has been made in the last few years, yet most of the materials now available have some drawbacks, so many researchers are continuing to work on this important problem. Presumably none will be considered "perfect," for no matter how deadly, how safe, or how selective one may be it will still cost money for the material, and labor for application.

Improvement can be looked for in the following ways—greater killing power against weeds, combined if possible with relative harmlessness to berry plants, less likelihood of damaging other plants, of persisting in the sprayer, of drifting fumes, and, of course, something that is cheaper. This may seem like asking for the moon, but 'twas ever thus with research. One thing we can be sure of— new, and better, weed killers will be developed.

Present weed killers, and presumably future ones, may be divided into certain groups or types, and are discussed under appropriate headings.

SOIL STERILANTS. These are materials which kill everything in the ground, roots, underground stems, and seeds. Some, of course, are more effective than others in actually giving a complete kill. Obviously such materials would have to be used before berry plants are set out. Some are effective only against weeds, others also kill insects, nematodes, and disease organisms and their spores. Some, such as methyl bromide, are gases which must be applied under a gasproof tarpaulin. Usually plants may be set in the soil soon after using these materials. Others are liquid, but kill by the gas formed after the liquid is dispersed in the soil. These may take a little longer, possibly a month or so, to clear out of the soil so it may be used with safety. Still others come as dry salts to be dissolved in water for application. These latter may sterilize the soil for some time so that planting may not be safe until next season.

All of these sterilants are a bit expensive, some quite expensive, for both material and labor of application. Obviously they should be used primarily for weeds which would be difficult to eradicate otherwise. The use of those which are triple threats is probably more often justified as a means of eradicating some disease, insect, or nematode, than it is for weed control. Some of the better known or more promising ones are listed in Table VI.

Another possible class of materials would be those which may be sprayed on the leaves to kill all plant life to the ground level, which, with some weeds, results in death of the roots as well. Nearly everyone working with weed killers of this, or any, type, for that matter, has hoped to find compounds which would kill the weeds but not the economic plant he was striving to protect. Such a material would be called a "selective" weed killer. As a matter of fact nearly all materials used as sprays for this purpose are selective, at least in some degree, some not quite selective enough so they can be sprayed over a berry row without injuring the plants, others seeming to have remarkably little effect on the berry plants, considering how deadly they are to certain weeds. So we will put in the following group all the materials which are sprayed on the foliage to effect a kill.

SELECTIVE WEED KILLERS. Several different types of chemicals would fall in this group, such as petroleum derivatives which kill by "burning," or direct injury to the tissues hit, and the hormone type of material, which may show little immediate effect but is absorbed into the leaf, translocated to all parts of the plant, and eventually kills by disrupting the normal process of cell development. The selectivity often depends on dosage, that is, a heavy dosage might kill almost everything, but a light application, of known strength, may be enough to kill certain weeds but do little or no damage to the berry plants. An example of the latter that is the hormone type is the well-known 2,4-D, which kills broad-leafed weeds in a lawn without killing the grass. Examples of the former are kerosene and paint thinner (Stoddard Solvent) which may be sprayed on cranberry plants early in the spring with little or no injury to the cranberries, but effectively killing many grasses and some broad-leafed weeds and burning other species to ground level. Some of these selective materials show great promise. Less than two weeks before this was written I saw a blueberry field at our state experiment station farm where the soil was mulched with sawdust in the rows and completely bare of weeds in the 3- or 4-foot strip between the sawdust ridges. In this field in previous years certain weeds, especially chickweed, had been a serious problem. The answer—Karmex, in this particular case.

These blueberries in the state of Washington are mulched with sawdust in the row. This largely prevents weed growth close to the plants.
Between the rows chemical weed killers plus some cultivation give
effective control.

PRE-EMERGENT WEED KILLERS. These materials are used to prevent
the emergence of weed seedlings. In certain cases it is feasible to
make only one spray application early in the spring, on bare
ground. Some materials can be used, with care, over crop plants
during the summer to prevent weed seed germination, or emergence, after each cultivation. These compounds have some value
for berries being grown under cultivation, which include most commercial, and some of the larger home garden, plantings. They may
make possible a decrease in the number of cultivations necessary,
and prevent the growth of some weeds which would be difficult to
reach with the cultivator and which might have to be pulled by hand.

SOME NEW PROBLEMS. Many special problems have arisen since
the chemical weed killers have appeared on the scene. Some tend
to drift in the wind, tiny droplets or gaseous fumes, to considerable
distances and kill or injure plants on neighboring farms or gardens.
Grapes are especially sensitive to 2,4-D. Commercial air applica-
tors flying over vineyards to get to wheat fields for which they had

TABLE VI
Some Chemical Weed Killers
Use according to directions of the manufacturer.

MATERIALS	REMARKS
Soil Sterilants	
Calcium Cyanamide	A partial sterilant, nitrogen fertilizer, leaves an alkaline residue. Apply in fall, plant in spring.
Methyl Bromide	Gas, to be applied under a tarpaulin. Kills insects, disease organisms also. Aerate a couple of days, then plant.
Sodium Chlorate	One of the older materials, some fire hazard, do not plant for several months.
Vapam	Liquid, seal in soil with water, kills some disease organisms, do not plant for at least two weeks.
Pre-emergents	
Crag Herbicide	Also known as SES and Sesone. For weed seeds, and seedlings not over ¼ inch high, can be used over growing plants. Do not spray newly set plants for at least two weeks.
Dinitros	Premerge, Sinox, and others; will kill foliage on contact. Use before planting or during dormant season for strawberries. May be used during growing season for bush fruits and grapes if kept off foliage.
IPC and CIPC	Especially for germinating grass seeds and small seedlings. Has been used with Crag Herbicide on strawberries.
Karmex DW	Known also as diuron; effective on broad-leaf weeds in bush fruits.
Selectives	
ATZ	Amino triazole. Especially for spot treating Canada thistle, other perennial weeds. Keep off berry foliage.
Kerosene	May be used for spot treatment of grasses.
Paint Thinner	Also known as Stoddard Solvent. For spot treating grasses or killing small annual weeds in bush fruit rows. Keep off foliage. Use full strength.
2,4-D	One of best-known selectives, especially for lawns; has been used with some success on strawberries but other materials are safer to use. Very injurious to grapes.

contracts to spray with 2,4-D have been charged with causing severe injury to the grapevines. Fortunately it is sometimes possible to alter a compound slightly to minimize the possibility of drift without losing the weed-killing ability. So now there are forms of 2,4-D safer to use than the volatile ester form which apparently caused most of the trouble with that particular chemical.

Some, and especially 2,4-D, have been extremely difficult to clean out of the spray tank, pump, and hose. I know of one experimental vineyard which had to be pulled out because, when it was sprayed with Bordeaux mixture, the sprayer, which had been used previously to kill dandelions in the lawn, had not been cleaned thoroughly enough.

When using any chemical weed killers, by all means read the instructions of the manufacturer, on the package, very carefully. I will not try to give specific directions here as formulations may change and new methods of cleaning the spray equipment may be recommended by the manufacturer.

EQUIPMENT AND APPLICATION METHODS. Some kind of a sprayer will be needed for applying weed-killing chemicals, although in certain cases an ordinary sprinkling can could be used. The trend recently has been toward application in as little liquid as possible, to cut down weight especially for air application, but also to leave the material on the leaves of the weeds in minute droplets which would not be large enough, or numerous enough, to have much tendency to run off. When 2,4-D was first used, very low pressures, possibly 25 pounds on the gauge, were recommended to give rather large droplets which would have less tendency to drift than smaller ones. With most materials it is probably best to use a pressure somewhere between this and the very high pressures, used in spraying fruit trees with pesticides, where a fog type with some drift is desired. The home gardener with the small sprayer often does not have the advantage of a pressure gauge on his equipment, so he will have to work out for himself the best way to get a thorough coverage of relatively small droplets, which will cling to the weed leaves but not drift to any extent. Drift will also depend on weather conditions. During certain parts of the year it may be necessary to do most of the weed spraying early in the morning or late in the evening, because there is usually less wind at that time.

The modern chemical weed killers are very potent materials and to be held in due respect. A pound or two of a chemical sprayed from an airplane to kill the vegetation over an acre was, a very few years ago, still in the realm of science fiction. There is an urge on the part of everyone, manufacturer, distributor, retailer, and consumer to try out a new material perhaps desperately needed. It may live up to all expectations for a while, then, reacting to some unusual weather, or soil conditions, it may cause unexpected and perhaps serious injury. So use any new material cautiously at first, until you are thoroughly convinced that it can be used safely under your conditions, or until it has been on the general market long enough for the building up of a real background of knowledge.

FLAME THROWERS. The elimination of weeds by fire has an appeal as we may think of fire as being the only fate sufficiently awful for some particularly noxious weed. But it isn't very effective, except where a trash pile has been burned, and then the accumulation of ash may raise nutritional difficulties with the berry crops, because of its excess of certain alkaline materials. Wood ashes carry a considerable amount of potash and certain other minerals, but ash piles should be well spread to utilize these nutrient materials without undesirable effects on the plants.

Fire might be used occasionally to clear off dry grass or weeds and eliminate most of the seeds still on the plants. I have a healthy respect for fire, and would much rather use some less dangerous method of weed control. The flame thrower will give some control and will permit the fire's being held on green weeds until the tops have been killed, but it is slow business, except possibly for singeing off newly sprouted seedlings. True, flame throwers have been adapted for use with certain field crops, but I do not consider them to be particularly useful in the small fruits planting.

GEESE AS WEEDERS. From time to time we see reports of the use of geese in berry fields, serving as weeders, not only working without pay but making a return in the way of meat. There is no doubt but what geese will graze down most of the common weeds, if confined and not given too much other food. During the dormant season they seem to do relatively little damage to berry plants, even strawberries. As the plants start to grow, the damage by trampling is more serious, and when the berries start to develop, the geese may eat some of them. For the small garden in urban areas, geese would be too noisy. For the larger garden, or commercial planting, I have always felt that the drawbacks to geese were probably greater than the advantages. They must have feed, not too much or their interest in weeding will lag. They must have water, shelter of some kind, fence to keep them where they are supposed to work, and pasture and quarters somewhere else when they must be moved out of the berry patch.

I have known of geese being used by commercial growers for strawberries, blueberries, and cranberries, but in most cases they were tried for a year or two and then given up, because the grower thought some of the chemical weed killers, or other methods, were less trouble. For the farm family which already has geese, and a berry patch, it would probably be worth while to try the geese as weeders. The lighter, more active breeds, such as the Chinese geese, have usually been considered better weeders and less destructive than the heavy breeds.

CHAPTER 8

Prevention of Plant Diseases

By and large the small fruits and grapes are relatively free of plant diseases and, in many home gardens, can be grown without control measures. However, there are various things which may cause the plants to die, or make poor growth, or show various types of leaf and stem injury. Probably the most important causes of these symptoms are insects and diseases, but there are a great many other things which may cause symptoms on the plants which are easy to confuse with disease symptoms. We could call these nonpathogenic troubles, and the actual diseases caused by fungi, bacteria, or viruses we would call pathogenic. It might be helpful to the gardener to describe some of these symptoms, so that he can arrive at some idea as to whether his plants are suffering from diseases which should be controlled.

OLD AGE. One of the causes of unhealthy appearance of the leaves is old age or senescence. All of the varieties of brambles, that is, the raspberries, blackberries, and dewberries, produce their fruit on canes that grew up from the roots, or crown, of the plant the year before. These canes die, after producing fruit, so that they are actually biennial. It is a desirable sanitary practice to remove these old canes as soon as the crop has been picked. They often have leaf spot, or cane spot, or cane canker diseases, and the spread of the diseases to the new canes will be lessened by just so much if the source of infection is removed.

Some beginners with berries do not know about these old canes dying. While I was in experiment station work I sometimes had such canes brought in with a query as to what was causing the leaves to turn yellow and brown. Actually, it is perfectly normal and there is nothing one can do about it. The rate at which the old leaves turn yellow and die is a fair index of the general well-being of the plants. If they remain green for a little while after the fruit has been produced it is good evidence that the growing conditions are satisfactory and that the plants are getting enough water and nutrients. However, if the plants are starved, the leaves on the old

111

canes will often start to turn yellow even before the berries ripen. Under extreme conditions they may actually die before the berries ripen, in which case the fruit will be worthless or, at the best, small and of poor quality.

Currant and gooseberry canes live for several years, and so yellowing of the leaves after fruit is produced is not the same as that just described for the brambles. Actually, currants and gooseberries do tend to mature their leaves rather early in the summer and drop them rather early in the fall. This early leaf drop, however, is often associated with certain leaf spot diseases. If it occurs too early, then the leaves should be examined for the characteristic small, brownish spots, and if the disease is serious enough a spray program can be planned for the following year. After the leaves start to turn yellow and drop it is too late to prevent it that season by spraying.

SYMPTOMS CAUSED BY WEED KILLERS. Some of the chemical weed killers, if they come in contact with the leaves of berry plants, will cause them to exhibit symptoms somewhat resembling those of a plant disease. If the leaves are blotched, with whitish or ivory-colored areas, especially near the ground, and a weed killer has been used, it is quite possible that it was responsible for the condition. Where a 2,4-D type of weed killer was used the young shoots and leaves may be somewhat twisted and distorted. At some stages these symptoms might easily be confused with the symptoms of certain virus diseases. Here we are not concerned with control, but rather identification, so that we will not waste money trying to control a disease that is not present. Of course the next time a weed killer is used we will want to be a little more careful about not getting it on the berry foliage.

FERTILIZER BURN. Fertilizer injury causes burning, or browning, of the edges of the leaves, usually the newer, more tender leaves, and may actually cause the death of new sprouts which have just come through the ground. It is frequently possible to connect this burning directly with the fertilizer, as you may be able to see heaps of the material concentrated in the areas where burning is evident. I have been invited to see strawberry fields where the grower was quite concerned as to why his plants suddenly looked sick. However, when we found little piles of still undissolved fertilizer in the spots where the plants had turned yellow and died, the cause was quite evident. Slight fertilizer burn is nothing to worry about, as the plants will usually grow out of it rapidly and make up in new growth what they had lost. However, if it is rather general and severe the plants may be set back materially. At any rate, it is better technique to apply the fertilizer at a time, and spread it in such a way, that no damage will occur.

DISEASE OR DEFICIENCY. Just the opposite condition may be responsible for quite similar burning of the leaves. For instance, extreme deficiencies of potash will cause brownish spots on the leaves, especially along the margins, followed eventually by dying of entire leaves and their dropping to the ground. Early stages of this deficiency may simply cause light-colored areas on the leaves, where the brown spots later develop. These light-colored areas, just as other deficiency symptoms, may resemble certain stages of virus diseases, and cause one to wonder what preventive measures he should be taking. Deficiency of nitrogen or to some extent of phosphorus and other nutrients will cause yellowing of the foliage, also quite similar to certain disease responses.

One way to help determine whether an unusual growth response is caused by a disease or a deficiency is to examine other plants growing under the same conditions. As a general rule, plant diseases are specific in attacking certain kinds of plants. For instance, the diseases which attack the raspberry in some cases attack blackberries, which are very closely related. These bramble diseases, however, do not appear on currants and gooseberries, or on strawberries. So if there are certain symptoms on the berry plants, which are also found on weeds growing between the rows, then a deficiency may be suspected, as the weeds will usually react to a deficiency in much the same way as the berry plants. If, however, the symptoms are strictly on the berry plants, and on just one kind of plant, then it is more likely to indicate a disease.

After one has become familiar with a few of the diseases, such as the leaf spots, and the spots produced by certain cane diseases, he will be able to identify them fairly easily. Usually the spots caused by one organism are of the same general shape, that is, you do not find one which is round, another triangular, another rather indefinite in outline being caused by the same disease. However, if you find numerous small roundish spots, and particularly if there is a dark center to the spot, they are very likely to indicate the presence of a so-called "leaf spot" disease. The darker center usually represents the fruiting bodies of the fungus. Examination under a hand lens may even disclose masses of spores being pushed out from this central mass.

SMOG. In certain areas it is possible for smog, or industrial gases in the air, under extreme conditions, to cause damage to plants. This damage may take the form of yellowing, and then burning of the edges, and turning brown of the leaves. It may be somewhat difficult to distinguish from symptoms caused by certain diseases or nutrient deficiencies. However, as with the deficiencies, if there is damage from air pollution it will usually show up on weeds and other plants as well.

Illuminating gas escaping into the soil will cause leaves to turn yellow and then die. Usually gas connections will come in to the front of the house and the pipe will not be near any berry plants.

EXCESS ACIDITY OR ALKALINITY. Soils that are too acid or alkaline will, of course, produce a restricted growth and the leaves will not be a good dark green in color. It is always safer, if one lives in an area where either extreme is to be expected, to have a soil test made and, if possible, adjust the soil to a relatively desirable pH reading before planting.

WEATHER INJURY. Just plain dry weather may cause the plants to be rather sickly looking under extreme conditions. It often happens that drouth occurs before the fertilizer is applied, and then it either lies on top of the soil or may dissolve just enough to go into the surface, but is not carried to a place where it is available to the plants. They may then show certain deficiencies, combined with drouth effects, which they would not show if there were ample rainfall.

Sun and wind burn may also be damaging in extremely dry weather. There are times when the evaporation rate is so high that the plants cannot take in water as fast as it is evaporated, and the leaves eventually become dry, and sometimes actually crisp, and then of course they will turn brown and die. The first thing to think of in a situation like this is to get more water into the soil, so that the plants will at least have an ample reservoir from which to draw. This type of injury may be prevented by turning the sprinklers on, if water is available, which will immediately reduce transpiration. The leaf tissues will be cooler, and conditions for normal growth will be much more satisfactory.

Of course, if the drouth is a condition which may occur for a long period of time, there may be a problem in continuing sprinkling. Perhaps water may be short, or the soil may be rather heavy, and too much sprinkling undesirable from the standpoint of soil aeration. Under such conditions, it would be desirable to use as fine a spray as possible. Small nozzles will break the water into fine droplets so that they will keep the leaves moist without a great deal of runoff to the ground. Much less water will be used. For actually applying water to wet the soil the coarser nozzles would be desirable, but for sprinkling to offset extremely high temperatures and drying winds the fine nozzles will be very useful. Of course, if there is a strong wind, and the nozzle is too fine, the mist will be blown onto the neighbor's yard and not hit where you want it to hit.

SYMPTOMS CAUSED BY POOR DRAINAGE. "Wet feet" caused by poor drainage is a frequent cause of trouble for all fruit plants, tree fruits as well as small fruits. It is mentioned again at this time because the plant responds to such conditions by producing rather weak growth, with slightly yellow to a rather strong yellow color. Where very poor, yellowish growth occurs on a low spot in the garden it can usually be connected rather definitely to too high a water table and consequent lack of aeration.

It does happen that there are certain soil diseases which are likely to be much more serious under such conditions. Regardless of whether it is just too much water or a specific disease, the first procedure is to correct the drainage situation. This may be done by any kind of drains, or, under certain conditions, ridging. However, it may be that a particular spot where this trouble is occurring cannot be well drained, especially if the soil is rather heavy and sticky, and that some other crop should be grown there. An annual crop, such as one of the vegetables, planted after the soil is dried out in the spring, may do extremely well.

FROSTED LEAVES. Several times this year I have been asked what caused certain deformities on the leaves of various plants. The leaves were rather below normal in size, a little uneven as to surface, and bore little greenish-yellow lines in a network pattern over at least a portion of the leaf surface. This type of injury is commonly caused by frost which occurred when the injured leaf was still enclosed in the bud or just opening. No damage was noticed at the time of the frost because the leaves which were already open were a little more resistant and did not show damage. Occasionally aphid injury to opening buds may cause somewhat similar markings on the young leaves. By the time the leaf has opened the injury is apparent, and it is too late to do anything except to realize what it is, and not be worried about a possible new type of virus disease.

The keen plantsman will spot these symptoms as they appear, and will usually be able to diagnose the trouble and act accordingly. The person who may be very much interested in plants, but who has had no experience, may notice these expressions of various types of injury and may be tempted to try a treatment which would be of no value for the cause of the particular symptom. Very often a little reasoning will indicate that the symptom does not indicate a disease at all, even though the gardener may never have seen it before.

THE TRUE PLANT DISEASES. Diseases which attack berry crops, as is true of all plant diseases, may be roughly divided into three groups, namely, fungus, bacterial, and virus diseases. There are good examples of each type which attack the various small fruit plants. It would be idle to speculate as to which is more destructive. If one has a fungus disease causing serious trouble, that is the most important at the time. Later, it may be another type on another berry crop.

VIRUSES. I will not try to distinguish technically between these three groups of diseases. However, as most people know from reading the popular science material in newspaper and magazine, the virus diseases are caused by some entity within the plant which is too small to be seen by the ordinary compound microscope. In the case of a number of virus diseases, however, it is possible to see the virus bodies within the plant cells by use of the electron microscope. There has been much study to determine whether or not the virus bodies are actually living organisms, or whether they are simply large protein molecules, which in some way have acquired the ability to reproduce themselves. From the standpoint of the gardener this is not too important as he is primarily interested in methods of avoiding losses.

BACTERIA. Bacterial diseases are caused by several types of organisms comprising the lowest form of plant life. Bacteria are without chlorophyll and must rely on other plants for their subsistence. They may, or may not, be motile, that is, able to swim around in surface water, or to move, on their own power, through the plant sap.

FUNGI. The bacteria are single-celled organisms, whereas the

A red raspberry shoot infected with mosaic, a virus disease. Note mottling and "bumpy" appearance of the leaves, a rather extreme case.

fungi are a slightly higher form of plant life, usually many celled. Some fungi produce motile spores which can move around like some of the bacteria. However, after they have passed through this stage, they settle down and produce certain long, threadlike growths called mycelia. These threads, which are microscopic in size, may penetrate a plant and go almost all the way through it. Certain ones may grow primarily on the surface. Some attack roots, others leaves, and still others fruits or flowers.

Our interest in the type of organism which causes a disease, that is, whether virus, bacterium, or fungus, is not entirely academic. Control measures for these three groups differ in several rather important respects. It is very helpful, therefore, when a disease occurs, if we do not know the specific disease, that we at least know that the organism is a fungus, a bacterium, or a virus. That will give us a lead in determining control measures.

DISEASE IDENTIFICATION. Actually, the identifying of fungi and bacteria, to say nothing of viruses, is a very difficult problem because of the extremely small size of the causal organism. In many cases, the identification can be made by, and only by, the plant response. In fact that is the only practical way at the present time of identifying virus diseases. It is true that bacteria or fungi may be cultured on artificial media and possibly the specific name of the organism determined eventually. However, this may be a very difficult problem because of the fact that there are likely to be myriads of other fungi and bacteria present, many of them relatively harmless.

In order to be absolutely sure that the particular organism suspected is the one actually causing a new or unknown disease, it must be grown on the culture medium, usually in a test tube, or a petri dish, in the laboratory, and then similar plants must be reinoculated and the disease symptoms reproduced. As can be seen, it is a long and tedious process and sometimes a fruitless quest. With some diseases the real trouble is caused by an organism which invades the host plant, grows rapidly, causes the disease symptoms, and then dies out, or at least recedes, while other organisms come in and attack the already injured tissues. Usually these secondary organisms are the ones which easily appear in the test tube, but they do not cause the specific symptoms when they are reinoculated into the plant.

CONTROL IS THE IMPORTANT THING. Small wonder the plant pathologist, while he is interested in this positive identification, finds, very often, that his most fruitful work is in developing control measures for a fungus which he may not know, or may only suspect as being a particular species. Of course, the more common diseases are rather easily identified because of the way they behave on the plant. A leaf spot may have a rather characteristic size and color and appear at a certain time during the summer on certain varieties more than on others. The pathologist has little hesitation in saying this is leaf spot "so and so." The same may be said of various stem cankers, rusts, and others.

Whenever a "new disease" appears then there is a real problem in identification. Usually the investigator starts to try certain control measures while he is still attempting to identify the organism. He can probably see at once the general type, that is, it may be a leaf spot, a stem canker, a root rot, or a fruit rot. If it is a leaf spot he knows that a spray program may control it. If it is a root rot he knows that it is likely to be a tough one, and that the final answer may be to change to a resistant variety, or even to stop growing that particular crop on that soil unless it can be completely steri- lized, which is a difficult problem.

In general, the fungi are responsible for the following types of diseases: most of the root rots, leaf spots, and cane blights and cankers, the mildewlike diseases, and most of the fruit rots. Bac- terial diseases of the small fruits and grapes are not as common as the fungus diseases. They may cause certain cane blights and some of the leaf spots and may, of course, be a factor in certain root rots.

MORE ABOUT VIRUSES. The virus diseases ordinarily are character- ized by weak growth and a mottling or distortion of the leaves, rather than specific lesions or spots. If there are spots they are usually fuzzy and indistinct, rather than being distinctly margined as are most fungus leaf spots. The virus diseases may be relatively harmless, or they may actually kill the plant very quickly. Usually they are somewhere in between, causing definite, but rather grad- ual, weakening of the plant. In some cases they may be present in a clone for many years without actually causing the plants to die. This was true of many of the strawberry varieties in years past, as it is now known that they undoubtedly had a virus disease over a long period of years, which simply made them weaker and less productive but did not cause death of the plants. In certain cases these viruses seemed to have very little in the way of specific symptoms other than the dwarfing and the cutting down of pro- duction. Until this was understood, and virus-free plants raised for comparison, it was usually thought that the type of growth observed was simply a varietal characteristic, and the presence of a disease was not suspected.

HOW DISEASES CAUSE DAMAGE. Referring to diseases of the human body for comparison, we do not consider the spots in measles, for instance, as being anything more than a symptom. The actual damage is done by the activity of the disease within the body, where it has a general weakening and debilitating effect. We might wonder if the same thing applies to plant diseases. The answer would be yes in some cases, and no in others. With the virus dis- eases we probably would give the same answer as for measles, and that is quite logical since measles, so far as we know, is caused by a virus.

Just how virus diseases damage plants is still somewhat mysterious. Especially since we know that some viruses may be carried
in certain varieties without showing any symptoms at all. They
do not interfere with normal growth and production, which may
be excellent. However, it can be determined that they are present
when another virus is brought in, because the two react together
to give injury of very specific type. Presumably, these viruses interfere in some way with the life processes in the cells.

The leaf spot diseases, caused by fungi or bacteria, do not ordinarily damage the plant except in so far as the spot itself is a
damaging agent. Of course, with a very heavy infection the lesions
may be so close together that the leaf cannot function normally.
Badly infected leaves will turn brown, die, and drop off. Where leaf
spots are more widely scattered, they can be considered as damaging about in proportion to the area of leaf surface covered by the
spots.

In the case of the rusts, however, such as the orange rust of
blackberry, there is more damage than may meet the eye. The
orange-colored pustules, which break and discharge spores, are
simply the outward expression of a growth within the plant. Young
shoots may be very badly distorted and actually killed since this
disease is systemic, which means it runs throughout the plant and
is not localized in a tiny spot, as many of the leaf spots are.

CANE CANKERS. Certain diseases cause cankers, or lesions, on the
canes. These may be quite superficial and interfere very little with
translocation of nutrients. Others go deeper, actually kill the cambium layer, and go into the conductive tissues inside, so that for
all purposes that part of the cane is entirely inactive. Such lesions
may grow completely around the cane and then the cane dies. In
general, we might say that cane cankers are damaging in proportion to their size and depth.

ROOT ROTS. The root rots, likewise, may be very aggressive and
soon kill the entire plant, or they may occur on certain portions of
the root system, killing part of it but never completely destroying
it. This group of diseases is not well understood, as it operates in
a way which is difficult to study experimentally. Sometimes the organism may invade the roots, then go on into the stem and plug
the conducting vessels so that there is no movement of water to
the top nor of elaborated plant foods to the roots. If this occurs
rather suddenly, while the plant is growing vigorously, the leaves

may suddenly wilt, and so we speak of that type of disease as a wilt.

Other root rots work a little differently, killing off a portion of the root surface and then spreading gradually to additional roots so that the plant becomes weak, the leaves turn yellowish, and death will come only after a rather long period. It is true that the leaves will wilt toward the end, but by that time they will be yellowish and show definitely that they had been injured long before they wilted.

DISEASES ATTACKING THE FRUIT. Any of the various types of diseases will damage the fruit eventually or will prevent its forming altogether. However, there are several diseases which attack the fruit directly. These, in general, belong to two classes, one of which is the leaf spot type. They make small spots on the fruit, as, for instance, anthracnose on raspberry, where one or more of the drupelets may be shriveled and gray, although the berry as a whole may not be damaged too much and is usually quite edible. However, if there are many of these spots on one fruit then the fruit becomes very unattractive, dry, and undesirable.

The other type of fruit disease is caused by various fungi which cause the berries to rot. One of the problems here is that the disease may continue to spread after the fruit is picked. It is very important therefore, that these diseases be controlled, especially if the berries are to be sold, or held for any length of time. Fruit rots on grape vary a little in that some of them are what we call soft rots, whereas others are dry rots. The terms are rather descriptive and will be discussed later in the chapter on grapes.

DISEASE RESISTANCE. One of the bright spots in this picture is that varieties have been found which are resistant to almost every important disease. Sometimes this resistance is slight, so that there is only slightly less damage. In other cases, resistance is almost complete. This indicates to the plant breeder that, if there is a little resistance present in some variety, it might be possible by crossing that variety with others to obtain seedlings which are still more resistant. The hope is that one may be found resistant enough to be satisfactory for production where susceptible varieties are undesirable.

Resistance, of course, is something hereditary, governed by the genes, and has to be discovered by the plant breeder. This has led to expeditions into remote parts of the world to find resistant strains of many different kinds of plants. Often these plants themselves are of no particular value, but their resistance may be bred into other varieties, so that eventually a good economic plant may be produced which is very resistant to some serious disease. This matter of resistance in all of the small fruits and grapes is especially important, important enough so that, for many of the common diseases, the pathologists' answer is that more resistant varieties should be developed.

THROW AWAY THE CRUTCH. Actually, a spray program is simply a crutch to lean upon. It is something that has to be applied every year, sometimes several times a year, and is expensive of time and material. If a variety resistant to diseases can be produced, resistant enough to grow without spraying, then countless thousands of gardeners, or farmers, as the case may be, will be able to throw away that crutch and grow the crop without having to carry on an expensive control program.

Dependence on resistant varieties is probably of more particular interest to small fruits growers than it is to growers of grapes or tree fruits. With those fruits there seem to be enough diseases and insects present, and few really resistant varieties, so that a spray program of some kind has to be followed anyway. The berry crops, however, under many conditions, can be grown in the home garden without any disease-control program at all. This is not true everywhere, but is true in enough places so that still further resistance is something that appeals very much to the berry grower, as it may mean the difference between having to spray regularly and not having to spray at all.

MUTATIONS OF DISEASE ORGANISMS. One of the big problems in resistance is that apparently mutations may appear in certain disease organisms. So even when a resistant variety is produced there is a possibility that the particular organism may mutate, or interbreed in some way, so that a more virulent strain is produced, one which will attack the formerly resistant variety. This does not minimize the importance of resistant varieties, as the cases where new and virulent strains of a disease have appeared have not been frequent. They do point, however, to the fact that scientists must be constantly aware of this problem and continue their breeding work, or be ready to start new projects if new disease strains appear.

There have been numerous actual cases where new varieties have been introduced, supposedly resistant to disease, but actually susceptible to some other disease, or new and virulent strains developed so that the breeder had to start over again. One may well ask what happened in years past, when there were no experiment stations, no plant breeders, and very little knowledge of plant diseases. It is true that berries were produced in those days and one wonders how. Actually the same problems existed then, as far as we can learn, because we read in the old accounts that flourishing small-fruits industries were built up in certain states, were very success-ful for a certain period, and then seemed to "run out." The pub-lished information frequently stated that the soil was exhausted, "strawberried out." It is evident now, from the descriptions, that certain diseases gradually built up in the area and forced it to give up the crop entirely.

COMMERCIAL INDUSTRY BASED ON RESISTANT VARIETIES. At the present time a large part of the commercial berry industry is based on varieties that have been bred for resistance to disease. Many of the varieties which were considered standard 25 or 30 years ago are now unheard of. If they were the only ones available there just would not be a commercial industry in many cases. The matter of breeding for resistance may not be so vital to the home gardener, as he can raise berries or not, as he feels like it. However, he does have the same problems, on a smaller scale, that the commercial grower has, and they have to be solved in essentially the same way, if he is to grow berries satisfactorily for his own use.

SANITARY MEASURES. Great progress has been made in chemical control of diseases, but sanitary measures are still important. If diseased leaves, or canes, or fruit can be burned, then the spores that would be disseminated from the spots on those plant parts can-not inoculate healthy plants. It is not feasible with many diseases to pick off the spotted material and burn it to such an extent that the disease will be controlled. However, in some cases control by spraying will be made less difficult and perhaps avoided altogether. The removal of raspberry and blackberry canes, as quickly as pos-sible after they have produced fruit, has already been mentioned. It goes without saying that these old canes should be burned as soon as possible after they are taken out.

Stem cankers, as found on blueberries, for instance, may be seen and removed by pruning. Usually the branch would die anyway, and taking it out is simply doing a necessary operation early enough to get an additional benefit from it.

Certain diseases tend to develop more rapidly and to a greater

The old fruiting canes in this Latham raspberry patch in New Jersey have just been cut out and will be burned. This is an important sanitary measure which helps in the control of several cane diseases.

extent where there is dense foliage and poor air circulation. Pruning to prevent such a condition will of course be an important sanitary measure. If there is to be spraying, then opening up the bushes will permit a more effective coverage.

ROGUING. Pruning will ordinarily not be effective in controlling systemic diseases, that is, those which spread throughout the plant. These would include the viruses, orange rust on the blackberry, and possibly others. With systemic diseases the method used is known as roguing, which means taking out the entire plant, rather than just pruning off an infected branch. Roguing is something that most commercial berry growers practice rather diligently. They do not always stop to inquire why a particular plant is weak, or off-color, or has some peculiar twist of the leaf, but if they think it is abnormal they suspect a virus disease and take it out and burn it.

Roguing is important for the control of virus diseases, but not so much because of the elimination of the one plant, which is under par but, even so, might have produced a fair crop. The main reason is that the viruses spread from diseased to healthy plants, usually by means of some insect, such as an aphid. Every diseased plant taken out of the field, therefore, lessens the likelihood of the disease spreading. Here is where a rather thorough knowledge of varietal characteristics is important. It might be easy for the home gardener to dig out plants, thinking they are virus infected, when actually they may have been struck by drift from a weed-killing spray, or they may have been injured by aphids, or frost, or other things which cause somewhat similar symptoms to those of a virus disease.

DESTROY DISEASED FRUIT. Another thing the home gardener may do is pick off and destroy diseased fruit. This is not so practical on a commercial scale, although growers may insist that strawberry pickers pull off and discard berries which have started to rot. These berries are usually thrown into the aisles and not destroyed, but if they are out where the sun can strike them they are much less likely to spread disease onto other berries or plant parts. It is usually down in the rather densely shaded and moist portions of the plant that these fruit rots develop. The home gardener can well go one step further and collect such rotten berries, by picking them into a separate cup, and destroy them.

Occasionally one or two clusters of grapes may be found with a little black rot starting. This will be a dark purplish spot on one side of the berry. If it is not general, then it would certainly be wise to pick off those berries or clusters and destroy them. If the spots are apparent on many clusters it would probably be a hopeless task, and one would have to rely on a better spray program next year.

CHEMICALS FOR DISEASE CONTROL. For many diseases sanitary measures are only partially helpful, or may not help at all, and for those we must rely on chemical sprays. Fortunately, great strides have been made in this field during the last few years. For a long time copper and sulfur sprays were the stand-bys, practically the only chemicals known which would control plant diseases. Copper and sulfur, though still widely used, have certain very definite drawbacks, particularly the likelihood of causing injury to the plants when used at a strength that will control the disease.

We now have a number of newer materials, such as captan, Fermate, and numerous others, which have proven quite satisfactory for many berry and grape diseases. These new fungicides have been a real boon to the home gardener, partly because they are much more effective in many cases than any previous material, but also because they are more pleasant to use than the older sulfur and copper compounds. This is not always true, but in general they are not too obnoxious to use, and they are not particularly corrosive to the spray equipment. As a matter of fact, many commercial strawberry fields are now sprayed or dusted with captan while the berries are ripening, in order to decrease the damage caused by gray mold, and without affecting flavor or odor of the berries.

ANTIBIOTICS. In general, the antibiotics, so important in the field of medicine, have not been effective against fungus diseases, but against certain bacterial diseases they have been useful. There is some evidence that certain ones, or combinations of two or more, may eventually prove successful for combating fungus diseases. Many of these new materials are the result of strict laboratory research, where literally thousands of chemical combinations have been tried out, first to see if they are toxic to disease organisms, and next to see whether they can be safely used on plants. Only a very few of the many materials tested have proven to be practical for actual disease control.

SOIL-BORNE DISEASES. In the field of soil-borne diseases there have also been some interesting developments. For a long time it was thought to be practically impossible to kill disease organisms in the soil, even after materials had been found which would kill insects and nematodes. More recently compounds like Vapam and methyl bromide have been developed and have proven remarkably effective. They may be useful to the home gardener in certain special cases.

These soil treatments are quite expensive when one considers the material and labor involved. Methyl bromide has to be applied under a gasproof tarp of polyethylene or similar material. Vapam has to be watered in thoroughly, and no planting done on the soil for at least two weeks afterwards. However, where there is a serious disease in the soil, which can be eliminated no other way, these materials may be very much worthwhile. Before attempting soil sterilization it would be desirable to talk with some local authorities, such as the county agricultural agent, or someone from the state experiment station about the problems involved. Under certain conditions, the organism for which you are attempting to find a control might also be in the soil surrounding the sterilized area, and it might come right back, in soil water, the following winter.

SOME OF THE NEWER CHEMICALS. A few of the present-day chemicals for the control of plant diseases are included in Table VII. This is not meant to be all-inclusive, but does give names of various types and a little information about the materials. Because of the large number of new compounds being marketed, manufactured names have been given to certain materials, and then the various manufacturers may use their own trade names for them. This is sometimes confusing to the gardener who may have used a material under one name, then hears about another name and thinks it is something brand new. He might even buy it, only to find that it is what he has already been using. Manufacturers include on the label, usually in fine print, a statement as to the active ingredients. By comparing the labels of two materials the gardener can determine if they are essentially the same, or if they actually contain different disease-controlling chemicals.

SPRAYING VS. DUSTING. There are two ways of applying chemicals to control insects and diseases, by spraying or dusting (three if we include the use of gas such as methyl bromide). For many years experiments were carried out to determine whether spraying or dusting was more effective, especially on tree fruits. In general these results indicated that spraying, for most diseases, was somewhat more effective, but in a few cases dusting was more satisfactory because of speed or other consideration. Somewhat the same thing applies to the small fruits and grapes. Often the most satisfactory coverage, and hence the best control, can be secured by spraying. However, there are certain pests which can be controlled quite well by dusts, even well enough so that, under certain conditions, the home gardener might be justified in purchasing only dusting equipment.

If the home garden is fairly extensive it is my feeling that both spraying and dusting equipment should be on hand, and the one used which best meets the immediate need. Certainly for treating strawberries with captan just before picking, dusting is more satisfactory, because the dust will float in under the leaves, and do a better job of covering the fruit. For most dormant applications spraying is superior because the canes are smooth and dust just doesn't stick. It is easier to direct the spray directly on the canes, whereas with dusting there is a large cloud of material, only a very small portion of which will actually hit a cane.

One of the drawbacks of dusting is that it is difficult to do when

TABLE VII
Some Effective Fungicides
Use according to the manufacturer's directions.

MATERIAL	REMARKS
Captan	Also sold as Orthocide. Has shown promise as a control for gray mold of berries and other diseases. No serious residue problem.
Copper	Used in Bordeaux mixture and various fixed copper fungicides. Usually effective but some may cause burning under certain conditions. Leave bluish residue. Corrosive to metal.
Ferbam	Also sold as Fermate. Black, so residue may be unsightly. Has come into rather general use for leaf and cane diseases.
Formaldehyde	For sterilizing flats, greenhouse benches, and seedbeds.
Methyl Bromide	A gas for soil sterilization, under a polyethylene tarpaulin. Will kill insects and weed seeds also.
Nabam	Also known as Dithane D-14 and Parzate Liquid.
Sulfur	Used as liquid lime sulfur for dormant sprays and in other liquid or dust forms for summer application. May cause injury to plants under certain conditions.
Vapam	A liquid for soil fumigation. Will also kill insects and weed seeds.

the wind is blowing. You will have to dust with the wind and there will be more dust on the windward side, even if you do not miss the leeward side altogether. Somewhat the same may be said for spraying, but usually you can direct the spray into the wind, if necessary, and at least hit both sides of the row.

POWER SPRAYERS. In considering spraying equipment for the home gardener, I would skip the large power sprayers, such as are used for commercial production. For a home garden on the farm, if there is a power sprayer available for other crops, it might be quite practical to use it for berries and grapes. If there are very few plants to be sprayed there is the problem of putting on just a few gallons, making it hardly worth while to use the big sprayer.

The small power sprayer, usually spoken of as an estate sprayer, on the other hand, is quite well adapted for use in the larger home gardens. These small sprayers, with tanks holding from 25 to 50 gallons, are usually mounted on rubber-tired wheels and can be pushed by hand, or towed by a car, or truck, or garden tractor. They have a gasoline engine and pump, patterned after the larger commercial outfits. As a matter of fact, the companies which make the large sprayers also make the smaller sprayers, and in most cases at least do a good workmanlike job on them. They can also be used for weed control in the lawn, spraying vegetable crops, spraying a few fruit trees, or shade trees, as well as spraying the berries.

These estate sprayers are good equipment, which can be used for many years to do a professional type job. Most of them have metal tanks. Fortunately, our newer insecticides and fungicides are much less corrosive than the old sulfur and copper and so the metal tanks are satisfactory. Certainly they eliminate the problem we used to have with wooden tanks which would dry out during the winter and have to be soaked up for several days before they could be used for spraying. Spraying with hand power equipment is tiresome if you have several rows of berries of considerable length. It is too easy then to justify skipping the spray application altogether.

HAND POWER SPRAYERS. The wheelbarrow type might be considered as "in between"—on wheels but hand pumped. They have their place, and yet I fancy many people who have bought this type would have been better served in the long run if they had gotten an estate sprayer. The latter usually has a propeller-type agitator, run by the motor, which will keep the material thoroughly mixed whenever the motor is running. The wheelbarrow type either does not have an agitator, or if it has one at all, it will be a paddle type, moving up and down as the pump handle goes up and down. This is not as satisfactory as the propeller type.

Another type which used to be popular was the barrel sprayer, a hand-operated outfit mounted on a barrel. It had a sturdy pump and a sturdy handle, and all that was needed was a sturdy boy on the handle to keep the pressure up. Given that combination it threw a good spray, and in the early days was even used for small commercial orchards. It is too bulky and laborious for modern-day ideas, and I mention it only to disparage it. Even though we may have exercised on the barrel pump handle we should think twice before trying to make our sons, or grandsons, do likewise.

SMALL HAND SPRAYERS. The knapsack sprayer was long a stand-by in European orchards and vineyards and has been used some in this country. It involved a tank of 5 or 6 gallons, flattened to fit a man's back, put on like a knapsack, with a pump handle extending forward under one arm. Some of these sprayers were very well made, and stood up under long hard usage, but the labor of getting the sprayer on and off, carrying it over the field, pumping and directing the spray at the same time, to say nothing of having spray material splashing over between one's shoulder blades, tend to make this equipment somewhat less than desirable. One place where this type has been used fairly satisfactorily is in spot weed control in cranberry bogs. Where the weeds were some distance apart portable equipment was needed and the knapsack worked out fairly well.

The so-called bucket sprayer is one with which many civil defense workers became familiar during the war. It is simply a pump which extends over a pail, with a suction tube on the inside and a foot rest on the outside. The plunger is worked up and down, like a bicycle pump, or there may be a handle like that on an old-fashioned water pump. These bucket sprayers were all right but difficult to move around. They were relatively cheap and have been used for washing cars, whitewashing chicken coops, and all sorts of things. If a person has one fruit tree he might do a fair job of spraying with a bucket sprayer.

For the person with just a few berries to spray, the compressed air sprayer is as satisfactory as any. This consists of a 3- or 3½-gallon tank with a brass cylinder running through the center. It is pumped up much as one would use a tire pump, and when the plunger can no longer be forced down easily it is locked in place. When the control valve is opened the air compressed in the tank forces out the spray in a fine mist. The sprayer can be carried by the pump handle or by a strap over the shoulder. Using it becomes pretty tiresome after a while, but for a small row of berries it can be quite satisfactory. One can mix up a small amount, perhaps as little as half a gallon, or even a quart, if he wants to spot spray some particular plant. It is convenient for weed control, and that is becoming increasingly important since the advent of chemical sprays. Agitation, of course, is by the sprayer's body motions.

HOSE SPRAYERS. There is another type of sprayer, designed specifically to appeal to the home gardener, about which I have some reservations. This consists of a small container that fastens on the end of the garden hose and contains spray material in solid form, which, presumably, erodes off at the proper speed to give the required spray concentration. Theoretically, this would be all right if the chemical dissolved at a uniform rate, which is a very difficult thing to work out. Some of these, which I have seen advertised, had a general-purpose charge of chemicals, designed to control all insects and diseases. It is well known that certain materials will control certain diseases fairly well but that for another disease another material may be better. The same applies to insects. True, the average home gardener might rather have a "shot gun" treatment such as this, but it will not, in the long run, give as good control as will tailoring the methods to fit the needs.

As of now, at least, the little compressed air sprayer strikes me as being a much more satisfactory tool for the home gardener than the hose sprayer. It can be a precision instrument, and is frequently used in spraying experiments where the amount of material, or concentration, must be carefully controlled, things which are difficult, at least, with any garden-hose attachment.

DUSTERS. Dusting equipment runs about the same gamut of size, complexity, and price as the sprayers. I do not know, just now, of any small power duster that is quite as satisfactory as the small power sprayers. However, there are hand dusters, particularly the crank-type duster, which will hold a gallon or more of the dust and with which one can cover a rather large area in a short time. As a matter of fact, one can cover more area, per unit of time, with this than he can with a small power sprayer. This duster hangs on shoulder straps with the crank convenient to the right hand. A flexible tube, or one that is adjustable, can be directed by the left hand to discharge the dust down or up, or to one side or the other.

There is another somewhat similar type called the knapsack duster, which, as the name indicates, fits over the shoulders and is held there by straps. A handle extends under the right arm and can be moved up and down like a pump handle. This duster has a small bellows arrangement near the bottom, and each movement of the handle sends out a puff of dust. This is particularly useful for dusting vegetables in hills, and for other places where application in puffs is better than a constant stream such as you get with the crank type. Either of these dusters is considerably cheaper than the smallest of the power sprayers. However, they are not particularly economical on materials. Partly because there is so much waste, one can depend on a dust program costing a little more than a spray program on the same area.

There are still smaller dusters which can be used for a small bed of plants, or for an infestation of caterpillars in a limited area. One of these is a Japanese miniature crank-type duster that is held in the left hand and the crank turned with the right. I have used one of these for three years and have found it very satisfactory around the greenhouse and occasionally for a plant or two in the field. However, when I tried to dust a row of strawberries with it, even a light breeze made it very difficult to get the dust to settle in where it was needed. There are some low-cost, bellows-type dusters available, which are operated much like the old fireplace bellows. Each puff takes a charge of dust with it. Somewhat similar is the type in which a plunger is operated through a tin cylinder, with a little dust compartment at the end of the cylinder. Neither of these is suitable for berries, except for a very few plants.

HOW TO APPLY SPRAYS AND DUSTS. Methods of application differ with the type of pest. If one is trying to control leaf-eating caterpillars working on top of the leaves, then spraying or dusting down onto the leaves will be the best. If one is attacking aphids, or some disease which might occur on the underside of the leaf, then the spray must be worked in from the side and directed upward as much as possible. This is where a power sprayer has an advantage. It throws a veritable cloud of fine droplets into the row and thoroughly saturates everything there. Leaves that were pointing the wrong way are blown around so that they get covered quite well, much better than is true with a small hand sprayer, where one has to rely entirely on changing the angle of the stream and position of the nozzle to hit all parts of the plant.

Under ideal atmospheric conditions, which usually occur about daybreak, a good duster will coat everything, probably doing a better job, in some respects, than would a sprayer. In the case of fungus diseases, the primary objective is to get the plant parts thoroughly covered with fungicide before a disease spore alights. Ordinarily after the spore has germinated and the mycelium has entered the plant, chemicals on the surface will not kill it. In other words, the spray is a preventive measure rather than an eliminative measure. It is true that certain sprays, such as concentrated lime sulfur, have some eradicative effects, but most of the modern sprays are strictly preventives. Since the disease spore is microscopic in size it is evident that a very thorough job has to be done so that no spores will find an unprotected spot.

SPREADERS AND STICKERS. In order to give better coverage and thus prevent unsprayed spots from offering a haven to spores, chemical materials called spreaders are frequently used. These have the ability to decrease surface tension so that, instead of collecting on the leaves as droplets and then running off, the spray with a spreader will tend to spread out, as the name indicates, and cover a larger area. Some of the spreaders are quite similar, or identical, to some of the materials we know as detergents; and some of the household detergents, used for dishwashing, are often used as spreaders.

Another problem is to get the material to stick on the leaf surface long enough to protect it against the invasion of germinating spores over a fairly long period, either until the danger of infection is past, or until it is time to put on another protective spray. Some of the materials will remain effective much longer than others, but it is quite desirable, in some sprays, to include a material called a sticker, usually with a spreading agent. In other words, the "spreader sticker" not only gives better coverage but tends to hold the material on the leaf for a longer period. Several brands of spreader sticker are available.

COMPATIBILITY. Modern spray materials have been checked very carefully to see that they do not cause injury to the plant at the concentrations recommended. However, sometimes it is desirable to combine them with other sprays, and occasionally the combination may form a material which does cause injury. If this occurs the materials are said to be "incompatible" so far as being combined as spraying materials is concerned. The table on the following page gives a brief summary of the compatibilities and incompatibilities of some of the available spray materials.

TABLE VIII

Compatibility of Some Spray Materials

	Aldrin, Endrin	Aramite	BHC, Lindane	Bordeaux	Captan	Chlordane	DDT, Methoxychlor.	Ferbam	Fixed Coppers	Karathane	Lead Arsenate	Lime	Lime Sulfur	Malathion	Nabam	Nicotine 40%	Oil—Dormant	Oil—Summer	Parathian	Rotenone	Sulfur—Wettable	Toxaphene	Urea	Zineb
Aldrin, Endrin			/d						/d			/	/											
Aramite			X						/	/		/	X											
BHC, Lindane			/d						/			/d	/			/								
Bordeaux	/d	X	/d		X	/		/d		/			X	X	/d					X	X	/	X	/d
Captan			X						/			X	X			/	X	X						
Chlordane			/									X	X			/								
DDT, Methoxychlor.												X	X				/	/						
Ferbam			/d						/d			/	/											
Fixed Coppers	/d	/	/		/			/d					X	/	/d					/				/d
Karathane		/		/					/				/	/	/		/	X	X					
Lead Arsenate													/d						/					
Lime	/	/	/d	X	X	X	/							/	/	/d				X	X		X	/
Lime Sulfur	/	X	/	X	X	X	X	/	X	/	/d			/	/	/d	/	X	/	X		X	/	/
Malathion			X						/	/		/	/											
Nabam			/d					/d				/	/											
Nicotine 40%		/		/	/				/				/d							/				
Oil—Dormant			X			/			X				/									/	/	
Oil—Summer			X			/			X				X									X	/	
Parathian			X						/		/	X	/				/							
Rotenone			X									X	X											
Sulfur—Wettable			/														/	X						
Toxaphene			X									X	X				/	/						
Urea													/											
Zineb			/d					/d				/	/											

X—not compatible　·　/—of doubtful compatibility　　　/d—decomposes on standing

CHAPTER 9

Insects and Their Control

Most of us as adults have an acquired, but almost involuntary, horror of insects of all kinds, especially "worms" as we usually call the larvae of various butterflies, moths, beetles, and sawflies. This seems to be an acquired revulsion, as small children are usually quite unafraid until conditioned by older people. The only reason for mentioning this here is to bring out the point that not all insects are harmful, and that we should not rush into an expensive spray operation at the mere sight of insects, before we are reasonably sure they are going to do some damage to the berry crop. This is not to intimate that insects may not be a menace to berries, but simply a caution to go slow and not scatter our shots, but direct them at the pests which we should control and at the time when the control methods will be the most effective.

KNOW YOUR INSECT ENEMIES. With insects, as with the plant diseases, it will be worth while to learn all we can about our enemies, their names if possible, but their habits especially. The U.S.D.A. and most experiment stations have bulletins and circulars on the subject, and there are numerous textbooks for any who become seriously interested in entomology, the science dealing with insects.

Space will not permit a full discussion in this book of all the small fruits insects. Some of the insects causing the most damage to specific small fruits will be discussed in the appropriate chapters in Part III. At this point we will consider some of the factors enabling us to determine whether insects we see are actually doing any harm and, if so, how we should go about trying to control them.

When I was in school the usual method of starting the study of insects was to consider their mouth parts. This was very helpful, for the type of mouth parts is not only an important character in identification and classification, but indicates quite definitely the type of injury to be expected and the method of control. So we begin by learning that insects may be divided roughly into the groups with chewing, sucking, and rasping mouth parts.

135

Clean foliage and fruit indicate insect pests are causing no damage. In some areas no sprays will be needed for insect control on blueberries.

CHEWING INSECTS. The grasshopper, Japanese beetle, both adult and larvae, the cutworms, larvae only, and many others are examples of insects with chewing mouth parts. They can chew holes in leaves, chew off young shoots, chew the margins of leaves, and in general consume plant tissues, leaving characteristic holes, notches, severed leaves or shoots. Since they actually chew up and swallow certain plant parts it indicates that one method of control would be to cover those parts with a stomach poison. For a long period the covering of plants with an arsenical preparation, usually arsenate of lead, was the only practical way of killing such insects. More recently a number of synthetic materials have been developed which will kill these, as well as other types of insects, by contact. They have not outmoded the killing by stomach poisoning, as some of these chemicals act as both contact and stomach poisons.

SUCKING INSECTS. The second type has sucking mouth parts, such as the aphids, leaf hoppers, and spittlebug. They feed, as does the mosquito, by inserting their tubular mouth parts and sucking out the plant juices. Obviously this enables the insect to push right through a coating of an old-fashioned stomach poison, without taking any of it into the digestive tract, hence only contact poisons are effective. It also means that there may be no scar, as the feeding puncture is usually invisible to the naked eye. This might complicate identification of the cause of injury but for the fact that aphids, and the young of the leaf hoppers, usually remain on one leaf or shoot, because they are wingless at that stage. In fact, some sucking insects may insert their sucking tube and stay in one place for a long period, or all their lives (some scale insects). Where leaf hoppers feed, a tiny yellowish spot may show on the upper surface of the leaf, even though the insect was working under the leaf. These spots may become so numerous the whole leaf has a yellowish color, and may turn brown and die. Other suckers, such as the tarnished plant bug, may leave no readily visible evidence of his feeding, on a fruit for instance, but later the tissues adjacent to the feeding puncture fail to develop and the fruit has a sunken spot there. So it is usually possible, without too much trouble, to find the type of insect which has caused damage.

Damage by a few, tiny, sucking insects might seem to be negligible when we think of the size of the insect as compared with the size of the plant, but some aphids may bring forth a new generation every two or three days, so that one stem mother, giving birth to living young, can multiply to tremendous numbers in just a few days. This is not the only risk, for many sucking insects inject some toxic material when they feed, which kills or stunts the tissues adjacent to the feeding punctures. Hence the potential injury is quite out of proportion to the actual loss of plant juices. Coupled with this is the fact that many virus diseases of small fruits may be transmitted from a diseased to a healthy plant by, and only by, an aphid or a leaf hopper. Hence the first appearance of these insects is cause for concern at least, and possibly serious consideration of control measures.

INSECTS WITH RASPING MOUTH PARTS. A third type of insect, such as the tiny thrip, has rasping mouth parts, with which it can scrape off portions of the epidermis of a leaf. Such spots usually become whitish yellow, and, if numerous enough, the leaf becomes brown and dies. With these insects some stomach poison might be taken in, but the most effective controls have been with the contact materials.

HOW INSECTS MAY INJURE PLANTS. We have already mentioned several ways in which insects can injure plants: by spreading diseases; by actually eating plant tissues, and thus reducing the functioning area of leaf, root or shoot; by sucking out the plant juices from root or leaf; and by injecting a poisonous material which will interfere with normal growth or actually kill plant tissues. There are girdlers, such as the larvae of the black vine weevil, which may kill young blueberry bushes by eating all the bark from the trunk in a zone, half an inch to an inch wide, just below the surface of the ground. This is out of sight, so there is no evidence of the injury until the plant starts to look yellowish, dull, and possibly to wilt, but by that time the injury may be a year old and the culprits escaped.

There are many kinds of borers, practically every kind of small-fruits plant being subject to its own particular species. Borers may damage by eating out a major part of an essential organ, as crown borers in the strawberry. Among the bush fruits the borers more frequently cause injury by breakage of weakened stems. The actual feeding of the borer larvae is most often in the pith tissues, more or less expendable, but as the larva increases in size it may eat into the strengthening or conducting tissues enough to permit breakage during stormy weather, and sometimes enough to cause the death of the cane aside from breakage.

Some insects cut off fruit buds, or new shoots, or web over growing tips, or cause the roots to become knotty and ill-functioning. And of course everyone is familiar with the fact that insects may attack the fruit, either internally or from the outside. Lest this list of possible ways insects may make life miserable for the berry grower discourage the reader before he even starts, let me hasten to add that many of these types of injury are not at all common. In many places berries of various kinds are grown without spraying, and with very little insect trouble, and when trouble does occur, it is most often caused by one or two insects and not by the whole list. But it should help to know how insects *may* damage the plants so one will be on the lookout for them.

The relative importance of the various kinds of insects is likely to be judged by what is bothering us at the present time. Those of greatest importance for the various fruits will be listed, with control suggestions, in later chapters.

INSECT PREFERENCES. Insects, like plant diseases, usually show preference for some particular kind of plant, although some, like the Japanese beetle, are almost omnivorous. But even the Jap beetle shows preference, not only for certain kinds of plants, but even for varieties. During several years of watching a variety vineyard in a bad Jap beetle section, I saw certain varieties almost defoliated every year, while others were harmed very little. Likewise the grape leaf hopper has distinct varietal preferences, as most other insects probably do, and as we will learn if there is a good opportunity to observe them. The preference for "kind" of fruit is often so strong that many insects are strictly one-host feeders.

HARMLESS AND BENEFICIAL INSECTS. Not all insects are harmful; some are harmless and some beneficial, from the gardener's standpoint. The more harmful ones would include the aphids, leaf hoppers, such gross feeders as the Japanese beetle, root-destroying insects as the strawberry root weevil, the borers, scale insects, thrips, fruitworms, and others for which no good word can be said.

On the other hand there are those such as the ladybird beetle which feeds on aphids; the praying mantis, also an insect eater; many kinds of little known or seen parasitic wasps; and of course the bees, which are generally beneficial from the standpoint of pollination but which may cause considerable damage to ripening grapes, once they develop a taste for the juice. There may be some argument as to which first breaks the skin, honeybees or the larger hornets and wasps, but the bees certainly do their share of cleaning out the pulp, leaving a cluster of dry, empty shells.

From the standpoint of the total number of insect species the greatest number do not affect the berry grower one way or another, so we may consider them harmless. Such obvious things as the dragonflies, most of the butterflies and moths, most of the ground beetles, and ants are of no immediate importance.

SANITARY MEASURES. Although there are modern insecticides, which may seem no less than miraculous to the older gardener, first attention should still be given to sanitary measures as a means of control. These sanitary methods are preventive in nature, directed at whatever harmful insects are present, but usually represent just simple good-gardening technique, relatively inexpensive as control measures because they should be done anyway. Take the matter of planting on sod or very weedy ground. It should not be done unless absolutely necessary because of inevitable trouble with weeds, and a year's preparation, perhaps while a short-season annual crop is grown, will help to eliminate, or greatly reduce, the population of such insects as white grubs, which often infest sod. This added time will also permit working in lime if needed, phosphorus, and organic matter, and an opportunity of assessing the fertility of the soil by observing the growth and appearance of the weeds.

Pruning is about the only way to eliminate certain borers which may have entered the canes. Be sure to cut down far enough to remove the larvae, and then burn the prunings. Some borers may be at least partially controlled by other means, but measures must be taken before the insect is actually inside the wood. Sometimes a borer which is not specifically a small-fruits pest, as the corn borer, may migrate to raspberry canes and hole up for the winter, usually causing the cane to break off where the borer entered. In regions where this insect is present the sanitary cleanup measures will be most important if practiced on corn and certain weeds, as well as the berries.

CHEMICAL SPRAYS OR DUSTS. By far the most effective method of controlling insects on small fruits is by chemical treatments. Most of the insecticides may be obtained either as dusts or wettable materials for use as sprays. If results of experiments have indicated either spray or dust is superior for a particular insect it will be so indicated in the discussion of that pest in the appropriate fruit chapter. When buying an insecticide be sure to get a wettable material, for use as a spray, as materials sold for dusting will usually be very difficult to mix with water. Likewise the wettable materials will ordinarily not be dry and fluffy enough to give good coverage as dusts.

STOMACH POISONS. For many years the stomach poisons, and especially arsenate of lead, were the most important factors in insect control, but they had many faults. There was a possibility of harmful residue on the fruit so such sprays could be used only up to a certain point before the date of ripening, unless the fruit were to go through an acid wash, not very satisfactory for the highly perishable small fruits. If the insects didn't like the spray they might refuse to eat enough to cause death, and if they did eat that much it meant just that much damage to the plants.

CONTACT POISONS. The modern trend is toward contact poisons which will kill adult insects or larvae and occasionally leave a residue on the leaves which will kill insects as they walk through it. In some cases this residue serves as a stomach poison for a short period, after which it changes chemically, weathers off, and is no

Spraying for pest control is nearly always necessary in commercial plantings. Fixed nozzles throw out a fog at rear of this North Carolina blueberry sprayer.

longer toxic to either insect or man. With most of these materials there is no build-up in the soil of chemicals which may injure the growth of plants, as there was with lead arsenate. This is not to be interpreted as condemning for all purposes things like lead arsenate. For a sudden plague of leaf-eating insects, such as tent caterpillars, at a time when there is no developing fruit on the plant, a spray of arsenate of lead may be economical, very effective, and entail no danger at all. Of course the chemicals, empty containers, and washings of the spray equipment should be kept from children, or, more appropriately, children kept from them. But we may have things just as deadly in the family medicine closet, or on the cleaning shelf.

Some of the earliest contact insecticides were lime sulfur and oil emulsions, used as dormant sprays for scale insects, and still effective. Later plant products such as nicotine, pyrethrum, and rotenone were developed and are still being used for some purposes. Nicotine is most effective when used at high temperatures, a distinct drawback in a climate such as ours, where we seldom have the required conditions. Pyrethrum and rotenone are somewhat expensive and have been largely superseded for agricultural use by the newer synthetics.

THE NEWER SYNTHETICS. Pioneer of the synthetics is DDT, which came into its own during the Second World War. Its toxicity to certain insects in very small amounts was phenomenal, but for other species it was much less effective. Other materials have proven much better for aphids, for instance. Unfortunately, two drawbacks to the use of DDT have shown up. One has been the development of resistance to its effect by certain insects. The home gardener probably should not worry too much about this as it usually takes a few years for resistance to build up, and with some insects it may not appear at all. If he does a thorough job even insects which may be somewhat more resistant than others will probably be killed. If, after a few years, DDT seems to be less effective one can then change to other available materials.

The more serious fault of DDT is that it encourages the build-up of certain pests, such as the red spider mites and woolly aphids. This has practically eliminated DDT for orchard use in certain areas where it had been hailed as the answer for the control of codling moth. In some cases it can still be used for part of the applications, or with supplementary control measures for the red mite. This build-up of mites and woolly aphids may be due, in large part, to the killing off of predators, other insects which have helped restrict the mite population.

More recently parathion has proven to be an excellent insecticide, but more toxic to warm-blooded animals than DDT. Except in very unusual cases I would suggest the home gardener leave parathion to the commercial grower, who will use an appropriate mask and protective clothing. Malathion is another material somewhat similar to parathion, very effective for many insects, and considerably safer to use than parathion. It is quite effective for aphids, leaf hoppers, and in fact most any insect that can be hit. Benzene hexachloride is a synthetic insecticide which is quite effective for many insects but unfortunately may cause an off-flavor in certain food crops, so it is not in favor for garden use. A number of other materials are listed in Table IX, and some will be further considered in later chapters.

INSECTICIDES FOR SOIL INSECTS. There are usually insects below the soil surface, some harmful, such as wireworms, Japanese beetle grubs, white grubs, root weevils, and some species of aphids. Some of the newer insecticides, including DDT, aldrin, and several others have been very effective, and one treatment may last for more than one year. Such soil treatments are expensive, and not to be used unless needed, but do offer a welcome control for some insects formerly thought to be practically uncontrollabe. In addition to the materials which were first developed for above-ground application there are others which are strictly soil fumigants, some gases, as methyl bromide, others liquids which turn to gas within the soil, as ethylene dibromide, but these are mostly deadly to plants, so usable only for preplanting preparation. Some, such as Vapam, are general-purpose fumigants for weeds, diseases, nematodes, and insects.

TABLE IX
Some of the Effective Insecticides
Use only as recommended by the manufacturer.

MATERIAL	REMARKS
Aldrin	Effective soil treatment for strawberry weevil.
Aramite	Specifically for mites, as red spider mite.
Arsenate of Lead	A stomach poison. Do not use on developing fruit because of poisonous residue.
BHC	Benzene hexachloride. Effective as a soil treatment for certain insects but may affect flavor of fruit.
Chlordane	Effective soil treatment for strawberry weevil.
DDT	Good contact insecticide. Where used mite population tends to build up.
Lime Sulfur	Used for scale insects at dormant strength.
Lindane	A form of BHC less likely to cause off-flavors.
Malathion	Effective contact insecticide, less dangerous to use than parathion.
Nicotine	Effective as contact spray for aphids but only at temperatures of 80 degrees or above.
Oil	Various emulsions used in dormant sprays.
Parathion	Probably the most effective contact insecticide but very poisonous to man. Not generally recommended for home garden use.
Pyrethrum	A plant product effective as a contact spray.
Rotenone	A plant product effective against certain insects.

POISON BAITS. Another time-tried method of control has been poison baits, effective for cutworms and a fair, but now outmoded, method for strawberry weevil. Cutworms may occasionally cut off young raspberry shoots, and climbing cutworms may cause considerable damage to young leaves by chewing holes in them, a mysterious problem as the cutworms go down to spend the day under a bit of trash or a clod of soil. These insects are not always present, but may suddenly appear in considerable numbers, often causing anxiety because the damage increases from day to day without any insects being seen, unless one looks by flashlight. Spraying soil and foliage with DDT or malathion would probably clean up the infestation, but so will the old-fashioned poison bait made up as follows:

Bran	1 lb.
Paris Green	2 teaspoons
Molasses	2 tablespoons
Water enough to moisten	

Mix bran and Paris green dry. Add water to molasses and mix thoroughly with the bran and Paris green. It should be moist but crumbly, not too wet. This should be placed in little piles near where the cutworms are working, or scattered on the ground in the evening. There may be potential danger to bird and animal life, but I have never heard of cutworm bait actually causing injury to anything but the cutworms. Raking over lightly next morning would so mix the bait with the soil as to eliminate danger.

Spray equipment for insecticides does not differ from that discussed for fungicides. As a matter of fact many times it is entirely practical to apply both in the same spray, and some manufacturers package formulas designed to control both insects and diseases. Such formulas provide a shotgun type of control, which may be satisfactory for a large number of pests, even though at times there may be no pest present of the type one of the components is designed to control, hence some wastage. For the casual gardener such possible wastage is minor, as compared to the convenience of buying one bag of spray material to control everything. But actually it may not control every possible insect, and so the alert gardener should know something about individual insecticides and be prepared to use the necessary treatment when such a pest shows up.

REPELLENTS AND ATTRACTANTS. Many other methods of insect control, or eradication, have been studied and are still under investigation; various forms of radiation for instance, promising for insects in packaged materials but not as yet for small fruits in the field. Repellents would, in many cases, be just as satisfactory as lethal materials if they would work, but so far it is usually easier to kill an insect than to repel it. At the opposite extreme are attractants, strange as it may seem, not to add to our insect woes, but to draw the pests to one spot where they can be more easily hit by spray or dust. Attractants have played an important part in trapping, to determine presence of certain serious pests such as the Mediterranean fruit fly. Repellents and attractants tested have included not only chemicals but light of different wave lengths. So far traps baited with attractants have been more effective in surveying to determine presence of insects than they have in actual eradication, although they do have some value as a control measure.

PARASITES. "Big bugs have smaller bugs to bite 'em, and these bugs have smaller bugs, and so ad infinitem," is a bit of doggerel I learned as part of my course in Freshman Entomology. This was used to introduce the subject of parasitism, in which we learned that most insects do have other insects which prey on them in one way or another, sometimes actually eating them, as the ladybird eats the aphids. In other cases the parasite lays an egg in a grub, which will hatch out, feed on the grub's "innards" and effectually prevent it from developing into a moth, butterfly, or beetle which would lay more eggs to hatch out more grubs. One example known to most gardeners is the tomato worm so often seen with the small white cocoons of the parasites hanging to its sides. Few parasites are so large and easily seen, but there are many of them. One important activity of the U.S.D.A. has been to search the world for parasites which could be introduced to this country to help control certain pests difficult to hold down by chemicals. There is little the gardener will be able to do in this field to help solve his own problems, but it is something he should know about.

This control of one living organism by another is called biological control, which would range from the grazing down of a noxious weed by livestock to introducing one virus disease to prey on another one. As a matter of fact there has been considerable progress made in control of insects by other insects. One difficulty is that the parasites can't give 100 per cent control or they will eliminate themselves by eliminating their food supply. And if we spray to clean up the few not parasitized we are very likely to kill off the parasites. The hope is to find a balance point where the insect causing damage to the berries, or other crop, will be reduced in numbers to a point where it is capable of causing very little damage, so little that spraying to control the remainder is not necessary.

Other biological controls involve fungi, bacteria, and nematodes, all of which have been used, experimentally, to control Japanese beetle and some other insects. We can look for further developments in the field of biological control. This may eventually be of more importance to the home gardener than the commercial grower, since he may be willing to settle for slightly less than perfect control and since spraying in a small garden, to help eliminate a pest, may not be so likely to kill off all the parasites as it would be in a commercial production area.

There are some gardeners who do not use chemical sprays because they are not "nature's way," or because they are afraid of being poisoned. However, at the present time, the chemical sprays or dusts, as recommended by the experiment stations, are undoubtedly the most effective for many insects. Furthermore, both state and federal authorities have been very careful to recommend only those materials which may be used with safety. Manufacturers are required to obtain approval before marketing spray materials and to include directions which, if followed, will insure that they are perfectly safe, both to the persons who apply them and to those who eat the fruit. The directions on the package should be followed carefully.

CHAPTER 10

Other Pests and Nuisances

Since we have just been discussing insects it might be best to start this chapter with the mites, insectlike animal life, allied to the spiders which differ from the true insects in having four, rather than three, pairs of legs. Some of the mites are called spider mites as they resemble spiders and even spin a slight amount of web.

RED MITES. The most prevalent is the red spider mite, a common pest in greenhouses. It attacks many species of plants out-of-doors in the warmer parts of the country, and especially in years of drouth and high temperatures. Strawberries and red raspberries are sometimes badly injured by these almost microscopic mites. An experienced gardener with good sight can see them well enough to know what the trouble is, but it requires a hand lens actually to see the mites moving slowly about, but with legs moving more rapidly and almost continuously. The comparatively large spherical reddish eggs can also be seen with a fair hand lens. Drouth symptoms make this pest doubly hard to spot, as it also tends to make the foliage duller and more yellowish. The mites themselves prefer the underside of the leaf, causing a tiny yellowish stippling to show on the upper surface. In a heavy infestation mites will be found over the entire plant.

In greenhouses the old preventive and remedy, not too effective, was frequent syringing of the undersides of the leaves with water. Certain chemicals, such as sulfur, applied as a dust, helped, but really efficient control of a heavy infestation in dry weather was extremely difficult until some of the newer organic insecticides came on the market. Malathion will give some control, but materials designed specifically for mites, such as Aramite, are usually more effective.

Not all mites are spiderlike in appearance. Some are so small they can be found with difficulty, even with a strong hand lens. These very small mites move around very little and are usually pinkish, or flesh-colored, and somewhat blimp-shaped. The damage they do, presumably by some sort of toxic injection, is out of all proportion to their numbers and the volume of juice they extract from the plant. Mites of this type, such as the cyclamen mite, are extremely hard to control. Sanitary measures, such as cleanup of infested refuse, planting only clean plants, hot-water treatment, and spray with certain chemicals for specific mites, make reasonable control possible, but not easy.

SYMPHYLIDS. Symphylids are small centipede-like creatures, about ¼ inch long, with voracious appetites, which are present in some soils, particularly in the Northwest. In spots where the concentration is heavy they can completely kill out strawberries and certain other crops by eating off the roots. Since they have no stage, as do most of the insects, where they are above ground, the control must be by injecting some chemical into the soil which will kill by gassing or poisoning. This is a tough problem in certain limited areas. If you have reason to think symphylids are present in your garden it would be well to get help from the local extension or experiment station staff in order to take advantage of the very latest research findings.

NEMATODES. Probably the most serious plant pests, aside from the diseases and insects, are the nematodes, or eelworms, microscopic (or almost so) one-celled worms of many species and well distributed over the world. Some are probably harmless, a very few beneficial in that they attack harmful insects, and many others harmful to certain plants. At least three different types attack the strawberry, which seems to be more susceptible to nematode damage than the other small fruits. However, it is by no means certain that all the kinds of nematodes attacking the small fruits have been identified and their importance evaluated.

A common type is the root knot nematode which causes swellings on the roots which interfere with their proper functioning and hence weaken the plant. Others pierce the roots, and may enter them, causing some direct injury and probably facilitating entry of fungi, bacteria, and possibly viruses. The "black root" of strawberry complex appears now to be based directly on nematode injury. Not all work below ground. The bud nematode of strawberry, as the name indicates, infests the growing points, or buds, at the tip of the crown, and causes malformation of leaves and blooms and sharply reduces the crop.

Here again the gardener can take comfort from the fact that if he has vigorous growth and good production it indicates that nematodes, although some species are probably present, are not building up to a point where he needs to worry about them. Even so, it is wise to rotate strawberries. That is, do not plant a new row immediately adjacent to an old row if you have any other place you can use, nor should you plow under a strawberry patch and immediately plant back in the same place. Allow two or three years in between if you can; it will help with certain disease and insect problems as well as with nematodes. It is very important also to set plants that are as nearly as possible nematode-free. If you are accustomed to getting plants from your own patch, or from a neighbor, be sure that the roots are straight and free from small knots, white and free from the typical black root lesions, and with leaves that are of normal size and shape and free from abnormal puckering. Just good common sense. And yet I have seen people pick out the poorer plants to set a new patch, because they wanted to save the best for fruit production.

DIFFICULT TO ELIMINATE. Once nematodes are inside a plant it is an almost impossible task to eliminate them. The home gardener shouldn't even try unless he is an incorrigible experimenter. It has been possible in certain cases to immerse fully dormant strawberry plants in hot water, 121 degrees for seven minutes, and kill the nematodes without killing the plants, or at least not all of them. The purpose was to get at least a few nematode-free plants, which could them be grown on fumigated soil, to produce more healthy plants and eventually a commercial stock of nematode-free, or almost free, plants to be offered to the public by the nurserymen. Hot-water treatment, where a degree too high may kill the plant and a degree too low will not kill all the nematodes, is for the experts.

Considerable progress has been made in developing treatments to kill the nematodes in the soil. By planting clean plants on clean soil the berry grower has a good chance of vigorous, productive growth. Since nematodes have been causing more trouble with strawberries than with the cane or bush fruits it is logical that most of the research has been directed to that fruit. To my knowledge, strawberries are the only small fruits now obtainable nematode free. If one is thinking of the possibility of fumigating his soil, an expensive process at the best, it would be well to consider carefully the whole range of pests, diseases, insects, symphylids, nematodes, and weeds. It may be feasible to use a material which will kill all of them, or at least all of the ones present in injurious numbers. As I see it now not very many home berry growers could profitably carry out soil fumigation, but, for those with pest problems which do not seem to yield to any other treatment, fumigation may be worth considering. Some of the available soil fumigants are listed in Table X.

TABLE X
Soil Fumigants
Use according to directions of the manufacturer.

MATERIAL	REMARKS
D-D	Also sold as Dowfume N. A liquid to be injected into the soil.
EDB	Ethylene dibromide. A liquid to be injected into the soil.
Methyl Bromide	A gas to be applied under a tarpaulin. Will kill weed seeds, insects, disease spores.
Nemagon	A granular material to be worked into the soil.
Vapam	A liquid to be used as a soil drench. Will kill most weed seeds and disease spores.

THE BIRD PROBLEM. In some places protection of berry plantings against depredations by birds is more of a problem than protection against insects or diseases. Certainly less real progress has been made in preventing damage by birds than by insects and diseases when we consider the newer insecticides and fungicides. In general the problem is one of repellency, as most of us do not want to kill off the birds, even if it were legal. Probably most of us would except the crows and starlings, but they have their friends. From my own experience I would not hesitate to recommend the shotgun for crows. You will be lucky if you ever hit one, as they are very wary of guns, but shooting occasionally when they come within sight will probably be effective in convincing them that other places are safer. I feel the same way about starlings, although they are likely to give the most trouble in urban or suburban areas where shooting is not permissible.

For other birds, also, a shotgun blast in the berry patch once or twice a day, just for the noise, will be as effective as anything in

A sure way to keep birds from stealing blueberries is to fence them out.

keeping them away. Certain manufacturers have used this knowledge to develop automatic noisemakers which make a loud report at irregular intervals. However, if the reports are too evenly spaced the birds may become indifferent to them. The youngsters of the family, with appropriate noisemaking equipment, could be very effective in this field, provided they get out early enough in the morning. Birds are early feeders, often doing the most damage soon after dawn.

Careful observation and many experiments conducted in various parts of the country with somewhat indifferent success have developed one important fact. That fact is that birds are much easier to keep away from the berry patch if they are never permitted to get a taste of the ripe berries. Once the taste is acquired they will sneak in at dawn or dusk, or even with pickers in the field, keeping as far away from people as possible, then grabbing a berry and flying away to eat it. Hence methods of scaring the birds away should be put in operation before the fruit ripens.

SCARECROWS, NEW AND TRADITIONAL. The use of scarecrows in the old traditional sense does not seem to be as effective as some other devices which involve motion. Running a string the length of the garden and suspending from it paper bags, blown up to make them balloonlike, and hanging on drop cords from one to three feet long, provides a number of objects which will sway in the breeze enough to discourage birds, at least to some degree. Instead of the bags, long strips of tin or aluminum, an inch wide and a foot or two long and slightly bent at intervals to encourage them to spin in the breeze, will provide motion and flashing reflected light. Some of the wind-activated objects used to call attention to filling-station advertising should work as well or better.

The bird-control problem in some oriental countries, in rice fields for instance, may be quite serious. A boy on a tower in the middle of the field, with strings running to the extremities, will jerk them from time to time to start suspended objects, such as metal strips, jumping around to scare the birds. What American boy wouldn't like to build the tower or tree house, but then to watch from it from dawn to dusk——Perhaps we should rely on the wind.

One of the most effective measures I have seen was the tethering of a captive hawk to a post in the middle of a berry field. A stuffed hawk or owl, if moved around occasionally, might work very well.

BIRDS MAY BE FENCED OUT. None of the methods of scaring birds so far devised is 100 per cent effective. A cage of chicken fence, or a cover of cheesecloth or netting of some kind, is a more positive method. I have seen screen houses over fairly large blueberry plantings, and also individual plant cages, both methods rather expensive. Cheesecloth or tobacco shade cloth, in pieces large enough to cover a bush, can be thrown over the top just before the berries start to ripen, to give effective protection. Usually it will not be necessary to make the enclosure absolutely bird-tight at the bottom, as they are not likely to crawl through a low opening to go up inside a net. Using snap clothespins to hold the cloth around the bush will make it fairly easy to remove for picking. If put on just before the berries ripen and removed and stored at the last picking the cloth should last for three or four seasons.

What has been said above refers to all small fruits to some extent, but to blueberries in particular, which seem to be especially attractive to many kinds of birds. Strawberries may be injured some, grapes and raspberries occasionally, the other berries less frequently.

A cheesecloth cover, held by snap clothespins, is effective in excluding birds, which will seldom come up inside even though there are openings at the bottom.

ENOUGH BERRIES FOR ALL. From the space that has been used to discuss birds some may wonder how it is possible to produce berries commercially, or why it is commercial growers do not seem to be bothered. Actually birds do cause blueberry growers considerable trouble, but they produce enough for the birds also. The birds of a particular neighborhood concentrating on half a dozen blueberry bushes can remove every berry as fast as it turns color, but the same number of birds working on an acre of blueberries might eat just as much without it being noticeable. In commercial fields there are usually pickers about and that helps to discourage the birds, especially if they can be scared away during the few days between the ripening of the first berries and the time picking starts.

DAMAGE BY ANIMALS. Rabbits may occasionally nip off a young blueberry plant, but unless there are lots of rabbits and other food supplies are scarce, there is not much to be feared. If trouble is anticipated, a chicken-wire protection around the individual plant or around the garden during the first year may be advisable. Repellent sprays may be obtained but the wire netting is positive, provided it is high enough so that it will not be covered by drifting snow.

In some localities moles are a problem in berry plantings, as well as in the lawn or vegetable garden, and of course the control is the same. We are in mole country, and trapping has been rather effective for us, available poisons less so. Occasionally a cat will develop into a mole catcher, for sport apparently, as they do not seem to eat the moles.

Since mulching is so desirable in the small fruits garden there is always the possibility of mice working in and under the mulch. Fortunately mice do not seem particularly anxious to feed on the berry crowns and roots as they do on young apple trees, and so girdling is not often found. However, if there is a large mouse population, as indicated by exit holes and burrows through the mulch or just under it, and there should happen to be a severe winter, there might be damage, as the mice may feed on anything available. In the home garden, cats are likely to keep the mouse population down. Poison baits are effective, and more recently spraying with endrin has given good control in some apple orchards. It would presumably work in the berry patch as well.

Deer seem to like certain varieties of blueberries, especially during the winter when other forage is less abundant. I have known of their causing damage in commercial plantings on the East Coast, and damage in home gardens here on the Pacific Coast is occasionally reported. Deer may be fenced out, but it takes a very high fence if they really want to cross it. Research work has been carried out on chemical repellents by various wildlife agencies. However, except in very unusual cases, the probable damage to be expected from deer is not enough to warrant most home gardeners' investing in either high fences or repellents. Any kind of a dog roaming the berry patch is usually enough to scare them away.

In certain localities slugs may cause some damage by feeding on ripening strawberries or foliage of young shoots of some of the bush fruits. There are satisfactory poison baits, as well as dusts, all based on the use of metaldehyde, which seems specifically toxic to slugs.

Unauthorized traffic through the small fruits planting by children, chickens, dogs, or farm animals can be provoking, especially if the trespassers belong to the neighbors. Fencing may be necessary. Blackberries or raspberries with a good wire trellis may be used around the outside, or at least on the side from which most of the traffic is likely to come. Ripening berries are an invitation to eat, and taking them, like "stealing" watermelons, doesn't seem exactly criminal to growing boys, so the fence may be advisable. But here again it may be well to consider the means suggested for avoiding bird damage, planting "enough for all."

CHAPTER 11

Designing and Planting a
Small Fruits Garden

Many a row of strawberries or other berries, and many a grapevine, has been planted without thought of garden design, just set in what seems the only vacant spot when the plants arrive as a gift from one of the neighbors, or as a result of impulse buying. Maybe they will bear just as well, but that is not the way to get the most out of small fruits any more than it is to get the most out of ornamental plants. So let's give a thought to design, or if that sounds too vague, to where we can plant the various kinds of berries to get the most out of them, in fruit, of course, but also in convenience, appearance, and general enjoyment. The fact that you already have some berry plants where you don't particularly want them should not lessen your interest in garden design, or planning, if you prefer that word, but stimulate it. For once you have a variety you like it is easy to propagate more plants, set them just where you have decided they should have been planted in the first place, and, as soon as the new planting is in production, dig out the old rows.

KINDS AND VARIETIES OF FRUITS. In planning the layout of a small-fruits garden we are concerned primarily with kinds rather than varieties, that is, with strawberries and grapes, rather than Catskill and Sparkle or Concord and Thompson's Seedless. Horticultural variety, or the recently suggested word, cultivar, is the term used to designate the different kinds of strawberries, or kinds of raspberries. I have heard some persons use the word "species" for this purpose, incorrectly of course, as species indicates the wild or natural groups of plants from which our cultivated fruits have been developed over a long period of time.

The horticultural varieties of all the berry crops are clones—that is, plants which have been propagated asexually by cuttings, layers, or runners from the one original seedling plant produced by the plant breeder, or picked up as a chance seedling by some keen

156

observer. Certainly the plants can be grown from seed, but the seedlings will all be different, mostly inferior, and none will be entitled to be called by the name of the horticultural variety from which the seed came. Actually every Concord grape is really a part of the original plant, and every one is exactly alike, genetically, unless a bud sport has occurred. If a plant is really different, except as such differences are caused by differences in soil, fertilizers, or diseases, then it should not be called Concord.

Horticultural varieties propagated by vegetative means do not change. One cannot "develop" them or "improve" them to make them genetically larger fruited or hardier, except by selecting a superior bud sport, all but impossible to find, or by raising seedlings, with or without cross-pollination. And the seedling should not be called by the name of the parent variety. Unscrupulous nurseries sometimes list an old and reliable variety but call it "improved," or some such term. Usually misleading!

TETRAPLOIDS. Modern science has found means of doubling the chromosome numbers of certain plants by treating growing points with the drug colchicine. If the plant treated had a "normal" chromosome number for the species, the plants with the doubled numbers are called tetraploids, which often produce larger flowers and fruits, although frequently somewhat fewer fruits. If a horticultural variety is actually a tetraploid, it is usually advertised as such, or by the variety name with the prefix tetra-. Incidentally, the production of tetraploid fruits is a difficult and time-consuming process, a job for the research man with laboratory training and equipment. The amateur who wishes to produce improved varieties will be much better rewarded if he goes in for making crosses and growing seedlings.

KINDS TO PLANT. The kinds of small fruits to include, one or two or all, is the first thing to be settled in planning that part of the garden. Some may wish to include only a few which can be grown under the special conditions of soil and climate; others may want only a certain one; and there are always a few, perhaps with the collector's instinct, who want them all. This is a question which will have to be settled after considering personal likes, climate, soil, space available, and time to care for the proposed planting.

Table No. XI gives an approximation of what may be secured per plant, or from 100 feet of row of vigorous plants in full production, in the units by which the berries are most commonly sold in the market. Admittedly yields will vary with the variety, the year, the soil conditions, and the care given, but these are estimates of what you might expect if your conditions are favorable. If you are shooting for a definite amount of fruit, better add a few plants to what the table would indicate. There are good and poor crop years, you know. In certain favored sections, of course, the yields may be higher.

TABLE XI

Suggested Planting Distances and Possible Yields from Small Fruits in the Home Garden.

| | Planting Distance | | Yield | |
FRUITS	BETWEEN ROWS	IN THE ROW	BASED ON UNIT OF	YIELD PER UNIT
Blueberry	6 feet	4 feet	1 bush	5 pints
Bramble				
Blackberry				
Bush	6 feet	3 feet	100 feet of row	30 quarts
Evergreen	8 feet	8 feet	1 plant	10 quarts
Dewberry				
Boysen	6 feet	3 feet	100 feet of row	70 pints
Logan	6 feet	4 feet	100 feet of row	60 pints
Lucretia	6 feet	3 feet	100 feet of row	50 pints
Raspberry				
Black	6 feet	3 feet	100 feet of row	50 pints
Red	6 feet	3 feet	100 feet of row	60 pints
Currant	6 feet	4 feet	1 bush	5 quarts
Gooseberry	6 feet	4 feet	1 bush	8 quarts
Grape				
Eastern	8 feet	8 feet	1 vine	15 pounds
Muscadine	10 feet	10 feet	1 vine	15 pounds
Vinifera	8 feet	8 feet	1 vine	25 pounds
Strawberry	4 feet	2 feet	100 feet of row	70 quarts

SELECT A SUITABLE SITE. Once the total amount of land needed is known one should use all his knowledge of soils and sites, frost pockets, drainage, and other factors to select an area for planting. If, as is more likely to be the case, only one space is available, then it should be studied to try to determine if all the fruits desired will grow satisfactorily on it. The farmer and estate owner frequently split up their berry planting to have certain fruits on one site, and others in another field, where conditions may be more to their liking.

BERRIES AND THE VEGETABLE GARDEN. On the smaller place there are three general ways of locating the berry crops. Very frequently they are combined with the vegetable garden. This is especially good for strawberries, as they should stay in one place only two to four or five years at the most. They would then be turned under, new plants having been set, preferably at some little distance, before the old ones are discarded. It is often practical, in the small garden, to shift the strawberries from one side to the other, alternating with some of the annual vegetable crops. But what of the bush fruits? They should be good for five to ten or even fifteen years in one place. There are perennial vegetables also, such as asparagus and rhubarb, and one solution is to place the bush fruits at one side of the garden, with the perennial vegetables between the ber-

A home berry garden in Maryland with blackberries, raspberries, and strawberries. It is unusual in that the berries are in cultivated and mulched strips with grass walks, extensions of the lawn, between the rows.

ries and the annual vegetables. This will concentrate activities, such as cultivating, fertilizing, and control of certain pests. A small, isolated berry patch is easily forgotten and may be allowed to grow up in weeds after harvest. This is less likely to happen if the berries are connected with a part of the garden where there is more traffic.

BERRIES AND THE HOME ORCHARD. If the home grounds include a planting of tree fruits, the small fruits may be made a part of that, again for convenience in the consolidation of necessary operations. Except where land is quite plentiful, where culture is to be sod from the beginning, or cultivation is to be by very large farm equipment, the common practice is to interplant tree fruits with some smaller growing crop as vegetables or small fruits. The trees are usually planted so they will use all of the land by the time they are six to twelve years old.

Dwarf fruit trees may be planted so close together that intercropping may not be very practical. And even with standard trees bush fruits may be squeezed out before they have produced for as many years as they would if planted at one side of the orchard. Strawberries make a fairly satisfactory intercrop, the number of rows between two rows of trees being reduced as the trees spread out. On the large place a good arrangement may be to have small fruits between the tree fruits and the vegetable garden.

BERRIES IN THE LANDSCAPE. The owner of the city garden, be it large or small, must give special consideration to the appearance of the small-fruits planting, and usually as viewed from all sides. His space is limited, and so is his time, and he has no large farm tools with which to run through the berry patch after cultivating some field crop. There may not even be a vegetable garden. And so the problem becomes one of integration with the present, or intended, landscape plan. Fortunately grapes and several of the small fruits lend themselves very well to such integration.

THE AGGRESSIVE TYPES. Here one must distinguish well those fruits, the brambles particularly, which are aggressive, and use them where their aggressiveness can be controlled without damage to other plantings. This is not to discourage the inclusion of the brambles, and especially red raspberries, even in the small garden, as they are delicious fruits, but just to point out the problems ahead.

GRAPES ARE WIDELY GROWN. Over the country as a whole there are probably more home gardens with a grapevine, or several, than

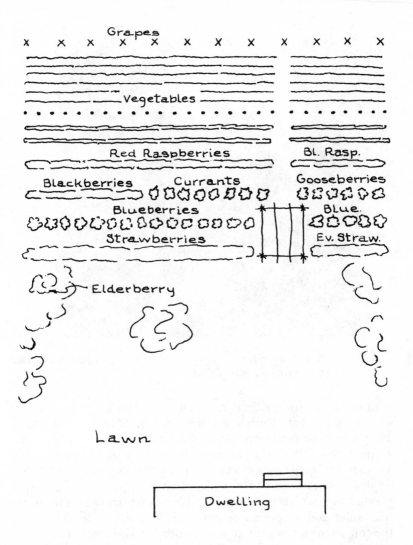

A rather extensive small fruit and vegetable garden layout for a suburban lot 100 feet wide in an area where blueberries and American bunch grapes can be grown. Path into garden may be grass, entered through a grape covered pergola, everbearing strawberries at the right. The elderberry bush is an integral part of an ornamental border planting. Additional ornamental border plantings might be used to soften the transition from lawn to fruit garden.

The little Delaware grape, red in color, delicious to eat out of hand, can provide many a pretty picture.

with any other fruit, although the newer homes are not so universally vine-planted. During my boyhood days in Indiana nearly every home, on the farms and in the smaller towns at least, had a grape "arbor." We didn't know about patio living, but during hot weather the grape arbor was the most pleasant place available. Typical arbors were 10 feet wide, of varying lengths, with grapes planted about 5 feet apart on each side and on the ends, if the arbor was wider and supported by posts inside. There were slats across the top so the vines grew to cover both top and sides. The family pump was frequently located here in the shade, with a shallow wooden trough, holding a pail or two, and a drain at the end. The ground under the arbor was usually paved with bricks, laid without mortar so a bit uneven, and stained green by the algae which flourished by grace of the shade and water occasionally splashed about. During hot weather there were usually a rocking chair or two and kitchen chairs as needed, and possibly a table where peas could be hulled and apples peeled. The grapes were somewhat secondary to shade, and frequently ripened unevenly because of insufficient pruning. But the musky aroma of ripening fruit was something to remember; a bit messy when the grapes began to fall, but by then it was cooler, time to think about school, and family living moved into the house.

The modern gardener might well consider a grape-covered pergola, but it will not have quite the place in family life that it once might have had. Other plant materials can make a better outdoor living room. But the grape is still an excellent home-garden fruit and can be worked into the landscape very satisfactorily to cover an unsightly fence, screen out an undesirable view, to cover a little arbor shading a garden seat, or frankly for fruit on a standard trellis back of the vegetable garden.

BLUEBERRIES IDEAL FOR LANDSCAPE USE. Of all the small fruits the blueberry is probably the best landscape subject. It stays put, does not spread, grows quickly to maximum size and then, if properly

A cool and attractive spot is provided by this simple grape arbor in California.

pruned, remains for years about the same size and shape. The foliage is attractive in summer, and some varieties have splendid fall coloration. The ripe fruit of most varieties is beautiful, and will remain beautiful for three or four weeks, if birds and hungry humans permit.

Much has been written about the difficulty of growing blueberries, and the so-called cultivated varieties do favor land that is acid and reasonably moist. Enough has been learned in recent years about the culture of these and related plants to warrant much more extensive planting than formerly thought advisable. Blueberries belong to the same family as rhododendrons and azaleas, the Ericaceae, and require somewhat the same growing conditions. At least if you can grow these ornamentals you can grow blueberries. As will be brought out in the chapter on blueberries there are types adapted to different conditions, from the Gulf Coast north to the Canadian border. Along the northern range the hardier types will be low growing, more of the ground-cover type, but still productive of delicious pie filling.

STRAWBERRIES VERY ADAPTABLE. Next in preference, for landscape use, I would place the strawberry, although, all things considered, it should probably go first as a home garden fruit. Strawberries can be so easily tucked into some corner of the vegetable garden, or some other out-of-the-way place that their use in the landscape has not been fully appreciated. They are very attractive as a ground cover throughout the growing season—shining green leaves, followed by pleasant white flowers, red berries, another green-leaf period, and then some autumn coloration. And they make a very good edging for walk or flower border.

It is quite quite practical to grow a few strawberries in pots, set them in place, fully grown, where they will flower and fruit, and then take them out if there is something else which would look better during late summer. They are attractive as a low border between lawn and vegetable area. Or they may be used to fill in a small bed somewhere toward the rear of the lawn, where they will turn out a surprising amount of fruit, and, although never so striking for color, if kept watered they never look bloomed out as some annuals and perennials do.

Currants and gooseberries are good landscape subjects, making trim bushes which do not spread beyond their allotted space, reaching 3 to 4 feet high and about as wide. They have rather small attractive leaves, and make good conversation pieces when loaded with their red or yellow fruit.

BRAMBLES IN THE LANDSCAPE. Red raspberries, grown on a suitable trellis, will make a wonderful screen planting or hedge, although not so effective as a screen after the leaves fall. But they will send up suckers in great numbers, particularly if mulched, which will reach out for 7 or 8 feet on each side of the row. They can be pulled easily when young, but it is a chore, and there are prickles which will make gloves almost a necessity. Cutting them off is not as satisfactory, as they will sprout up from the stump. Root barriers of sheet metal or plastic might help, if deep enough, but they would probably concentrate the shoots rather than decrease their number.

Black raspberries do not sucker, but the canes root at the tips

A rather formal grape arbor during the dormant season. In summer a cool and sheltered pathway.

to form new plants, which, if not taken out, may result in the planting's expanding through the fence into the neighbor's lawn. The canes are rather silvery in appearance, gracefully arching, and can be fairly attractive even during the winter months, when properly groomed.

The various dewberries, including types like Lucretia, Boysen, and Logan, have relatively little landscape value in themselves. They are trailers, lying flat on the ground unless supported. Some landscape use may be made of them by erecting a suitable trellis. However, the fruiting canes should be removed after harvest and the new canes not tied up until the following spring. This means that the trellis will be standing bare except during spring and early summer. Dewberries spread by tip layering the same as black raspberries.

The so-called bush blackberries also send up suckers, not so many as the red raspberries, but wide ranging and armed with vicious spines. I would consider them somewhat less desirable for the small garden than red raspberries, except in some southern areas where the latter do not thrive.

Trailing blackberries, such as the Evergreen, Himalaya, and Brainerd, can be very aggressive where they grow well, sending out heavy, viciously thorned canes 10 to 15 feet long, which take root at the tips. They will have to be put on a trellis if the fruit is to be where you can reach it, although, if left to their own devices, they will make a broad mound, higher than a man's head and perhaps 12 feet in diameter. They will remain evergreen or semievergreen, and the mound of green is not unattractive if viewed from a little distance, but certainly not a landscape subject for the small lot. They are very productive in the milder climates but will usually be killed back to the ground at temperatures below zero.

I have not tried to fit the more unusual small fruits into a scale of desirability for landscape use. The elderberry is quite attractive in bloom and in fruit, and quite tall. If used at all the proper place would seem to be in the landscape planting. Somewhat the same may be said for the highbush cranberry, probably more valuable for its ornamental properties than for its fruit.

SOIL PREPARATION. Although too few of us do it, it is very desirable to prepare the soil a year in advance by growing some annual crop. In this way weeds can be brought under reasonable control, organic matter worked in, pH adjusted if necessary, and facts learned about the soil fertility or lack of it. If you plant in an old garden or crop area the answers to those questions may already be at hand.

It may occasionally be desirable to set a blueberry or an elderberry in an established lawn as a specimen plant. In such cases the grass should be removed from a circle at least 3 feet in diameter, the soil prepared, and the plant set carefully as you would plant any other ornamental shrub.

For general garden planting the soil will need to be plowed and harrowed or rotavated. If there is a likelihood that the soil may need lime or phosphorus, these elements should be plowed under or worked in deeply, as it is somewhat difficult to get them down into the soil later by surface application. The phosphorus may be applied in a complete fertilizer suited to the particular area. A 5-10-5 formula is recommended in a number of states for soil of average fertility. If the soil needs conditioning by addition of a large amount of organic matter such as sawdust or peat moss, by additions of sand or clay or the laying of drains, these should all be done before planting.

TIME TO PLANT. Spring vs. fall planting has been discussed for years. In most places outside of the Far South, I would suggest spring, as early as the soil can be gotten in the proper condition. Early-fall planting does permit the plants to become established during late fall and winter and to start off promptly in the spring. But weeds also may become established during the winter, and spring-set plants have the advantage of the soil preparation for planting, which at least starts them off free of weeds. Where a mulch is applied in the fall, immediately after planting, the weed problem will be partially solved. Fall-set plants, in northern climates, may be somewhat more subject to winter injury than they would be after a season's growth in place. Fall-set strawberry plants will produce some fruit the following spring, if properly mulched and protected during the winter, which may be of interest to the person who decides during the summer that he wants strawberries, and as soon as possible. Spring-set plants will produce very little that same spring, and will be stronger if all blossoms are picked off.

In the Far South danger of damage from hot, dry summer conditions is greater than danger of winter injury, so fall planting is often more desirable. Strawberries may be "summered over" in a nursery bed under sprinklers and possibly some shade. Plants may then be taken from the nursery bed in late summer and set out to fruit during winter and early spring, after which a few plants are again placed in the nursery bed. With the bush fruits not much can be expected the first season, anyway, so the best time for planting depends on the conditions which will give best survival and vegetative growth.

In Far Northern gardens, spring planting seems more desirable from the standpoint of survival during the first winter.

Where the winters are rather mild and moist as in the Pacific Northwest, fall-set plants will survive easily enough but the weed growth by spring may be terrific. Unless a mulch is applied in the fall right after planting I would prefer spring.

Planting in summer is justified in only a few circumstances. Strawberry runners rooted into pots plunged beside the mother plant may be moved as soon as established, if set under irrigation or properly watered in. Red raspberry shoots may be dug when a few inches high and transplanted successfully, although they are quite soft and will need watering and possibly shading, and even then the mortality will usually be greater than when dormant plants are used. These "green" plants were preferred in the commercial raspberry section of southern New Jersey, probably because the dormant plants were nearly always infested by larvae of the raspberry crown borer.

The laying out of rows may be done by garden line, measuring stick, sighting, or other methods to the degree of refinement justified in the particular garden. Contour planting is desirable on slopes which will erode badly, unless the whole area is to be kept heavily mulched. Even with mulching, slopes that are quite steep would be better on the contour.

ROOT PRUNING. Some writers place great emphasis on root pruning before planting, especially the removal of broken roots and the making of a clean cut where the end of a root has been somewhat frayed in digging. To insure a neat and workmanlike job such root pruning might be done, but I do not believe it could be proven that it will result in any better or healthier growth. I would shorten any extra-long roots to a length which would fit into a hole of the size described, and that is mostly for the convenience of the planter. Blueberries, having a rather compact mass of small fibrous roots, should need no root pruning, even if planted bare root, unless there is such a mass of fiber that soil could not be worked into it, in which case a little judicious opening up may be desirable.

TOP PRUNING AT PLANTING TIME. The pruning of the tops of these particular fruits is more important, for two reasons. In the first place there may be a long shoot growing over to one side, so the bush, if left unpruned, would make a one-sided growth instead of the well-balanced bush usually desired. But more important is the fact that when the plant was dug, unless with a fairly large ball and certainly if bare root, a large part of the fibrous root system and probably all the absorbing rootlets and root hairs were lost—they just break off as the soil falls away. This materially reduces the water-intake organs of the plant, and it will be very helpful if the potential leaf surface is reduced somewhat to balance water intake with water loss, by removing shoots or parts of shoots bearing leaf buds. Probably a third of the top growth could be removed with beneficial results.

PLANTING. Bush fruits and grapes should be set about an inch deeper than they were before digging, which will leave them just slightly deeper after the soil has been well compacted by rain. Strawberry plants should be set as deep as possible without covering the tip of the crown, the fleshy organ to which the leaves and roots are attached. If the tip is covered the plant may fail to make new leaf growth; if most of the crown is uncovered it will dry out and be slow in starting.

If the soil has been well prepared, planting may be done with a trowel or small spade. For blueberries, which are frequently moved with a ball of soil, and for currants and gooseberries, which may have a rather large root system, it will be desirable to dig a hole at least a foot across and 8 to 10 inches deep. If the plant is bare root, spread out the roots and work the soil around them, occasionally "jiggling" the plant slightly so the soil will sift down within the root mass, and firming by stepping, with full weight, around the plant when the hole is full.

Where blueberries are being planted on unfavorable soil it may be desirable to dig an extra large hole and incorporate some peat or leaf mold as indicated in Chapter 16, but for the other small fruits it is usually better to work any manure or organic matter into the plot as a whole. Fibrous material, except peat moss, put directly into the hole may cause undesirable drying out. Fertilizers are best worked in during soil preparation. A top dressing after planting may be added if needed, scattered around the plant in a ring, no closer than 4 inches from the stem and extending outward to about 10 to 12 inches. If the soil is one known to be very deficient in phosphorus a half a teacup of superphosphate could be mixed with soil in the bottom of the hole, below the root zone, and covered with an inch or two of unfertilized soil.

Unless the soil is very moist it will help to fill the hole only halfway, then pour in half a gallon of water, allow it to sink away, and then fill the hole. In fall planting, mounding the soil a bit around the trunk will help to drain water away; in spring planting it may be advisable to leave a little depression so the rain water will sink in instead of running off.

PLANTING WITH TROWEL OR SPADE. Strawberries, raspberries, blackberries, and even small plants of currants and gooseberries, can be

Blueberries in tubs may be moved where desired to fit in the garden picture. If soil conditions are unfavorable it may be easier to prepare a suitable mixture for use in such a container, above ground or sunken, than to prepare a special plot of ground.

planted with a spade or trowel without actually digging a hole. The soil should be moist and deeply worked. Thrust the trowel straight down to a depth of about 6 inches, pull toward you, trying to move the point of the trowel as well as the handle, so the soil will be opened up back of the trowel to form a more or less rectangular hole as deep and wide as the blade; the other dimension depends on how far you pull the trowel. Obviously if the soil is too dry the slit will fill up, and if not loose enough it will be impossible to open up the bottom of the slit when you pull on the handle. When you have a proper opening, insert the plant behind the trowel, seeing that the roots go down and are not looped up over the edge of the hole. Hold the plant firmly in place with one hand, withdraw the trowel with the other, turn the blade up, and firm the soil with the fist which holds the trowel. It may be desirable, depending on condition of the soil, season, and whether water is available, to step firmly beside and somewhat against the plant.

With a little practice, by dropping the plants a short way ahead, one can proceed at a slow walk across the garden, doing a good job of planting in the meanwhile. Commercial growers follow this general procedure where they have not gone over to planting machines. Some writers describe much more careful methods for the home gardener, involving the spreading out of the roots and other niceties, but it seems to me the gardener is just as much entitled to speed up his methods and save his back as is the commercial man.

For larger plants, such as husky red raspberry canes, the garden trowel is obviously inadequate. However, the method of planting can be essentially the same, using a spade or a long-handled, pointed shovel. It will not be practical to try to pull the point back in some soils, although if the soil is loose one can push the handle forward a bit, then pull it back and open up the bottom of the slit. It will help to have another person insert the plant so the shovel operator can work his implement back and forth, or even pull it out and insert it again to make the opening large enough. After the plant is inserted and the shovel withdrawn the soil should be compacted with a firm step, pushing toward the plant as well as down.

WATERING IN. If the soil is dry, and irrigation not available, it will be very desirable to pour a cupful of water about the roots of each plant before pushing in the soil. If this can be done by another person it will not slow the operation unduly. If the planter makes a separate operation out of watering he will probably let it soak in, then later pull in the soil with a long handled hoe and firm it with his foot.

STARTER SOLUTIONS. It has been found very helpful, especially in soils of low fertility, to use a starter solution as the plants are set. Most commercial plant-setting machines are arranged to deliver about a cup of starter solution around the roots as the plant is set and before the soil is compacted. The home gardener can accomplish the same thing by watering in with starter solution instead of with plain water. A suitable solution may be made from one of the complete fertilizer formulas, especially designed for such use, hence containing only salts which are readily soluble. In most cases nitrogen seems to be the element which will do the most good at this point, and so a soluble nitrogenous salt may be used, such as sulfate of ammonia, at the rate of a rounded tablespoon dissolved in 3 gallons of water in pail or sprinkling can. As the solution goes directly on the roots, injury is inevitable if the solution is too strong, so if you use a mixed material be sure to follow directions.

Some materials for use at planting are said to contain hormones which will lesson transplanting shock and stimulate immediate root growth. There is some experimental evidence to justify the use of these hormones, but other investigators have not always been able to duplicate the results. We do know that, under most conditions, transplanting can be successfully done without adding such materials; in some cases they might be helpful. If you decide to try them, leave a few plants for a check, giving them just starter solution alone without the hormones.

Part Three

SPECIAL REQUIREMENTS FOR,
AND INFORMATION ABOUT,
THE VARIOUS FRUITS

CHAPTER 12

Start with Strawberries

In our previous chapters we have attempted to give some suggestions about small fruits in general, including cultural methods adaptable to all. In the chapters ahead each fruit will be considered in light of its peculiar attributes and requirements, attention being given to specific needs as viewed against the broader field already covered.

There is reason for the heading of this chapter. For the person who has never grown small fruits, or who may be somewhat doubtful whether his conditions are suitable for such plants, the strawberry is the logical starting point in practically any part of the United States. In the first place there are varieties which are especially adapted to Florida and the Gulf Coast, to the Middle West, the East, the Pacific Coast, and the Northern Plains.

LARGE PRODUCTION FROM SMALL SPACE. A worth-while amount of strawberries may be grown in a very small space. For instance, a dozen plants could be set in a bed 3 feet wide and 25 feet long, permitted to make a matted row, and could be expected to reward you with at least 25 to 35 pints of berries. This is enough for 50 to 75 servings of what many consider to be the ultimate in desserts. For just plain return on the investment this is hard to beat. Of course no plants may be considered investments to be planted and forgotten, they must have reasonable care.

If that reasonable care is furnished, and barring extreme frost conditions during bloom, strawberries can be expected to yield well every year, but not on one original planting, of course. New beds are usually most productive, but may remain satisfactory for up to three or four years. The replacement program is an integral part of strawberry management.

UNIVERSALLY LIKED. There are people who do not like strawberries, but I have yet to meet one, and it would not be hard to defend the thesis that they are the best loved of the berry crops. Unfortunately a few people, a very small minority, are allergic to them and after eating break out in a "strawberry rash." Even the reactors, whom I have known, have liked the fruit. Medical science may yet come up with a tasteless salt to mix with the sugar which will prevent the allergic reaction; then the preference for strawberries will be just about universal.

If we need more reasons for suggesting that you start with strawberries consider the fact that they do not have thorns, as many berry crops do, no trellises are needed, and in most places the home gardener can produce good crops without sprays or dusts. No other fruit is so quick to produce a crop. A full crop from a spring planting will ripen just a little over a year later. In the south a winter crop will be produced from fall planting, and further north fall planting will yield a partial crop the following spring.

What has been said about the universality of strawberries does not mean they will thrive under all possible conditions of soil and climate, but they are adaptable to a relatively wide range of conditions. If the water supply is controlled—enough but not too much—they can be grown in almost pure sand to a rather heavy clay, but a medium sandy loam is generally considered to be best. Because of the small space involved the home gardener who especially wants a few strawberries but has unfavorable soil could make up a soil to specifications, adding sand, clay, or organic matter as needed. Incidentally an area made up for strawberries would also be excellent for lawn, ornamentals, or vegetables. An ideal soil might well be of moderate fertility, as nutrients may easily be added when needed. A soil of very high fertility is likely to be infested with weeds and may cause the strawberries to make a very vigorous but soft growth somewhat more susceptible to certain fungus diseases.

THE VARIETY IS VERY IMPORTANT. The horticultural variety is the basis of all gardening. A poor variety, or one not adapted to local conditions, may be entirely worthless, whereas the same amount of effort expended on a desirable variety would give a rewarding crop of excellent fruit. Of course there are personal preferences as to flavor, and not all gardeners will agree on one single variety as being the best. But don't just plant strawberries from an unknown source, unless you have sampled the berries and know they will do well in your neighborhood. Knowing the name of the variety isn't necessary, if you have one you really like. But it is just like owning a car; it doesn't ride any easier if we know the make, but it gives us satisfaction to know, and is essential if we want to order another of the same make. If you share your berries someone is sure to say, "That's a fine berry. What's its name?" and you will want to be able to answer.

ORIGIN OF THE STRAWBERRY. The strawberry as we know it is essentially American, the main components being *Fragaria chiloensis* from western South America, taken to France in 1712, presumably combined with the eastern meadow strawberry, *F. virginiana*. Varieties resulting were reintroduced to America in the early part of the nineteenth century. The European hybrids were improved by a long line of American breeders, many still working to make further improvements. The original strawberries of Europe are of a different chromosome number so do not ordinarily cross with our cultivated varieties. They are much smaller fruited and some do not produce runners so must be grown from seed.

SEX IN THE STRAWBERRY. *F. chiloensis* is normally dioecious—that is, there are male and female clones, berries being produced only on the female plants, and only if they are pollinated by a male plant. All of the important varieties today are hermaphroditic— that is, the flowers are perfect, having functional stamens as well as pistils, and so a field of one variety will produce a normal crop through self-pollination. Earlier in the century, several of the more important commercial varieties were pistillate, producing no pollen, and had to be interplanted with a perfect flowered variety for pollination. Some of these pistillate sorts were exceptionally productive, but the inconvenience of having to plant pollinizers gradually resulted in their elimination as breeders worked almost exclusively with the perfect flowered kinds.

TYPES OF VARIETIES. There are various ways of classifying varieties, one being as to fall-bearing (everbearing), as contrasted with, June-bearing (spring-bearing). In central and southern California and the Gulf Coast most varieties produce berries over a period of several weeks or even all winter; in general the further south the longer the fruiting season. Toward the northern part of the country most varieties have a picking season of two to three weeks. Under the same conditions, however, the everbearers will start producing about the same time in the spring, and fruit more or less continuously until frost, although some of the everbearers may tend to produce a spring and a fall crop. What we have to say will deal with the June-bearing varieties except where everbearers are specified.

AFFECTED BY LENGTH OF DAY. For many years people from northern states going to Florida for vacation were impressed by a variety in one location, north or south, and took plants with them to grow in the other latitude. As a general rule the results were disappointing, as a variety transported over a long distance, north to south or the reverse, never seemed quite satisfactory. Varieties were said to be "adapted" to the South or to the North. Some years ago Dr. George Darrow of the U.S.D.A. carried out length-of-day experiments and found that the southern varieties produced normally during short days, whereas the northern varieties, if given short days, grew slowly and irregularly. They seemed to need a rest period during the winter, but the southern varieties did not.

Commercial growers know there is little to be gained by trying a variety from a few hundred miles, or more, south or north of their own latitude. Length of day does not influence adaptability east and west, but, for various reasons, only a very few varieties have proven satisfactory over an area as large as several states. So it is important to plant only those varieties well adapted to your own locality, but that does not necessarily mean that you will have to buy the plants in your own neighborhood. Some strawberry nurserymen grow plants for distant producing sections, varieties that, in their own locality, would not be well adapted for fruit production.

RUNNING OUT OF VARIETIES. For many years strawberry varieties seemed to "run out." That is, they would become progressively less vigorous, and less productive, and within a few years practically disappear from cultivation, so that any variety recommendations soon became out-of-date. In recent years it has been shown that this "running out" did not indicate any genetic deterioration, as once believed, but was the result of certain diseases, principally virus diseases and a fungus disease known as "red stele." It is now possible, therefore, to make up a list of varieties which will probably be good for many years if these diseases are controlled. However, many will be superseded by better ones, as the breeders are sure to continue to make improvements.

It would be interesting to describe and discuss individual varieties at length, but for the home gardener a rather brief treatment may be useful. Table XII lists some which are adapted to various regions. Local recommendations and the experience of local people should be considered if available.

TABLE XII

Strawberry Varieties Suggested for Home Garden Planting
in Various Regions of the United States

New England	New York	Other Middle Atlantic States	Great Lakes Area
Catskill	Catskill	Blakemore	Catskill
Fairfax	Empire	Catskill	Fairfax
Howard 17	Fairfax	Fairfax	Howard 17
Maine 55	Howard 17	Jerseybelle	Sparkle
Sparkle	Sparkle	Pocahontas	
Temple		Redcrop	
Vermilion		Sparkle	
		Tennessee Beauty	

Southeastern States	Florida	Other Gulf States	Southern Mississippi Valley
Albritton	Konvoy	Konvoy	Blakemore
Blakemore	Missionary	Massey	Dixieland
Dixieland		Missionary	Pocahontas
Massey			Redglow
Pocahontas			Surecrop
Surecrop			Tennessee Beauty
Tennessee Beauty			

Central Mississippi Valley	Northern Mississippi Valley	Prairie States	Great Plains States
Armore	Armore	Arrowhead	Arapahoe
Blakemore	Arrowhead	Dunlap	Radiance
Catskill	Blakemore	Howard 17	
Fairland	Catskill		
Howard 17	Dunlap		
Pocahontas	Fairfax		
Tennessee Beauty	Howard 17		
Vermilion	Pocahontas		
	Sparkle		
	Tennessee Beauty		

Rocky Mountain States	Southwest	California	Northwest
Arrowhead	Blakemore	Lassen	Marshall
Dunlap	Lassen	Shasta	Northwest
Howard 17	Missionary	Solana	Puget Beauty
Redcrop			Siletz
Shasta			

BRIEF VARIETAL DESCRIPTIONS

The following descriptions are necessarily brief but they do indicate the state of origin. In most cases the varieties have been given extensive local tests and selected on their merits before being named by their originators, so may be considered as especially well adapted to their state of origin. Home gardeners who become especially interested in strawberries might well try out additional new varieties, as they are introduced by their state experiment station.

Albritton—late midseason, deep red, firm. U.S.D.A. and North Carolina Experiment Station.

Arapahoe—midseason, firm, very vigorous, hardy, drouth tolerant. U.S.D.A. (Cheyenne, Wyoming).

Armore—late, productive. Missouri Experiment Station.

Arrowhead—medium late, vigorous, productive, hardy. Minnesota Experiment Station.

Blakemore—early, productive, firm, tart. U.S.D.A.

Catskill—midseason, large. Experiment station, Geneva, New York.

Dixieland—early, large, very firm. U.S.D.A. and North Carolina Experiment Station.

Dunlap—early midseason, small, soft but hardy. Originated in Illinois about 1890.

Empire—midseason, light flesh color. Experiment station, Geneva, New York.

Fairfax—early midseason, large, very good quality, dark. U.S.D.A.

Fairland—midseason, large, good quality, resistant to red stele. U.S.D.A.

Howard 17—known also as Premier, early, rather soft, very productive, fair quality. Introduced by A. B. Howard, Massachusetts, 1918.

Jerseybelle—late, large, showy. New Jersey Experiment Station.

Konvoy—early, productive, vigorous. Louisiana Experiment Station.

Lassen—productive, for central to southern California. California Experiment Station.

Maine 55—midseason, vigorous, resistant to red stele. Maine Experiment Station.

Marshall—early, large, soft, good quality. Originated in Massachusetts, 1890.

Massey—late, large, bright red. U.S.D.A.

Missionary—early, long season. Chance seedling in Virginia, about 1900.

Northwest—midseason, vigorous, productive, tolerant to virus diseases. Washington Experiment Station.

Pocahontas—early midseason, firm, deep red. U.S.D.A. and Virginia Experiment Station.

Puget Beauty—medium late, especially adapted to heavy soils, attractive, good quality, partially resistant to red stele. Washington Experiment Station.

Radiance—early, fairly firm, hardy, drouth tolerant. U.S.D.A. (Cheyenne, Wyoming).

Redcrop—medium early, vigorous, at least partially resistant to red stele. New Jersey Experiment Station.

Redglow—highly flavored, moderately productive, resistant to red stele. U.S.D.A.

Shasta—long fruiting season, for central to northern California. California Experiment Station.

Siletz—late midseason, productive, good quality, resistant to red stele, tolerant of virus diseases. U.S.D.A. and Oregon Experiment Station.

Solana—for same general area as Lassen, better quality, not quite as productive, large, bright red. California Experiment Station.

Sparkle—late, vigorous, firm, good for freezing, resistant to red stele, leaf spot, leaf scorch. New Jersey Experiment Station.

Surecrop—early, firm, attractive, resistant to red stele. U.S.D.A. and Maryland Experiment Station.

Temple—early midseason, vigorous, resistant to red stele. U.S.D.A.

Tennessee Beauty—midseason to late, large, bright red. Tennessee Experiment Station.

Vermilion—productive, a bit soft, resistant to red stele. Illinois Experiment Station.

EVERBEARING STRAWBERRY VARIETIES

A few everbearing varieties have been suggested by the Extension Service for planting in certain states. However, most of these have some undesirable characteristics and, up to this time at least, are probably close to 100 per cent virus infected. Which will be superior when virus-free plants are available is hard to say. Furthermore, about the same varieties are recommended in each region, indicating either that they have a wider range of adaptability than the June-bearing sorts, or, more likely, that we do not have enough accurate information on which to base more specific recommendations. The following varieties have been suggested for planting in widely scattered areas and probably include the best available at this writing.

Evermore—dark red, good quality, very hardy, recommended primarily in Minnesota, where it originated at the experiment station.

Gem—light red, fair quality, originated in Michigan. Brilliant and Superfection very closely resemble Gem.

Red Rich—large, bright red, good quality, vigorous. Originated in Minnesota.

NUMBER OF VARIETIES TO PLANT. "Should one plant more than one variety?" is a question likely to occur. Unlike some tree fruits the modern, perfect flowered strawberry seems to produce a maximum crop without cross-pollination, so there is no advantage in mixing varieties. However, it will be possible to extend the fresh berry season somewhat by planting an early ripening and a late variety. In the northern part of the country the earliest sorts are likely to ripen not more than ten days before the latest ones, each variety producing ripe fruit over some three weeks. As one goes further south this interval may be somewhat greater, and each variety will have a longer picking season.

The interested gardener may wish to try out several varieties to determine which best satisfy his taste and which are best adapted to his soil and climate. This is fine, if one is sure that all the plants are virus-free. Many a gardener has ruined a variety which was doing reasonably well by bringing in something new which happened to be carrying a contagious disease. Certain varieties may be excellent for dessert but not suitable for freezing, and vice versa, although good general-purpose varieties are usually available.

PROPAGATION. Strawberries may be propagated in two ways, by seed and by runners. Plants grown from seed will be quite variable —that is, they will not reproduce the variety, so this is a method primarily for the plant breeder. There is one exception, a type of European strawberry which does not make runners, hence must be grown from seed. This is a novelty, small-fruited but flavorful, and of little interest to most American gardeners.

The standard way of propagating strawberries is to remove the runners and transplant them, usually as early in the spring as the soil can be gotten in condition. In the Gulf States, fall planting for

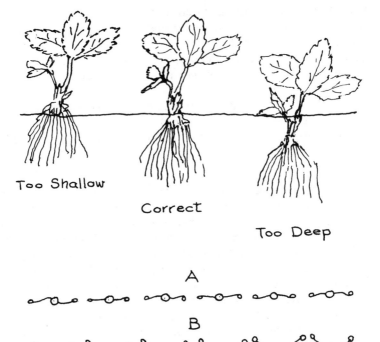

Too Shallow

Correct

Too Deep

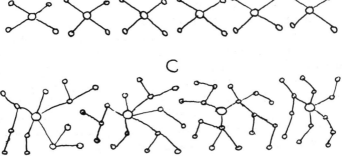

A

B

C

TOP: Correct planting depth is important. If there are several leaves on a plant, prune to one or two of the younger leaves at planting time.

BOTTOM: A. Strawberries trained to single hedge row. Large circles represent mother plants, small circles runner plants. B. Double hedge row of runners with mother plants retained. C. Matted row with runner plants spaced about 6 inches apart.

An ordinary posthole digger used to lift out a strawberry plant with a ball of soil intact. The same tool may be used to prepare a hole to receive the plant.

winter production is the usual procedure. Further north, spring-set plants are usually allowed to produce runners to make a matted row of plants which will produce a crop the following spring. Fall-set plants in the northern part of the country, if they become well established before winter and are protected by mulch over winter, will produce a good crop per plant the next spring. However, it must be remembered that, in fall planting, if you set 100 plants and all survive, you will harvest fruit from only 100 plants next spring. If you set in the spring, 100 plants may have increased, a year later, to 1000 or 5000, depending on the variety, from which you will pick fruit.

EARLY PLANTING DESIRABLE. The primary reason for planting very early in the spring is to get the plants well established while the weather is still cool and the soil moist, especially important in commercial operations. In the home garden, where the plants may be watered and given special attention, later planting may give very good results. In the small garden the efficient use of space is very important, and tying up a sizable area for a year to grow a matted row of plants may seem uneconomical. With water and proper feeding it will usually be possible to plant late, even after picking, when new runners may be available. The row which fruited may be turned under, to be followed by a late vegetable, while the new row is set where some early vegetable has been taken out. Such a late-set row may not make many runners, not necessarily a disadvantage, as we shall see.

Expert gardeners have long followed the practice of plunging pots, filled with a good compost, alongside the strawberry row, and pegging runners so they will take root in the pots. As soon as well rooted they may be severed from the mother plant and transplanted to their fruiting location with very little interruption in their growth. The later the planting is made the less will be the weed-control problem.

Research has shown that strawberry plants may be kept in cold storage, if properly protected and handled, for several months, so that it is possible to purchase good plants, from some nurserymen, practically any time of the year. For late planting it is much better to use properly stored plants, which were dug when they were dormant, than those dug at the time, which may be in full bloom or even starting to produce berries.

THE MATTED ROW SYSTEM. Planting distances will depend on many factors. Varieties which are prolific runner makers may be set as much as three feet apart in the row for matted row culture, poor runner makers as close as 18 inches. If planting is unduly late, then closer planting will be necessary to produce the same density of matted row. The distance between rows in commercial plantings is usually about 4 feet, sometimes as close as 3½ feet. As the runners spread out, the cultivated area becomes narrower, the last cultivation usually stirring a strip of about 12 to 15 inches, so the matted row of plants is then about 30 inches wide. In the home garden where space is more valuable, and where quite a bit of hand work can be done, the rows may be as close as 3 feet, although I prefer the 4 feet distance.

PLANT SPACING. One of the real problems with strawberries, whether in the commercial field or the home garden, is the crowding of the runner plants. Breeders have been hesitant about introducing varieties which produce few runners, as that would mean the plants would always be expensive, and under poor growing conditions they would not produce enough runners. The problem

Setting a strawberry plant dug with a posthole digger. This is a good
way to move plants during the summer after the regular spring planting season.

of too many runners can be attacked in a number of ways. Numerous experiments have been conducted to determine the optimum
spacing of runners. Results have varied with the variety and growing conditions, but usually about 6 inches between plants, center
to center, at fruiting time has given a maximum crop and berries
of maximum size.

Commercially the advantage to be gained from any known
method of spacing, within the matted row, has usually not been
sufficient to pay the cost. What the grower most often does, and
this should be a valuable hint to the home gardener, is to set the
plants as far apart as he thinks his particular variety can be spaced
and still close up the row. This is followed by a feeding, and possibly water, program which will give enough but not excessive
growth. As the plants start to make runners he will cultivate close
to the original row, which will drag the runners around into the
row. There will probably be a second cultivation close to the row,
after which the runners may be spread out by raking or by hand,
an operation usually accompanied by hand hoeing. If the runners
at this time cover an area considered sufficient for the final width

of matted row it would be ideal if there were some way to prevent the formation of any more runners. This has been studied and may eventually be done by chemical sprays, although the problem is complex. It is possible to put rolling disk cutters on the cultivator so as to cut off the runners which project into the cultivated strip.

So far there is no economical way to remove the excess new runners which grow between the older runners. Usually these superfluous plants will be left, the resultant crowding possibly causing some reduction in fruit size, making pest control more complicated and picking more tedious. The home gardener may be just as busy as the commercial grower, and interested in maximum production at the least cost of effort and money, and so follow commercial methods. The more meticulous gardener, who wants size and beauty of fruit, and a garden of which he may be justly proud, can do some hand spacing and thinning of runners to good advantage.

Some commercial growers, as well as home gardeners, plant the rows closer together, as close as 3 feet, space the plants as described, and develop what is known as a narrow matted row. This gives more "outside" plants per unit of area, and anyone who has picked strawberries knows that the best berries are usually on the outside of the rows, where they have more light, nutrients and moisture.

THE HILL SYSTEM. It is rather obvious that a plant growing with ample space all around it will be most favorably situated with respect to moisture and nutrients and will probably give optimum production. This is what we have in the "hill" system. Plants are set 12 to 18 inches apart—a little further in some areas with large growing plants—in rows 3 feet apart. In the home garden where plants are to be kept mulched, or hand hoed, the rows may be closer together, even to the extent of having the rows the same distance apart as the plants in the rows. Usually in such a case a wider space will be left, every 4 or 5 rows, to provide ease of access as the plants grow large and tend to cover the entire area. A double-row system is often seen.

There are various intermediates between the hill and matted row systems. A fairly common one consists of setting mother plants in a single row, at least 30 inches apart, after which, from each mother plant, four runners are permitted to develop and are trained outward at about 45 degrees from the row, to form a double row of runners, one on either side of the mother row. If desired the mother plants may later be removed to leave a double row. A factor to be considered is that the best yield will be secured from plants that took root fairly early the previous season. Late-formed runners produce small plants with small crowns and fewer flowers.

PLANTS BEAR MORE THAN ONE YEAR. Plants may live and bear fruit for 3 or 4 years, but will become progressively less productive, partly because of root diseases and partly because the new roots tend to come out above the old ones on the new crown growth. Throwing soil onto the old bed, after picking, will help these new roots get established. A matted row can usually be expected to produce at least two crops, the second somewhat less than the first. Some commercial growers try for two crops, but many feel that it is more profitable to set new fields each year, plowing the old beds under after harvest, unless they happen to be especially fine and comparatively weed-free. With the wide use of virus-free plants it may be practical to keep a planting somewhat longer, provided weeds can be kept under control.

IS A PERMANENT STRAWBERRY BED POSSIBLE? Some gardens which I have seen in the past had what was considered a permanent strawberry bed, usually somewhere in the background of the other plantings. Such a bed can be fairly productive for quite a long time, barring weed and disease problems. Taking out the older, weaker plants after every harvest is almost essential to maintain vigor. In fact Dr. George Darrow writes of certain large fields he studied in Ecuador which had apparently been in strawberries continuously for some 300 years. There was no virus disease evident. The Indian owners pulled out the worst weeds and the older plants each year. Since this planting antedated the development of cultivated strawberry varieties, the plants were a selected clone of the native *F. chiloensis.* Under usual garden conditions, however, I am convinced that frequent, if not yearly, replanting will be most satisfactory.

THE STRAWBERRY BARREL. A method of growing strawberries, frequently written about but less frequently seen, is the strawberry barrel. This involves a stout wooden barrel into the staves of which holes 1¼ to 2 inches in diameter, are drilled at 10- to 12-inch intervals. This container is then filled with a good composted soil, a strawberry plant being set in each hole as the barrel is filled. A refinement is to place porous tile down through the center, filled with sand or gravel, and through which water may be applied. Straw-

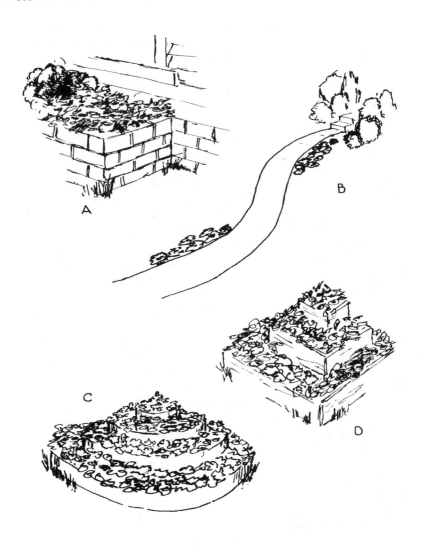

Some novel methods of planting strawberries. A. Strawberries with taller plants, in a brick planter under a window. B. Two small groups of strawberries as a border planting for a back walk. C. A pyramid made of metal strips. D. A wooden pyramid.

berry jars are terra cotta containers with openings on the sides, in which plants may be grown, although I have more frequently found them in use for succulents, or other ornamental plants. My feeling about the strawberry barrel is that it is more of a conversation piece than an efficient method of raising berries, granting, however, that very nice berries can be produced in this way.

It is quite easy to grow strawberries in a planter, window box, or similar container if one so desires for novelty, or ornamental purposes, as well as for fruit. This may appeal to the owner of a tiny garden and under certain conditions may be more practical than the barrel.

Some nurseries sell a combination of strawberry plants and three or four aluminum strips which are used as retaining walls to build up a three-tiered conical mound. The berries hang over the little terraces and may make quite a pretty picture. Such a mound will have to be watered carefully to prevent drying out. From the standpoint of production I would feel that just as much high-quality fruit could be produced by conventional methods with less effort.

CARE AFTER PLANTING. After the plants are set the principal cultural operations, during the first season, will include control of weeds, fertilizing, watering if necessary, possibly some spacing of runners, and finally application of winter mulch. However, one of the first operations, on spring-set plants, will be removal of the blossoms by pinching out the entire flower cluster shortly after the first blossoms open. In the gardens where watering can be adequate it may be practicable to permit these fruits to ripen if the plants were set early enough to be well established, but the berries will be rather small and probably covered with sand. If growing conditions are not very favorable the presence of the fruit will retard runner formation, and may seriously weaken the plants. The decision as to removal of blossoms may be based on the appearance of the plants at the time, and whether there is an older planting to furnish berries for the table.

MULCHING AT PLANTING TIME. It is quite practical and desirable to mulch the plants when they are set, if you are going to use the hill system. If the matted row system is contemplated the mulch may interfere with the rooting of the runners, although on a small area they may be poked through to the soil and will then root even better than under cultivation. Even with no assistance some runners will send roots down through the mulch if it is not too thick. If the mulch is applied at planting time some weeds will probably have to be pulled out by hand. They will pull easily through the mulch, but should not be allowed to get very large, as pulling them then would bring up quantities of soil. This would be scattered over the mulch where it would undoubtedly encourage more weeds to start, and would largely offset the effectiveness of the mulch in keeping the berries clean at picking time.

The usual procedure is to cultivate to kill the weeds during the first season, preferably as shallowly as possible. This may be supplemented with chemical weed killers, if you want to experiment, and almost certainly by hand hoeing or pulling. This is the time when one can really appreciate a good job of weed eradication the season before planting.

IRRIGATION. The trend is more and more toward sprinkler irrigation for commercial strawberry fields, and there are probably few home gardens, anywhere in the United States, where extra water is not badly needed at least sometime during the year. Where water is available it is a good idea to be especially careful that the soil does not become too dry during spring and early summer, when new growth is being made, and while the fruit is sizing up. At this time of year the plants will need something like an inch of water a week to maintain optimum growth, rain and irrigation combined, of course.

It would be well to have the soil relatively moist before the fruit starts to ripen, so as to apply as little water as possible during the picking season. Wetting foliage and fruit at this time, whether by rain or irrigation, will likely increase fruit rots and foliage diseases. But if it is so dry that the plants show they need water, by starting to wilt, I would irrigate right after a picking. At this particular time surface or rill irrigation would be a very desirable way of getting the water on the soil without wetting the plants. However, sprinklers can be used satisfactorily, even at this time, and in many ways are more flexible than surface irrigation.

Newly set beds will need water throughout the growing season, either natural rain or otherwise. In late summer, however, if good rows have developed, it may be desirable to keep the plants on the dry side so as not to encourage too many superfluous runners.

FERTILIZING IN THE FALL. Strawberries start the development of their blossom buds in the fall and bud differentiation may continue through the winter. If the plants have not made a vigorous growth in late summer an application of fertilizer in August may be useful in encouraging fruit bud formation. Broadcast over the rows, and brush off, 100 to 150 pounds per acre, 2½ to 4 pounds per 1000 square feet, of nitrate of soda or sulfate of ammonia. On very poor soils a complete fertilizer, as 5-10-5, might be used instead, up to 500 pounds per acre, 12 pounds per 1000 square feet.

THE FROST HAZARD. As the flower buds begin to appear in the spring one becomes conscious of the frost hazard. Some varieties are less susceptible than others, either because they are genetically hardier, or because they bear their flowers down under the leaves where they have some protection from frost. Except in bad frost areas I prefer the varieties which hold their flowers up level with, or above, the leaves, as they are easier to pick and possibly less likely to rot, being up where they are better aerated.

If one must plant in a frost pocket then he should be prepared to fight frost or take the consequences. One way to give some protection, where there is a straw or hay mulch, is to fluff up the mulching material and cover the plants with it on the nights when frost is expected. A less laborious way is to turn on sprinkler irrigation when the temperature falls to about 31 degrees at the level of the blossoms. This may be some 5 degrees colder than at the usual thermometer height of 5 or 6 feet. If water is kept on the foliage until the temperature has risen to about 32 degrees, it will protect against several degrees of frost, because of the heat given off as the water turns to ice crystals.

If the soil is poorly drained it may not be desirable to apply too much water, so if sprinkling for frost control is used at all it should be with relatively small nozzles, allowed to run only as long as necessary. Orchard heaters could be used, but the hazard of fire and smoke around the home makes them somewhat less desirable than they might be in a commercial planting. Fortunately strawberries bloom fairly late and frost damage is usually not serious. Even when some of the early flowers are killed a partial crop will usually develop from the blossoms which open later. In the North there will be a period of about two weeks from the time the first flowers open until the last ones appear. In the South the blossoming period will be much longer.

Frost damage to strawberry flowers causes the central, greenish cone of pistils, which would have developed into the berry, to turn black; usually the petals and stamens are uninjured so one may not realize injury has occurred unless he looks closely.

SOIL ACIDITY. Lists of plants with their requirements as to acidity often include strawberries with the acid-loving group. Of course, we must realize that practically all economic plants prefer the soil reaction to be on the acid side of neutral, so it is a question of how acid, rather than acid vs. alkaline preference. The pH at which plants will grow best may vary somewhat in different soils, as the degree of acidity has an effect on the availability of certain elements, some beneficial, some harmful. Usually pH 5 to pH 6 will be satisfactory for strawberries, but they may do well at higher or lower pH values. If the soil in an area has a history of responding well to lime it could be expected to benefit the strawberries also.

On very alkaline soils it may help to use some sulfur, trying perhaps 100 pounds per acre, 2½ pounds per 1000 square feet at first. Ammonium sulfate used as a source of nitrogen will help to counteract akalinity. Under alkaline conditions the iron in the soil may be tied up in a form unavailable to the plant, resulting in poor growth and chlorosis, yellowing of the leaves which then do not function normally as they are short of chlorophyll. This problem may be attacked by acidifying the soil, or by using an iron chelate, an organic form of iron which the plants are able to use even if the soil is alkaline. There are types of chelates for acid and for alkaline soils so it would be best to consult your county agent. If the soils in your area are deficient in available iron he will be able to give you suggestions as to what to buy and how to use it.

FERTILIZERS. In discussing fertilizers for the specific small fruits it would be well to stress again that one should fertilize to make up the nutrient deficiencies of the particular soil. In general what is good for other crops, such as vegetables, in your community, and more specifically in your own garden, will also be suitable for strawberries. On the average sandy loam soil this will probably mean the application of a complete fertilizer, such as a 5-10-5, to be turned under before planting. Suggested rates per 100 feet of row, covering 4 feet in width, are 20 pounds for very poor soil, 10 pounds for average, and 5 pounds for a relatively fertile soil.

Where soils are especially deficient in phosphorus it may be desirable either to turn under a very heavy application of superphosphate, or put the material in a strip, or, band, where the strawberry row is to be set, preferably a little to one side of the row, and about 4 inches below the surface. This concentration of the phosphorus in a band will prevent the soil from "fixing" it immediately, or making all of it insoluble before the plant roots have had a chance to get what they need. Since this special treatment for phosphorus-deficient soils will be needed only in limited areas, local information as to amounts of phosphate to apply should be sought.

SIDE DRESSING. On some soils no additional fertilizer may be needed, from planting time until after the crop is picked a year later. On the lighter soils, however, a side dressing with a readily available nitrogen fertilizer during early summer may be desirable. Depending on the soil, this might run from 100 to 200 pounds per acre, 1 to 2 pounds per 100 feet of row, of ammonium sulfate or nitrate of soda. The choice between these two materials can probably be made on the basis of which is being used in your community for other crops. The ammonium sulfate contains about 21 per cent nitrogen and leaves an acid residue in the soil. The nitrate of soda runs about 16 per cent and leaves an alkaline residue. Other similar materials, such as calcium nitrate, or ammo-phos (16–20) might be used. On very poor, sandy soils a second side dressing during midsummer might be helpful.

On soils of average fertility it is usually possible to fertilize well enough the first, or plant-growing, year so that no additional feeding will be needed the spring of the fruiting year. It is easy to get too much nitrogen into the plants which are about to produce a crop, resulting in overvegetative leaf growth, and berries that are especially susceptible to rots such as gray mold. Here the gardener will have to call on his experience with other plants, and his ability to read the signs showing in the strawberry foliage as growth starts in the spring. If growth is rather slow, leaves small, and yellowish rather than a good dark green, then a light top dressing of readily available nitrogen will be needed. This may be broadcast directly over the rows, care being taken that there are no lumps or piles of fertilizer to cause burning of the foliage. If the leaves have started to grow enough to catch the fertilizer material and hold it in visible quantities, it would be advisable to remove it by sprinkling, or by "sweeping" with a branch covered with reasonably fine twigs. Needless to say the foliage should be dry when the fertilizer is broadcasted.

If irrigation is available it is always a good idea to give the soil a soaking as soon as fertilizer is applied, partly to be sure all is removed from the leaves, but especially to insure it dissolves and is washed into the soil. I have seen side dressings, of even so soluble a material as sulfate of ammonia, stay on the surface for a month after application. Even when there is a light rain, enough to dissolve the material, it may not wash it down more than half an inch. Then the soil dries out and the fertilizer stays in the dry surface layer, mostly out of reach of the roots, although it has all disappeared and the gardener is puzzled as to why no response can be seen. The next good rain, perhaps a couple of months later, may make the nitrogen available and growth starts off vigorously, possibly so late in the fall that the plants enter the winter in a freeze-susceptible condition.

MULCHING FOR WINTER PROTECTION. We have already discussed mulches from the general standpoint of keeping weeds down, conserving moisture, and keeping the soil cool. There are two additional functions of mulches for strawberries, winter protection and keeping the berries clean.

In any area where the soil is likely to freeze hard enough to hold up a man's weight there is danger of the plants heaving partially out of the soil as it freezes and thaws. This breaks off many of the feeding rootlets and exposes the remainder, as well as the lower part of the crown, to drying out. Where the temperature goes below zero most winters, mulching to prevent heaving is almost a necessity, except, possibly, those fields that are so weedy that the weeds serve as a mulch—but a very poor substitute. The nature of the soil also has a decided effect on the amount of heaving, the light sandy soils being less subject to heaving, at the same temperature, than are loams, clays, or mucks. On a medium sandy loam I have often seen stakes, driven in to a depth of 8 inches, heaved out and lying flat by spring.

Another phase of winter protection is the actual covering of the plant with mulch, which keeps the temperature of the covered plants from getting quite so low and prevents them from thawing quite so fast, both effects tending to prevent actual injury to the plants. In the northern part of the country this latter effect of mulch is probably the most important. Depth of mulching is of special importance where it is used for winter protection, up to 6 inches of strawy material being needed where winter damage is most to be feared.

One excepion to the general desirability of winter mulching seems to be the western half of the central Great Plains. The very hardy varieties originated at the U.S.D.A. Station at Cheyenne, Wyoming, apparently do not need protective mulch to survive. Furthermore, under the conditions of very little rainfall and very low winter temperature, the mulch has some directly harmful effects, partly, if not entirely, modified if the plants are irrigated.

MULCHING MATERIALS. A number of materials may be used for mulch with satisfactory results. Probably straw, or some strawy material as spoiled hay or salt hay, is most commonly used. They not only give good protection but do not mat down, like leaves, for instance, to such an extent that the plants are smothered. They may also be moved off the plants into the "middles," the strips between the rows, fairly easily in the spring, and can be spread back over the plants for frost protection if necessary.

In regions where heaving may be a problem but actual freeze damage to crowns and roots not so likely, the mulch may be somewhat thinner, so that it will not have to be removed but the plants will grow up through it. If straw is used some of it may be blown into piles by winter winds, and these thicker spots will need to be respread, or pulled off the plants into the alleys. Sometimes the straw can be chopped before applying so the plants can grow through it easily. Chopped cornstalks, chopped corncobs, peanut hulls, sawdust, and a number of other materials may be used if available. The city gardener, in order to get straw, may have to take it in baled form, easier to deliver but harder to spread. The bales will usually have to be torn apart by hand.

In northern regions it is usually satisfactory to wait until the soil is frozen, right after the first freeze of the season if possible, before putting on the mulch. Then you can walk over the plants without doing damage, and the leaves will have been flattened enough to permit easy coverage. On soils which heave badly one may have to judge the timing rather closely. But if the plants are well covered before they are dormant, and then there are several days of warm rains, there may be some rotting of leaves and crowns.

MULCHING TO KEEP THE BERRIES CLEAN. In those regions where there is no winter heaving—that is, where the soil seldom freezes, or where there is a very sandy soil with winter temperatures not too severe, the mulch may be put on during late winter or spring to keep the fruit clean. I have seen berry fields along the Gulf Coast

A sawdust mulch has kept weeds down and berries clean. This is the Sparkle variety grown in the state of Washington.

with just a small handful of long leaf pine needles tucked in around each of the plants, which were grown in rows, essentially the hill system. It does not take very much material to prevent splashing, as it tends to break the impact of the raindrops on the soil, and also to interfere with the upward splashing of mud or sand. This is not to be interpreted as recommending against a permanent mulch for the home garden under southern conditions. However, if only a small amount of material is available, best use of it would be to put it around the developing berries to keep them clean. True, sand or mud may be washed off the berries, but the pleasure of eating clean fruit that has not been scrubbed, which still retains its natural sheen, is one of the significant rewards awaiting those who have properly grown their own strawberries.

HANDLING THE FRUITING BED. Spring treatment of the fruiting bed will consist primarily of removing, or thinning, of mulch if necessary, pulling weeds if present, and pest control. Except under unusual conditions cultivation between the rows at this time is undesirable. The loosened soil, if not covered by mulch, will splash more and damage will be done to the roots which will have grown several inches out into the alleys during the winter. Cultivating close to the rows can cause very definite injury to the outside plants, the ones which would ordinarily produce the most and the biggest berries. If there are weeds which must be removed, pull them, shave them off with a sharp hoe, or, if cultivation seems necessary, cultivate just as shallowly as possible.

HARVESTING. The gardener who has come this far will probably have little trouble with harvesting, doing just "what comes naturally." But a few hints may help. The berries just won't wait for you; other operations can usually be put off a few days, but not picking. A berry will remain in edible condition from one to three days, depending on variety and weather. The ideal time for picking is just when the individual berry is ready to eat. If you are going to keep the fruit for a couple of days, or take it to someone at a distance, it would be better to pick earlier than that, when the berry is just pink instead of full red. Berries which are to be shipped long distances commercially are picked when only partially colored, not the best for flavor, but best for arrival before they become soft and decayed.

Best flavor, and minimum loss from spoilage, will be secured if the picking is done every day. Every other day is about the limit, unless quite a few berries are to be lost. Unfortunately such loss is cumulative, as overripe berries will usually rot and the rot may spread to adjacent fruit that is just ripening or still green. For that reason it is desirable when picking to remove spoiled berries and discard them at some distance from the plants. When you pick, pick clean is good advice, not only to secure all the berries that are coming to you, but to protect the green fruit.

HOW TO PICK. Even a two-year-old can pick strawberries, but not very efficiently. If the berry is grasped firmly between thumb and fingers it can be pulled off, but will be badly bruised, the cap or calyx will usually remain on the plant, and the fingers will soon be sticky and dirty. The berry is covered with a thin cuticle which is valuable in excluding decay spores. When the calyx is pulled off, a corelike projection may come with it, thus opening the very center of the fruit to spores of decay organisms. Here they will find a moist, protected area, ideal for their germination and rapid invasion of the whole fruit. To avoid bruising, grasp the pedicel, or stem, of the fruit just back of the cap, and give it a twisting pull which should cause it to break, leaving ¼ to ½ inch attached to the berry. Some varieties may be a bit difficult, in which case the fruit stem can be pinched between thumbnail and finger and given a sharp little jerk which should do the trick.

Only one or two berries should be held in the hand at once or bruising is bound to occur. Have the berry cup, or other receptacle, handy, so the fruit can be laid down quickly but gently. Berry cups are good to pick into because they are shallow, but any other shallow container may be used. The trouble with larger ones, kitchen pans for instance, is that there is always a temptation to pile the fruit too high; looks harmless at the time but it will bruise.

WHEN TO PICK. The best time to pick is early in the morning while the fruit is still cool, and the poorest is during the hottest part of the day. It is better to pick when the berries are dry, but unless there has been considerable fruit rot, picking when wet will not cause any serious trouble, especially if the fruit is promptly taken in to the refrigerator, or other cool, well-ventilated place. Picking in the rain may not be much fun, but eating the berries, which might otherwise be lost, will be fun.

TREATMENT AFTER HARVEST. After the crop is picked there is a natural tendency to forget the strawberry patch for a while, but one to be resisted. If it is to be turned under, either because it is old, or because you are following the short cycle, "plant every year" system, then the quicker it goes under the better. By turning under the plants you will also destroy disease spots and spores, insects and spider mites, and prevent, by that much, their going over to the new plants which by now should be well established and making new runners.

RENOVATION. Renovation is the term generally used for the after-harvest treatment of a strawberry patch which is going to be kept for another season. These are various methods, but all of them, on most soils at least, will involve fertilizing the plants. A complete fertilizer, about the same mix and amount as used before the plants were originally set, may be broadcast over the plants and brushed off the leaves in some way. For plants which are in hills little more can be done, if they are mulched, except to water in the fertilizer if water is available. If cultivated, then the fertilizer may be worked into the soil.

There is some disagreement about the advisability of mowing the leaves after fruiting. It is done in some regions, but I have felt that the plants would be stronger if the old leaves were permitted to function. There are occasions, where pests such as red spider, or leaf spot, or mildew are bad, when mowing, followed by burning, would destroy a lot of pest-carrying material. Commercial growers sometimes burn over mowed fields, after letting them dry just enough for a quick fire, but not dry enough so the crowns would burn. I am mentioning this, not as a recommendation, but to indicate to home gardeners that it is sometimes done, but is rather dangerous, and the objectives can be accomplished by safer means. Modern spray materials make it possible to control pests without burning, and we now realize that organic matter is much better as a mulch, or turned into the soil, than it is as ashes.

RENEWING THE MATTED ROW. The matted row may be renovated by chopping out a portion of the plants to provide room for new runners to take root. Sometimes most of the new runners are cut off, leaving the job of fruit production to the old plants, but they are not usually as productive as younger plants.

Commercial growers may plow under part of the matted row, leaving a strip of plants, possibly 15 inches wide, standing on a ridge, then plow or cultivate the soil back against the ridge. This leaves a row of plants, 12 to 15 inches wide, from which new runners will grow to produce a new matted row of full width. This may be accompanied by a crosswise harrowing, with spike tooth or spring tooth, to tear out part of the remaining plants. In other cases the harrowing, usually in both directions without the plowing, is the only renovation.

The home gardener may not have a plow available, but the old matted row may be narrowed by hand hoeing, or the small garden rotavator, to provide a suitable place for new runners to root on either side. Whatever the method used, weeds should be cleaned out as completely as possible. All in all, renovation is one of the hardest jobs in strawberry growing, but if it isn't done crop and size will run down. There is a limit to the number of times an old strawberry bed may be profitably renovated, probably once, sometimes twice, and rarely three or four times. I feel that frequent planting of new plants, every year or two years, and turning the old plants under after picking, is likely to be more satisfactory in the long run.

STANDARD VARIETIES VS. EVERBEARERS. There is a great temptation to look over the nursery catalogs and decide the only berries worth

growing are those that will give "large, delicious berries all summer," and pass up the June-bearing varieties altogether. My own
opinion is that the so-called standard varieties will give a better return for the effort expended than the everbearers. The best combination would seem to be the June-bearing sorts for main crop,
for freezing and preserving, and for daily use over a three-week
period, followed by enough everbearers for occasional treats the
rest of the summer.

Everbearers differ from other varieties principally in the peculiar
faculty of producing flower buds at many of the growing points
which, in other varieties, would become runners, hence they are
often shy in runner production. Some will produce flowers at the
regular spring blossoming time and then bloom almost continuously until frost. Others will produce a spring crop and then a fall
crop.

CULTURE OF EVERBEARERS. If only one everbearer variety is being
grown, spring as well as fall fruit will be wanted, although in many
ways it is better to depend on a June bearer for the spring crop. If
everbearer plants are set each spring, and the flowers pinched off
until mid-June, or the first of July, a better fall crop will be produced than if they were allowed to start fruiting in the spring, and
better than would be secured from plants grown the year before.
Under certain conditions at least, some of the everbearers will produce good fruit on old plants, even three or four years old, but
young plants set early each spring will normally be better.

Everbearers are usually planted in hills, about a foot apart.
Sometimes they are grown on built-up beds of one kind of another,
and lend themselves well to this kind of culture, which has a flavor
of novelty. It should be remembered that any arrangement built
up above ground level will require special attention to watering. A
permanent mulch of sawdust, or some other satisfactory material,
is very desirable, as the plants will be starting to produce their crop
during the hottest and driest time of the year.

Fruit which matures during the cooler weeks of the fall will ripen
rather slowly, as compared to the spring crop. This is an advantage
in that picking every four or five days will be sufficient. It is a disadvantage in that the more slowly ripening berries seem to offer
more temptation to birds and some of the ground beetles. And
while ripe strawberries in the fall are a real treat, the flavor of the

berries at this time is likely to be somewhat below that of those ripening in warmer weather.

Up to this time I do not know of any virus-free stock of any everbearing variety, although such stock will undoubtedly be developed soon. When that occurs it could make everbearing strawberry varieties considerably more attractive.

THE VIRUS PROBLEM. Unquestionably the most important pest-control problem with strawberries has been the virus problem. For generations it has been known that new varieties were likely to "run out" within a very few years. Sometimes it was said the soil was "strawberry sick." Some years ago scientists in the Northwest and the South proved that certain viruses were involved, and that they were transmitted by the strawberry aphid. A few years later it was shown that most of the strawberry plants in the East also were infected with virus, although most did not show the previously described symptoms—just weakening of plants and unsatisfactory production. A method was worked out whereby plants could be tested for the presence of a virus by grafting the runners to an indicator plant, which would show certain known symptoms if the virus were present. Such plants were said to be "indexed."

Scientists of the U.S.D.A. made an extensive search for virus-free individual plants of the more important varieties, and were successful in finding at least one plant of most of them. These were propagated in a screen house free of the transmitting aphid, and stock released to nurseries, who further increased it in their own screen houses to produce mother plants for field production. Aphid sprays were used in the nursery fields. The result has been plants of unusual vigor and productiveness.

SET ONLY VIRUS-FREE PLANTS. Home gardeners should insist on virus-free plants. They should also realize that to set them in the same garden with others, which probably have virus, is going to result in the new plants picking up the disease. Aphid control would prevent such transfer of the virus, but 100 per cent control is very difficult, and would involve dusting several times a year with an aphicide such as malathion.

It would be wise to eliminate entirely the old plants before attempting to make a new start with virus-free plants. If you can't bear to be without strawberries one season, order virus-free plants for late delivery, about the time your other plants are starting to form little green berries, or about three weeks before ripening. Set the new plants as far from the old ones as possible, and at that time dust the old bed thoroughly with malathion. In a couple of weeks dust the new plants. Just as soon as the crop is picked turn under the old patch and then give the new plants another dust. To be effective this schedule will have to have the co-operation of your neighbors, for aphids are no respecters of property lines.

It would be still safer to purchase virus-free plants out of cold storage after the old, virus-infected plants have been destroyed. However, this would mean planting in relatively hot, dry weather, and special care, especially irrigation, would be needed to insure survival and a fair matted row by the end of the growing season.

THE VIRUS DISEASE COMPLEX. There are a number of distinct viruses which affect strawberries, some occurring only occasionally and resulting in striking distortions as witches'-brooms, or curled leaves. Some of these more striking manifestations are relatively unimportant, partly because they can so readily be seen and rogued out. The more destructive virus trouble is usually the result of a plant's being infected by two or more, possibly up to five, different viruses, the cumulative effect of which is more serious than the effect of any one of them. Some may cause mottling of the leaves, some yellowing of the edges, most of them cause some dwarfing of the plant, especially of the new leaves. These typical symptoms appear only on certain varieties, and are almost entirely masked on others, even though the disease may be causing very poor growth and production.

RESISTANT VARIETIES. Some varieties have more or less resistance to the virus complex, to the extent that they may show no symptoms and remain relatively vigorous and productive, even when grown beside diseased plants. They might seem to be the answer to the problem, but there are two drawbacks. First, such varieties may be weakened and production cut appreciably, without its being evident enough to permit a satisfactory diagnosis. In the second place, they usually carry the virus, and any susceptible varieties growing in the vicinity will be infected. If we could find varieties resistant enough so that production would not be affected, and suitable for all soils and climates, the question might be solved. But viruses have a way of appearing from time to time, from another country perhaps, or by way of mutation, which may combine with some other relatively innocuous virus to cause real damage. It is probable, therefore, that virus-free plants will be in demand as the most satisfactory solution for many years.

CERTIFIED PLANTS. Almost as soon as the virus troubles were first discovered, programs of inspection, and roguing of fields for plant production, were carried out in some states, and plants were certified. In most cases the certified plants were superior to the general run. However, the inspectors, relying on appearance, could not spot plants recently infected, and varieties which have no distinct leaf symptoms were a baffling problem; hence the best of field-certified plants nearly always developed virus troubles within two to four years.

The so-called virus-free plants, from indexed mother stock, are much superior but will very probably pick up one or more of the viruses eventually, depending on how close they are planted to infected wild or cultivated plants. The home gardener who uses his own plants, therefore, should keep close watch on growth and production. If either begins to decline for no apparent reason, and especially if the new leaves, as they emerge from the crown, show yellowish edges and a crinkled or mottled appearance, then he should consider getting new, virus-free plants and getting rid of the old ones.

THE MORE IMPORTANT DISEASES

Viruses: *Symptoms:* Decline in vigor and production, possible leaf distortion, crinkling and curling, yellowing of edges of new leaves, witches'-broom effect.

Control: Plant disease-free plants away from infected plants, control aphids by spraying or dusting with an aphicide such as malathion, at two-week intervals, twice before the berries are half grown and twice during late summer. Consult local authorities for more precise timing to suit your locality.

Red Stele: *Symptoms:* Plants suddenly wilt and die during the first dry spell in the spring of the fruiting year, especially in low, poorly drained places or in heavy soil. The main roots will be rotted off at the ends, most side roots gone. Splitting the stumps of the main roots will show the central cylinder of conducting tissue (stele) reddish brown instead of white. Caused by a fungus.

Control: As there is no known way of killing the organism within the plant, set disease-free plants on disease-free soil. The fungus may remain viable in the soil for several years. Avoid poorly drained spots. Fortunately there are several resistant or partially resistant varieties, including Fairland, Puget Beauty, Redcrop, Redglow, Siletz, Sparkle, Surecrop, Temple, and Vermilion. Unfortunately, at least three strains of the fungus have been found, and a variety may be resistant to one but not the others. Stelemaster is said to be resistant to all the presently known strains.

Remarks: Soil fumigation might eliminate the disease from a particular area, but the resting spores are very tenacious and if your soil is infected it would be better to rely on resistant varieties. At one stage of the disease there are swimming spores which will be carried by surface runoff to any lower spots, to your neighbor's garden—or from it to yours.

Verticillium Root Rot: *Symptoms:* Plants wilt and die, often while ripening their crops, the outer leaves wilting first. Roots will be rotted off, but the steles will be whitish, not reddish. Often found where tomatoes or peppers have preceded the strawberries, especially on the West Coast.

Control: Set clean plants on clean soil; avoid following tomatoes if possible. Soil sterilization is possible. Not too much is known about varietal resistance. Will persist in soil for several years.

Leaf Spot: *Symptoms:* Small purplish, roundish spots, with whitish centers, $\frac{1}{16}$ to $\frac{1}{8}$ inch diameter, sprinkled over the leaves, and even on the calyces and fruit in very susceptible varieties. Usually the effective leaf surface is reduced considerably. In bad cases the leaves turn brown and dry up.

Control: Some varieties are fairly resistant. Keep plants growing vigorously. Spray with Bordeaux mixture or one of the other copper sprays, or with ferbam, when new foliage appears and again when first blossoms open.

Leaf Scorch: *Symptoms:* Somewhat resembles leaf spot, but the lesions of scorch are somewhat larger and have indistinct margins instead of the sharply defined margins of leaf spot; color is about the same but does not develop a lighter colored center.

Control: Same as for leaf spot.

Mildew: *Symptoms:* Leaves become covered with a powdery, whitish sprinkling of fungus growth, followed by browning and eventual death of those areas.

Control: There is definite varietal resistance. The disease will be worse where the growth is excessively vegetative and plants are too thick, resulting in poor aeration. The mildews are hard to control by sprays. A sulfur dust at the first indication of the disease has long been the standard recommendation. Materials developed particularly for mildew on other fruits may be effective.

Fruit Rots: *Symptoms:* Watery, brownish spots appear on the ripe or green fruits, rapidly enlarging to include the whole fruit and leave it a sodden mass covered with a grayish mold. There are several fungi which cause fruit rot, and the symptoms may differ in the color of the spot and the rapidity of its spread. Probably the most common one is a botrytis.

Control: Keeping the plants from being over vigorous and too thickly crowded in the row will help to hold down fruit rot. Rain during the picking season nearly always increases rot. If you have to irrigate while the fruit is ripe, do so right after a picking; give a good soaking so you will not have to do it again soon. Recently satisfactory control has been reported by some researchers from the use of a 7½ per cent captan dust, applied just before first bloom, 10 days later, and 10 days after that. Unfortunately, in other experiments such good results were not obtained, but at present Captan seems to be the most promising fungicide for fruit rot caused by botrytis.

NEMATODES

Black Root: *Symptoms:* Blackish lesions on the roots, destroying the outer cell layers. Sometimes the entire root will be blackened. The root system of a plant may be of normal length but blackish and dried up, not rotted off as in red stele. This was long considered as a disease caused by some unknown fungus or bacterium, but more recently rather definitely associated with injury by a root lesion type nematode, possibly accentuated by some secondary fungus.

Control: Clean plants on clean soil, hence rotation of strawberries with other crops. The U.S.D.A., in co-operation with various nurserymen, is working in the direction of nematode-free plants. Soil can be fugimated with D-D or ethylene dibromide to kill nematodes. Black root has been very widely distributed over the country, although more serious in some localities and in some years than in others. Immediate damage to the plant is probably associated with lack of water due to the loss of feeding rootlets and root hairs. Keeping the soil moist may permit the plants to produce a fair crop with that part of the root system still functioning.

Root Knot: *Symptoms:* Shortened, knotty roots, resulting in poor functioning, hence poor growth and production. Caused by the root knot nematode, more serious in the southern states.

Control: Clean plants on clean soil. Most nurseries are inspected for this pest, as the symptoms are easy to see, but a few may slip by and infest your soil. The soil may be fumigated as described for black root.

Bud Nematode: *Symptoms:* Leaves narrowed, slightly crinkled, some of the new leaves may fail to develop, plants are low—that is, the leaves do not stand up normally.

Control: This nematode does not ordinarily survive in the soil, so must be brought in on infested plants. Buy clean plants, first plowing under infested plants if you have them. Sprays and dusts have usually been unsuccessful. The home gardener will do better by relying on clean plants than by trying chemical control.

INSECTS

White Grubs: *Symptoms:* Plants suddenly wilt, usually in early summer, and when pulled up are found to have had all roots chewed off just below the crown. Search may reveal a fat, whitish grub, 1 to 1½ inches in length. This is the larva of the June beetle, the big brown fellow which bumbles around outside lights on warm spring evenings.

Control: These grubs are usually worse in old sod land, so plant strawberries in soil that grew a cultivated crop the year before. Incorporation of a suitable insecticide in the soil should give control. It will seldom be profitable to do this just for white grubs, because they usually do not do a great deal of damage, but if wireworms, Japanese or Asiatic beetle grubs, or strawberry weevils are present the use of a soil treatment may be worth while. Aldrin, 3 pounds per acre, 1.1 ounce per 1000 square feet, or chlordane, 10 pounds per acre should give control. These figures are for actual active material, hence use twice as much for a 50 per cent, 4 times for a 25 per cent, brand. These materials should be applied uniformly, in spray or dust form, and thoroughly incorporated in the top 6 inches of soil.

Japanese Beetle: *Symptoms:* Adult beetles will feed to some extent on the foliage of certain varieties, skeletonizing the leaves. The beetles have a bluish black color, with a metallic sheen and are about ⅜ inch in length. The grubs, somewhat smaller than white grubs, are light grayish in color and, when dug, curl up in a circle. They eat the roots.

Control: The adult beetles may be controlled, or at least repelled, by spraying the foliage, after the fruit is picked, with DDT, ½ ounce to 3 gallons water. More damage is likely to be caused by the grubs and they may be controlled by incorporating aldrin, chlordane, or DDT into the soil as for white grubs. This insect is present primarily in the Middle Atlantic and some adjoining states. It will not be worth while to worry about Japanese beetles on strawberries unless they are prevalent enough in your neighborhood to be causing considerable damage to other plants, such as roses and grapes.

Strawberry Weevils: *Symptoms:* Plants wilt down in early summer and examination reveals the roots have been chewed, some of the lower part of the crown may have been eaten away, and small, pearl-white larvae, about ¼ inch long, may be found. The adults are jet-black snout beetles, about ¼ inch in length, which have wings but do not fly. There are three closely related beetles in this group, the strawberry weevil, the rough strawberry weevil, and the black vine weevil. The eggs are laid during May and June around the base of the plants, the larvae descend to the roots where they feed until the next spring, when they emerge for a few weeks above ground.

Control: Apply aldrin 7½ pounds (actual) or 15 pounds chlordane per acre (3 or 6 ounces respectively per 1000 square feet) and work into soil before planting. Or dust with aldrin, 2½ per cent, when the adults have emerged and before they have started to lay eggs. Strawberry growers often check the timing by laying a board in the field and looking under it, as the adults feed at night and like to spend the day under some protective material. Do not dust while fruit is developing. A weevil bait, obtainable in most areas where the weevils are prevalent, can be used but is not as effective as a thorough job of spraying properly timed.

Bud Weevil: *Symptoms:* Another, and smaller, snout beetle is sometimes prevalent in the East and Southwest, where it lays its eggs in the flower buds just before they are ready to open. The female then nips the pedicel, just below the bud, so it will never develop, giving meaning to the common name, strawberry nipper. A sulfur-lead arsenate-lime dust was found useful before some of the modern insecticides appeared. If you have been bothered in previous years dust with 5 per cent DDT or 5 per cent chlordane (sometimes combined with sulfur to prevent build-up of mites) when the first flower buds are pushing out of the crowns. This insect overwinters in trash on the ground, often in a fence row or similar place next to the strawberries, so cleaning up trashy areas around the berries may help.

Crown Borer: *Symptoms:* A reddish brown snout beetle, about ⅙ inch long feeds on the leaves in early spring. The larvae tunnel through the crowns and stunt or kill the plants.

Control: This insect is somewhat localized so it might be best to check with your county agent if you think it is present. Spraying with toxaphene has been successful in some commercial plantings.

Spittle Bug: *Symptoms:* Masses of spittle-like material on various weeds and grasses, as well as on strawberries, is an all too common sight during early summer in many parts of the country. Examination will show an immature leaf hopper, light greenish in color, in each foamy mass, which is a protective device. The insect stays in one place, sucking juice from the host plant, until it reaches its final adult stage, when it becomes a rather large, winged leaf hopper, and may be seen flying around near the ground.

Control: Dust, when the first spittle masses appear, with rotenone, methoxychlor, or chlordane.

Aphids: *Symptoms:* Very small, yellowish green aphids may sometimes be found on the undersides of the new leaves. Probably they seldom do very serious damage directly, but one species is the vector for the virus complex which can make the plants practically worthless.

Control: Dust at the rate of ¾ pounds per 1000 square feet with 4 per cent malathion dust.

Strawberry Root Aphids: *Symptoms:* Occasionally in eastern strawberry fields there may be a general lack of vigor, associated with a great deal of ant activity as evidenced by small anthills, often adjacent to the crown of the plant. If the plant is dug, a number of dark greenish aphids will be found clinging, by their sucking mouth parts, to the main roots just below the crown.

Control: Since the ants move the aphids from one plant to another some help will come from exterminating the ants. Dusting the surface of the soil with chlordane should take care of the ants as they will pick up the insecticide as they walk through it. Killing the aphids directly after they have gone down to the roots is almost impossible, and the potential damage hardly warrants the expense. If there is considerable trouble it may be desirable to eliminate the old bed and secure plants known to be free of the aphid.

Red Spider Mite: *Symptoms:* Rather pale color, dullness of leaf, very tiny yellowish spots occurring during hot, dry weather may indicate attack by this mite. The underside of the leaf may be webbed in severe cases. Good eyes can see the tiny, reddish mites constantly moving about, and with a hand lens the comparatively large, spherical, reddish eggs can be easily seen. In severe cases the leaves will become brownish and dry. This mite also attacks many other plants, such as raspberries, beans, and several species of weeds.

Control: This being a dry-weather pest, keeping the plants growing vigorously, with ample water, will tend to discourage it. The old remedy was to dust with sulfur but was not very effective. There are several materials on the market now, especially formulated to control mites of this type, including aramite, which should be used according to manufacturer's directions. A 5 per cent malathion dust, not closer than 4 days to harvest, should give reasonable control.

Cyclamen Mite: *Symptoms:* Plants lower than normal, leaves slightly puckered, foliage rather sparse, few flowers produced. This is a tiny mite, difficult to find, even with a hand lens. It does not move about as much as the spider mites. The damage is out of all proportion to the actual feeding and is apparently due to the injection of some toxic material as the mite feeds.

Control: By far the most satisfactory situation is to set clean plants. If you suspect that you have this mite, destroy all old plants before bringing in new ones. It will not persist in the soil for long, but it would be a wise precaution to plant the new bed as far as convenient from the old one. Sprays have not been very effective, although endrin and kelthane have been reported as giving control.

Strawberry Leaf Roller: *Symptoms:* Leaves rolled upward and the margins webbed together. An active greenish yellow larva will be found inside, up to ⅝ inch long. It feeds on the inside of the folded leaf, eventually skeletonizing it and causing it to turn brown and die. In bad infestations there may be a roller to almost every leaf, and then the damage may be severe.

Control: After the leaf is rolled it is difficult to reach the insect with a spray, except with some material, such as parathion, which kills by gas penetration. It is much better to spray with a less dangerous material, as DDT, or malathion, at the first evidence of the presence of the insect, and before many leaves are rolled. On a small scale the leaves may be picked off if a few rollers were missed by the spray.

CHAPTER 13

Fresh Raspberries—How to Grow Them

One of the most delectable of the small fruits, and one of the most difficult to buy fresh, in most places, is the raspberry. This scarcity is associated with the fact that raspberries are extremely perishable, and frequently a disappointment both to the grocer and the housewife. The result is that this crop has become concentrated in a very limited number of localities, usually where canning and freezing facilities are available. The tendency then is for all fruit to go to the processor, rather than to the more uncertain channels of trade leading to the fresh market. Even near important commercial raspberry-producing sections fresh berries may be difficult to find in most stores. And so if you like them, and who doesn't, why not grow some for yourself?

Raspberries are relatively easy to grow in the home garden, except in the Far South and the semi-desert areas. They are generally adapted to the cooler parts of the country, roughly the northern two thirds to three fourths. They are not too particular as to soils, except that they do not like poorly drained ones. They will do well on very light, sandy soils if mulched or irrigated. However, a medium sandy loam to clay loam is preferable. They are not particularly fussy as to pH; fertility is important but can be built up.

RED, YELLOW, BLACK, AND PURPLE. Raspberries belong to the genus *Rubus,* as do the blackberries and dewberries. There are two general types, the red raspberries, which group includes a few yellow-fruited varieties, and the black raspberries, usually referred to as blackcaps. Although these two types differ in a number of ways they are closely related, as evidenced by the fact they can be crossed fairly easily, the hybrids between the two types being called purple raspberries, or purple canes. The term "purple" really refers to the color of the fruit, which is intermediate between red and purplish black.

The cultivated raspberries, like many other fruits, are the result of many years of hybridizing, bringing together the best qualities of several different species. The black varieties are derived from

211

the native American species, *Rubus occidentalis.* The red sorts have resulted from combining certain species, primarily *Rubus strigosus,* native to North America, and R. *idaeus,* a European species. From the American types have come hardiness and adaptability to our climate, and from the European, large size and high dessert quality. More recently breeders in the South have been using certain Asiatic species, in attempts to breed in resistance to high temperatures, and extend the potential raspberry-growing area further south.

THE RED RASPBERRIES. Differences in plant characters as well as the color of the fruit distinguish the reds from the blacks. The reds have stiff, erect canes, more or less covered with prickles, although the breeders have been producing varieties that are almost smooth caned. These canes are produced freely from adventitious buds on the roots. These sucker plants may come up several feet from the original row and so must be kept down by cultivation, or pulling, if the plants are mulched. The bark color is some shade of brown,

A fruiting lateral of the Puyallup red raspberry. This whole shoot developed from a single "fruit bud" on the overwintering cane.

from rather light to quite dark. The fruit is quite tender, juicy, and separates easily from the whitish receptacle which is usually roundish conic to long conic. The berries range from roundish to long conic, and from rather light to dark red. Some of the less desirable sorts have a tendency to crumble—that is, the individual drupelets of the berry break apart, a very undesirable characteristic. Some also are hard to pick because they cling tightly to the receptacle until fully colored, so they cannot easily be removed just before they have reached their full mature, red color, when they will have good keeping quality but also good flavor.

The yellow raspberries resemble the reds in all except color, having presumably arisen from the red type by mutation. They occur rather rarely as seedlings of a cross between two red varieties.

THE BLACK RASPBERRIES. The black caps produce long arching canes which may grow erect to about 3 feet and then arch over, eventually reaching the ground and perhaps trailing for several feet. These canes all come from the original crown, as this type does not produce suckers. During late summer and early fall the tip of the cane will thicken and then take root. The canes are light yellowish green when young, changing to a reddish brown, and covered with a dense, whitish bloom, which gives them at a little distance the appearance of being almost white. The prickles are stouter than those of the red varieties.

Fruit of the blackcaps is rounded, rather than conic, and much firmer than the reds. Some may think them too seedy. They have a rich-flavored, highly pigmented juice, sometimes used to make a harmless vegetable dye for stamping meats. The ripening fruit changes from green to red to purplish black.

THE PURPLE RASPBERRIES. The purple varieties, as might be expected, are somewhat intermediate, usually resembling the blacks in type of cane growth and rooting at the tips. Some, however, may make sucker plants and others do neither. The fruit is large, usually a dusty, light purplish in color. As additional crosses are made, purple on purple, and backcrosses to either type, the variation naturally increases. Fruit of the purple varieties has never proven very popular, except for preserve manufacture, but is, in my opinion, very good for dessert purposes also, although usually quite tart.

The Asiatic species used in hybridization have mostly been red fruited, usually with an orange cast rather than a rich red.

TABLE XIII
Red and Black Raspberry Varieties
Suggested for the Home Garden

New England

RED	BLACK
Latham	Bristol
Milton	Cumberland
Newburgh	Logan
Sunrise	
Taylor	

New York

RED	BLACK
Latham	Bristol
Milton	Dundee
Newburgh	Logan
Taylor	

Other Middle Atlantic States

RED	BLACK
Latham	Bristol
Sunrise	Cumberland
Taylor	Logan
	Morrison

Great Lakes Region

RED	BLACK
Early Red	Black Hawk
Latham	Dundee
Newburgh	Logan
Willamette	Morrison

Southeastern States

RED	BLACK
Dixie	Bristol
Latham	Logan
Mandarin	

Lower Mississippi Valley

RED	BLACK
Chief	Black Hawk
Latham	Bristol
Sunrise	Morrison

Upper Mississippi Valley

RED	BLACK
Chief	Black Hawk
Latham	Cumberland
Newburgh	Morrison
Sunrise	

Prairie States

RED	BLACK
Chief	
Latham	

Great Plains

RED	BLACK
Chief	

Rocky Mountain States

RED	BLACK[1]
Chief	Bristol
Latham	Cumberland
Newburgh	Logan

California

RED	BLACK
Ranere	
Willamette	

Northwest

RED	BLACK
Canby	Dundee
Puyallup	Morrison
Sumner	Munger
Washington	Plum Farmer
Willamette	

[1] Black varieties need winter protection.

BRIEF VARIETAL DESCRIPTIONS

Red Raspberries

Canby—midseason, large, bright red, good quality, U.S.D.A. and Oregon Experiment Station.

Chief—early, small, fair quality, very hardy. Minnesota Experiment Station.

Dixie—tart, soft, a cross between Latham and an Asiatic species, for south of usual raspberry region. North Carolina Experiment Station.

Early Red—early, productive, good quality. Michigan (South Haven) Experiment Station.

Latham—late midseason, widely grown, hardy, quality fair. Minnesota Experiment Station.

Mandarin—hybrid of an Asiatic species for trial in the south. U.S.D.A. and North Carolina Experiment Station.

Milton—very late, large, good, apparently has some resistance to mosaic. New York (Geneva) Experiment Station.

Newburgh—midseason, large, firm, fair quality. New York (Geneva) Experiment Station.

Puyallup—midseason, large, good. Washington (Puyallup) Experiment Station.

Sumner—midseason, large, attractive, good quality, appears resistant to root trouble in heavy soil. Washington (Puyallup) Experiment Station.

Sunrise—very early, makes excessive number of plants, a bit small, quality only fair. U.S.D.A.

Taylor—late, large, good quality. New York (Geneva) Experiment Station.

Washington—late, medium size, very good quality. Washington (Puyallup) Experiment Station.

Willamette—midseason, very productive, large, a bit dark, good quality. U.S.D.A., Oregon Experiment Station.

Black Raspberries

Black Hawk—late, very large, very good quality, hardy. Iowa Experiment Station.

Bristol—medium early, large, very good. New York (Geneva) Experiment Station.

Cumberland—midseason, good size and quality but rather susceptible to virus and anthracnose. Originated in Pennsylvania about 1896.

Dundee—midseason, large, very good. New York (Geneva) Experiment Station.

Logan—midseason, medium size, good, resistant to leaf curl. Originated in Illinois.

Morrison—late, large. Originated in Ohio.

Munger—midseason. Originated in Ohio.

Plum Farmer—early, fair size and quality. Originated in Ohio.

Yellow Raspberries

Although no yellow varieties were listed in Table XIII some gardeners may wish to try them as a novelty. The state of origin will give some inkling as to where they may be well adapted.

Amber—large, high quality. New York (Geneva) Experiment Station.

Goldenwest—resembles Washington, except in color. Washington (Puyallup) Experiment Station.

Purple Raspberries

Of several purple raspberry varieties which have been available during recent years, Sodus has seemed to be most disease resistant, productive, and generally satisfactory. It could be grown in most areas where the reds or blacks are satisfactory and is even recommended by some horticulturists for planting further south than either red or black types.

Sodus—large, firm, fair quality, very vigorous. New York (Geneva) Experiment Station.

Fall-Fruiting Red Raspberries

Although the fall bearing varieties were not specifically recommended in Table XIII, they are worthy of trial on a small scale by any gardener who especially likes fresh raspberries. The summer bearing sorts are usually superior for the main crop, and for processing, with the fall bearing varieties producing that occasional out-of-season treat. September may do well farther south than most raspberries.

Durham—good fall crop but poor to fair summer crop. Cutting canes to ground in spring will eliminate summer crop and give better fruit in the fall. New Hampshire Experiment Station.

Ranere—early, small, fair quality, bears light crop in the fall. Originated in New Jersey.

September—quality fair in summer, good in fall, will produce a summer and fall crop. New York (Geneva) Experiment Station.

RASPBERRIES FOR THE SOUTH. In the practically frost-free parts of southern Florida the tropical species *Rubus albescens* is sometimes grown. Northern Florida and the other Gulf states are not adapted to present varieties, although fair success might be achieved in exceptionally favorable spots, especially at the higher altitudes. Breeding work is under way in southern states which will, in all probability, produce good home garden raspberries for that part of the country.

PROPAGATION OF RED RASPBERRIES. The method of growth gives a clue as to how plants may be propagated. Suckers of the red varieties may be dug in early spring and set in a new row. Strong canes about 3 feet long are desirable. Most plants which make suckers from adventitious buds on the roots can be propagated readily from root cuttings, and red raspberries are no exception. It is easier simply to dig up the suckers, but occasionally it is desirable to propagate rapidly some new or scarce variety, and then root cuttings may be made during late winter. Use fairly large roots, the size of a soda straw to the size of a lead pencil. Cut them into sections about 3 inches long and lay in a trench 3 to 4 inches deep, cover with sand, or soil if it is reasonably light in texture. Transplant to their permanent row the next autumn or the following spring.

Soft sucker shoots of the red varieties may be transplanted in late spring when they are 6 to 9 inches high, although they wilt easily and will have to be watered if the weather is dry. The necessary care for such soft plants is considerably greater than for dormant plants, and the mortality is usually higher. However, it is a way of getting a new planting started in late spring if you didn't get around to it earlier. This method was used almost entirely in a commercial raspberry section with which I was familiar in New Jersey, where the raspberry crown borer was prevalent. Most dormant canes had tiny, over-wintering larvae present at the base of the canes, ready to start burrowing around under the bark, whereas the green shoots did not and were thus assured of one season's growth free from damage by the borer.

PLANTING THE RED VARIETIES. The red raspberry dormant plants may be set with a shovel as described in Chapter 11. Their root system will be rather meager, consisting mostly of a section of the large root from which the sucker had grown, with a few smaller laterals. Early spring planting is preferable in northern areas but fall planting has advantages in the South as it permits the plants to become well established over winter, before the hot, dry days of summer.

Pruning at planting time is done for two reasons—to cut down on transpiration or water loss until new roots are grown, and to reduce potential disease infection. The red raspberry cane is ordinarily cut back to a few inches. If you are very eager to get some fruit, and you plant early in fertile soil, and maintain a good supply of moisture and nutrients, you can cut a 3-foot plant to 18 inches at planting time and get a few berries the first year. Commercial growers prefer to use all the plants' strength in making cane and root growth, so they may prune to as short as 6 inches, or longer, if growing conditions are quite favorable. This will result in no fruit worth picking the year of planting but a fair crop the next year when the plants are said to be one year old. There should be practically a full crop the following year and from then on, as long as the plants remain healthy and vigorous.

SYSTEMS OF PLANTING. Most red raspberries are grown in a hedgerow system. The plants are set about 3 feet apart in the row, but the new shoots soon fill in the row. This means cultivation can be in only one direction. Sometimes the plants are set about 4 feet apart in the row so cultivation can be in both directions. In this hill system a post or heavy stake is set to support each hill. Blackcaps and purples may be grown in hedgerows or hills, although as they do not produce suckers the original plant remains as a distinct "hill," even when handled as a hedgerow and tied to a trellis.

SOIL MANAGEMENT. Managing the soil for raspberries involves nothing unusual. Mulch is desirable if available, and may be applied at planting time, or during early summer after a thorough cultivation. Mulch, however, does provide a good run for red raspberry roots and suckers will come up in great numbers, to a distance of several feet on each side of the row. They pull rather easily, fortunately, as they will have to be taken out in that way. A lawn mower would cut them off easily enough, but the stumps would continue to grow. When they are pulled they usually break off cleanly where the sprout grows out from the cross root.

The use of any systemic weed killer to keep the middles free of suckers and weeds is out of the question, as the material would also be translocated to, and probably damage, the fruiting canes. Possibly a strictly contact material, one which injures only the plant tissues which it hits directly, could be used. Paint thinner would be

Red raspberries trained to a trellis of poles. This was done for economy, but a rustic trellis, thoughtfully designed, might add interest to the garden in winter.

effective in burning down grass in early spring, but it would not kill the roots of perennial grasses. Without killing them, it would probably burn the leaves off the rasberry suckers which might be covered by the spray. Any weed killer at all to be used between red raspberry rows should be tried out on a small spot first, to limit the amount of damage if it does not work as you had hoped.

Practically all commercial red raspberry plantings, and most home garden plots, are cultivated, which works out well, as the main roots are fairly deep. Even with cultivation there will have to be hand weeding in the row, and pulling, or hoeing off, of excess suckers, many of which will be missed by most cultivating implements.

FERTILIZING RASPBERRIES. This fruit will stand heavy feeding, as indicated by the growth attained in the best commercial sections, where canes of some varieties 8 feet long, and longer, are not unusual. The home gardener, unless his conditions are unfavorable, should shoot at such a mark for his own plants. If he is not getting it, he should try increasing his fertilizer application, especially nitrogen, being sure that his soil is not actually deficient in the other major nutrients. Water supply, possible presence of mosaic disease in the plants, and other pest problems should be considered, however, before extending oneself too far with fertilizers. But it is true, I believe, that more home garden raspberries are underfertilized than overfed. One must remember, too, that the more cane and leaf growth being made, the more water will be required.

On most soils it will be advisable to start with a basic application of a complete fertilizer before planting. On soils of medium fertility or below, an annual early spring application of 5-10-5, or similar formula, should be made. The amount to use can be estimated accurately only by one who knows local conditions—the gardener himself, usually. As a hint to the beginner it will probably be somewhere between 500 and 1000 pounds per acre or 12 to 25 pounds per 1000 square feet. Usually it will be necessary to supplement this with some readily available nitrogenous fertilizer. This may be applied as a side dressing after growth starts, when it will be possible to judge from the color of the leaves and the general vigor of growth whether or not the plants are deficient in nitrogen. Of course soils known to be deficient in any of the other elements should receive special treatment to correct those deficiencies as indicated in Chapter 5.

The water requirement may be lessened by pulling out excess suckers while they are small, rather than letting them grow to full height and removing them at the dormant pruning. This summer thinning will also let more light reach the lower part of the canes. This, in turn, will cause the lower leaves to hang on longer and "fatten up" the lower part of the cane. Spur blight and certain other diseases will be less prevalent where light and moving air may reach the canes more readily.

IRRIGATION. Because of their relatively deep rooting, red raspberries may get by without irrigation where some other crops might require it. However, they will respond to watering when the soil becomes very dry. It is best not to sprinkle during the picking season, if possible, as the berries will mold very quickly if picked when wet. Try to water enough, before the fruit ripens, to carry through the picking season.

Too much water—that is, poorly drained soil—may cause injury or death to red raspberries. Certain varieties seem especially susceptible. Sometimes such a variety will at first grow fairly well on soils where it will later refuse to grow. This would seem to indicate that some harmful organism—fungus, bacterium, or nematode—may be associated with the seeming aversion to poorly drained soils. The assumption is that this pest, whatever it is, does better with poor drainage so that it kills the plants there, but not where drainage is good, hence less favorable for the pest. This has been a serious commercial problem in the Northwest. At this writing the Sumner variety seems to be more resistant than others.

PRUNING RED RASPBERRIES. The raspberries, like all the brambles, have biennial canes, which make their entire growth in length, including any side branches, in one growing season. The next season they put out fruiting laterals, leafy shoots a few inches to a couple of feet long, considerably branched with each branchlet terminating in a cluster of flowers. By the time the fruit has all ripened, the leaves on these fruiting canes will be rather pale, and duller than those on the younger canes. Within a few days most of these leaves will drop and the canes which have borne fruit will be dead or nearly so. Where growing conditions are unfavorable because of drouth, heat, insufficient nutrients, or other causes, the fruiting canes will die earlier, even before all of the berries have ripened. When that happens start looking for the cause and a possible remedy.

It is better to remove the fruiting canes as soon as the crop has been picked, in order to eliminate the disease spots, almost invariably present, and the spores which they would produce. Some thinning of young canes may be advisable at this time, at least with certain varieties, to permit better air movement which may help in controlling certain fungus diseases. The old canes will have to be cut out with shears or loppers, although if they are left until the following spring they may, by then, have been dead long enough to be brittle so they may be broken out.

DORMANT PRUNING. The regular dormant pruning for red raspberries may be done any time between leaf fall and the start of growth in the spring. Fall pruning will remove a lot of disease spots and cut down by that much the amount of spores to be produced in the early spring. On the other hand, in many areas, there are likely to be some winter injured canes, and spring pruning will permit a clean job of removing them, whereas in the fall one is likely to remove some canes which would have survived, and leave some

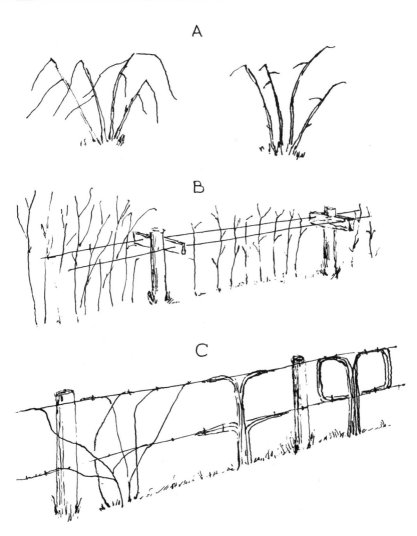

Methods of training and pruning brambles. A. Unpruned and pruned black raspberry. B. Bush blackberries supported by two wires on cross arms, unpruned at left, pruned at right. C. Methods of trellising the trailing blackberries, such as dewberries, boysenberries, and loganberries. Left to right, canes spread out and tied individually; canes tied in four bundles; canes in two bundles which extend to top wire and are looped to lower wire.

which will be killed during the winter. Late winter or very early spring is better than late spring as there will be no growing shoots to break off, but if you can't get it done early it is better to do it late than not at all. Unpruned raspberries will produce smaller fruit, although probably a greater number of berries, which will be more difficult to pick. There may be more diseases such as spur blight because of poor aeration if the canes are very close together.

THINNING OUT AND HEADING BACK. The pruning will consist of two operations, thinning out surplus canes and shortening, or heading back, those which are left. Naturally the thinning comes first. In general, the fewer canes that are left, the larger the berries will be, but eventually a point is reached where the removal of more canes will appreciably reduce the crop. Just how many to leave per foot of row, or what distance between, will depend on the variety, soil conditions, and freedom from weakening pest injury, so that it is difficult to make specific recommendations. In the East, with varieties like Latham, from 6 to 9 inches between canes, with the canes scattered over a row some 18 inches in width, has seemed about right. In the Northwest extensive experiments have indicated that, under good commercial raspberry-growing conditions, the more canes per hill, the larger the crop, and without seriously affecting the size of the berries. The home gardener, because no one else has conditions identical with his, can well do a little experimenting by spacing the canes differently in various parts of the row and then observing the results.

After excess canes are removed, the ones remaining should be cut back. In the East I have seen canes cut back to one half or less, where there was no trellis, and each cane had to be self-supporting. These plants were also in dry, sandy soil, with no irrigation, and in some cases partially girdled by crown borer larvae. On heavier soil, with a reasonable amount of moisture and free of crown borers, the same varieties could have a much smaller portion of the cane removed and still produce good fruit. Under the unfavorable conditions, canes which were not cut back severely produced very small berries, mostly toward the tip of the cane, and in times of drouth were inclined to die back from the tip, during or just before harvest.

TRELLISES. Although it is possible to prune raspberries short enough so the canes will stand up without support, a trellis of some kind is nearly always advisable, even where the canes are relatively short or where severe cutting back is indicated.

Where red raspberry canes have no other support they may be made
to support themselves by tying the canes together, "tepee" style.

In the Northwest, red raspberry canes grow much taller than in
the East or South, or even the Midwest, so that support of some
kind is essential. This eliminates the requirement of pruning back
specifically so the cane can support itself with its crop. Where
canes are very long they may be tipped back 2 or 3 feet and still
be too high to reach, and so they are woven over the top wire of
the trellis and tied to the lower wire.

Trellises vary, but a good one for the home garden consists of
posts every 12 feet or so, with two wires at the top, from 4 to 5 feet
from the ground, and two other wires halfway between the ground
and the top wires. The wires may be stapled directly to the posts,
or, better yet, put near the ends of short cross pieces, some 18
inches long. This will permit the new canes to grow up between the
wires, and possibly be tied to the wires on one side, while the bearing canes are tied to the wires on the other side. Some such method
of separating bearing from new canes will facilitate picking.

Red raspberries may be trained on stakes, in hills some 4 to 5
feet apart, so the land may be cross cultivated, but the hedgerow
system is probably more satisfactory for the home garden. Where

no trellis is used, but the canes are cut a little too high to be self-supporting, it is a good plan to tie half a dozen canes together, "tepee" style, greatly decreasing the tendency to bend down when loaded with fruit.

Another method sometimes used is to provide temporary support while the crop is developing. Strong stakes are driven into the middle of the row at intervals of 15 to 25 feet. Binder twine, or other strong cord, is then tied to the end stake, run along each side of the row, wrapped around each stake and pulled as tight as possible. It will still bulge out between stakes, but a few ties, pulling the strings on either side together, will straighten up the canes and hold them reasonably erect. If the string stretches, more cross ties can be put in. By holding the upper parts of the canes together in this way they tend to support each other.

BLACK RASPBERRIES DIFFER IN GROWTH HABITS. The blackcap raspberries differ markedly from the reds, even though so closely related that they will intercross fairly easily. The blacks do not make suckers at all, and they have many fine roots instead of a few larger ones, such as the reds have. The canes have the peculiar habit of bending over, and running for several feet on the ground. Late in the summer the ends of the canes, both primary and lateral, swell a bit, become somewhat fleshy, and put out roots, forming what are known as tip layers. These rooted tips may be dug up the following spring and used to set a new planting.

Since tip layers of the blacks and purples have a mass of small fibrous roots, it is a little better to dig a hole with trowel or shovel, and plant with the roots spread out somewhat. If the plant is dormant it will consist of, in addition to the roots, a large bud, and a portion of the cane which took root, which may be used as a "handle." The bud should be some 2 inches below the surface when the hole is filled. If the bud is starting to grow, covering it entirely may injure it, so the hole may be left partly filled, to be filled at the first hoeing, when the new shoot will have grown enough so it will not be hurt.

The preferred method for the blackcaps is to remove all the "handle" at planting time so the entire plant will be covered. A cane and leaf spot disease, known as anthracnose, is very commonly present, and is transmitted from over wintering spots to the new growth. Removing all above-ground wood will give the young plant a chance to get started free from this disease. The handle usually dies off anyway, and seems to contribute nothing to the young plant, merely serving as a marker to indicate the location of the row, which can just as well be done with stakes. As the blacks do not produce suckers it may be possible to use weed killers between the rows somewhat more safely than with the reds, although any such use should be on a trial scale at first. It will help to place the canes on the ground beside the rows, where they may be held by stakes or by weaving them together, rather than permitting them to run in all directions, which would effectively prevent weed control during late summer. In regions where winter injury is likely to occur, however, the growth of weeds or a cover crop of some kind may be desirable to hasten maturing of the wood growth.

PRUNING BLACK RASPBERRIES. With the blackcaps, as with the reds, the removal of the old canes immediately after picking is a desirable practice from the standpoint of sanitation.

Summer pinching of the canes when they have reached a height of about 30 inches will cause the production of several lateral growths, and so increase the number of fruit buds. Such summer pinching is not practiced with the red varieties as they do not respond by producing husky laterals, but rather a few very weak laterals and some additional new canes. This tipping of the blackcaps may be easily done by thumb and forefinger when the tips are still soft, which is the correct time to do the work.

Winter pruning then consists of cutting back the laterals to about 6 to 12 inches in length, the longer length being used only for vigorous varieties under good growing conditions. Canes which had not been tipped should be cut off at about 30 inches. Blackcap canes are stiff, and will hold themselves up fairly well, but it will help considerably to put a stake in each hill and tie the canes to it. They might be tied to a wire also but that is not so common. Small or weak canes, or those heavily diseased, should be pruned out.

THE PURPLE RASPBERRIES. The purple raspberries, hybrids between the red and black species, have achieved little popularity, except in New York State, where they have been grown for processing into jam. The purple varieties are mostly very vigorous, the spines are stiff and rather objectionable, and they are rather susceptible to virus diseases. The berries are very large, dusty purple in color, and usually rather tart, with a flavor somewhat intermediate as compared to the parents. They are very good for jam or jelly. I like them for dessert, with plenty of sugar and cream, and, in my experience, when they are available many persons will buy them in competition with either red or black varieties. If we could get some varieties a little less rampant, and more resistant to mosaic, they should be more popular, in spite of their rather unattractive color.

Most of the purples resemble the blackcaps in type of growth, making no suckers but rooting at the tips. They may be handled as the blackcaps, pinched during the summer, and tied to stakes.

OTHER TYPES USED FOR BREEDING. There are several species of raspberries, from the Orient mostly, which have been imported for use in breeding with our present varieties to make them more resistant to disease, or better adapted to hot, dry conditions. Most are red, or yellowish red, with a raspberry flavor, but not a very good one. None of these species can be recommended for the home garden, and most of the hybrids have been inferior in quality to our standard varieties. However, as the breeders continue to work with them, types adapted to locations presently unfavorable for raspberry growing should be forthcoming.

The Japanese wineberry, *Rubus phoenicolasius,* resembles our raspberries, the fruit being orangey red and of rather poor quality. The shoots are covered with reddish bristles, rather soft, but interspersed with stiffer spines. It has been grown some in home gardens, but the same effort expended on red raspberries would produce a greater abundance of superior fruit.

WINTER PROTECTION. Although most raspberry varieties are apparently best adapted to the cooler parts of the country they may be seriously injured during cold winters in the northern Prairie and Great Plains states. The likelihood of such injury will be decreased by encouraging vigorous growth in spring and early summer; then by applying no nitrogen fertilizer after midsummer, by watering moderately if at all, and by seeding a cover crop, the canes may be "hardened up." Even this may not be sufficient to prevent injury where winters are especially severe. In such localities protection may be given by bending the canes over and covering the ends with soil. In extreme cases it may be necessary to cover the entire canes. They should be uncovered before the buds swell in the spring.

HARVESTING SUGGESTIONS. For best quality of fruit the red varieties should be picked every day, or every other day at the most if fruit is not to be lost by decay. Rainy weather may be disastrous. Berries picked in the rain, or while still wet, from dew as well as from rain, will mold within a few hours, but if processed at once are all right for canning, jam, or freezing. If left on the plant they will spoil quickly, and the gray mold may spread to green berries which are touching, hence picking off moldy berries is advisable after a rainy spell. If wet berries are to be kept overnight they may be crushed with sugar, 1 cup sugar to 4 cups berries, using only sound berries, and placed in the refrigerator.

Blackcaps do not decay as readily as the reds and commercially are picked only two or three times to get the crop off, as compared to eight or ten times for the reds.

The softness and juiciness of raspberries, particularly red varieties, make careful picking essential. Because the berries come off the receptacle they cannot be picked by the stems as with strawberries. One must grasp the berry between thumb and fingers, as gently as possible, and pull it free. Varieties which color up before they are ready to separate from the receptacle are unsatisfactory because so many will be crushed.

The picking container should be very shallow; probably nothing is much better than the one-pint berry cup. If these are used, a carrier to hold 6 to 12 cups will be very useful. Commercial growers' carriers are usually constructed to stand up on four legs so the picker does not have to bend over so much. Another timesaving method is a belt-type carrier, to hold one cup, which is put in the larger carrier as soon as filled.

CONTROL OF PESTS. In many localities raspberries are relatively free from damage by insects or diseases and are raised year after year in the home garden without spraying or dusting. For that reason the development of a universal spray calendar is hardly feasible.

DISEASES OF RASPBERRIES

Mosaic: *Symptoms:* Yellowish foliage which cannot be corrected by use of fertilizers, usually accompanied by a mottling of light and dark green, and sometimes an uneven puffing of the leaf surface. Cane growth becomes weaker, and very susceptible varieties may die out, but more resistant sorts may go on for years making poor growth and producing a few rather small and inferior berries. There are apparently several virus strains, each with its specific symptoms. Transmittal is by means of aphids which feed on diseased plants, then go to healthy ones. Strangely, not all aphids will transmit a particular virus, often only one. Some four species of aphids apparently are effective transmitters of raspberry mosaic. Plants once infected do not recover, and the virus, once in a plant, is soon transferred to all its parts, to attached suckers in the reds, and to the tip layers in the black.

Control: Set only clean plants, as far as possible from an older infected planting. Diseased plants in a neighbor's garden, even a city block away, may provide a source of infection. Eradicate wild brambles nearby, as they very likely carry viruses. Some black varieties are very susceptible, whereas some red kinds are more resistant. It is better, therefore, to keep these two types well separated if you have sufficient space to do so. At this time virus-free raspberry plants are not on the same basis as virus-free strawberry plants, the latter based on carefully controlled production from indexed mother plants, whereas field inspection is about as far as raspberry plant growers are going. At any rate get the best plants you can obtain. Do not use your own, or your neighbor's plants, unless they are vigorous with a uniform dark-green leaf color. Become familiar with virus symptoms if possible and rogue out diseased plants, especially while they are young and have not intermingled with healthy plants. If a red raspberry plant is infected, all the suckers will be also, and removal will serve a useful purpose only if the whole colony is removed. Control of the aphids which spread the disease should be effective but has not proven so as yet, possibly because many of the plants in the tests were already infected but did not yet show the symptoms.

Leaf Curl: *Symptoms:* The leaflets are crinkled and curl downward at the edges, and are crowded together on stunted shoots.

Control: This is a virus, and the only control is by planting healthy plants at a distance from other brambles and then roguing out diseased plants as fast as they appear.

Streak: *Symptoms:* Yellowish leaves which tend to curl downward. Streaks, bluish to purple, appear on the new canes, which are usually stunted.

Control: As for the two previous virus diseases.

Anthracnose: *Symptoms:* More or less circular grayish white spots ⅛ to ¼ inch in diameter. These may be so numerous near the base of the cane, or on fruiting spurs, as to practically girdle the cane or spur, greatly weakening it or actually killing it. These spots appear on the leaves and fruits as well. Anthracnose is somewhat more severe on the black varieties but occurs on the reds as well, usually as less conspicuous, darker gray spots on larger areas.

Control: This is a fungus disease, the spores of which are spread in rain water. Infection occurs mostly when the shoots are young and succulent. When setting blackcaps remove the stubs of old canes from the field and burn them. Spray with liquid lime sulfur, ½ cupful per gallon at the delayed dormant stage, when the new shoot growth is pushing out of the winter buds about ½ to ¾ inch. Newer chemicals, such as Elgetol, 1 tablespoonful per gallon, may be used. A household detergent, used at the rate of one teasponful per gallon will cause better spreading and wetting and should make control more effective. Where this disease is especially severe, summer sprays of ferbam or captan should be made just before bloom and again after bloom.

Crown Gall: *Symptoms:* Rough, warty growth, sometimes as large as an egg or larger, at the base of the canes or on the main roots near the soil surface. Infected plants may grow almost normally or may be greatly weakened, according to the location of the gall.

Control: Set clean plants in land that has not been in raspberries previously. This is not a virus but is caused by bacteria, but no effective chemical control method has been worked out.

Spur blight: *Symptoms:* Purplish spots appear on the lower parts of young red raspberry canes, causing little injury except when conditions are right for rapid growth of the organism when it can spread completely around the stem.

Control: This disease is often associated with dense growth of canes and weeds with consequent poor air movement, so prevention of weed growth in the row and thinning of canes in summer should help. The spray schedule recommended for anthracnose should hold spur blight down to a point where it will cause little damage.

Verticillium Wilt: *Symptoms:* Vigorous young plants will suddenly wilt and die, usually during midsummer. A bluish stripe extending from the base upward on infected canes is another symptom.

Control: This is a fungus disease caused by a verticillium organism which also may infect strawberries, and especially members of the family which includes the tomato, pepper, potato, and eggplant. In areas where this disease is known to be prevalent raspberries should not be planted after one of these vegetable crops. In the home garden this may present a difficult problem if these vegetables have been grown in various parts of the garden. Soil sterilization would probably be effective but expensive. No spray program would help, as the organism is in the soil, enters the roots, and works up inside the woody tissues. The home gardener may have to "take a chance" with this disease and hope he will not have many diseased plants. Fortunately it has not been serious in most of the country.

Root Rots: *Symptoms:* The plants turn yellow and die with no apparent cause except that the roots are dead when the plant is examined. It is often associated with poorly drained soils.

Control: Little can be offered, as we may be dealing with a symptom resulting from various causes. Planting on well-drained soil and keeping the plants growing vigorously is about all that can be done until the actual cause is determined.

Leaf Spots: *Symptoms:* Small, usually roundish spots on the leaves, often grayish underneath and brownish purple above. These may be caused by the anthracnose organism, as previously mentioned, or by other fungi, such as septoria leaf spot.

Control: These spots are usually not very serious. Sanitary measures plus the sprays recommended for anthracnose will usually keep these fungi under control.

INSECT PESTS

Raspberry Cane Borer: *Symptoms:* The tips of red raspberry canes wilt during the active growing season. Close examination will show the wilting is all beyond two girdles around the cane about ¾ inch apart. These are made by the female beetle, one above and one below the spot in the shoot where she has deposited an egg. If the egg hatches, the larva will bore down through the pith of the stem, coming out to the surface occasionally and causing the death of the cane before it has fruited.

Control: As the wilted tips are so easily seen it is quite practical to pick them off and burn them, being careful to break the cane below the lower girdle so as to remove the egg or young larva.

Red-Necked Cane Borer: *Symptoms:* Cigar-shaped swellings or galls near the bases of the canes. Cut one of these with a knife and small tunnels around the cane will be found, and possibly the larva of

the borer. Canes with galls usually die above the gall during the
following winter and before the cane has produced fruit.

Control: Cut out and burn the galls, which will reduce next
year's infestation. This pest is often found on wild blackberries and
dewberries and wild roses, so elimination of these in the immediate
neighborhood will help. Where the infestation is very severe and
destruction of the galls seems ineffective, a spray of DDT or rotenone may be applied just before the first blooms open.

Raspberry Crown Borer: *Symptoms:* There is little external evidence except poor growth and production. If the cane is pulled up late in
the summer and split with a knife, a white larva about an inch long
will be found in the pith just above ground level. During early
spring the tiny larvae may be found under pinhead-sized domes of
bark particles, just below ground level. This insect very rarely attacks blackcaps.

Control: As the eggs are laid on the leaves in the fall, by the adult
clear-winged moth, coating the base of the canes with a DDT spray
at the proper time should be effective. The proper time in New
Jersey, where this pest has been of considerable economic importance, would usually be from mid-September to mid-October, so
two applications would suffice, or one, if properly timed and not
subject to extended rainfall.

European Corn Borer: *Symptoms:* Red raspberry canes sometimes break
off during late summer or fall, and investigation reveals a borer a
little over an inch long, rather slender, and greenish brown. This
insect does not normally feed on the raspberry cane, but toward
the end of summer may leave its preferred food plant and may occasionally select a raspberry cane in which to spend the winter. It
simply eats in from the side of the cane and hollows out a hole in
the pith little larger than just enough to hide in, but enough to
cause the cane to break off or die beyond the burrow.

Control: Little can be done specifically with the raspberries.
Where the borers are common there is usually a well-developed
local control program designed to protect the borer's food plants,
such as corn. By following control and prevention measures for
other crops the raspberries will be protected.

Various Leaf-Eating Insects: *Symptoms:* There are a number of insects,
such as Japanese beetle, various "green worms," climbing cutworms,
and leaf rollers, which occasionally may cause more or less serious

damage. In most cases they are not serious enough and predictable enough to warrant a regular preventive spray program. They may usually be eliminated by a dust or spray with DDT or malathion, which should not, of course, be applied while the fruit is developing.

Fruitworms: *Symptoms:* Small larvae burrowing through the receptacle, or even into the fruit.

Control: This may be one of two or three different insects, depending on the locality, none of which is easy to control. Consult local authorities for control methods adapted to your particular conditions.

Spider Mites: *Symptoms:* Leaves turn pale, dull; mites may be seen on the underside of the leaves with a hand lens. This occurs during hot, dry weather.

Control: Keep the plants growing well and well supplied with water. If the infestation promises to become serious, dust with malathion or one of the new miticides such as aramite.

CHAPTER 14

Blackberries and Dewberries

Although these are often considered as two different kinds of fruit, both might be, and often are, spoken of as blackberries. They differ from the other bramble fruits, the raspberries, in fruit characters. The receptacle, the whitish central core, comes off and is eaten as an integral part of the berry. In the raspberry, on the other hand, the receptacle pulls out of the berry and remains attached to the bush. There are other differences, of course, but the fruit differences are most important to the home gardener. More important, perhaps, are the points of similarity between raspberry and blackberry and between the different groups of blackberries. Scientifically important is the fact that they may be intercrossed, practically important is the fact that cultural requirements are quite similar and that a number of pests, both insects and diseases, attack all of the bramble groups.

THE VARIOUS TYPES. For purposes of convenience we may divide these fruits into four groups as follows:

1. The upright or bush blackberries, derived from the native American wild blackberries so abundant in some sections of the Northeast and Middle West. As might be expected, these are the hardiest types and are what one thinks of when blackberries are mentioned in New England, New York, and the Middle West. They produce upright, rather stiff, well-armed canes, black fruit of medium to large size ripening after the dewberries and before the trailing blackberries. They spread by sending up suckers from the roots.

2. The trailing blackberries include primarily two European types, the Evergreen, called Black Diamond in the East, and the Himalaya, and their hybrids. They are not as hardy as many of the upright types and so are grown primarily on the East Coast, from New Jersey south, and along the Pacific Coast in the Northwest. They produce very long, sturdy, stoutly armed canes which may start up at an angle of about 45 degrees, then droop to continue their growth on the ground, unless they find some support. They

Two quarts of luscious bush blackberries. The plants, taller than a
man, are supported by posts and wires.

root at the tips but produce practically no suckers unless the roots
are cut by cultivation. They come true from seed which is produced
by apogamy—that is, without fertilization. This explains how these
two varieties have succeeded in covering hundreds of acres of pasture land in the Northwest, with plants which are identical to those
under cultivation. The bush blackberries do not ordinarily reproduce
this way, and so all colonies in a wild area will be different, although
the various canes within a single clump will be identical, having
grown up as suckers from the original plant. Fruit of the trailing
blackberries is black.

3. The black-fruited dewberries are derived from the native
eastern dewberry, found on very poor sandy soil along the East
Coast. The canes are prostrate, or nearly so, from the beginning,

and are about one fourth the diameter of the canes of the trailing blackberry. They root at the tips and do not produce suckers. The fruit ripens even earlier than the bush blackberry.

4. The reddish-fruited dewberries are somewhat less hardy than the black-fruited ones which they resemble in type of growth. The canes, however, are somewhat more vigorous, and the spines are tinged with red. They do not produce suckers but root at the tips, although somewhat less readily than the black varieties.

Hybridizers in recent years have crossed the various types, so there are intermediates between most of the types described above. Waldo, in Oregon, has used the native western blackberry to produce some high quality hybrids.

THORNLESS BLACKBERRIES. For many years thornless varieties of blackberries have been the desire of the breeder, the grower, and especially the small boy who has fought through the barbed-wire entanglements of wild blackberry patches and the no less forbidding jungle of thorny canes in many home plantings gone wild. Unarmed, or lightly armed, species are known, but thornless hybrids have been slow in appearing—that is, with good fruit, hardy and productive. More important have been thornless bud sports, of which there are several.

The Thornless Evergreen is one that is being grown commercially. It is a periclinal chimera—that is, the epidermis is thornless but the inner layers are genetically thorny. Tip layers produce thornless plants, but suckers, which fortunately seldom develop, are thorny. However, if roots are injured, a sucker may develop and if cut out will usually stimulate formation of other suckers, all thorny of course. Seedling plants will be thorny. The home gardener who finds one of his thornless plants becoming thorny may just as well start a new one from a tip layer and, as soon as it is large enough to produce fruit, remove the objectionable one.

WHICH TYPES TO GROW. Home gardeners in favored climates might grow varieties representing all four of the types discussed, but actually few would want to do that, except possibly experimentally to determine the best sorts for a specific locality where all four will grow. The trailing blackberries, because of their rampant growth and strong spines, have not generally been recommended for the small home garden. True, some home gardeners who know these fruits may have a specific place for them where they will be useful and not a nuisance. Thornless varieties will be desirable unless you are planting a barrier. Fruit characters of the older trailing types are not as good as might be desired, although they are extremely productive. Fruit of the Himalaya is soft and that of the Evergreen, although quite firm, is seedy, and of only fair edible quality.

Overaggressiveness may also be charged against some of the bush blackberries, but because of the superior hardiness of some varieties they may be grown where none of the others are practical. They are not adapted to landscape use as they will send up suckers where least wanted, but may be kept under reasonable control in a cultivated row in an inconspicuous part of the garden.

The black dewberries are especially adapted to very sandy soils in the southeastern and Gulf states and will not be too difficult to control if the young canes are trained along the row instead of being allowed to grow in any direction. Spreading by means of the rooted tips may be eliminated by cultivation or pulling at least once each spring. They are not landscape subjects, however, and should also be relegated to the background.

Probably the highest quality in the blackberry group is found in the reddish-fruited dewberries, such as the Boysen. Unfortunately, they are not as hardy as the others but are well adapted to the coastal areas of the Northwest and may be successful, if leaf diseases are controlled, in the southern and southeastern states. They grow more vigorously than the black-fruited types and under ideal conditions are quite productive. Where growing conditions are not really satisfactory they may make good cane growth, but much of it will not survive the winter and fruit production will be disappointing. These also are not landscape plants.

Perhaps the hybrids of the western blackberry should be considered as a separate group; at least they do not fit exactly into any of the above four types. They have excellent quality, but some are rather subject to leaf spot diseases. For gardeners on the West Coast they are well worth trying.

BUSH BLACKBERRY VARIETIES
Bailey—midseason, large, medium, firm, good quality, productive. New York (Geneva) Experiment Station.

Early Harvest—very early, good, fruit rather small. Originated in Illinois.

TABLE XIV

Suggested Blackberry and Dewberry
Varieties for the Home Garden

REGION	BUSH BLACKBERRIES	TRAILING BLACKBERRIES	BLACK DEWBERRIES	RED DEWBERRIES
New York and New England	Hedrick Bailey Eldorado			
Middle Atlantic	Jerseyblack[1] Hedrick Bailey	Evergreen	Lucretia	
Southeast	Eldorado Lawton	Brainerd		Boysen
Central	Eldorado Jerseyblack			
Gulf	Early Harvest Lawton		Lucretia Mayes	Boysen
Southwest	McDonald Lawton Eldorado		Lucretia	Boysen Young
Prairie	Eldorado Snyder			
Rocky Mountain	Eldorado		Lucretia	
Northwest	Eldorado	Marion[2] Chehalem[2] Evergreen		Boysen Cascade[2]
California	Lawton	Olallie		Boysen

[1] Semitrailing, needs trellis.
[2] Hybrids of Western trailing blackberry.

Eldorado—midseason, firm, good quality, most widely grown upright blackberry. Originated in Ohio.

Hedrick—early, large, medium firm, good. New York (Geneva) Experiment Station.

Jerseyblack—midseason, vigorous, semitrailing, large, good quality. New Jersey Experiment Station.

Lawton—early midseason, large, soft, good quality. Originated in New York but mostly grown in the Southwest, Texas and Oklahoma.

McDonald—very early, semitrailing, good quality. Originated in Texas.

Snyder—early midseason, only fair in size and quality but hardy. Originated in Indiana.

TRAILING BLACKBERRY VARIETIES

Brainerd—early for this type, large, high flavor but very tart, extremely vigorous and thorny. U.S.D.A.

Chehalem—early, excellent flavor, good for freezing, one of the western trailing blackberry hybrids, U.S.D.A. and Oregon Experiment Station.

Evergreen—late, very vigorous, productive, quality only fair. Thornless type most satisfactory. Of European origin.

Marion—midseason, medium size, good quality, vigorous with large thorns, a western trailing blackberry hybrid. U.S.D.A. and Oregon Experiment Station.

Olallie—medium-sized, firm, large, being grown in California; too tender for Oregon although origin is U.S.D.A. and Oregon Experiment Station.

BLACK DEWBERRY VARIETIES

Lucretia—large, firm, quality good, usually protected in winter where grown in northern states. Originated in West Virginia before 1886.

Mayes—also known as Austin, earlier than Lucretia, soft, fair quality. Originated in Texas.

RED DEWBERRY VARIETIES

Boysen—later than Young, larger, otherwise very similar and more widely grown, large, rather tart, not as hardy as the black dewberries. Also sold as Nectar. First introduced in California.

Cascade—early, small to medium size, somewhat soft, excellent wild blackberry flavor. This is a western trailing blackberry hybrid but put in this class because the fruit is dark red. U.S.D.A. and Oregon Experiment Station.

Young—early (as compared to Boysen), large, sweet. Possibly preferable to Boysen in the South, although the latter is planted to a greater extent in other parts of the country. Originated in Louisiana.

All three of these red dewberries are excellent for freezing and for jam.

ADAPTED TO RATHER POOR SOIL. All of the blackberries can be grown on rather poor soil, but the black dewberries are adapted to the poorest and sandiest. As a matter of fact they cannot seem to stand prosperity, and on fertile loam are inclined to grow rather lush and are more subject to disease and winter injury. The three other groups will do well on sandy loams of medium fertility.

PROPAGATION BY SUCKERS AND TIP LAYERS. Propagation was discussed incidentally to classification. The bush types are usually increased by the simple expedient of digging up the suckers in early spring, cutting them back about a third, and replanting where they are wanted. Suckers of medium size are best. Where rapid propagation is wanted, as with new varieties, root cuttings may be taken in late winter. Use roots about the size of a soda straw to the size of a pencil, cut into sections 2 to 3 inches long, and plant in a nursery row, covering with about 3 inches of soil, somewhat less if it is heavy.

With the tip-layering types the procedure is somewhat the same —take the tip layers where you find them and transplant in early spring. However, although some varieties will root readily and because of numerous shoots will make lots of plants, others may need assistance if you are looking for a large number of rooted tips. Ob-

Left to right: Jerseyblack, Brainerd, and Evergreen, trailing or semi-trailing blackberries.

viously the canes will not take root unless they are in contact with the ground, so where the new canes are permitted, or encouraged, to grow up over a trellis, or over the old canes, many will not reach the ground in time to take root.

Even where the canes lie on the ground there may be enough disturbance by wind, or by the operations of weeding, or cultivation, to effectively prevent rooting, or delay it until so late in the season that the roots formed are very meager. If tip layers are wanted, therefore, keep the new shoots on the ground and disturb them as little as possible during late summer. When they are ready to root, the shoot will thicken up, and the leaves near the tip will be very small, giving what is sometimes called a "rattail" appearance. With some varieties it will be necessary to cover the tips with soil early in the fall. Varieties which are difficult to root may have the tips stuck down, at the appropriate time, into a vertical shovel cut, so there will be less opportunity for the cane to grow on through the soil covering without rooting.

The dewberries are subject to anthracnose, and, like the black raspberries, when the tip layers are planted, should have the portion of old cane removed in order that the new shoot, when it breaks the soil surface, may not find a potential shower of disease spores waiting above it.

PROPAGATION BY SEED. Even though some of the trailing blackberries come true from seed, because the seeds develop from nonfertilized cells, they are normally propagated by tip layers, as seedlings would require a year longer to produce bearing plants. The other blackberries and dewberries, as most other fruit plants, do not come true from seeds. Hence propagation by seed is for the plant breeder who is looking for variation, and is willing to grow thousands of worthless seedlings to get a few that are really superior.

MULCH FOR CERTAIN TYPES. Because of the numerous thorny suckers, which do not pull as easily as the suckers of red raspberries, mulch culture is not well suited to bush blackberries, unless you wish to cut off the suckers with a heavy hoe. Clean cultivation during spring and early summer is the usual custom. Where erosion may be a problem during winter a cover crop may be sown, or the natural weed growth may suffice.

Mulching is more satisfactory for the nonsuckering, tip-layering varieties, although some might need a little assistance if you especially want to get a good supply of layers for a new planting. However, the blackberries are naturally adapted to rather dry soils, and may not be benefitted by the moisture-conserving properties of the mulch as much as some other plants. Using the same reasoning, if water is short it would seem wise to use it on these fruits, and particularly the black dewberries, after most other fruits have had their share.

FERTILIZERS FOR BLACKBERRIES. The fertilizer program for these fruits should be about the same as for raspberries, with major emphasis on nitrogen, but including a basic amount of phosphorus and potassium in areas where these elements are known to be deficient as indicated by the response of other plants. If there is doubt about the need for these two elements it would be advisable to apply about 15 pounds of 5-10-5, or similar formula, per 1000 square feet early in the spring. Additional nitrogen, in the form of ammonium sulfate or nitrate of soda, should then be applied, if needed, a little later in the spring.

Blackberries and dewberries thrive on acid soils, but it is quite possible that some are too acid. On soils below pH 4.5 it would seem to be worth while trying some lime, enough to bring the reaction to at least pH 5.

PRUNING BUSH BLACKBERRIES. Removal of fruiting canes immediately after harvest is desirable as an aid to pest control on all types and varieties. Obviously methods of pruning and training will vary with the different growth habits. Bush blackberries may be grown with or without a trellis. If no support is provided the shoots should be summer pinched when they have reached 30 inches to 3 feet so they will throw out side branches. At the regular winter pruning time these laterals should be shortened to 8 to 16 inches, depending on the amount of growth.

Occasionally the upright types are provided with a trellis, such as two wires about 16 inches apart and 30 inches above the ground. For very vigorous growing plants, four wires may be used, two about 16 inches apart at 4 to 4½ feet high, with two others directly below these at approximately half that height. This means two crossarms on each post. With either type the canes are encouraged to grow up within the trellis, and those coming up outside are removed by cultivation or, if close, tucked inside the wires. It is not so important, with such a trellis, to summer pinch the shoots to give sturdy treelike plants which will support themselves. Some pinching may be done, or the canes may be allowed to grow tall.

At winter pruning time the terminal foot or so of the cane—that part that is likely to be thin, with weak buds—may be removed and the cane tied down to one of the top wires of the trellis. On poor, light soils, especially if no water for irrigation is available, it will be necessary to prune more severely than where conditions are more favorable, in order to prevent the small twigs from drying up before the crop is ripe. The exact amount of cutting back, which will depend on the variety as well as the growing conditions, can best be learned by observing. If the berries are small and ripen slowly and unevenly, it is a sign that something is wrong. If there is no indication of pest damage which could cause the trouble, and if the plants have been well fertilized, then more severe pruning should be tried.

PRUNING THE TRAILING BLACKBERRIES. Although we do not highly recommend the trailing blackberries for the home garden, they are very productive, and if you have the space and are willing to do the necessary pruning you may find them worth while. Pruning of the thorny varieties is a real job, requiring thick gloves, a stout pair of pruning shears, and some determination.

On very light, sandy soil it is possible to train these berries on stakes, as described for dewberries, using longer stakes of course, and cutting the canes at the top of the stake, usually about 6 feet. A trellis is more satisfactory. It may be a one wire trellis, 4 to 5 feet high, with the canes bunched and tied up a stake and out along the wire.

On stronger soils the growth will be too great to be handled conveniently in one bundle. For such conditions a four-wire trellis is suggested, two wires 18 inches apart at a height of 4½ to 5 feet and two other wires 2 feet from the ground, supported by crossarms on the posts. Sticks with notches near the ends are placed across the wires at intervals of about 30 inches. The young shoots are trained up between the lower wires and supported by the crosspieces. The following spring they are raised so they rest on the crosspieces on the top wires and the new shoots are again trained on the lower wires. There is somewhat more danger of winter injury if the canes are on the wires over winter than if they are laid down on the ground.

Summer pinching of the new shoots when they reach a length of 2 or 3 feet will cause them to branch and produce several canes 5 to 10 feet long instead of a few which might reach to 20 feet. The

Lucretia dewberries growing on a low two-wire trellis. Fruiting canes are tied to the wires, the new shoots are on the ground but tucked in under the wires.

spring pruning will consist of removing late-formed or weak canes, and those which inevitably stray beyond the confines of the trellis. The canes on the trellis may be shortened somewhat, at least back to where they are plump with well-developed buds.

PRUNING DEWBERRIES, BLACK-FRUITED VARIETIES. The black-fruited dewberries are usually tied to stakes but may be tied to single wires 24 to 30 inches high. The shoots are permitted to sprawl on the ground during the summer, or they may be crowded into the row to leave room for walking between the rows. In areas where there is any danger of winter injury it is best to leave the canes on the ground all winter and tie them up as late as possible, usually when the buds are starting to push in the spring. At that time the canes from one plant are gathered into a bundle and tied firmly to the stake, or up to the wire and out on the wire in one direction or in both directions. It would seem that the canes would be able to produce more if they were spread out and tied individually to the wire. It is true that some of the canes inside the bundle may be crowded so that part of the buds will be prevented from growing, but the total crop does not seem to be appreciably reduced, at least not enough to warrant the extra trouble of tying the canes individually.

In the South this type of dewberry may be grown without staking. A sharp, heavy hoe is used to cut off the entire top, immediately after the last berries are picked, preferably cutting just below the surface of the ground. The tops are taken off the field and burned. This eliminates a very large part of the leaf and cane diseases, such as anthracnose. New shoots are made the same season and will reach a height of a few inches to possibly 2 feet. At the winter pruning they are merely clipped back to about 6 inches, too short to be tied up, but because they are so short they tend to stand up off the ground. However the fruit is produced so close to the soil surface that it is desirable to use mulch to keep it clean. Dewberries pruned in this way will probably not produce as much as those trained on stakes or trellis, but where anthracnose is especially severe it would be worth trying. North of the Carolinas the growing season is usually not long enough to get the necessary second growth of canes if the tops are all cut off after fruiting.

PRUNING THE RED-FRUITED DEWBERRIES. The red-fruited dewberries grow more vigorously than the black-fruited varieties, at least in those areas to which they are adapted. They may be trained in much the same way, but taller stakes or higher trellises will be needed. A two-wire trellis, one wire above the other, may be used, with the canes bunched into "ropes." There may be one rope extending to the top wire, out along the wire, and twisted around it for about 3 feet, then down to the lower wire and back toward the plant. More commonly the canes would be divided into two ropes, one going in each direction, or four ropes, one going in each direction on each wire.

With certain varieties, such as some of the newer western blackberry hybrids, which are semitrailing but have stiffer canes than the typical dewberries, a trellis of three to four wires, one above the other, will permit weaving the canes between the wires, up and over the top wire and down again. In this case each cane must be woven in individually. This weaving is most easily done during the summer as the canes grow and while they are most pliable. This will keep them up out of the way and out of the cover crop or weeds if under cultivation. However, where there may be danger of winter injury it must be remembered that they will come through the winter in better condition if on the ground. The Loganberry, Cascade, Pacific, and Chehalem may be handled as belonging to this group.

DISEASES OF BLACKBERRIES AND DEWBERRIES

Orange Rust: *Symptoms:* The shoots are spindling and the young leaves narrow and poorly developed. During the summer the undersides of the leaves discharge millions of bright, orange-colored spores. The disease is systemic—that is, it travels throughout the plant, and suckers from an infected plant will themselves be infected.

Control: The only remedy is to dig out and burn infected plants. All suckers of the clump must be removed, even though at the time they do not yet show the typical symptoms. This is primarily a disease of the bush blackberries. It should not be difficult to secure plants which are free of the disease, but where wild blackberries are prevalent in the neighborhood it may keep appearing. It may be possible to eradicate wild plants near your garden, if you find them to be spreading rust, by use of some of the weed killers such as 245-T, which is especially deadly to blackberries. Be very careful such weed killers do not drift onto plants you do not want to kill.

Double Blossom: *Symptoms:* The flowers, of the Evergreen variety particularly, develop extra, somewhat deformed, petals and do not produce fruit.

Control: The buds which are going to produce the double flowers can be distinguished early in the spring as they start to grow, being somewhat more fleshy and reddish than healthy buds. They may be easily broken off and burned, which will eliminate the fungus that would develop in the deformed flowers and produce spores to infect additional buds.

Anthracnose: *Symptoms:* Small ash-gray spots on the canes, especially near the base, sometimes running together to encircle the cane entirely, especially on the black dewberries. Spots also appear on the leaves and fruits, causing the individual drupelets of the latter to be gray and sunken instead of plump and shiny black.

Control: Spray at delayed dormant when new shoots are about ¾ inch long with lime sulfur 1-12. Where the disease is bad, spray again just before bloom and again after harvest with ferbam, 1 ounce to 3 gallons of water.

Virus Diseases: *Symptoms:* Occasionally the upright blackberries, and the dewberries, may show mottling of the leaves accompanied by weak spindly growth, resembling the symptoms of raspberry mosaic. This may be a bit difficult to diagnose accurately. If all the plants show the condition rather uniformly it might be well at first to suspect some nutritional trouble. The amount of nitrogen might be increased and a complete fertilizer, preferably one fortified with the minor elements, applied the following spring. If the symptoms remain it is quite likely that a virus disease is present.

Control: Whether or not to destroy the plants will be determined by their value for fruit production as you estimate it. If there are only a few plants showing the symptoms and the others are vigorous and the leaves uniformly dark green, it is somewhat easier to conclude that a virus is present, in which case removal and destruction of the diseased plants would seem desirable. There is need for more research in the field of virus diseases of this group of berries.

INSECTS THAT ATTACK BLACKBERRIES AND DEWBERRIES

The Red-Necked Cane Borer: *Symptoms:* Cigar-shaped swellings near the base of the canes, especially on dewberries, but appearing on the bush and trailing blackberries as well and, as already mentioned, on raspberries also.

Control: Prune out the galls and burn at the regular dormant pruning.

The Raspberry Crown Borer: *Symptoms:* No visible symptoms are evident except weak growth. If the presence of this insect is suspected inspect the old canes when you remove them right after harvest. The larvae at that time would be about two thirds grown and in the new canes, but the old canes would have the pith hollowed out at ground level and some would probably show exit holes where the adult moth had escaped from its cocoon the previous fall. This insect has been quite destructive to the Evergreen variety on the East Coast. The young larvae which hatch out during October spend the winter burrowing through the bark, just below ground level, of the canes which will fruit the following summer, weakening and sometimes killing them outright. I have counted over a hundred of the tiny larvae on the base of one cane, although usually only one or two will reach the adult stage in each cane. Buds for the new shoots develop from the base of the old canes, from 2 to 6 inches under ground, and where there is a bad infestation of crown borer most of these buds will be killed and only one or two weak canes develop where normally there would be a dozen. This insect is less prevalent on bush blackberries and dewberries.

Control: Spraying the base of the canes with DDT early in October and again two weeks later should be effective in the latitude of New Jersey. Timing can be checked by observing the presence of the adults, clearwing moths that look like yellow jackets, and by the presence of the eggs. The eggs resemble mustard seeds and are deposited at the margin and on the underside of the leaf. They begin to hatch in about two weeks and the spray should be applied before hatching begins, as the larvae descend the canes immediately, and once under the ground they are very difficult, if not impossible, to kill.

Scale Insects: *Symptoms:* Various scale insects may be found on the blackberries, but usually they are not present in sufficient numbers to warrant special control measures.

Spider Mite: *Symptoms:* Leaves become dull and pale, with tiny yellowish dots on the upper surface. The under surface may show some webbing. The tiny reddish mites may be seen moving about if examined with a hand lens. The damage is most likely to occur during very dry weather.

Control: Keeping the growth vigorous by giving adequate water and plant food will minimize the likelihood of damage. If chemical control seems necessary, spray or dust, being sure to cover the undersides of the leaves, with malathion, aramite, or one of the other special materials developed for mite control.

Red Berry Mite: *Symptoms:* The berries of the Evergreen or Himalaya varieties fail to ripen normally, all or part of the drupelets of the berries becoming bright red instead of black. This injury is caused by a microscopic mite which may also be found on other varieties of blackberries and raspberries, but usually shows no characteristic symptoms except on the two varieties mentioned. It is present all along the Pacific Coast, but damage has not been general in recent years.

Control: In the late fall apply a spray of a commercial summer-oil emulsion or of liquid lime sulfur at the rate of 1-12. Follow with a delayed dormant spray of lime sulfur 1-12. Very thorough spraying must be done to reach all the mites.

CHAPTER 15

Currants and Gooseberries

Interest in these fruits has never been very high in the United States, at least compared to what it is in European countries. Black currants, particularly, have never found great favor here, except among people of English or Canadian descent. Most of the other berries are commonly used fresh for dessert purposes but currants and gooseberries must be cooked, except for certain European gooseberry varieties which are excellent for eating out of hand. That has probably been the main factor in their decrease in popularity, which has occurred at a time when the housewife has been doing less and less home preserving and cooking of desserts.

Currants are used almost entirely for jelly, either by themselves or combined with red raspberries or other fruits. Gooseberries have mostly been used for pies, although gooseberry pie has come to be a rather infrequent visitor to the American table. Gooseberries may also be used for various types of conserves, which are very good if you like something that is rather tart. As one who is not especially fond of either of these fruits, I still feel that they are a desirable part of the small-fruits garden, and like to have a few on hand for occasional use.

WELL SUITED TO THE HOME GARDEN. These two fruits are especially well adapted to the home garden as they make nice neat bushes, some 2 to 4 feet in height, and do not spread as do many of the other berry plants. During spring and early summer their foliage is attractive, and when loaded with fruit they are nice additions to the garden. Unfortunately, the foliage drops early, often during late summer. This is partly due to attacks by various leaf spots, or other pests, which could be controlled, but still the normal leaf drop is relatively early.

Since the average gardener will probably want only a few plants of each they can very well be worked into a shrub border or a corner of the lawn where they will be thought of, primarily, as part of the ornamental planting. For those who especially like these fruits a short row in the garden, where they may be cultivated, is a good way to handle them. Currants and gooseberries are usually considered together, partly because they are closely related, both belonging to the genus *Ribes*. These fruits are a little unusual in that they do not belong to the Rose family, which includes so many of the other fruits, but to the family Saxifragaceae. Their close botanical relationship is evident to the casual observer only by the fact that the same pests are likely to attack both kinds of fruits. They do not intercross.

SEVERAL TYPES OF CURRANTS. There are red, white or yellow, and black currant varieties, which have been derived from several different species. The red and yellow currants are very much alike, really being different colored forms of the same fruit, but the black currant is somewhat distinct and belongs to a different species, *Ribes nigrum*. The black currant, of course, is the one with the rather strong flavor, which makes a jam that is either liked very much, or left alone with considerable enthusiasm. The jelly currants are primarily the red ones, the yellow varieties being more of a novelty than anything else.

Chautauqua gooseberries. This is a very large, green fruited variety.

GOOSEBERRY COLOR TYPES. The gooseberries, which have been developed from both American and European species, may be classified by color of fruit. Some remain green until they are ripe, others turn yellow, while still others become a deep red. The green gooseberry is one of the sourest fruits that can be found, although when it begins to get ripe, by putting enough sugar with it, a delicious pie may be made. Some varieties, even when fully ripe, never lose their tartness; others become quite sweet and can be eaten out of hand with considerable pleasure.

Unfortunately most of the gooseberries which have high quality are of the European type and seem to be somewhat unsuited to our conditions, not resistant enough to low temperatures and some of the pests which are prevalent in this country. It is hoped that the breeders will eventually have hybrids which show the vigor and disease resistance of the American types, together with the large size and higher flavor of the European sorts. The following list gives the more important characters of some of the common varieties.

CURRANT AND GOOSEBERRY VARIETIES FOR THE HOME GARDEN

Although grown in this country since early in the seventeenth century, not a great many varieties of these two fruits have been tried, and these few have not been extensively tested. It is apparent that none are especially adapted to the South and that certain ones have been introduced primarily because they are exceptionally hardy. The remainder are fairly cosmopolitan in their requirements and are grown across the country where soil conditions are suitable and where gardeners have a taste for them.

Red Currants

Perfection—midseason, large, not as generally reliable as Red Lake. Originated in New York.

Red Lake—midseason to late, fruit large, clusters very long, vigorous, hardy, productive. Minnesota Experiment Station.

Wilder—midseason, medium size, long an important commercial variety. Originated in Indiana.

White Currants

White Grape—similar to the red varieties in plant characters but fruit is ivory white; of interest only as a novelty. Of European origin.

Black Currants

No varieties are recommended because of the white-pine blister
    rust problem. If you are in white-pine country you'll probably
    just have to forget about black currants. If there are no white
    pines in your area you might possibly find some plants locally,
    if you have a yen for that black currant jam.

Gooseberries

Chautauqua—one of the European varieties supposedly subject to
    mildew and other troubles, but I have experienced no particu-
    lar difficulty in growing it. Very large, green, becoming yellow-
    ish green when ripe. Quite tart, even when allowed to hang
    until fully ripened. Bush relatively small.

Como—midseason, medium size, fair quality, green slightly tinged
    with yellow, hardy. Minnesota Experiment Station.

Fredonia—late, rather open bush, red fruit of good size and quality.
    English type. New York (Geneva) Experiment Station.

Oregon—also known as Oregon Champion. Late, medium size, fruit
    green. Originated in Oregon.

Pixwell—medium size, pink when ripe, very hardy, few thorns.
    North Dakota Experiment Station.

Poorman—midseason, medium to large, vigorous, fruit ripens to a
    rich red, quality excellent. Probably the best for eating out of
    hand. Originated in Utah.

SOIL AND CLIMATIC ADAPTATION. These fruits are particularly adapted
to the climate of that part of the country extending from New
York, or the Middle Atlantic States, west through the central and
northern part of the Middle West to the Northwest. Some varieties
are extremely hardy and adapted to even the coldest parts of the
United States, where few other fruits can be grown. Most of them
are not well suited to the southern states, where the high temperature seems to encourage the development of diseases and perhaps
interferes with the normal growth of the plants themselves.

Most of the small fruits prefer a light sandy soil, and currants
and gooseberries can be grown on that type. However, they seem
well adapted to a somewhat heavier soil.

PROPAGATION. Propagation is normally by cuttings, although
either fruit can be grown from layers. For the ordinary gardener,
who may want to grow a few more plants for his own use, or to
give away, the currant can be grown quite readily from cuttings

made during late winter. These plants start growth very early in the spring, and in order to get good dormant cuttings they should be taken not too long after midwinter. Currant cuttings may be 6 to 8 inches long, and can be rooted directly in the soil or in a propagating bench in a greenhouse or cold frame. For cutting wood, use vigorous growth on year-old shoots, about pencil size or a little smaller.

Gooseberries do not root so readily, and for the casual propagator layers will probably be more satisfactory. The branches tend to grow close to the ground anyway and often root of their own accord. It is a simple matter to cover a few of them with soil, leaving the branch tips uncovered, of course. Notching the branches where they are covered will help them to root more rapidly. After they are in place for one growing season they should be ready to dig and transplant.

EARLY PLANTING ADVISABLE. Because of the fact that these fruits start growth so early in the spring, it is advisable to plant either in the fall or very early in the spring. A good plant will have a fairly extensive root system and three or four shoots which have branched off from the original cutting. Except for rather small plants they are a little too bulky to set with a spade as suggested for strawberries and raspberries. Usually it will be better to dig a hole and plant them as you would plant a fruit tree or flowering shrub. They may be set a little deeper than they were in the nursery row.

Pruning at planting time should consist of removal of any shoots which are rather weak or broken, and tipping back the ones which are left to a length of 6 or 8 inches, so that they will branch out and form a rather broad bush. Root pruning may be helpful in reducing the root system to a convenient size for planting, but is not so terribly important, provided you dig a hole large enough to accommodate the roots.

SOIL MANAGEMENT. These fruits respond very well to mulching, especially if they are grown in the ornamental border. In the garden they may be either mulched or cultivated. Because of their normally early leaf drop they are not so likely to be hurt by late, hot, dry weather as are some of the other small fruits. For that very reason, however, it is probably a good idea to keep them growing rather vigorously in order to hold the leaves as long as possible, both from the standpoint of appearance and the manufacturing of enough reserves for a good crop next season.

Fertilizer could well be applied quite early in the spring, or even during late winter, especially if the plants are mulched and you have to depend on the spring rains to wash the nutrients down to the plant roots. In some localities fertilizing in the fall might be worth considering for these plants, which start growth so early in the spring. The amount to use will, as previously indicated, depend on the natural fertility of the soil. However, a complete fertilizer, such as a 5-10-5, would be satisfactory for soils of average fertility, if used at 15 to 20 pounds per 1000 square feet.

IRRIGATION. I do not know whether these fruits are being grown commercially under irrigation, although possibly they are. It does happen that they have been grown largely in the so-called nonirrigated parts of the country. However, there is no doubt but what they will respond, as will all other plants, to an adequate supply of water. They will be able to withstand drouth, especially if growing on good soil, perhaps a little better than some of the other fruits.

Too often the weeds are neglected, during the middle and latter part of the summer, so that there is tremendous competition for water with the currant or gooseberry plants, which of course have produced their crop for the season. It is at this time, however, that the leaves should be functioning to build up thick twigs and fat buds for next spring's early bloom. Of course, if the leaves have all dropped by the latter part of the summer the demands of the plants for moisture will be much lower than if the leaves were still present. You will recall that the leaves are the organs through which the plant transpires the moisture which it takes in through the roots.

FRUIT SPURS AND BUDS. Both the currant and the gooseberry produce their fruit a little like a cherry tree. That is, they have branches which will remain productive for at least three or four years, in contrast to the brambles which have canes able to produce fruit only once. On these branches there will develop, on wood two years old and older, short fruit spurs which will produce flower buds around the terminal leaf bud. Flower buds will also be produced in the axils of the leaves, on one-year-old shoots, just as they are in the cherry.

From each flower bud of the currant comes a cluster of flowers which will produce several fruits, not unlike a miniature cluster of grapes. The value of the variety depends somewhat on the number of berries per cluster. In the case of the gooseberry there is one

A well-pruned red currant bush. The various stems are one, two, and three years old; all older wood has been removed.

flower, or possibly two, per bud, so that while sometimes the berries are borne in pairs, or even in triplets, they are not in long clusters like currants.

PRUNING CURRANTS. The pruning of currants will naturally begin with the removal of those canes which are three or four years old, or older. Whether the dividing line is three or four years will depend on the variety, the soil conditions, and how well you are taking care of the plants. However, the canes which have become old enough to have slowed down in their production of new growth should be removed, because they will produce a large number of weak flower buds, which will be so crowded, and so many per unit of leaf growth, that the fruit will be quite small and unsatisfactory. As long as the new growth, at the end of one of the main canes, is 6 inches or more in length it may be concluded that that particular branch is not too old, and it may be retained for another year.

The straight, unbranched shoots 2 to 3 feet in length are the youngest, called one-year-old wood, although actually less than a year old. At the regular pruning time they are usually tipped back slightly to encourage branching. The next summer such a cane should produce three or four branches, each 6 inches to a foot in length. The following year any laterals produced, as well as the terminal growth, will be still shorter.

Sometimes an old, neglected bush is so weak that it has nothing but old canes, with very short annual growth at their tips. In such a case, most of them can be cut out, leaving perhaps two or three to form the basis of a new plant. These in turn will be removed, as soon as vigorous new canes have been produced from the crown of the plant. This will happen only if you give good treatment, of course. Pruning will help to stimulate the plant, as will the addition of fertilizers, cultivation, and irrigation if needed.

Beside taking out the old canes there is sometimes the problem of thinning out the ones which are younger. With good growing conditions there may be so much cane growth that the bush will be crowded, and the fruit will not develop normally, and certain leaf diseases, such as mildew, may be encouraged. On soil of average fertility it may be feasible to leave three or four canes three years old, three or four two years old, and three or four one-year-old unbranched canes. Usually there will need to be no tipping back of the lateral branches, only of the one-year-old unbranched canes. The entire pruning of a currant bush can, therefore, be done with a pair of strong loppers which take out large canes right down to the crown of the plant.

PRUNING GOOSEBERRIES. In the case of the gooseberry the essential pruning is somewhat the same. However, under good growing conditions so many laterals may be produced, especially around the base of the plant, that some thinning out will have to be done. Some varieties are rather sprawly, and would produce part of their fruit so close to the ground that it would be splashed with sand and mud. These low-hanging branches should be removed.

The best time for pruning is during late fall or midwinter or very early spring. Just remember that these plants start growth very early in the spring. More than one home gardener has been surprised, when he went out to perform what he thought was dormant pruning, to find the plants in full bloom. If pruning had not been done by that time, of course, it would be better to do it then than to let it go altogether. However, the earlier pruning would be more satisfactory.

It used to be rather common to find these fruits growing as standard plants. That means that they were trained to a single trunk, and branches permitted to develop only from that trunk. Of course, the trunk could not be very high, perhaps eighteen inches at the most, and it might have to be held up by a stake. However, these plants do make rather decorative little trees. The problem is to maintain vigor in the main stems, which have a tendency to weaken after they are a few years old. Of course, a new shoot can be trained up beside the old trunk, from which to develop a new head before the old one has completely served its usefulness. One of the objections to this form, in addition to the extra work involved, and the somewhat lesser production, is that borers may get into the single cane. In that case, one insect could eliminate the entire top of the plant, which would not be true if there were several trunks. All things considered, I would suggest the standard plants only as a novelty in your garden.

Both currants and gooseberries are grown much more frequently in European gardens than in our own. They have a larger list of available varieties and some different methods of growing the plants. They are sometimes grown, as we occasionally see dwarf apple trees, as espaliers or cordons. This means the plants are trained on trellises or other supports, usually being pruned to single trunks with a single vertical or sloping branch, or a single short trunk branching to form two or three vertical shoots. Such systems require considerable training during the summer, with removal of all shoots except those required to form the desired framework, which are then tied in place. Such plants are used to edge walks, or to cover a low wall or fence. The extra labor is justified by their ornamental value and not by any extra fruit production, although they do produce quite well per cane or spur, and the fruit is of good size and quality.

HARVESTING PROBLEMS. Currants and gooseberries of a particular variety ripen essentially at one time, unlike the other fruits, such as strawberries, raspberries, or blackberries, where ripening covers a long period, and you will have to pick every other day for a period of two or three weeks. With currants and gooseberries the fruit may all be harvested at one picking, although it may not be completely uniform in color.

It would be advisable to consider picking currants, which are designed primarily for jelly, a little on the green side, rather than fully ripe, as their jelling qualities will be better at that stage. Fruit that is quite green should be avoided as it will not yet have developed its normal flavor.

The usual method of picking currants is by the cluster, grasping the stem by thumb and forefinger and removing the entire cluster. The individual currants will have to be stripped off the clusters later, before going into the jelly kettle. It is possible to strip them right on the bush, but this is rather messy and some of the clusters will come off anyway, so the best way seems to be to pick by the cluster. This is especially true if any of the currants are to be sold, or given away, as the keeping quality will be much better if the berries are still firmly attached to the cluster stem.

GOOSEBERRY PICKING, A THORNY PROBLEM. The picking of gooseberries presents something of a problem, as all of the important varieties are very strongly armed with stout thorns. People who work with thorny plants learn to handle them judiciously and know just how firmly they can grasp a branch or leaf without forcing the spines or prickles into the fingers. This is certainly true with gooseberries. Some people can pick them rather easily, without much damage to the fingers, but the novice is likely to have trouble.

Commercially, gooseberries are often stripped from the plants by pickers wearing heavy leather gloves. They use a round bushel basket, or some other large container, and strip the branches directly into this receptacle. Of course, this means that there are lots of leaves and other trash with the berries, and a cleaning job has to be done. On a large scale this is sometimes done with a fan mill such as is used for cleaning wheat and other seed grain. The home gardener who tries this method of stripping with gloves will have little difficulty in cleaning the berries. He can usually pour the mixture gently onto an inclined surface, such as a heavy piece of cardboard, and the berries will tend to roll down leaving trash and leaves on the cardboard.

For the gardener who is getting the makings for his first gooseberry pie it should probably be explained that the stems and the petals, both of which will still be adhering to the fruit, should be pinched off with thumb and forefinger. I can recall being served gooseberry pie in a restaurant and the stems and blossoms were still attached—not a very appetizing dish.

Usually when gooseberries have reached their full size, and are still quite hard and green, they may be used for pies with good results, if properly sweetened. They will stay on the bushes for a couple of weeks after this, not gaining much in size but becoming sweeter. Some varieties never become sweet enough to eat out of hand, while others do become quite flavorful and sweet enough to be eaten raw, provided they are left on the bushes long enough. With the colored varieties, those which develop yellow or red color, the amount of pigment can be taken as a measure of the degree of ripeness. Many of the varieties grown in this country, however, do not become colored, but simply lose their deep green and become a whitish green when ripe.

DISEASES OF CURRANTS AND GOOSEBERRIES

White Pine Blister Rust: *Symptoms:* This is one of those strange cases in which a disease passes one stage of its existence on one type of plant, and then must go through a cycle on another plant, in this case the white pine, before coming back to the gooseberry or currant. The great interest in this particular disease, of course, has been from the standpoint of protecting the white pine and not of protecting the currants or gooseberries.

Control: Primarily eradication of currants and gooseberries where white pine is of any importance. As a result of the federal quarantine it is forbidden to ship black currants interstate because they are the worst offenders. In some areas, where white pines are numerous, the planting of any variety of currants or gooseberries is frowned upon or actually forbidden. However, in much of the country where white pines occur as only a very occasional shade tree, the disease is not of major importance. On the berry bushes it develops as a leaf spot which in itself would be of no particular concern. The main caution, with respect to white pine blister rust, is that before planting currants or gooseberries, and especially black currants, which you might perchance find in your own neighborhood, it would be desirable to consider state regulations as well as the presence of white pine within an area of several miles.

The breeders have attacked the blister rust problem, just as they have other plant diseases, from the standpoint of varietal resistance. Their efforts have been crowned with success so far as the production of resistant black currant varieties is concerned. However, these resistant varieties are still frowned upon because it is not sure that some of their seedlings, if they are crossed with a susceptible variety, for instance, may not be susceptible. These seeds may be scattered by the birds in nearby woods, and the result would be another infestation of wild black currants susceptible to the blister rust.

Leaf Spot: *Symptoms:* Small roundish spots about a sixteenth of an inch in diameter, often associated with the early dropping of the leaves.

Control: Spray with one of the copper sprays, just before bloom, and again right atfer picking.

Cane Blight: *Symptoms:* One or two canes in a bush may die back, frequently in early spring, while they are bearing immature fruits. These fruits turn red at the same time the leaves on the affected canes turn yellowish, quite a conspicuous symptom of the presence of this disease.

Control: Usually there is just a cane here and there which should be cut out and burned. The program recommended for leaf spot should help to keep this disease in check.

Crown Gall: *Symptoms:* A swelling, hard and warty in appearance, occurring usually just at the crown—that is, partly underground and partly above ground—is sometimes found on currants and gooseberries.

Control: There is not much to be done, once this disease is on a plant. There is no particular point in destroying the plant as soon as you see the gall. It might just as well be left to bear as long as it will. Sometimes infected plants may remain productive for quite a long period, if the gall is just on one side and does not choke off all the root system. It is important to secure plants free of crown gall, which will usually be found at a good nursery where plants are inspected for this disease by a state inspector.

INSECT PESTS OF CURRANTS AND GOOSEBERRIES

The insects are somewhat more conspicuous, and probably more damaging, on these fruits than are the diseases.

Aphids: *Symptoms:* On the currants particularly, aphids are very commonly found. They congregate on the undersides of the leaves and cause a warty swelling of the leaf surface. This swelling may become yellowish and reddish as viewed from above, giving a very unusual, colorful appearance to the leaf. Sometimes the gardener does not look underneath the leaf and is sure that he has some strange new disease.

Control: The usual treatment is with an aphicide, such as Black-leaf 40, in the warmer areas. Malathion is probably as generally satisfactory as any of the aphicides, especially where the temperature is rather cool at the time the sprays should be applied. It will be necessary, of course, to spray up under the leaves and actually hit the aphids in order to get a satisfactory control.

Currant Sawfly: *Symptoms:* The larvae of the currant sawfly are greenish worms or caterpillars, growing up to three quarters of an inch in length. They have black spots down the sides and are usually found in clusters. As a matter of fact, they work together so well, and so rapidly, that a plant may be entirely defoliated within a short time. They attack both currants and gooseberries.

Control: These insects present something of a problem, as they usually are at their worst while the fruit is developing. The old remedy was to use hellebore, an almost forgotten spray material from a plant source, which was toxic to the insects but not to humans. Malathion, or DDT, could be applied, if several days before the fruit is to be harvested. If these materials are used, the fruit should be thoroughly washed before being consumed. This insect may not appear at all, so it is usual to wait until it is seen before applying the insecticide. Even then, it might be just as well to spray only the bushes on which the clusters of "currant worms" are found.

Borers: *Symptoms:* An occasional cane may die, from some point on its length out to the tip. If you check back to where normal, live wood begins you will find that the cane has been hollowed out to that point.

Control: Because the infestation is usually very spotty, control, unless there is unusually serious damage, would consist of cutting out the infested canes and burning them, but you must make sure, of course, to cut down below where the borer is working.

European Corn Borer: *Symptoms:* The larvae of this insect may go into currant canes to pass the winter. They do not normally attack the currant as one of their food plants, but when the mature larvae are looking for a place to hole up for the winter they may go into currant canes, raspberry canes, or similar woody plants. Usually the entrance hole is sufficiently large to weaken the cane so that it will break off, or at least die beyond that point.

Control: Measures should be directed toward control of the pest on its preferred food plants.

Currant Fruit Fly: *Symptoms:* The currant fruits are attacked by maggots, indicated by discolored areas and premature ripening.

Control: Spray or dust with DDT as soon as most of the flowers have wilted.

CHAPTER 16

The Cultivated Blueberry—
Our Newest Fruit

The blueberry and cranberry are two fruit plants of a family usually thought of as providing strictly ornamental subjects. This is the family Ericaceae, which includes such plants as rhododendrons, azaleas, mountain laurel, the heathers, and manzanitas, among others. A closely related group of ericaceous plants, the huckleberries, is very often confused with blueberries. According to modern terminology, we consider as huckleberries those species whose fruits have ten large, bony seeds—mostly edible fruits, but not as high in quality as the blueberries. The blueberries have many seeds which are so small and soft that one is hardly conscious that seeds are present when the fruit is being eaten. In many areas blueberries are called huckleberries, and in some cases the reverse situation is true.

BLUEBERRIES IN THE WILD. These native American blueberries have been harvested in the swamps and on the hills for as long as the country has been settled, and long before that by the American Indians. In the Northwest certain Indian groups still celebrate a blueberry festival, or feast, each year. The harvesting of wild blueberries in Maine and other New England states, as well as in northern Michigan, Wisconsin, and Minnesota, and in the upland sections of some of the southern states, is, even now, a very extensive business. There are many species of blueberries with edible fruits, but only half a dozen or so are harvested in any quantity, either in the wild or under cultivation.

In New England, especially in the hills near the coast of Maine, there are thousands of acres of the lowbush blueberry, *Vaccinium lamarckii,* formerly known as *V. angustifolium,* and before that as *V. pennsylvanicum.* These native, lowbush berries are processed and shipped all over the country, the annual value of the crop running up to as much as $5,000,000. Along the Atlantic Coast the highbush blueberry, *V. australe* and *V. corymbosum,* is found in the wild over large areas, and considerable quantities are harvested annually. The dryland blueberry, *V. pallidum,* is harvested in the upland areas of Alabama and Georgia and northward to West Virginia.

Along the Pacific Coast, in the Northwest, the evergreen blueberry, *V. ovatum,* is harvested from natural stands, both fruit and leafy branches being important products. The leafy branches are shipped to florists throughout the United States, to be used as "greens" in floral make-up work. In the mountain area of the Northwest the mountain blueberry, *V. membranaceum,* is harvested by Indians and others who come out from the cities and villages in that area. In the South, the rabbiteye blueberry, *V. ashei,* formerly known as *V. virgatum,* is found rather extensively in Florida, and as far north as North Carolina, and west to Mississippi and Louisiana. Other species are harvested in somewhat smaller amounts in limited areas.

FRUIT NEW TO CULTIVATION. One of the reasons why the blueberry came under cultivation comparatively recently undoubtedly is the abundance of these wild berries. At the present time the value of the cultivated crop exceeds that of the wild crop, being some $10,000,000 in 1955. However, the value of the wild crop, including all types and producing areas, was certainly well over half of that amount, and possibly two thirds.

Another reason why the blueberry merits the title given in the chapter heading, "Our Newest Fruit," is that it has growing requirements somewhat different from the other cultivated fruits. Undoubtedly plants were dug and moved into gardens in many many cases, of which there is no record, at a relatively early date. There is a scanty record of certain plantings made in the latter part of the nineteenth century with results which were unsatisfactory, as presumably was true of the earlier efforts.

THE BEGINNINGS OF BLUEBERRY CULTURE. The romantic story of the beginning of our modern blueberry culture starts with the efforts of Dr. F. V. Coville of the U.S.D.A., who in 1906 began experiments in the culture of the highbush blueberry. He made selections in the wild in New Hampshire and New Jersey, and began breeding work in 1909. Miss Elizabeth White, of Whitesbog, New Jersey, reading of his experiments, and having had considerable experience with the wild blueberries in the vicinity of her family's extensive cranberry plantings, became interested, and wrote to Dr. Coville, offering co-operation. The result was many years of co-operation, including an extensive planting of blueberry seedlings at Whitesbog. Soon the White Company was establishing some of the first commercial fields with plants which had been propagated from wild selections. Miss White later began an extensive breeding project of her own.

SPECIAL REQUIREMENTS. The most important feature of Dr. Coville's work probably was his recognition of the fact that the blueberry has special nutritional requirements. Dr. Coville was a botanist and physiologist, and accustomed to looking for the explanation when plants refused to grow when given what was apparently good care. He reasoned that, since blueberries grew in swamps, and swamps were quite acid, soil acidity was the primary reason why failures had resulted when plants were taken from the bogs and set in upland soil. Dr. Coville's conclusions, since developed and, to some extent, modified by others, paved the way for successful commercial culture. His second contribution, that of breeding better varieties, has been almost as important as the other. About thirty selections from his breeding work have been named and propagated.

In recent years investigators in a number of experiment stations have studied the blueberry, and added greatly to our knowledge of its requirements. The breeding work started by Dr. Coville has been continued by Dr. Darrow of the U.S.D.A., and more recently by Dr. Scott, in co-operation with experiment stations in various states

The first shipments of cultivated blueberries, on a commercial scale, were made in 1916, and some forty years later the value of the cultivated crop throughout the country was over $10,000,000. This development of a cultivated crop from wild plants within forty years is almost unheard of in the history of our economic plants. The state of New Jersey, where blueberries were first successfully brought under cultivation, has remained in the lead so far as total acreage is concerned, but is closely pressed by Michigan. North Carolina is third in total acreage, and there are also commercial plantings in the states of Washington, Oregon, Massachusetts, New York, and a few others.

SOIL ACIDITY. Since the blueberry is rather widely distributed, although not all of the same species, the occurrence of wild blueberry plants may be helpful in determining whether soil requirements in a given locality are favorable. As the same general conditions are required by rhododendrons, azaleas, and mountain laurel, the presence of those plants may also be a helpful indicator. One of the things to check first, of course, is the soil acidity, or pH. Probably a pH of 4.5 is about right, with a range of from pH 4 to pH 5 being quite satisfactory. If the soil is more acid than that, or more alkaline, then some soil amendment might be desirable. If more acid than pH 4, and the plants are not growing well, an application of ground limestone might be tried. I have seen blueberries on soil so acid that the leaf tips were burned, and growth was very poor until after lime had been added. However, it is true that blueberries are very sensitive to an oversupply of lime, and the addition of this corrective material should be made only after considerable study, and then only on a small scale. It would probably be desirable to compute the amount of lime necessary to bring the pH up to 4.5, and use no more than that.

Where the soil has a pH above 5 and the plants are not growing well, or in any case if the pH is above 6, some thought should be given to acidifying the soil. If growth and production are satisfactory, then it may be better to let well enough alone and not use specific acidifying measures. However, it has been shown during recent years that the blueberry prefers ammonium, as a source of nitrogen, rather than nitrate. Ammonium sulfate is a relatively cheap and satisfactory source of ammonium nitrogen for blueberries, and it also has a tendency to make the soil more acid as the sulfate remains in the soil. So here we have a cheap means of acidifying the soil while providing nitrogen, an essential nutrient deficient in most blueberry soils, in the form in which the blueberry can best use it. The amount to apply will have to be determined by the amount of nitrogen the plants can use, rather than the extent of acidification desired. If the soil is a little too alkaline, using ammonium sulfate over a period of two or three years will probably bring it into the proper degree of acidity.

If the soil is much more alkaline than pH 6 or 6.5, then it will probably be desirable to use ground sulfur to produce a more acid condition. It has been suggested that, on sandy soils, ¾ pound of sulfur be used to each 100 square feet, for each full point that the soil acidity is above pH 4.5. On medium loams the amount of sulfur would need to be at least twice this much to get the same results. Aluminum sulfate has occasionally been recommended as a chemical to use to acidify soil. I do not like it, as aluminum is toxic to plants if present in the soil in sufficient quantity.

Recently there has been a considerable amount of research on this particular phase of blueberry nutrition, and there is some evidence that it is not entirely the pH which is the controlling factor. Some experiments show that the presence of calcium in considerable quantity is harmful to blueberries, even if the pH is satisfactory. There is also evidence that the presence of nitrate, as contrasted to ammonium, is not only of no value to the plant as a source of nitrogen, but may actually be harmful.

LIGHT, WELL-DRAINED SOILS PREFERRED. Blueberries in nature are found mostly on sandy soil, from very light sand to a sandy loam. For the highbush blueberries, which are the most important from the standpoint of cultivated fruit, there must be an ample water supply. Ideal blueberry soils are usually rather open and well drained, but have a water table within 2 to 3 feet of the surface. They do not like a soggy soil condition, and even though they are often found growing in swamps, they usually are up on an old stump, or a hummock, so that the water does not actually stand around the roots at any time. Where the soil is heavier it will undoubtedly help a great deal to incorporate into the soil sawdust, peat moss, or other sources of organic matter, in order to provide porosity as well as the organic matter itself, which seems to be especially needed by this group of plants.

CLIMATIC REQUIREMENTS. The highbush blueberry will stand reasonably cold temperatures, to about minus 20 degrees, or a little lower for some varieties, without being injured if the plants are well matured. This determines the effective northern limits of the highbush type, so that it may be usefully planted in southern New England, southern, and some places in central, New York, west into southern Michigan. In the Midwest this potential climatic zone would go south somewhat, although in this area other factors are limiting. On the West Coast, the Pacific Northwest, west of the mountains, seems to be ideally adapted. The southern limit of the highbush blueberry is determined by the effects of high summer temperatures, limited water supply, and in some regions soil alkalinity. Light shading, and a plentiful supply of water on a porous soil would undoubtedly permit the southern limits to be pushed further than it is commonly thought to be possible. In Florida, and along the Gulf of Mexico, the cold period may be so short that the bushes do not complete their rest period and blossom normally. This phenomenon is well known, as it applies to peaches in that area. In the South the varieties of the rabbiteye type are well adapted to local conditions, and will be discussed later in this chapter.

The blueberry is quite sensitive to moisture conditions, as might be gathered from its preference for lowlands. Regions where there is very low humidity during the growing season may be rather undesirable.

WHAT TO PLANT. The collecting and establishing of wild plants in the home garden is not impossible but may be disappointing. However, if you do find a superior-appearing plant growing wild it might very well grow satisfactorily in your garden. As a matter of fact there is one variety which originated as a wild seedling, the Rubel, still being grown commercially. However the hybrids produced by various breeders, notably the U.S.D.A. group, are certainly superior in size, quality, and appearance. Most gardeners will want to purchase plants of the best varieties rather than collect from the wild.

The table on the opposite page gives some suggestions as to varieties and some of their characteristics.

THE NEWER BLUEBERRY VARIETIES. In the preceding table most of the varieties listed are relatively recent introductions from the breeding work of the U.S.D.A. and co-operating experiment stations. Some of these may eventually develop faults of some kind, but in rather extensive tests they have seemed so superior to the older sorts that home gardeners are justified in planting them as being the best available.

VARIETIES FOR THE SOUTHEAST AND SOUTH. The southeastern area, especially the Carolinas and Georgia, have three different lists suggested. For the southern part of this section, especially at the lower altitudes, the highbush varieties are not so well adapted, because of high summer temperatures and not enough chilling during the dormant season. The varieties recommended therefore are of the rabbiteye type.

A little further north, but in the coastal plain area, the blueberry canker disease has been very serious, and so only varieties relatively resistant to this disease are recommended. Further west canker is not so prevalent, and about the same varieties are recommended as for the Middle Atlantic States.

Along the Gulf Coast and in the lower Mississippi Valley the rabbiteye varieties listed for the southern part of the Southeast are

TABLE XV

Blueberry Varieties Suggested for Home Gardens

Northeast, Colder Areas
- Bluecrop
- Blueray
- Earliblue

Other Northeast
- Atlantic
- Bluecrop
- Blueray
- Coville
- Dixi
- Earliblue
- Herbert
- Jersey

Middle Atlantic
- Berkeley
- Bluecrop
- Blueray
- Coville
- Earliblue
- Herbert
- Jersey

Southeast, Southern Part
- Callaway
- Homebell
- Tifblue
- Walker

Southeast, Coastal Area
- Angola
- Croatan
- Murphy
- Scammell
- Wolcott

Southeast, Western Part
- Berkeley
- Bluecrop
- Coville
- Earliblue
- Ivanhoe
- Jersey

Central States
- Bluecrop
- Earliblue
- Jersey

Great Lakes
- Bluecrop
- Blueray
- Coville
- Earliblue
- Jersey
- Keweenaw

California
- Bluecrop
- Earliblue
- Jersey

Northwest
- Berkeley
- Bluecrop
- Blueray
- Coville
- Dixi
- Earliblue
- Jersey

suggested. Further north, especially at the higher altitudes, some of the highbush varieties may be tried.

With our present knowledge and varieties there are great areas in the Southwest, the Prairie States, the Great Plains, and the Mountain States where conditions are generally unfavorable for blueberries. The factors responsible include high summer temperatures, low rainfall and low humidity, soil alkalinity, and, in the North, low winter temperature. Gardeners in these areas who would like to try blueberries and who could give them special care to offset, as much as possible, the naturally unfavorable conditions might well try Jersey as it is apparently adaptable to a wider range of conditions than most. If it grows reasonably well additional varieties might be tried.

HIGHBUSH BLUEBERRY VARIETIES

The following are arranged in order of ripening, the early varieties listed first. All have been produced by the U.S.D.A. breeding project.

Earliblue—as early as Weymouth, the earliest of the older varieties, but of much better color and quality than that variety.

Ivanhoe—very vigorous, large, light blue, excellent dessert quality. Not dependably hardy north of Maryland.

Blueray—very vigorous, very large, highly flavored, promising from New Jersey northward.

Bluecrop—very light blue, consistently productive, very firm, may tend to overbear so pruning should be carefully done.

Berkeley—open spreading bush, fruit clusters loose, berries very large, very light blue, firm.

Atlantic—open spreading bush, good color, size and flavor, one of best for freezing. Subject to bacterial cane blight in Northwest, liked in New England.

Jersey—vigorous, productive, fruit large, round, good color, fair quality, most widely adaptable of all.

Dixi—very large, a bit dark, good quality, cracks in wet weather.

Herbert—very large, clusters loose, fair color, productive, very good quality.

Coville—very late, of good color and size, quality good but tart, productive.

CANKER-RESISTANT VARIETIES FOR EASTERN NORTH CAROLINA

The following varieties are being grown commercially in eastern North Carolina partly because of their resistance to canker. Scammell is one of the older U.S.D.A. varieties, the other four were developed by the U.S.D.A. in co-operation with the North Carolina Experiment Station specifically for canker resistance They are arranged in order of ripening but the first four are all very early.

Angola—productive but a bit dark and soft, fair quality.
Wolcott—very vigorous, large, dark, firm, fair quality.
Croatan—vigorous, medium size, dark, good quality.
Murphy—large, dark, firm, of fair quality.
Scammell—midseason, fair size and quality.

FOR NORTHERN MICHIGAN

Keweenaw is a variety developed by the Michigan Experiment Station and named because it would ripen in the short growing season of northern Michigan. Good color and quality, firm.

RABBITEYE VARIETIES

These varieties have possibly not been tested as extensively as some of the highbush varieties. Gardeners in the South who are interested in blueberries might well try several, or all, of the following. They are arranged in order of ripening. Plant two varieties for cross-pollination.

All except Walker are from the U.S.D.A. breeding work in cooperation with the Georgia Experiment Station.

Callaway—early, medium size, excellent quality, productive.
Tifblue—large, light blue, excellent quality.
Walker—one of the better selections from the wild, fair size and quality.
Homebell—large, fair quality, very vigorous and productive.

ARE POLLENIZERS NEEDED? Quite a bit of work has been done in studying the self-fertility of blueberry varieties. There seems little doubt that a somewhat better size of berry may be secured if there is provision for cross-pollination. Most home gardeners will want to have more than one variety, anyway, in order to extend the ripening season and to provide some variation in the type of fruit. Most commercial plantings have been of two or more varieties, although some varieties have been self-fertile enough so that growers have set out large fields of one kind. It is of course much easier to keep varieties separate at harvest if there is only one variety in a field.

The home gardener may want to experiment by planting several varieties. This is especially worth considering if you live in an area where blueberries have not been grown, and you are not too sure whether your conditions are going to be suitable. Varieties react differently to local conditions, and, by trying several, you may find that one or two are superior, which you might have missed altogether if you had planted only one kind to begin with. In the older commercial plantings it was the practice, in many cases, to plant two rows of one variety and then two rows of another to provide for cross-pollination. In the ordinary small garden, the arrangement of the plants will not make very much difference, as they will be close enough together to insure the cross-pollination desired, provided there are two or more varieties.

GOOD LANDSCAPE SUBJECTS. The highbush blueberries fit very well into the landscape, being medium-sized, well-rounded bushes which, at maturity, may be anywhere from 4 to 6 feet in height. They are a pleasant green in summer, the fruit is beautiful when ripe, and most varieties show very attractive autumn coloration. The bushes do not produce suckers or seed themselves, so there will be no danger of their spreading beyond their assigned space. They may be used in a border planting, or as a hedge, or simply lined out in the garden. Although they do look very nice in an ordinary border, if they are mixed in with other easily damaged shrubs there may be trouble at picking time, especially if there are children in the family who want to run back and forth to the bushes while the berries are ripening. If used in the landscape it would probably be best to have special groupings of blueberries in a place that is relatively accessible and not enclosed by other low-growing shrubs to fence out the pickers.

PROPAGATION OF BLUEBERRIES. Blueberries are normally grown from cuttings, either softwood summer cuttings or hardwood cuttings—usually the latter. They may also be grown from layers made by pegging down some of the lower branches and covering them with soil. A cut about half through the branch on the underside of the bend where it is pegged down will hasten rooting. Blueberry cuttings do not root very easily, so it will usually be better to purchase plants unless you have good facilities for propagation.

If you do want to try, hardwood cuttings are made during late winter, and may be rooted in granulated peat moss, or a mixture of peat and sand. They make shoot growth promptly in the cutting bed but it will be several weeks later before the roots are formed, hence the problem of the leaves transpiring water but no roots to supply it. Enough will soak into the base of the cutting to maintain the leaves, provided the rooting medium is kept moist, and the humidity is fairly high around the leaves. Softwood cuttings, made during the summer, must be kept in a propagating case or under mist, and root-inducing hormones should be helpful.

It will be advisable for the home gardener to purchase fairly large plants, as they will produce a crop sooner than will small plants. I do not mean large fruiting plants, which some commercial grower might be discarding, although they may be all right, but rather plants about three years old which would have a good-sized root ball attached. A three-year-old plant is one which has been in a nursery row for two years, after one year in a propagating bed or cold frame. The larger plants are desirable especially if your conditions are likely to be somewhat unfavorable. Under such conditions it will take a considerable time for very small plants to become established, and there may be some loss, certainly more than there would be with larger plants. Plants with top growth some 18 to 24 inches in height should be about right.

PLANTING TIME AND METHODS. If plants are bought with a ball of soil, as blueberry plants should be handled, they may be moved at almost any time of the year, provided they are kept well watered afterwards. However, as with all other plants, fall and spring are

A well-branched two-year-old blueberry plant with a good root system.

to be preferred, because moisture and temperature conditions are more favorable at those times. By spring planting is meant about as early as the soil can be gotten into suitable condition for planting, which by the calendar would be considerably later in the North than in the South.

As the blueberry root system is rather fibrous and spreading, and usually includes a ball of soil, it will be necessary to actually dig a hole, rather than set the plants with a spade or a trowel, as was suggested for strawberries and raspberries. In favorable soil it will suffice to dig a hole only large enough to accommodate the root system, setting the plant at about the same depth as it was in the nursery. If the soil is unfavorable, then any changing or conditioning should be done before the plants are set. Depending on what the soil needs, this might consist of working in any acidifying chemical that may seem to be necessary, and also incorporating organic matter in the form of peat or sawdust. If conditions are quite unfavorable, it would be advisable to try to improve the whole mass of soil where the blueberries are to be grown. That might involve rotavating in several inches of peat or sawdust. If conditions are not very unfavorable it may be sufficient to dig a rather large hole, perhaps 2 feet in diameter, and fill in around the plant with a mixture of soil and peat moss about half and half. Any fertilization at planting time should be done on top of the soil, or, if a large hole was dug, well out from where the roots are located, in order to avoid the possibility of injury.

CULTIVATION MUST BE SHALLOW. Blueberries, like other ericaceous plants, have very shallow, fibrous root systems. Any cultivation, unless it is extremely shallow, will cut many of the roots and effectively hold back satisfactory growth. Of all the small fruits, perhaps the blueberry is best adapted to growing under mulch, or, to put it another way, it is more important to mulch blueberries than most of the other fruits, because of this shallow rooting characteristic. If it is impossible to secure satisfactory mulching material, cultivation, at least close to the bushes, should be done preferably by hand hoeing, simply scraping off the weed and grass seedlings while they are small. A sharp, hoelike tool on a garden cultivator would give the same results, but it is hard to get in under the bushes with a motor-driven cultivator without special attachments.

SAWDUST MULCH IS GOOD. Peat moss may be used as a mulch, but it is not very satisfactory as it is so water-repellent after it becomes dry. A mulch of sawdust will be just as effective, and the water will penetrate through it much more readily when it becomes thoroughly dried out. Wood shavings, crushed corncobs, straw, or spoiled hay may also be used. However, from the standpoint of permanence, fire risk, and effect on the plants, sawdust is hard to beat if you can find it. A depth of about 4 inches should be satisfactory to start with. It will probably be necessary to apply another 2 or 3 inches the following year and then more or less per year, depending on the rate of decay and settling, which you can easily gauge by digging down to the soil. The depth of mulch covering at any time should not be less than 1 inch, and preferably 2. This will be much more effective in keeping down weeds and conserving moisture than will a shallower layer.

Whenever one thinks of mulching in the garden he must also take into consideration the matter of soil fertility. As stated in Chapter 4, it will be necessary to increase greatly the amount of nitrogen applied if the plants are mulched, as compared to what they would need if not mulched.

FERTILIZERS FOR BLUEBERRIES. Blueberries, like other crops, require all of the essential nutrient elements, but nitrogen is the element most likely to be needed. As previously stated, ammonium sulfate makes a very satisfactory source, providing nitrogen in the form in which the blueberry plant can use it, and leaving an acid residue in the soil. The amount to use naturally depends on the soil; however, in a typical blueberry soil, which would be rather light, sandy, and probably infertile, one might estimate a need for about 250 pounds of ammonium sulfate per acre per year, or about 6 pounds per 1000 square feet. For the first year, under mulch, this should be at least doubled, and possibly almost doubled the following year. This would be a rather heavy application to put on at one time, especially if the soil were to dry out soon after it is applied. It would be better to split the amount and make at least two applications, and possibly three. One might be in late winter, just before growth starts, another soon after growth starts, and the third about full bloom.

In the home garden it would usually be possible, and certainly quite practical, to irrigate, or sprinkle in some way, as soon as the fertilizer is applied. Otherwise it will stay on top of the mulch or on top of the soil until there is a rain. If there should be a slight rain, just enough to dissolve the material but not enough to wash it down into the soil, the solution within the mulch may become concentrated enough to cause injury to the roots, which often grow up out of the soil into the lower part of the mulch.

The amount of phosphorus, potash, and possibly magnesium to use will have to be determined either by your experience with other plants or a general knowledge of the abundance of these elements in the soils of your neighborhood. If you are not sure, it would not hurt at all to use a complete fertilizer, such as a 5-10-5, at the beginning of the season, in order to be certain that phosphorus and potash are available to the plants.

YELLOW LEAVES. A not uncommon reaction of blueberries to unfavorable soil conditions is a yellowing of the leaves, sometimes with the veins remaining green. If the drainage is good and the yellowing cannot be corrected by the addition of nitrogen, it would indicate that it is probably due to deficiency of iron or possibly magnesium. If the veins are dark green and the area between the veins is yellow, it may indicate lack of magnesium, in which case magnesium sulfate should readily correct the deficiency. If it does not, then lack of iron is pretty definitely the cause, especially if the pH is rather high. The difficulty is not that iron is actually lacking in the soil, but that in this particular soil, and under these specific conditions, it is tied up in insoluble form and is unavailable to the plant. It might be partially released by acidifying the soil with sulfur. However, some of the new iron chelates, which are organic forms of iron that are not tied up by the soil, should be considered. If iron chlorosis, or yellowing of foliage, is prevalent in your community and likely to appear on your blueberries, the chances are that your county agent will have had some experience with chelates and can give you suggestions as to their use.

UNDER DRY ALKALINE CONDITIONS. There are many places, of course, where blueberries are completely unadapted, principally the hot, dry areas, with soils that are fairly alkaline. In these areas the water is likely to be alkaline, also, so that even though the soil were acidified, it would gradually turn alkaline again. If you live in an area like this and wish to try highbush blueberries, it would probably be advisable to grow them in pure peat moss, or in soil that has at least half peat moss mixed into it. Even then you would have to watch the pH, as the watering may bring it up. The proper use of chelates in such soil may make it possible for you to get reasonably satisfactory growth. As always, the harder it is to raise a plant, the more of a novelty it is and the more to be desired by those of us who like to grow plants which are not the common thing in our neighborhood.

THE USE OF WATER. The preference of blueberries for adequate moisture, but combined with a well-drained soil, was stressed earlier. This should be kept in mind during the summer as you irrigate or sprinkle during dry weather. If the soil is inclined to be a little compact, it will be especially necessary to avoid putting on so much water that the soil becomes waterlogged. If the plants are under mulch, the soil will tend to remain more porous and percolation will be more satisfactory. Although most commercial plantings are grown without irrigation, most growers would admit that many times they would like to have more water available for their plants. Many home gardeners at least can furnish that water when their plants need it. Ordinarily, when the other plants in the garden need watering, the blueberries will also.

PRUNING BLUEBERRIES. Most blueberry varieties make nice-shaped plants, and so pruning to develop a desirable shape is usually unnecessary. However, many varieties tend to overbear. They will produce a very large crop of fruit buds which may easily be distinguished during late winter by the fact that they are rather plump and roundish, compared to the smaller, rather flat, pointed leaf buds. When one considers that from six to eight flowers, and possibly that many berries, will be produced from each fruit bud, he can see what a load a particular twig will carry. A large crop is desired, but the leaf area and root system of a bush are able to produce and ripen only a limited number of berries, possibly one fourth as many as the number of flowers produced, especially by weak bushes.

Very frequently it is desirable to thin the fruit buds, either by cutting back the end of the twig to a point where the fruit buds are widely scattered, or by removing entirely some of the spurlike growths, which may be very tiny and yet have four or five fruit buds on them. Where there is a heavy set of buds and all are allowed to produce fruit, none of it will be very large, and in extreme cases it will not mature but simply remain green and inedible. This detail of thinning out the fruit buds, because the problem does vary with varieties, size, and age of the plant and its relative vigor, is something that the gardener will, to a large extent, have to work out for himself.

The young bush should probably not be permitted to mature any

This bush of Atlantic blueberry has been well pruned to produce berries of good size and quality. Some blueberry bushes have an attractive appearance even when the leaves have fallen.

fruit the first year it is set out. Although if it is a fairly large, vigorous plant, with a good root ball, and set in the fall or early spring, it might be allowed to produce a few berries. Usually the easiest way to prevent fruit production on small plants is to rub off the blossom clusters as they emerge from the buds. By the second year the bush should be making a normal growth and could produce a dozen or two good clusters of fruit. However, this would range from none for a plant which has made a poor start to perhaps twenty-five for an extra-vigorous plant. Soon the gardener should have a fairly good idea of how many buds to leave or how close together they should be in order to get a good crop. Usually it is best to remove the very thin, weak spurs entirely, because it is an endless job to try to cut them back and because they are not vigorous enough to do a good job even with one fruit bud. They may be cut off with the pruning shears or simply rubbed off with the hands protected by leather gloves.

The ideal pruning, perhaps, would be accomplished by doing a rather fine job throughout the bush, cutting back most twigs and carefully thinning the spurs, but this is rather time consuming. Commercial growers have found that by cutting out some of the older branches, which have a lot of the fine spurs bearing a large number of rather weak fruit buds, and leaving the younger, more vigorous canes, which have stronger fruit buds but fewer of them, they can do a good job with relatively few cuts per bush.

Pruning may be done at any time during the winter or even in late fall. Toward spring the fruit buds are a little larger and easier to distinguish.

HARVESTING HINTS. Blueberries will hang on the bushes in good condition for several days after they turn blue. Picking crews of

This blueberry picker in Michigan is picking with both hands into a small pail attached to a string around her waist.

large growers may go over a field every week, or as infrequently as every ten days, depending on the variety. This permits the berries to become fully ripe and attain their maximum flavor. The objection to this, in the home garden, is that the birds are not so backward in waiting for full maturity, but are inclined to pick off a berry as soon as it turns color. If you are protecting your blueberries, as you may have to with a screen or a cage or a cover of some kind, then you can let them mature fully. The point is that they do not spoil, or mold, nearly as quickly as strawberries, raspberries, or blackberries.

One of the problems in picking blueberries is that the fruit is borne in clusters and the berries in a cluster do not all ripen at once. The ones at the base of the cluster will be fully grown and ripe while the ones at the tip may be only half grown and still green. This means that the individual berry has to be picked from the cluster without knocking off the green ones. An experienced picker will grasp the berry lightly between the thumb and the first two fingers and roll it to one side. It will easily break loose from the stem and may be permitted to roll down into the palm of the hand until there are perhaps half a dozen berries. The more berries you hold the more they will be bruised.

One of the nice things about blueberries is the bluish gray bloom which is responsible for their name. This bloom is made up of minute scales which will easily rub off the berries and leave them rather blackish and unpleasantly streaked, although of course just as good to eat. Blueberries may be picked in pails, as they do not crush as easily as the other berries, but it will be somewhat better to pick in shallow containers, such as the one-pint berry baskets. Usually a small pail will be very satisfactory, if it is dumped into shallow containers before it is completely full.

Some varieties have better picking qualities than others. In some there is a tendency for the pedicel, or short stem by which the berry is attached to the cluster, to remain on the berry. This is hardly noticed when the berry is eaten, but when you see the stems in the dish at the table you would rather they had been removed. Another problem is that some berries tend to have a large scar or hole where the stem was attached. If this is rather large, and inclined to be juicy, and perhaps the skin is torn a little, you can expect that these berries will mold fairly readily. If the scar is very small and relatively dry, it will usually indicate better keeping quality.

THE RABBITEYE BLUEBERRY. The foregoing has applied specifically to the highbush blueberry, which has been commonly thought of as the cultivated blueberry. During recent years there has been increasing interest in the rabbiteye blueberry for the Gulf Coast states. In the first place it will grow satisfactorily under conditions of rather high winter temperatures and a short dormant season. It is also adapted to dry land, and thrives over a wide range of conditions. The plants are vigorous, tall growing, and productive, but yield their crop over a long period, which is more desirable for the home garden than for commercial planting.

Between 1920 and 1930 there was something of a boom in northern Florida in the planting of rabbiteye blueberries, collected from the wild, into cultivated fields. Although many of the wild seedlings of this species produce rather small berries which have gritty flesh, the thousands of plants moved into field culture offered a good opportunity for selection. Many of the selected berries have good size, color, and quality. There are now named varieties available, some being selections from the wild, others the result of breeding. The varieties most recently released by the breeders usually represent the highest development of the species and are worth trying as soon as stock is available. Some of the new varieties, usually very few, may prove susceptible to some disease, or not adapted to certain growing conditions, so there is a slight gamble. Since the rabbiteye blueberry tends to be self-sterile, the planting of at least two varieties insures cross-pollination and lessens the risk of relying on a new sort which might conceivably prove to have some hidden fault. Varieties suggested for the home garden are included in Table XV.

The rabbiteye bush grows considerably larger than the highbush blueberry, so it is necessary to plant them further apart. For home gardens about 8 by 8 feet would be satisfactory. I have not seen rabbiteye plants used in landscaping the home, but see no reason why they should not be quite satisfactory if properly located. This type of blueberry will respond to mulching and fertilization, although it will grow under conditions of partial neglect where the highbush type would not survive. Pruning should be relatively light, and only the older stems and branches which have borne fruit and become rather weak should be taken out.

Propagation may be by summer cuttings, preferably under mist. However, for the home garden, propagation by offshoots or suckers, which come out from the crown of the plant, are probably more satisfactory.

About the same list of pests that attack the highbush varieties may be found, from time to time, on the rabbiteye, but usually in the home garden they will produce satisfactorily with no spray schedule. Apparently some of the better varieties are rather resistant to pests. For instance, canker, which is a serious disease on most highbush varieties in the South, does not seem to bother the selected rabbiteye varieties to any extent.

THE LOWBUSH BLUEBERRY. The lowbush blueberry, in areas where it is prevalent, is usually picked in the wild, so it may hardly be worth trying to introduce it into the garden. However, it does make a very pretty ground cover and may be used for that effect, with fruit production as a secondary result. It ripens a little earlier than the highbush blueberry and has a similar flavor, although usually quite mild. Commercially the fruit is picked by rakes or scoops similar to the cranberry scoop, but for home use it can readily be picked by hand.

The lowbush blueberry produces best on canes which are two to three years old. Commercially the blueberry barrens are often burned over, so that the crop is sacrificed in order to assure a good crop the second and third year.

THE DRYLAND BLUEBERRY. In the Southeast the dryland blueberry is also commonly harvested from natural stands rather than from cultivated plantings. It would be possible, of course, to bring selected wild plants into the home garden, and it might be of considerable interest. However, where these do well the chances are there would be wild ones in the neighborhood to offer an easier method of getting the season's supply of berries.

NORTHWESTERN SPECIES. In the Northwest, especially along the coast, the evergreen blueberry is quite often found as an ornamental plant, used as a hedge, or as an evergreen shrub for a border planting. Such home-garden plants, even if considered as ornamentals, may be harvested for their fruit, but most of the berries still come from wild plants. Somewhat the same thing may be said for the branches used for florists' greens, which come almost exclusively from plants on cutover forest land. These branches are usually broken from the plant, rather crudely, which leaves the plant itself in very poor condition as far as appearance is concerned. Within its climatic range it is quite practical to have a few bushes of this species growing in an inconspicuous place where it can be cut for greens, as well as produce fruit. However, it is probably not hardy where temperatures would go much below plus 5 degrees.

In the same area the red-fruited blueberry, *Vaccinium parvifolium,* is commonly found in the woods, and is frequently seen growing as an ornamental plant. The fruit is seldom used, as it is borne rather sparsely. It does have a translucent, bright red color, however, and makes a jelly quite comparable to, and in many ways better than, currant jelly.

In most places where the lowbush, the evergreen, or the red-fruited blueberries may be grown fairly easily the same effort on the best varieties of the cultivated, highbush blueberry will undoubtedly be more satisfactory from the standpoint of fruit production. In the Far South there will be places where it is too dry, and the winters are too short, for the highbush blueberry, and there the rabbiteye finds its natural place. In the northern part of New England, New York State, northern Michigan except near the lake, and in the northern Great Plains states the highbush blueberry is of doubtful hardiness. In those areas, if any blueberries are to be grown, they may have to be the lowbush type, or certain related, extra hardy species that grow close to the ground and may be covered with straw or hay, which in turn will be covered with snow; and in that way they may come through the winter where the highbush type would be killed to the snow line.

PEST CONTROL. In many areas blueberry pests are rather uncommon, and in home gardens no pest-control program will be needed. In others, however, some one or more of the insects or diseases may cause trouble, unless you use the prescribed control measures.

BLUEBERRY DISEASES
Blueberry Stunt: *Symptoms:* Plants do not grow vigorously, and the leaves are first yellowish, then become reddish, or mottled reddish, during late summer, before normal fall coloration should start. This is a virus disease.

Control: It is important, of course, to set plants which are free of this disease. Normally you will not get diseased plants from a nursery which has been inspected, so be sure that the nursery from which you buy has been inspected specifically for stunt. Rogue out, and burn, any plants which show evidence of stunt after they are set.

This is rather difficult to determine, as the symptoms are likely to be confused with certain nutrient deficiencies or lack of moisture. If you suspect stunt, and are in a locality where it is known, it would be best to have some experienced person diagnose the trouble before taking out the plant. As the disease is spread by a leaf hopper, the control of this insect, called the vector, would effectively prevent its spread. However, it is difficult to prevent all leaf hoppers from coming in from a neighboring field or garden, or from the wild, and feeding for a few days in between sprays. Fortunately, stunt seems to be concentrated in a few areas, mostly where blueberries are commonly grown commercially. In most of the country you will probably never have occasion to worry about stunt if you get disease-free plants to start with. There is, of course, no control, or remedy, for the disease, once it is established in a particular bush.

Other Virus Troubles: *Symptoms:* There are some other virus diseases of blueberries which may cause rather spectacular symptoms on individual bushes but which are so uncommon, and spread so slowly, that they are relatively unimportant. Some of these make the leaves narrow and rather long, shoestringlike, and others cause certain types of curling and mottling.

Control: If there is a bush which exhibits such unusual or abnormal foliage symptoms, and you can find no evidence of direct cause by aphids, or other insects, or by frost injury, then it would be best to eliminate the bush. The chances are that the disease will not spread to your other plants, but the one which does have the disease will be practically worthless and might as well be destroyed as a precautionary measure.

Galls: *Symptoms:* Swellings may occasionally develop on the branches, near the ground, or on the main trunk. These may be more or less conspicuous, rough and warty, and will usually cause a decrease in vigor of the plant. It would be advisable to cut out and burn diseased branches, and to burn any plants showing several of the galls. The diseases causing these galls are not very common and it would be well not to let them go unchecked in your particular planting, even though under your conditions they might not cause very much damage.

Canker: *Symptoms:* Cankers are produced on stems and branches of susceptible blueberry varieties, particularly in the North Carolina area. So far this disease has not proven very serious in other blue-berry districts. The new cankers are reddish swellings, which later spread, and in some cases the canker will completely girdle the branch and cause its death. A survey made a few years ago indi-cated that the following varieties have sufficient resistance to pro-duce crops even where stem canker is prevalent: Jersey, Atlantic, Scammel, Murphy, and Wolcott. The cultivated rabbiteye varieties seem to be quite resistant to this disease.

Control: Up to the present time the main reliance, in areas where canker is severe, must be put on the growing of resistant varieties. We must remember, of course, that it is fairly well localized in the Carolina region, and, while present in some neighboring states, has not been nearly as destructive. Even in North Carolina the amount or severity of the disease seems to vary in different growing sections. The home gardener will probably need to rely on securing disease-free plants of varieties that are resistant in his particular locality.

Mummy Berry: *Symptoms:* Ripening berries turn whitish, or salmon colored, rather than the normal blue. These infected berries shrivel, drop off, and turn to mummies, which then provide spores for infecting the plants again next spring. The spores, which form from these overwintering mummies, attack the buds as they push out in the spring, causing a twig blight, from which additional spores are formed, to infest the blossoms and fruit, again causing mummy berries and thus completing the cycle. There is some difference in resistance of various varieties, and in many places the mummy berry is not prevalent enough to be serious.

Control: Spraying experiments have shown some control by keeping the flowers covered with a protective spray such as ferbam. This usually involves about three or four sprays, at weekly intervals, beginning as the buds push out in the spring. Certain ground sprays, to kill the fungus as it starts to produce spores in the spring, have been promising. Partial control may be secured by raking under the bushes, in early spring, to destroy the mummy cups, which will pro-duce the spores to be carried up to the developing buds. This raking of course should be very shallow. In most gardens, especially where there are only a few bushes involved, it may be practical to pick off and burn the mummy berries as you see them during the picking season, and at the end of the season pick up from the ground any which have been missed.

Botrytis Blight: *Symptoms:* In areas of high humidity the developing shoots in the spring may be attacked by botrytis, which will cause the growth to first appear water-soaked, and then be covered with a gray mold. This very commonly starts during the blossoming season, the infection getting its first entry into the petals and moving from there into the developing fruit cluster and into the twig, sometimes killing it back for several inches. This will be markedly affected by weather conditions during blossoming, very serious when there is rain during most of the blooming season, very little if it is fairly dry.

Control: In areas where this type of injury is likely to occur, it may be desirable to spray the bushes, just as they are coming into bloom, with a copper fungicide, or possibly with Fermate. Very little experimental work has been done so far on this disease as it affects blueberries.

Leaf Spots: *Symptoms:* Various small, roundish spots may appear on the leaves during the growing season. These are likely to be more numerous on plants that are making rather poor growth. They may be caused by various fungi, and as a general rule the damage caused is not serious.

Control: A spray or two during early summer with one of the copper sprays or Fermate will probably hold the leaf spot trouble under control. Actually, however, the damage done usually does not warrant a regular spray program. It would be advisable, however, to consider whether plants affected by leaf spot are making a normal growth, and whether they should not have more fertilizer, or possibly a better water supply during the summer.

BLUEBERRY INSECTS
Black Vine Weevil: *Symptoms:* Young blueberry plants sometimes wilt suddenly and the leaves dry up, indicating that the plant has been seriously injured in some way. If such a plant is pulled up it will be seen that the bark has been eaten from the main stem, the injury usually making a complete girdle just below the surface of the ground. By the time the injury is evident there will be spongy callus tissue formed at the upper rim of the girdle. This damage was caused by the feeding of the larvae of the black vine weevil the previous season. By the time it occurs, of course, there is nothing that can be done to save the plant. Sometimes older bushes are partially

girdled, and if the insect is then controlled, and the plant well cared for, it may recover; but the small plants completely girdled do not recover.

Control: Poison baits may be scattered around young blueberry plantings in areas where the black vine weevil is known to exist. More satisfactory, in recent years, has been the use of one of the newer insecticides, such as chlordane or aldrin, as a spray around and onto the base of the plant. Use according to the directions of the manufacturer.

Borers: *Symptoms:* Occasionally the tips of blueberry canes will wilt during midsummer and it will be found that the pith of the cane, at and somewhat below the wilting point, has been hollowed out by a borer.

Control: If this wilted tip is broken off a couple of inches below where injury is evident, as soon as the wilting is observed it will usually be possible to destroy the larva. Generally these borers are not prevalent enough to make necessary the complicated control measures which might be worked out to control the adults, or the eggs before they hatch.

Leaf-Eating Insects: *Symptoms:* Various types of injury may be caused by leaf-eating insects. In most cases both the insect and the injury will be evident, as with Japanese beetle.

Control: If there is sufficient likelihood of damage being done, one of the contact sprays such as malathion or DDT may be used, being careful, of course, not to apply it while the fruit is approaching the ripening stage.

Leaf Hoppers: *Symptoms:* The presence of these pests may be indicated by the insects themselves as they fly up when disturbed, or by a general yellowing of the foliage, accompanied by tiny yellowish dots on the upper surface. The insects, of course, feed on the under surface. Actually leaf hoppers would, in most cases, not be particularly damaging to blueberries, except that they are the agents for the spread of blueberry stunt.

Control: In areas where stunt is prevalent, controlling leaf hoppers by use of contact sprays, such as malathion, should be considered.

Blueberry Maggots: *Symptoms:* In some localities blueberry fruits may be infested with small white maggots, which are the larvae of any one of several insects, such as the blueberry fruit fly, cherry fruit-worm, plum curculio, and cranberry fruitworm. Unfortunately the presence of these larvae is not easy to observe, as they develop completely inside the berry. In some cases there will be a sunken place on the berry to indicate where the insect is feeding, or the berry may color up unevenly or prematurely.

Control: In general, where fruitworms are prevalent it will be advisable to apply preventive sprays or dusts. Since the material to use, and the timing of the application, will depend on what species of insect is causing the infestation, it will usually be necessary to check with local authorities for control measures. Control measures of any kind are likely to be needed only in areas where blueberries are quite commonly grown as a commercial crop. The isolated home garden planting is not likely to have much trouble with wormy berries. Furthermore careful picking for home use will enable most of those which do occur to be readily culled out.

CHAPTER 17

Some Other Berry Crops

THE CRANBERRY

The cranberry is the one commercial berry crop which is not well adapted to the home garden. The reason is that it is essentially a bog plant. The commercial plantings, which are largely restricted to five states, Massachusetts, New Jersey, Wisconsin, Oregon, and Washington, are mostly on peat swampland. However, this does not mean that cranberries can be successfully grown in any swamp. Drainage during the growing season is an important factor.

AMPLE WATER NECESSARY. It is rather necessary that the plants may be covered with water at certain times of the year, and uncovered at the will of the operator. It is true that in recent years cranberries have been very successfully grown on the West Coast with no flooding. In the other parts of the country, however, flooding is used as means of protection against high temperatures, against frost, and against low winter temperatures. Furthermore, certain important pests are controlled, at least partially, by flooding for a definite period at a definite time. On the West Coast the winter temperatures are not low enough to require flooding to prevent winter injury, and frost protection by the use of sprinklers has been quite successful. The sprinklers are also used to irrigate during dry periods of the summer, and to prevent damage by high summer temperatures.

HARDLY FEASIBLE IN THE HOME GARDEN. It is quite possible that cranberries could be successfully grown in some home gardens, if the soil is satisfactory, by use of a mulch for winter protection, and sprinklers for irrigation. As a matter of fact, one commercial planting in Wisconsin was made on upland soil and mulched for winter protection. Some promise of success was indicated, but the invasion of certain hard-to-control grasses finally caused the abandonment of the project.

At our present state of knowledge, I would suggest that the cranberry in the home garden is strictly on a novelty basis. If you do want to try growing it, use plenty of organic matter in the soil, peat moss preferably. The pH should be on the acid side, probably around pH 4.5 to 5.5. Use sprinklers to avoid damage by frost, and by heat, and to prevent drying out during the growing season. The southern limits of commercial cranberry culture have been determined by summer temperatures and by pests, particularly the fungus diseases which are encouraged by high temperatures. So the cranberry would seem to be strictly out in the dry parts of the West and Southwest, and in the Gulf states because of the high summer temperatures. Of course, no breeders have tried to produce varieties particularly adapted to upland culture, or to the home garden, so we should not say that cranberries will never be grown in the home garden, but just now it does not look very feasible.

The cranberry is an evergreen, trailing member of the Heath family, rather closely related to the blueberry. The cultivated form is *Vaccinium macrocarpon,* native in the Northeast. In the Northwest we have *V. quadripetalum,* a smaller berry, but prized by the Indians along the coast when the first white men appeared.

THE LINGONBERRY

Another ericaceous plant is the lingonberry, *Vaccinium vitis-idaea,* well known to Americans of Scandinavian descent. It can be grown in the cooler parts of this country, under conditions suitable for blueberries, although I would not generally recommend its culture, even if you do like Swedish pancakes with lingonberry sauce. The fruit resembles a miniature cranberry and is borne rather sparingly, too sparingly to compete with the cranberry.

The form native to the United States, and found in the Northeast, is *V. vitis-idaea* var. *minus.* It makes a beautiful little evergreen ground cover with its bright red berries, edible but almost too pretty to pick.

THE HIGHBUSH CRANBERRY

The native American *Viburnum americanum* produces a bright red fruit which looks something like a cranberry. This is a bush which may grow to 7 or 8 feet in height, and hence has been given the common name of highbush cranberry. This contrasts with the cranberry itself, which is a trailing vine, growing flat on the ground, and producing fruit on short uprights a few inches long.

The highbush cranberry does have an edible fruit, although the quality is not high. Its main claim to fame has been that it is ex-

The cranberry is hardly a home garden fruit, but this cranberry grower has a home garden strawberry patch adjacent to the cranberry bog.

tremely hardy, and can be grown as a fruit for jelly in the northern Great Plains area. It does of course have some ornamental value, and I would consider it of most importance from that standpoint. If you have plants growing in a border, and want to make jelly from them, that is fine, but I would hardly consider it an important small fruit for the home garden.

THE ELDERBERRY

There are two types of elderberry which have edible fruit and which, at least under certain conditions, have some place in the home garden. In the East the native elderberry is *Sambucus canadensis,* a rather common wild plant, found from the Atlantic Coast to the Middle West, and as far north as the Canadian border and south into the southeastern states. This makes a nicely rounded bush to about 8 feet in height. It is rather coarse and rapid growing with large, compound leaves. Certain types have finely cut leaves which have been selected for their ornamental value. There is also a golden-leafed form, occasionally used in the landscape.

Two varieties of elderberry growing in New Jersey. The one on the right is the Adams, a vigorous and productive sort. A well-shaped elderberry bush in full bloom is a very attractive landscape subject.

The flowers are produced in flat umbels, sometimes 8 inches to a foot across. They are quite attractive when in bloom, and also attractive when the fruits have obtained a rich, dark, reddish black in color. The individual berries are rather small, with large seeds. Elderberries make a delicious pie, so far as flavor is concerned, but the large seeds are rather objectionable. Undoubtedly someone, sometime, will produce or discover a plant with no seeds, or very small seeds, and that should be a very good pie berry. The present forms make excellent jelly, although one has to be careful to use the proper amount of pectin to get the proper consistency, but the flavor is very good.

On the West Coast, primarily in the Northwest, there is a native elderberry, *Sambucus coerulea.* In the wild this produces a magnificent bushy plant to 20 feet in height. It has a show of white, with its umbels of flowers in the spring, and in late summer and fall is attractively covered with clusters of fruit from 6 to 8 inches across. This fruit is very light blue in color, contrasting with the almost black color of the eastern species. The western type is more tree-like, and the older growths do not die back as early as is the case with the eastern one. It can probably best be grown as a tall bush for the first few years, then to a single-trunk, or a multiple-trunk, small tree. This means, of course, that it is a landscape or orchard plant, rather than one to include as part of the cultivated vegetable or berry garden.

The fruit of the western elderberry is a little milder than that of the eastern, and is not used very freely by people who have access to it. Still it is an edible fruit, and can be used about the same as the eastern type. Perhaps we should consider it primarily an ornamental plant. There is another western species, with conspicuous red fruit, inedible, but a striking, if somewhat rampant, ornamental.

CULTURE OF THE EASTERN ELDERBERRY. The eastern elderberry does very well under a wide variety of conditions, but does like plenty of moisture. It will grow on dry soils, but will be small and not very vigorous. On a mature plant a number of shoots will be sent up from the ground each year, usually attaining the full height of the plant in one season. These shoots are rather soft and thin walled with a large pith. The older trunks lose vigor and become weak after two or three years and should then be pruned out. Usually the shoots make no side branches, or very few, the first year. They can be tipped back slightly during the winter, and will make several side branches the following summer, which will be good fruiting wood. By the third year, however, a stem will begin to be weak and should be removed then or the year after. The usual fertilizer program as outlined for other berries will be quite satisfactory, depending on the nature of the soil and its nutrient supply.

ELDERBERRY PROPAGATION. Propagation of any of the elderberries may be by seed, by winter cuttings, by dividing an old plant, or digging some of the side shoots away from it. Named varieties, of which there are a few, should only be grown from cuttings or by division. If propagation is by seed there will be some variation in

Ripe fruit of Adams elderberry seen against blue sky and white clouds makes a pretty picture.

the seedlings. In the past, one or two of the named varieties have been grown from seed, and hence may not now be what we would consider a true, or satisfactory, horticultural variety.

Good plants may often be found growing wild in the neighborhood, and transplanted, or propagated by cuttings, and moved into the home garden. Actually this plant will fit into the landscape better than in a cultivated part of the garden. The plants grow quite large and should have room to spread out, as they will be several feet in diameter, possibly 8 to 12, when fully grown, and will tend to shade out smaller-growing nearby plants.

Not very much is known about the problem of self-sterility in the elderberry. I do recall one planting of the golden-leafed eastern type which was apparently self-sterile. In a planting of a half acre or so the outside rows, which were nearer some wild plants, set a good crop, whereas the ones toward the center of the plot produced very poorly. It would be a wise thing to set at least two plants if you are growing seedlings. If you are growing some named variety, and there are no wild elderberries in your neighborhood, it might be well to put a wild plant, or a second named variety, nearby.

These plants as they grow in the wild do not seem to have many pests. Occasionally borers get into the soft pith of the trunks and weaken them so that they break off. One planting, with which I was familiar in the East, was attacked by a very small mite, which caused the leaflet margins to roll inward. Whether it did very much damage is doubtful, but we were able to clean it up with a dormant lime sulfur spray.

THE WONDERBERRY

One of Luther Burbank's introductions which never amounted to very much is the wonderberry. It is a type of *Solanum* and closely related to the tomato. When the blueberry was first becoming established as a garden fruit, people frequently got the idea that the wonderberry was closely related, as it has somewhat the same bluish black color. It is very productive, but tastes somewhat like a tomato, and so far as I can see has little value except, perhaps, as an ornamental annual plant. From the standpoint of producing fruit for use, I believe that I would prefer one of the tomato types.

The wonderberry has not been heard from very much during the last few years. However, there was a period when several nurseries were advertising it very highly as a plant producing delicious fruit for pies and other common fruit uses. A number of experiment stations tried it and published statements about its true nature, but interest in it has apparently died down, even on the part of those nurseries which were exploiting it.

SALAL

On the West Coast the salal, *Gaultheria shallon,* is a very common wild plant, forming a large proportion of the underbrush in certain localities. This is an ericaceous plant, distantly related to the blueberry. The fruit is about the size of a blueberry—reddish black, and edible, although rather insipid. It was used extensively by the Indians and the early settlers, and does make a fairly nice jelly. However, from the standpoint of actual results from a given amount of effort, it would seem that the cultivated blueberry, or some of the other berries, would more amply repay gardening effort. In the area where I live, salal is very common, and in general the fruit is left pretty much alone. Under certain conditions salal may be grown as an ornamental plant, although where it does well it is likely to spread more than one might wish. It would probably be best to consider it as a coarse-leafed ground cover for ornamental planting, rather than as an edible fruit. It needs a fairly mild winter, acid soil, and will grow where it is moist or where it is relatively dry, producing under the latter conditions rather short plants.

In the wild, salal may make a very vigorous growth and the leafy shoots are collected in large quantities for shipment as florists' greens. The leaves are rather coarse, perhaps 3 inches long and 2 inches wide, but they are evergreen, tough, and leathery, and will hold up for a long time. They are often used as Christmas decorations after being dipped in aluminum or bronze paint. They will dry and hold their shape without curling as most leaves would do.

THE SALMONBERRY

The salmonberry is a native in this same country, with the salal, growing much like a raspberry. There are two types—red and yellow—which are essentially coarse raspberry fruits when they are ripe. The fruit is rather tasteless, there being some acid, but a relatively small amount of distinctive flavor. Salmonberries are eaten by the youngsters in the woods and occasionally picked in the wild, but are not considered as good fruit-producing plants. It is doubtful if they would be of any importance in the home garden, except as a novelty in the milder sections of the Northwest. In some areas where they do grow so vigorously one wonders if they will not eventually be hybridized with some of the better-quality fruits, and transmit some of that vigor to their offspring.

There are other kinds of berries which have not been touched upon, which may be found in limited quantities in certain areas. None of them would be considered as important small fruits for the home garden. Some of them may be studied by plant breeders in the future and used for hybridizing with some of our present fruits. This is especially true with respect to some of the odd species of blackberries, raspberries, and blueberries. Where any of these are found growing wild and seem to be worth transplanting, it is always an interesting project to carry out, although the results are often disappointing. It seems that some of the wild berry plants just do not appreciate good care, and do not do as well in the garden as they did in the wild. This simply means that the environment created for them by the gardener is not as satisfactory as the one which they had found in the wild. This may be due to lack of shade, or lack of organic matter in the soil, or soil that is a little too heavy, or too light, or even to the development of certain pests under cultivation which had been relatively unimportant in the wild.

CHAPTER 18

Grapes Are Fine for the Home Garden

The vine and the fig tree vie for honors as the oldest of the fruits used by man. I do not say "cultivated," because undoubtedly they were used for many centuries, and even thousands of years, as collected fruit before being put under cultivation for the first time. We do know, however, that from the earliest written records there is evidence that grapevines were known and appreciated by mankind. It may be assumed then that the natural habitat of the species of grapes, from which our present varieties have been derived, coincides with the area where man first emerged from the savage state. Even in modern times the Mediterranean area and the Near East are noted for production of grapes, where, in many localities, no other fruits are being grown.

From the earliest times in this country the grape was also known, even to the Norsemen, who, apparently finding wild grapes, gave the name Vineland to the unknown continent which they had discovered. The early settlers of more modern times also noted the abundance of wild grapes, and reckoned that this would be a wonderful place for the kinds of grapes which they had known in the Old World. Consequently, great efforts were made to establish plantings of Old World grapes, and great fortunes were lost in these attempts in the early part of the nineteenth century. The Old World grapes just did not thrive in the eastern part of the United States. They were about given up as a bad job for the New World, until California came into the picture, and, as everyone knows, the European grapes found conditions to their liking there, and so we now have California as the prime factor in grape production in this country.

DEMAND FOR WINE STIMULATED INTEREST. At the beginning the interest in wine was the primary factor in the development of grape vineyards, both in the Old Country and the New. At least as far back as we have written records references to the fruit of the vine almost invariably bring in some mention of wine. However, there are other aspects to this remarkable fruit that we do not find so often in the written story of the past because they are of comparatively modern development. They include the desirability of some present-day varieties as dessert fruit, of others for sweet grape juice, for raisins, for jelly and conserve, and, much later, the possibilities as a plant in the landscape design.

The desire for a profitable wine enterprise has undoubtedly been instrumental in starting most of the commercial plantings which have been and which are still being made in this country. From the home garden standpoint, however, the dessert qualities of this fruit have been quite important from the beginning. The production of the Concord variety by Ephraim Bull, introduced in 1854, really marked the beginning of the use of grapes for the home garden, as well as of successful commercial planting in the eastern states. Since that time many varieties have been introduced to grace the tables of grape lovers everywhere.

CLIMATIC REQUIREMENTS. Historically grapes are inhabitants of warm and relatively dry climates. They grow in some of the North African countries, and certain islands where rainfall is almost totally absent and moisture comes primarily from mist-laden clouds which never quite reach the point of precipitation. There are exceptions of course, even in the Old World type of grape, as we find varieties adapted to northern Germany and that general latitude. In this country we have another exception, in that varieties of the Concord type seem to be adapted to a cooler climate. There are other grapes, native American species, which are adapted to areas in this country still further north. These far northern types, however, are generally not as high in quality as the Concord type and are grown for jelly and juice because so few other fruits will produce at all in those rigorous climates.

The grapevine is a deep-rooting plant, going down in a relatively dry, sandy soil some 8 to 10 feet. This ability to survive in very dry climates and dry soils has perhaps been a factor in the apparent preference of the grape for this type of soil, rather than the moister and heavier clays.

THE EUROPEAN GRAPE. The grapes grown in this country might be placed in four different groups. The first group, and by far the most important from the standpoint of production, but not most important from the standpoint of wide distribution, and adaptability to the home garden, is the European grape, sometimes called the California grape, botanically belonging to the species *Vitis vinifera.*

Vinifera grapes, used in California to cover a simple arbor, provide an effective and attractive screen.

This is a variable species as it includes the tiny seedless varieties, from which dried currants are made, the larger ones, which make the conventional type of raisins, and others, which are especially adapted for wine making, in addition to the well-known dessert varieties.

These vinifera grapes so far have proven to be adapted almost entirely to conditions as they are found in California. The horticulturists and plant breeders of other states have been working, with some success, to develop varieties of this group and hybrids with other species, which would be well adapted to their own conditions. In general, the vinifera varieties are rather tender to cold, and where grown in more northern climates may be killed, or injured, during severe winters. Further than that they frequently show their dissatisfaction with the climate by failing to mature normally, or to reach a high sugar content, because of the lower temperatures.

THE EASTERN GRAPES. The grape of the eastern coastal regions and Middle West, and to some extent of the Northwest, is the Concord type, derived mostly from the native American species *V. labrusca.* These varieties are hardier than the viniferas, and will ripen normally as far north as the milder parts of the Great Lakes region and New England. They are not generally hardy enough for the northern states of the Great Plains. These are the home garden grapes of the Midwest, the eastern coast, as far south as the Carolinas, and to a lesser extent of many areas in the West, and probably comprise the most important group, or at least the most widely grown, of all of the home garden fruits.

Many breeders have made an effort to combine the good qualities of the viniferas and labruscas, but as yet there is more of promise than of actual fulfillment in this line of work. The labruscas, in general, have a rather musky flavor, and have the "slip skin" characteristic, whereas the viniferas have a solid, meaty flesh with a tender skin, practically inseparable from the pulp. The labrusca skin is tough and so is the pulp, which pops out of the skin when you squeeze or bite it.

THE MUSCADINE GROUP. Another strictly American type of grape is the one commonly known as muscadine and belonging to the species *V. rotundifolia*. This species is adapted to the Far South, where the labruscas do not seem to thrive. Incidentally, there are indications that this dislike of the labrusca varieties for the Far South may be due to the prevalence of certain virus diseases there. Once they are controlled or eliminated in some way, it may be that the Concord and its cousins will be at home much further south than they are now. But the muscadine is the native grape of the South and has been widely used there for the home garden.

The muscadine has several peculiarities. It is a rank-growing, long-caned vine, accustomed to growing on the taller trees along the riverbanks of the South. The fruit is produced in clusters of only two or three berries, rather than in clusters bearing a large number of berries, as many of us ordinarily think of grapes being borne. Muscadine grapes then cannot be picked as a bunch but must be picked individually, or, what is probably more often done, they may be shaken and picked up from the ground. This might indicate that they have a tough skin, and that is true. As a matter of fact, the skin is so tough that it prevents their being a very desirable fruit for dessert purposes. They do have good qualities for juice and for certain culinary purposes that are adapted to the peculiar flavor and flesh character.

This species in nature is dioecious—that is, there are male and female plants. This means that any planting to be successful must include at least a male and a female plant. Where there are a number of plants the pollenizers may be distributed at the ratio of perhaps one male to twenty or twenty-five females. The breeders have been working for many years to produce perfect flowered varieties and have some now available. It would seem wise to plant these, rather than the older ones, because of the necessity of including a male plant with the latter, which of course does not produce any fruit.

OTHER AMERICAN GRAPE TYPES. The fourth group of grapes includes those derived from native American species and particularly adapted to the colder regions of the country. An example would be the variety Beta, put out some years ago by the Minnesota Experiment Station. Where varieties of the Concord type can be grown their superior flavor would make them desirable, but where they are subject to winter injury, hardy varieties of this miscellaneous group, derived from several species, are the only ones which can be grown.

MOST INTEREST IN CONCORD TYPE. Probably more home gardeners will be interested in the Concord type of varieties than in the others, so we consider that group as typical for the main part of our discussion, indicating occasionally how methods would be modified in areas where either the vinifera or the muscadine varieties are to be preferred.

GRAPE VARIETIES. Grapes are rather sensitive to local growing conditions and so it is difficult to make general recommendations. Even in a single state there may be several "climatic zones," each of which would be different from the others with respect to the varieties which could be considered as well adapted. The twelve divisions shown in Table XVI are based on similarity of growing conditions. However there are some areas in each region which are not really suited to any variety, so these lists should be used for general guidance and be reinforced with whatever local information is available.

In New England, Concord would ripen satisfactorily only in the southern part, whereas Beta would be recommended only for the northern part where varieties of better quality would not be hardy. The New York Experiment Station has introduced many varieties not listed in the table. I have included those which seemed to me to be most strongly recommended. Possibly others would be well worth while for the home gardener, especially if he is quite inter-

TABLE XVI

Grape Varieties Suggested for the Home Garden in Various Regions

New England
- Beta
- Concord
- Delaware
- Fredonia
- Ontario
- Portland
- Van Buren

New York
- Concord
- Fredonia
- Golden Muscat
- Interlaken Seedless
- Ontario
- Romulus
- Seneca
- Sheridan
- Steuben

Great Lakes
- Beta
- Concord
- Fredonia
- Red Amber
- Seneca
- Sheridan
- Steuben
- Van Buren

Middle Atlantic
- Concord
- Fredonia
- Golden Muscat
- Interlaken Seedless
- Ontario
- Portland
- Romulus
- Schuyler
- Seneca
- Sheridan

South

BUNCH
- Concord
- Delaware
- Extra
- Fredonia
- Lake Emerald
- Niagara
- Portland

MUSCADINE
- Burgaw
- Creek
- Dulcet
- Higgins
- Hunt
- Scuppernong
- Tarheel
- Topsail
- Wallace
- Yuga

Central States
- Concord
- Delaware
- Fredonia
- Golden Muscat
- Niagara
- Van Buren

Prairie
- Beta
- Concord
- Fredonia
- Niagara
- Portland
- Van Buren

Great Plains
- Beta
- Bluebell
- Fredonia
- Red Amber
- Van Buren

Rocky Mountain
- Concord
- Fredonia
- Niagara

Southwest

VINIFERA
- Black Monukka
- Cardinal
- Muscat Hamburg
- Ribier
- Thompson Seedless

AMERICAN
- Carman
- Concord
- Delaware
- Niagara
- Pierce

| | *California* | | *Northwest* | |
VINIFERA	AMERICAN	VINIFERA	AMERICAN
Delight	Concord	Black Monukka	Buffalo
Muscat Hamburg	Golden Muscat	Pearl of Csaba	Concord
Muscat of	Pierce		Early Giant
Alexandria			Interlaken
Ribier			Seedless
Scarlet			Ontario
Thompson			Van Buren
Seedless			

ested in grapes. In the Great Lakes area, Beta and Red Amber are for the colder localities only.

In the South the bunch grapes and muscadines may intermingle somewhat with the latter preferred in the Far South. Lake Emerald was introduced in Florida as desirable there; whether it would be as desirable in other parts of the South I cannot say. The Southwest is a large area and includes parts of Arizona and New Mexico where vinifera grapes would be best adapted to the hot, dry, climate. Further north, and at higher altitudes, some of the American bunch grapes would be more satisfactory, so both types are included in the table. A somewhat similar situation prevails in California. Even where the vinifera varieties are grown commercially the American type may be preferred for home-garden "arbor" use because of less trouble with mildew, hence less necessity for a dust or spray program. In the South, Southwest, and California, grafting on resistant rootstocks may be advisable in certain areas.

In the Great Plains area even such extra hardy varieties as Beta and Red Amber might have to be protected, and Fredonia and Van Buren certainly would.

AMERICAN (BUNCH) GRAPES

Beta—early, black, suitable for juice and jelly but not very good for dessert purposes, very hardy. Originated in Minnesota about 1870.

Bluebell—bluish black, about size of Concord, sweet, sprightly, hardy. Minnesota Experiment Station.

Buffalo—midseason, black, good quality, prune to spur system in Northwest. New York (Geneva) Experiment Station.

Carman—late, black, medium size, quality fair. Originated in Texas, 1883.

Concord—midseason to late, black, good quality, the most widely grown American variety; for coastal and intermediate valleys and lower foothills in California, good for sweet grape juice. Tends to ripen unevenly in the South. Originated in Massachusetts over 100 years ago.

Delaware—midseason, small, red, very good quality, of medium vigor. Introduced in Ohio in 1849.

Early Giant—very early, large blue-black berries, sweet and juicy.

Extra—midseason, black, flavor sprightly, agreeable. Originated in Texas in 1886.

Fredonia—ripens about two weeks before Concord, black, quality fair to good, vigorous, productive. New York (Geneva) Experiment Station.

Golden Muscat—late, golden yellow, large, excellent quality when well ripened, somewhat tender, suggested for California except along the Coast. Resembles the European type. New York (Geneva) Experiment Station.

Interlaken Seedless—very early, berries small, golden yellow, sweet, good. New York (Geneva) Experiment Station.

Lake Emerald—light golden color, berries small, sweet. Has grown in Florida where most other varieties have failed because of degeneration presumably caused by a virus. Florida Experiment Station.

Niagara—standard white grape, midseason, quality fair to good, large. Originated in New York about 1872.

Ontario—very early, greenish white, productive, reasonably hardy, of excellent quality. New York (Geneva) Experiment Station.

Pierce—similar to Concord but better adapted to warm climate. Originated in California about 1882.

Portland—about same season as Ontario, larger but with a rather foxy flavor, greenish amber. New York (Geneva) Experiment Station.

Red Amber—amber red in color, best flavor of the very hardy varieties. Minnesota Experiment Station.

Romulus—midseason, white, seedless, clusters large, berries small, good. New York (Geneva) Experiment Station.

Schuyler—very early, black, European type, only moderately hardy, requires rather severe pruning. New York (Geneva) Experiment Station.

Seneca—very early, golden yellow, medium size, skin thin, tender, flesh firm, quality very good, of the European type. New York (Geneva) Experiment Station.

Sheridan—late, black, very good quality, keeps well, must be pruned rather severely. New York (Geneva) Experiment Station.

Steuben—ripens shortly after Concord, black, good quality, vigorous, hardy. New York (Geneva) Experiment Station.

Van Buren—ripens about three weeks before Concord, black, fair size, good quality. New York (Geneva) Experiment Station.

MUSCADINE VARIETIES

Burgaw—midseason, reddish black, skin medium thick, tough, fair quality. Perfect flowered. U.S.D.A.

Creek—late, reddish purple, skin thin, good. Georgia Experiment Station.

Dulcet—midseason, reddish purple, skin medium thick, good. Georgia Experiment Station.

Higgins—midseason, bronze, skin medium thick but tender, good, very large fruit. Georgia Experiment Station.

Hunt—early, black, skin fairly thin, excellent quality. Georgia Experiment Station.

Scuppernong—early, green to bronze, skin fairly thick and tough, quality very good. Discovered in the wild, North Carolina.

Tarheel—midseason, small, black, thin skin, very good. Perfect flowered. U.S.D.A.

Topsail—midseason, green to light bronze, skin medium thick, tough, good. U.S.D.A.

Wallace—midseason to late, yellow to bronze, skin thin, sweet. Perfect flowered. U.S.D.A.

Yuga—late, reddish amber, skin thin, very good. Georgia Experiment Station.

The muscadine varieties not specifically listed as perfect flowered are pistillate and will require a pollinator, which may be one of the perfect flowered sorts.

VINIFERA GRAPE VARIETIES

Black Monukka—early, reddish black, seedless, excellent quality. Originated in India. Prune to spurs or cordon.

Cardinal—very early, dark red, large, slight muscat flavor, very good. U.S.D.A. (Fresno, California.)

Delight—very early, fruit resembles Thompson Seedless, with a muscat flavor. California Experiment Station. Should be spur pruned. For California valleys and lower foothills.

Muscat Hamburg—midseason, reddish black, sweet, distinct muscat flavor. For interior and intermediate valleys and lower foothills in California. Probably originated in England. Requires spur pruning.

Muscat of Alexandria—late midseason, large, dull green, strongly muscat flavored, for hot, warm valleys, but not desert heat. Probably originated in Africa. Spur pruning required.

Pearl of Csaba—very early, yellowish white, muscat flavor, very good. Prune to spurs.

Ribier—early midseason, very large, black, very good. For interior valleys in California. Prune to cordon.

Scarlet—midseason, black, sweet, good for sweet grape juice. California Experiment Station.

Thompson Seedless—also known as Sultanina, early, light golden yellow, seedless, very good. Probably originated in Persia. Cane pruning required.

GRAPES AS LANDSCAPE MATERIAL. Where grapes are desired solely for fruit, a row or more in the garden or at the edge of the orchard will be the proper way to handle them. This row, in the way it is trellised, trained, pruned, and cultivated is essentially the same as a row in a commercial planting. There are certain landscape considerations around the home, however, and a row of grapes, even though designed primarily for fruit, may as well be located where it will be the most pleasant to look at. Certainly one would not want it across an area where there is a nice view, as it would provide an efficient screen during most of the summer. By the same token if there is an undesirable view, then the placing of the grape trellis across that view is worth considering, so that it may be either screened out, or at least so subdued that one thinks, not of the unpleasant view beyond, but of the green of the grapes in the foreground. And so one landscape use is as a screen.

There is always need for climbing vines around the home—to cover an old building, or an old dead stump of a tree, or perhaps a fence which is not particularly decorative in itself. The grape provides a vigorous, rampant growing vine which will cover in a relatively short time. Of course it is not evergreen, and the screening effect is primarily during the summer months, but that is when it is most important.

FOR SHADE. Grapes have been used for shade, at least in this country, from the very beginning, and quite possibly in olden times as well, for the poets write about sitting under a vine as a kind of symbol of the idyllic existence. The early settlers of America, at least in the areas I knew as a boy, usually had a family pump at the back of the house which needed some sort of shelter, and the grapevine, or rather several vines growing on an "arbor," was used extensively. Usually the vines were trained up the sides and across the top of the wooden trellis so that the area was quite completely screened in. This gave protection against wind, and to some extent against rain, and certainly to a great extent against the heat of the sun. In many parts of the country the grape arbor was the summer sitting room of that day, the forerunner of our outdoor living rooms and patios, which still occasionally have a grape arbor as an important element.

In the South the muscadine plants were often placed at some little distance from the house and trained on an overhead trellis made of wire, or boards, or both, so that the grapes could be permitted to fall under the trellis and be picked up in the shade. I have seen trellises like this, covered by one or two vines which extended over an immense area, perhaps 50 to 60 feet square.

The vinifera varieties vary a great deal in their fruiting habits and tendency to vine. Many of them are grown commercially without any trellis at all, being pruned back to self-supporting stumps each year, obviously not a very decorative thing for the home garden. However, other varieties do range much more widely, and can be used for covering a trellis for shade, or for screening, or for any other similar purpose. As a matter of fact, some of the largest vines in the world are undoubtedly of the species vinifera. We read of some in the Old Country of great age covering half an acre or more.

PROPAGATION BY CUTTINGS. Propagation of the grape is normally by cuttings taken during the winter. These are made from one-year-old canes, which are well matured and of medium size, usually about the thickness of a lead pencil. This simply means that the weak-growing, spindly canes and the overly vigorous, so-called bull canes are not ideal for cuttings. Usually the cuttings are of two or three nodes, in those varieties where the nodes, or buds, are 6 to 8 inches apart. With varieties that have shorter joints more buds per cutting would be called for.

Suppose we consider a cane some 8 or 9 feet long of a variety like Concord. Toward the base of the cane the buds will be close together, perhaps less than an inch apart for the first two, and 2 or 3 inches for the next, then increasing to 6 and possibly 8 or 9 inches. If we are making cuttings of the entire cane, then the one from the base of the cane might include as many as four nodes, some others three, and others two, so that all the cuttings will run from about 8 inches to a foot in length. The buds near the tip of the cane tend to be closer together than those near the midpoint, but are inclined to be weak and immature. The terminal 20 to 25 per cent of the cane is usually discarded as being poor cutting wood.

The basal cut is made just below a node, as that is where the roots will most easily be formed. The distal end of the cutting is usually made about an inch beyond the upper node. This is partly to identify the two ends, so that if they get mixed up as they are being made there will be no likelihood of their being put in the nursery row upside down. As is usual with cuttings, if they are put in upside down they will fail to root.

PROVIDING BOTTOM HEAT. A time-honored method of handling the cuttings is to tie them in bundles, with the butts of the cuttings together, and then bury the bundles upside down in a place where the soil is rather light and warm. They should be buried deeply enough so that there will be about 2 inches of soil over the base of the cuttings. If the cuttings are made about midwinter they should be buried as soon as the ground can be worked and left buried upside down for at least three or four weeks, or until conditions are favorable for lining out in the nursery. The purpose of burying the cuttings in this way is twofold. First it provides a cool moist place to store them until it is time to put them out in the open field, where they are usually rooted. In the second place, it provides a natural bottom heat, as the surface of the soil warms up considerably more than that further down, so we have a desirable situation, warmer where the roots are desired, and cooler, to hold back development of the buds, at the other ends of the cuttings.

When the soil is ready to work, the cuttings may be placed in a nursery row, right side up, and deep enough so that the top bud is just above the surface of the ground. A common fault is to insert the cuttings only about halfway. This may not get the base of the cutting down where the soil will remain damp all summer, and more of it is in the open air to be dried out by wind and sun.

Single bud cuttings can be made. These have about an inch of cane on either side of the node and are dropped in a shallow trench and covered completely.

LAYERING. A good way for the home gardener to propagate a grapevine or two is by layering. The long canes are ideal for bending down to the ground and covering with soil. It helps to make a cut on the underside of the cane, right at a node if possible, at the point where it is to be buried. There should be at least 3 or 4 inches of soil above the cane at this point, so that it will not dry out. After roots are formed, which should be within a few months, the entire layer can be removed from the mother plant and set out in its new location.

GRAFTING. Grapes may be grafted, and as a matter of fact very commonly are, in the commercial grape regions of California, to provide a root system resistant to phylloxera. The home gardener, however, will probably seldom have occasion to try out his skill as a grafter on grapes. If he does, the scions may be whip grafted onto small seedling stocks, or may be top worked onto older vines during late winter. In the latter case the vine is cut off at ground level, split, and a scion, cut to wedge shape, inserted so cambium layer of stock and scion will be in contact. Usually the spring of the split stump will hold the scion firmly enough so that it will not have to be tied or waxed. The soil may be pulled up over the stump to prevent drying out.

PLANTS AND PLANTING. Grapes may be planted either in the fall or early spring, the latter being perhaps the preferred time. Most nurseries offer either one- or two-year-old plants. Probably the best plant is a real good one-year-old, as it has to be really vigorous if it is big enough to sell at that age. A good, vigorous, cutting-grown plant, by the time it is two years old, will have a very long cane which will probably be branched in several places. The nurseryman will cut this back in order to handle it more easily, and while it would be satisfactory it would probably be no better than a one-year-old plant.

At planting time the usual procedure is to prune the top to one cane, the best one, of course, if there are two or more, and then shorten it to two buds. This takes practically all of the top, at least in the eyes of the home gardener who is not used to pruning grapes. There should be a good root system, which it would be better to spread out in a hole, rather than planting with a spade as was described for raspberries and strawberries.

The roots may be quite long, depending on how well the plant was grown and how carefully it was dug. Usually they may be shortened to a length of 6 inches, which means when spread out they will fit in a hole a little over a foot in diameter. There is probably little point in leaving them longer, as, in the process of digging, the fibrous roots and the root hairs will have been broken off anyway and they will have to be regenerated. If the main roots are left 2 feet long, most of the regeneration will occur out at the ends of those roots; if only 6 inches long it will still occur at the ends of the roots. After the vine is set it would be desirable to water it in, if possible, and perhaps put a little fertilizer on the soil surface around the plant. This latter will depend entirely on the nature of the soil in which you are planting.

At planting time one is always inclined to wonder how long he will have to wait to harvest some fruit to pay for his labors. Grapes will not be quite as prompt in this repayment as the small fruits. However, there should be a little fruit the second season, more the third season, and a full crop the fourth season if all goes well.

SOME FACTORS AFFECTING PRUNING. Before planting, the gardener has probably decided how he intends to train his vines. That is, whether they will be cut back every year to a stump which will stand up of its own accord, or will be tied to a stake or to some type of wire trellis or arbor. Since the type of trellis and the pruning system are very closely interrelated, a discussion of pruning will probably throw a little light on the training problem, a subject which covers the type of support used and shaping the vine to make the best use of that support.

Grapes are borne on the current season's growth which, after developing blossom clusters at two or three or four nodes near the base, may continue on to produce a cane several feet in length. These canes the following spring are known as one-year-old canes, and it is from them that new shoots will develop, produce fruit and more canes. After the cane is more than a year old it develops

These Delaware grapes are ripening uniformly because the vine had been pruned to limit its crop to the optimum number of bunches.

fibrous bark and is easily distinguished. This older growth, usually known as an arm, does not produce buds, except occasionally adventitious buds when heavily cut back.

The problem then, at pruning time, is to leave enough buds on one-year-old wood to produce the fruit desired for the season. One might say, if that is true, why not leave all of them and get a maximum amount of fruit? Actually a very heavy yield can be obtained in this way, but if it is beyond the capability of the plant to mature, the fruit will not ripen and will be relatively worthless. Furthermore, the vine, in putting all of its energy into the development of this excess crop of fruit, will make very poor shoot growth so that there will be a lack of good canes for the following year.

Grape pruning, therefore, becomes a matter of finding the proper balance between fruit production and cane production and pruning so as to maintain that balance. It has been studied enough so that it has become something of a science. With a particular variety, on a particular soil, and at a particular cultural level, the grower knows that he can leave just so many buds on a vigorous vine to get a maximum yield and at the same time sufficient growth for adequate renewal canes for the following year.

HOW TO JUDGE THE SEVERITY OF PRUNING. For the less experienced grape grower there are schedules which will enable him to judge how many buds he should leave on vines with different rates of growth. The rate of growth may be calculated by the number of pounds of prunings to be removed. It may sound like an impossible thing to weigh the prunings to find out how many buds to leave or, to put it another way, how much to prune. Actually, the pruner estimates about how many buds he should leave and then prunes a few vines and weighs the prunings. Then he can estimate other vines and prune them on the basis of the weighing of the few criterion plants. In New York State the following schedule is recommended for the Concord variety. If weight of cane prunings is less than 1 pound, leave less than thirty buds; if 1 pound, leave thirty buds; if 2 pounds, leave forty buds; if 3 pounds, leave fifty buds; if 4 pounds, leave sixty buds; if more than 4 pounds, leave more than sixty buds.

Others have based the number of buds to leave on the number of long canes and the total number of canes. Actually, most grape growers do this judging or estimating subconsciously, and simply prune more severely where the growth is poor or weak, thus cutting down on the potential crop, and encouraging the plant to get back into a vigorous condition. The more vigorous plants are capable of maturing more fruits, and so more buds are left.

Total number of buds is one very important part of the picture, but another part is: just what types of buds should be left, and where are they to be located. There are two general methods of pruning involving this distribution of buds. One is called the spur system, in which a number of canes are cut back to spurs, 3 or 4 inches in length, each carrying a definite number of buds, usually two or possibly three. If one leaves two-bud spurs, therefore, and wants forty buds on a particular vine, he leaves twenty spurs, as simple as that.

With a good many varieties, however, better fruit will be produced from buds out beyond the base of the cane. That is, if we prune a cane to ten buds, and weigh the fruit, and count the number of bunches produced from the shoots coming from each of those ten buds, we will find that the best clusters and the most fruit are produced, not on the first two buds, but out at buds three, four, five and six, and even beyond. That means, that if we cut to two bud spurs we will be saving the poorer producing buds. Actually, if we are interested only in weight of fruit, for juice, or jelly, or wine, then the size of cluster doesn't make very much difference, and we can leave enough two-bud spurs to be sure that we get the maximum amount of fruit that the vine can mature. However, if we want to have large, attractive-looking clusters for dessert purposes, then we are interested in leaving buds that will produce clusters of maximum size.

THE CANE RENEWAL SYSTEM. Apparently, many of the vinifera varieties do fairly well in producing good clusters from spur pruning. However, Concord and related varieties and some viniferas seem to do somewhat better with the so-called cane renewal pruning. There are, of course, many factors involved in this choice of pruning systems. For one thing, if a vine of the Concord type is pruned to spurs for a few years, there is a tendency for the fruiting wood to be moved further and further out from the trunk, and there will be a considerable amount of older wood, which soon becomes weakened.

The most common system of pruning, for the Concord-type varieties, is known as the four-cane Kniffin system. This involves a trellis of two wires, one about 5 feet high and the other halfway between the top wire and the ground, supported by posts every 12 to 16 feet. The vines are trained so that they will have a straight trunk, reaching to the top wire, and a one-year-old cane extending in each direction on each wire, making four canes in all. This is developed as follows: Prune to two buds at planting time, one cane to the top wire at the end of one year's growth, and the 4 arms at the end of the second year. If growing conditions are such that growth may be rather slow, it will likely take a year longer to develop the vine to the four-arm stage.

RENEWAL SPURS. In order to provide a source of renewal canes near the trunk for the next year, when pruning a mature vine, four spurs are ordinarily left, one near each of the canes. If this is not done, the more vigorous shoots, suitable for renewal canes, will be

A grape vine, American type, which has made a fairly vigorous growth on a Kniffin trellis.

produced out near the ends of the arms, and each year the fruiting wood will get further away from the trunk. The further away it gets, the less productive it is likely to become, and certainly the more complicated management would be, as the canes from one vine would grow over, and even beyond, the vines on either side. By leaving a spur, usually on the main trunk if possible, a good vigorous shoot is usually produced, since the cane had been cut back so severely to form the two-bud spur. Each year then, the cane which has produced fruit is removed, with all of its branches, and a new cane is laid down, having been produced from one of the spurs or sometimes from a cane near the base of a previous year's fruiting cane. Sometimes it is impossible to find renewal spurs on the main trunk and one may have to go out somewhat further on the fruiting arm. Perhaps a year or two later an adventitious bud may develop on the main trunk, and that shoot can be spurred back and used to provide a fruiting cane, thus getting back near the trunk.

The vine pictured on page 314 after pruning. Note the four canes and the four renewal spurs from which will come the four arms a year later.

MODIFICATIONS OF THE KNIFFIN SYSTEM. There are other systems of pruning which may be used with the Kniffin trellis. One may even use the spur system, or a fan system, in which canes are simply fanned out without any very definite order, or one may make a fan of three, four, or five fruiting canes and plan to renew them each year. There are various other systems which have been tried out, but almost all experiments have indicated that the Kniffin system, as described, is more satisfactory for this particular type of grape. Some people may prefer to use a single wire, training only one cane in each direction on this wire, or they may train two canes in each direction on the same wire. The objection to having two canes together is that the clusters will be more or less intertwined with the growing shoots, and more difficult to pick. Where only one cane is trained on a wire, the clusters hang free and can be cut loose at picking time without being so entangled that the berries will be crushed as they are picked.

Occasionally, a three-wire trellis has been used. Arbors or ornamental trellises usually go considerably above the normal 5 feet suggested for the Kniffin trellis, which requires the leaving of as many as eight arms on the various elements of the trellis. The difficulty with this is that the more vigorous growth will be made toward the top, and it will eventually be difficult to find good renewal canes near the bottom. Furthermore, if a vine appears able to produce fruit efficiently from forty buds, and eight canes are desired, that means only five buds to a cane or even less if we count the buds on the renewal spurs. Where grapes are used primarily for shelter of an outdoor living area, or to cover a building, or something of that kind, one may sacrifice quality of fruit for foliage and leave more buds, getting more fruit but of poorer quality. Quality could be maintained by thinning out part of the clusters soon after blossoming.

When a young vine starts to grow it is quite general practice to put a stake by it and tie it to that stake, as the trellis may not be built for another year or two. If the plants are to be trained to the spur system they may be left permanently on stakes. There are certain varieties which seem to do fairly well trained in this way. None of the Eastern-type varieties, however, are well adapted to being pruned to unsupported stumps, as may be done with certain vinifera varieties.

PRUNING THE MUSCADINE VARIETY. The muscadine varieties may be grown on a Kniffin type of trellis, and are able to carry a somewhat larger number of buds than the Concord type. From what I have seen in years past in the South, the more common method of handling these, for the home garden, has been the large overhead arbor. The vines are allowed to grow on such a support with very little pruning, since the berries are to be permitted to drop to the ground to be used for juice. Apparently it is not so important that vigor be revived by severe pruning as it is with other kinds of grapes.

PRUNING THE VINIFERA VARIETIES. Certain vigorous-growing vinifera varieties may also be trained on such an overhead trellis, if one wants to cover a courtyard or outdoor living room. However, if the vine is planted primarily for fruit, rather severe pruning will be advisable. Depending on the variety, as previously indicated, no trellis may be used, or the plant may be tied to a single stake and headed back to half a dozen spurs each year. Other varieties seem to do better by being trained to four arms as suggested for the Concord type.

TIME FOR PRUNING. Much has been written about the time of pruning grapes. It is a well-observed phenomenon that grapes pruned late in the spring will "bleed." That is, sap will drop from the wounds, sometimes in practically a steady stream. This has been considered by some garden writers as very devitalizing, and the statement made that the vines "will bleed to death." Actually, this bleeding seems to have very little harmful effect on the vine. Most of the liquid that comes out is simply water from the roots, with a little sugar and other material dissolved in it. Certainly there is nothing comparable to the bleeding of an animal, where there is only a limited amount of blood, and where severe damage or death will occur if a very large portion of it is lost.

It may be somewhat better to prune during the winter or very early in the spring than to prune late enough so that the vines will bleed. However, it is certainly better to prune late than not to prune at all, because the grape is one fruit which does require rather severe pruning, and annual pruning, in order to maintain reasonable vigor and productiveness. I recall a series of experiments conducted at one of the experiment stations a few years ago, in which grapevines were pruned every month in the year. There was very little effect on productiveness or vigor, in the long run, which could be attributed to late spring pruning. Where winter weather is severe it is better to prune in the spring than in the fall. This will give an opportunity first to remove injured canes and then select renewal canes and spurs from wood that was not damaged.

SUMMER PRUNING. Some people have done summer pruning with the idea of admitting more light to the fruit. It is a well-known fact that fruits such as apples must have light to color up. Occasionally people cut their initials out of black paper and paste them on a green apple so that it will develop a red color around the initials in green. It is not surprising then that people have the idea that the development of color in any fruits is dependent on light. That is not true with grapes, as they will develop color even in a black paper bag. Actually, the use of paper bags to protect clusters of grapes from insects and diseases used to be quite common.

Certainly it is not necessary to pick off the leaves, or defoliate the vine, in order to encourage grapes to color, even though they may be covered with a dense mat of foliage. As a matter of fact, the results obtained will be exactly the opposite of those desired. The coloring matter in grapes is carbohydrate in nature, hence manufactured in the leaves and not brought in from the soil. Reducing the leaf surface will delay maturity and development of color pigment and result in a lower sugar content. This is quite evident when the vine has been defoliated by Japanese beetles, or by leaf hoppers, or by any other pest or disease. Cutting the leaves off with a knife has exactly the same effect.

I realize that certain well-trained private gardeners have, for years, followed the practice, on certain varieties, of cutting off the tips of the growing shoots at perhaps the fourth node beyond a cluster. I doubt if their tipping has resulted in better size or color, but it has probably not been harmful. As the tipping has been done while the shoots were relatively young, branching was induced, so that, in the long run, the leaf surface per cluster was about as large as if the tipping had not been carried out.

SOIL MANAGEMENT. In commercial vineyards grapes are ordinarily cultivated. They do not seem to take too kindly to sod culture, which, under certain soil conditions, is commonly practiced for some of the tree fruits. One of the difficulties with sod would be the mowing in between the rows of vines which are usually not more than 9 feet apart, and often less. The closeness of the rows also poses somewhat of a problem for cultivation. In the home garden it can be accomplished by using a small garden tractor, or Rotavator, plus a little hand hoeing around the vines and around the posts. For commercial vineyards, there are certain implements which enable one to guide a tractor-drawn blade in under the trellis, and close to the vines, while riding along on the implement.

Cover cropping is common practice in commercial vineyards, probably not resulting in a great increase in organic matter, but certainly helping to maintain the current level, and also helping to prevent erosion during the winter, and having other beneficial effects. Grapes adapt themselves to mulching, although, because of their deep roots, they are probably benefitted to a less extent than some of the small fruits. In other words, if a limited amount of mulch is available it would probably be better used on the small fruits than on the grapes.

As has already been mentioned, grapes are adapted to a rather dry soil, so less irrigation is needed than with most of the other fruits. However, extreme dry weather will definitely affect the crop and the shoot growth, which in turn affects next year's crop, and so, if your grape soil becomes exceedingly dry, adding water is certainly desirable.

MAINTAIN SOIL FERTILITY. The discussion of pruning brought out the fact that that operation is a matter of regulating vegetative growth, so that it will be in balance with fruit production. The more severe the pruning, the better will be the vegetative growth, and the smaller the crop; less severe pruning will result in more fruit and less vegetative growth. However, soil fertility, including the use of fertilizer if needed, plays its normal role with grapes, as with other plants. That is, if you have a rather poor soil, you can probably grow grapes fairly vigorously by very heavy pruning, but your yield will be relatively low. By increasing the fertility of the soil, you can leave more buds at pruning time, get a larger crop, and still have good cane growth.

On most soils where grapes are grown commercially the use of a nitrogen fertilizer has seemed to be desirable. A complete mixture, such as a 5-10-5, may be better in soils which normally respond to the use of phosphorus and potassium, especially if a cover crop is being grown. Since the root system of the grape, or much of it at least, is at considerable depth, it may not be so easy to influence immediately the growth of the plant by the use of fertilizers. Rather one should work out the long-term plan which seems best, and follow it, even though it may be difficult to be sure of the results obtained from any one application.

GRAPES UNDER GLASS. A century ago there was considerable interest in the production of grapes under glass in this country, as well as in Europe. That interest has lagged, and is now found only on a few of the larger estates, where there are ample greenhouse facilities and gardeners to do the necessary work. A book such as this, a hundred years ago, would have devoted half, or perhaps more than half, of its space on grapes to their culture in the greenhouse, or grapery as it was called. Growing grapes in a glass house was quite a ritual. Books of that day give detailed directions for planting, pruning, pinching back, and for heating and ventilating. This was based, not on research, of course, but on practical experience handed down from gardener to apprentice, from generation to generation. These were cool greenhouses, ordinarily, often just a glass house with little or no artificial heat.

There are several reasons why grapes were grown under glass to such an extent then and not now. At that time there were no good varieties of American grapes that could be grown out-of-doors along the North Atlantic Coast, where the centers of population were located. Accordingly, those who wanted grapes tried to grow the European sorts, and they were too tender to take the outside temperature. Furthermore, there was no grape industry in California to ship fancy dessert varieties to the East, so that they could be obtained at any corner grocery. If one wanted dessert grapes he had to produce them himself. It was also a time of more gracious living, or at least more expansive living.

The cool greenhouses were also devoted to peaches, apricots, melons, strawberries, and other things which were particularly desirable "out of season." Such houses were not particularly productive per square foot, as we think of modern commercial greenhouses. Therefore, they were relatively expensive to build and maintain, and the increasing cost of labor and materials and heating facilities have contributed to the dying out of this art of growing grapes under glass. There is little interest in it now, but I might just add that I have had Muscat of Alexandria grapes, greenhouse grown, given to me early in the summer, and they were excellent. I am sure they were the best grapes I have ever eaten. The bunches were very large and came packed in cotton in a cardboard box, somewhat like the florist uses to deliver a fine bouquet of flowers. There was a bouquet here also, but in this case the term refers to the aroma of the grapes, which was very rich and very pleasant.

DISEASES OF GRAPES

Black Rot: *Symptoms:* Of the various diseases affecting grapes the most serious one in the East and Middle West has been black rot. This is a fungus which causes dark purplish brown spots on the green berries, and eventually the berries shrivel up and "turn to raisins." However, don't be misled and try to eat one of these black rot mummies, for it will not be very tasty.

Control: The standard control method for black rot, for many years, has been Bordeaux mixture or other copper spray of similar attributes. Bordeaux mixture was discovered by a grower in France who mixed up the first lot to scare away prowlers, hoping to make them think that the vines were poisoned. It was observed that certain diseases were controlled, and so the material came to be used as a fungicide rather than a scarecrow. Ferbam may be used in place of Bordeaux mixture at the rate of 2 pounds per 100 gallons or 2 level tablespoonfuls per gallon. The most important times to spray for this disease are (1) when new shoots are 7–10 inches long (2) three to five days before bloom and (3) soon after the petals fall. Where the disease is hard to control, an additional spray may be made about ten days after (3). In the South black rot on bunch grapes may be somewhat more difficult to control and additional applications may be needed.

Virus Diseases: *Symptoms:* Recently, we are learning that there are virus diseases on grapes as there are on other plants, and quite likely they have done more damage than has been realized. The symptoms are not as well understood as they are with virus diseases of some of the berry crops. In the South a disease called Pierce's disease is now considered to be caused by a virus. This has killed the branches of vines and eventually the entire vine.

Control: At the present time there is no cure for these diseases. The only thing to do is to rogue out the diseased plants and thereby reduce the likelihood of infection of healthy plants.

Downy Mildew: *Symptoms:* A white, moldy growth appears on the leaves, which later turn brown and die. This is common in the East and Middle West.

Control: The Bordeaux mixture sprays suggested for black rot should control mildew also.

Powdery Mildew: *Symptoms:* This is a disease of both leaves and fruit in California, causing the leaves to turn brown and the infected grapes to become russeted on the surface and fail to mature.

Control: In the East the Bordeaux mixture sprays for black rot will keep it under control. In California frequent dusting with sulfur, beginning when the shoots are 6 to 8 inches long, is recommended.

DISEASES OF MUSCADINE GRAPES

This type of grape is usually grown successfully without spraying. Several diseases, especially foliage diseases, may be found, but they do not usually cause enough damage to warrant spraying. Where it is desirable to keep the foliage attractive in appearance, the use of a fungicide such as ferbam might be tried.

INSECT PESTS OF GRAPES

Leaf Hoppers: *Symptoms:* The leaves become pale, and close examination shows numerous yellowish white dots on the upper surface. Although these appear on the upper surface, which is the one you normally see, they are caused by leaf hoppers sucking the juice from under the spots and working from the underside of the leaf. Where this symptom occurs you can usually see plenty of hoppers by shaking the vines; if they are in the adult stage they will fly out in swarms. The younger leaf hoppers, however, do not fly, and so you may have to look on the underside of the leaf where you will see them running around. They are small, about the size of an aphid, but much more active.

Control: A contact spray such as Black Leaf 40 can be used if the air temperature is above 75 degrees F., but DDT or malathion are more effective. DDT, at the rate of 2 or 3 tablespoonfuls per gallon of water is the usual recommendation. Spray before the young hoppers acquire wings, or many will fly away as the sprayer approaches. It will be necessary of course to hit the underside of the leaf to kill the insects.

Brown Aphids: *Symptoms:* Rather conspicuous brown aphids may be found clustering at the tips of the canes during midsummer or later. Usually they are very numerous on a few tips but do not do much damage.

Control: Any contact insecticide will get them, such as malathion.

Root Aphids or Phylloxera: *Symptoms:* On eastern grapes, small galls, possibly an eighth of an inch in diameter, may be found, frequently several on the underside of a single leaf, of certain varieties. The aphids also attack the roots and causes them to be distorted and knobby, but injury to the eastern varieties has seldom been considered as very serious. It is possible that, under certain conditions, it does more damage than has been realized. On vinifera varieties, especially those growing on certain soils, the insect interferes with the functioning of the roots to the extent that the plants are very much weakened, and, if not killed, are practically worthless. This is a pest native to the eastern United States, which was taken to Europe, where it infested the vineyards, and probably from there came to our West Coast, where it caused very serious damage to the vinifera vineyards of California.

Control: Efforts to control phylloxera by chemical means have been unsatisfactory. However, a relatively simple treatment was found which, while it did not kill the insect, successfully circumvented it. It was found that certain American species of grapes were practically immune to attack by this pest. The simple expedient of grafting the susceptible vinifera varieties onto resistant American varieties did the trick. It was not as simple as all that, of course, because a great deal of work had to be done in testing out various possible understocks. Not only did the understock have to be vigorous and adaptable to a wide range of conditions, but it also had to be compatible with the varieties which it was proposed to graft on it. Vineyards on certain soils in many portions of California are producing successfully only because they are on resistant stocks. Most nurserymen who handle vinifera varieties will offer them grafted onto suitable rootstocks.

During the grafting experiments it developed that some vines, which had been relatively weak growing and not too productive, grew much better on the more vigorous stocks, even when phylloxera free. That gave an idea to researchers that possibly the American varieties, such as Concord, should be grafted, not because they were bothered by phylloxera but because more production might be obtained. It was found that vigorous rootstocks did give increased yields, on a number of varieties, particularly those like Campbell's Early, which on its own roots is a notoriously weak grower and much inclined to overbear unless severely pruned. As a general rule, however, varieties like Concord are still grown on their own roots, and seem to be quite productive and vigorous in that way.

Japanese Beetle: *Symptoms:* In certain sections of the East the Japanese beetle has been a rather important grape pest, feeding in great numbers on the foliage of certain varieties.

Control: Various types of repellents have been tried, but DDT has been found effective in controlling the beetle.

Grape Berry Moth: *Symptoms:* Greenish larvae, about ⅜ inch long, feed in the flower clusters and later in the berries. Several berries may be stuck together as the larva moves out of one into the others.

Control: Use DDT, 2 tablespoonfuls of 50 per cent wettable per gallon of water just before bloom, again after bloom, and 10 days later.

CHAPTER 19

What the Plant Breeders Are Accomplishing with Small Fruits

The home gardener who has grown, or even tasted, some of our best modern varieties may well ask the question, "Why bother with plant breeding to improve what seem to be almost perfect berry varieties?" That is a good question, but the plant breeders and the administrators of the research institutions which are doing the work have good reasons for continuing the research on breeding superior berry varieties.

There are many reasons for further breeding experiments. The first and best one, perhaps, being that no present variety is perfect. For that matter, no variety likely to be produced in the foreseeable future will be perfect either, so that improvement can be looked for about as long as the breeders want to continue their work. For the average home gardener most of the final decision as to whether a variety can be improved upon or not may be based on edible quality. That is rather natural, but we must remember that people's tastes vary. I used to work with a prominent plant breeder who preferred things much more acid than I did. The berries he selected as ideal were too acid for me, and the ones I liked were too flat, insipid, and sweet for his taste. That means that, in order to produce varieties which will be liked by everyone, we cannot rely on one best variety but will need an assortment of varieties to meet the various tastes.

MANY FACTORS AFFECT VALUE OF A VARIETY. When we get down to the fine points of breeding, it is obvious that there are many factors affecting the desirability of a variety. It is not only flavor we look for, but size and color as well. Even season of bloom is important, because an early-blooming variety in some cases may be much more subject to frost than one blooming later. Shipping quality perhaps doesn't appeal very much to the home gardener. However, good shipping quality might be defined as the ability to withstand rough handling and to keep in good edible condition over a long period. This is a valuable consideration even in the home garden, as there are many times when one would like to have the berries keep longer than they do. Our pickers, even though members of our own family, may not be too careful, and berries that do not bruise and rot quickly are of extra value, even in the home garden.

Of considerable importance is the season of ripening. One of the main reasons why berries are grown in the home garden is so fresh fruit will be available. Since berries will not keep very long, if we are going to eat fresh berries over a period of several days, or several weeks, it will involve the growing of early, midseason, and late-ripening varieties. One of the aims of the plant breeder, working with all kinds of fruits, is to extend the season of ripening, either at the beginning or end of the season.

THORNLESS BLACKBERRIES. Then there are many plant characters which may be improved; to take a very striking example, the thorns on blackberries. I can't imagine anyone wanting to punish himself by picking blackberries from thorny bushes, if he could get just as good fruit, and as much fruit, from plants without thorns. We do have a thornless type of the trailing Evergreen blackberry which is grown commercially on a wide scale, but it is a bud sport, with a thornless epidermis, and the seedlings are thorny. However the breeding of truly thornless blackberries is well under way and there is no reason why we may not have thornless varieties of all the blackberry types in the foreseeable future. The main problem is to find the first thornless plant, and one which is thornless genetically and not just a chimera with a thornless epidermis. The same thing might be said about the desirability of thornlessness for raspberries and gooseberries.

There are many plant characters less obvious than thorns. A very important one is relative hardiness. Many berries cannot be grown in the northern part of our country because they cannot stand the low winter temperatures. The breeding-in of greater resistance to low temperature, and also greater resistance to high summer temperature, are important factors in the breeding work at several experiment stations.

RESISTANCE TO PESTS. Another important phase of breeding is the attempt to produce varieties resistant to serious insects and diseases. This is a difficult problem because the disease organisms may not be present in sufficient numbers when the seedlings are ready to be selected. Sometimes artificial innoculation with the disease has to be resorted to in order to observe the resistance, if any. No matter how successful the chemists are in producing spray materials that will give better and better control of plant pests, it is still better to have varieties that are resistant to those pests. No spraying at all is certainly superior to spraying with even the best type of fungicide or insecticide.

Pests frequently occur in cycles. A berry grower, either home gardener or commercial, may have little trouble with a particular disease for four or five years, and then, because of some peculiar combination of environmental conditions, it may be extremely serious for a year or two. Probably he has saved money by not spraying, during the four or five disease-free years, even though he loses the year the disease is bad. However, if he had a disease-resistant variety it would be still better, and he would not have to worry about a bad disease year coming up.

There is little likelihood that the breeders will ever produce a

Small fruits plant breeders, C. D. Schwartze (left) and George M. Darrow (right) looking over some promising new raspberry selections.

variety that is resistant to all pests, because the pests tend to change over a long period, and even vary from year to year. This is true with both insects and diseases. It is rather well known for instance that certain insect pests of fruit trees have developed considerable resistance to DDT and certain other of the newer insecticides.

NEW DISEASES FROM OLD ONES. It is also known that diseases mutate or change in the same way as higher plants. This is well illustrated by the situation with respect to the red stele disease in strawberries. When red stele first appeared in this country only one variety, the Aberdeen, seemed to have any appreciable amount of resistance. Based on breeding with Aberdeen, it was not too long before varieties apparently completely resistant to red stele were found. Within a few years, however, some of these varieties began to show symptoms of the disease. Careful tests indicated that the organism itself had changed, and that there was a new strain to which the supposedly resistant varieties were not actually resistant. Then varieties resistant to the two strains were developed, but more recently there are indications that there is a third strain.

It is evident that we can never be sure that a variety resistant to a disease will always continue resistant, because of the possibility of mutations in the disease itself. There are no indications that a variety loses any of its inherent resistance, but rather that the disease itself changes by mutation or hybridization. This means that a plant-breeding project may profitably go on almost indefinitely, or in some cases that the industry simply cannot afford to let it stop.

We can always imagine improvements in size, color, firmness, and quality. As a matter of fact, certain flavors, aromas, or other characters may appear in plants which are entirely unthought of at the present time. But most important is the fact that the breeder must watch for the changes in diseases and insects, and the appearance of new pests from other countries, or from goodness knows where. As soon as a new disease appears, the breeder must immediately try to find some plant, somewhere in the world, which has some resistance, even though it may be almost worthless otherwise, and then go on from there.

RESISTANCE TO NEMATODES. Our knowledge of nematodes is increasing rapidly, but we do not have much, if anything, in the way of small-fruit varieties which are resistant to nematodes. Eventually the breeders will probably provide some of these resistant types, but the nematodes may mutate, and the breeders then will practically have to start over. This is by no means a bleak or hopeless project, and we should not necessarily think of it as a continuous battle for survival in keeping ahead of these harmful pests. As a matter of fact, the increases in productiveness, in flavor, shipping quality, hardiness, and many other qualities which appear in the breeders' plots are undoubtedly sufficient to more than pay for all of the effort and expense put into these breeding projects. This is in addition to the resistance to pests, which might be considered as the most important long-range objective of small fruits breeding.

BERRY BREEDING AND THE HOME GARDENER. It might be thought from the above that the breeding work should be done in, and financed by, the states where commercial berry culture is an important part of the state economy. This is not necessarily true. Some of the best breeding work, and most profitable in many ways, has been done in those states where certain types of berries did not grow and produce satisfactorily enough to encourage the development of a commercial industry. These states have developed breeding projects, in many cases, so that their own residents could grow berries in varieties and qualities which were previously impossible, because of too cold or too hot weather, or some other environmental factor. It is true, of course, that some of the biggest breeding projects have been in the important berry-producing states, and that is also logical. Some projects have been aimed directly at producing better varieties for the home gardener, but many good home garden berries have been developed by breeders whose primary objective was varieties for commercial planting.

STRAWBERRY BREEDING. By far the largest number of breeding projects with small fruits is with strawberries, which is rather logical, since they are so universally grown and liked. As a matter of fact, a large number of the states of the nation have official experiment station strawberry-breeding projects, both in commercial strawberry states and in others where strawberries are grown very little. There would be little point in including a list of these states, as these projects occasionally lapse and new ones may be started. However, if you are interested in new varieties of strawberries, or any of the other berries for that matter, it would be desirable to keep in close touch with your experiment station and find out when new introductions are being made.

There will be field days or other opportunities for you to see some of the newer things before they are actually made available for general distribution. In this way you will have some basis for evaluating the new varieties and determining whether you should substitute them for older standard sorts that you are already growing. Just a hint at this point would be that, if you have a variety which you like very well, and are well satisfied with its performance, then perhaps it would be better to stick to it. Sometimes a new variety is introduced because of some degree of disease resistance, or hardiness, or other factors which might not apply to your particular garden. A variety of the desired flavor and edible quality, and which you are able to grow fairly easily, is the thing to be desired.

BREEDING OTHER SMALL FRUITS. Fewer states are involved in the breeding of raspberries. Some of the leading ones are New York, Washington, Oregon, North Carolina, Maryland, and Illinois.

Strawberry crosses can most easily be made on potted plants in the greenhouse. Here the flowers are being emasculated, pollen-bearing anthers removed with forceps. The bottle contains alcohol for sterilizing the forceps.

Blackberry breeding is also restricted to a few states including New York, Oregon, New Jersey, and others.

Comparatively little breeding has been done with currants and gooseberries. The Minnesota Experiment Station has done some work with both, introducing the Red Lake currant variety, which is now well known.

Blueberry breeding has been under way in the Department of Agriculture for many years, often in co-operation with workers in the various states. There are breeding projects in New Jersey, North Carolina, Michigan, Washington, Georgia, and possibly other states.

Grape breeding has been carried out by the U.S.D.A. and in California, New York, North Carolina, South Carolina, Mississippi, Minnesota, and others.

In naming the above states where breeding projects are carried on, no attempt has been made to compile a complete list, but simply to indicate certain states which have been involved in this work for some time, and to give an idea of the importance of this type of work in the agricultural research of the nation.

ARE NEW VARIETIES REALLY BETTER? In general, the new varieties which have been introduced are improvements on the old ones, usually with respect to edible quality, as well as other characters. However, new varieties are not necessarily better than old ones, from the consumer's standpoint. A good example of this is the Cuthbert raspberry, which, for many years, was the standard variety in the Northwest. It has qualities which made it a very desirable variety for processing. Newer varieties have largely supplanted it, but many processors would still like to get the Cuthbert if they could be assured of a sufficient supply. In other words, newer varieties have been planted because they were more resistant to certain diseases, or more productive, and not necessarily of better edible quality.

SOME ACCOMPLISHMENTS. A book could be written about what has been accomplished in the field of small-fruits breeding, although it is not intended to give any general survey of the specific accomplishments at this time. However, a mere glance at the list of varieties of small fruits and grapes now being grown commercially, and offered for sale, will illustrate that the accomplishments have been very solid and extensive. It is true that there is commercial production of a few varieties which originated in the wild and were simply discovered by some lucky person. Some of our blackberries are in that category. In the raspberry field, however, especially red raspberries, the varieties now being grown, both home garden and commercial, are almost entirely the result of plant-breeding projects.

In the case of strawberries we find the same situation. The Blakemore, for instance, has been the leading variety of the entire country, in acreage. It is the result of breeding work by the U.S.D.A. Practically all the important varieties now are the product of breeding projects, mostly from the U.S.D.A. or experiment stations. There are some private strawberry breeders, and one variety, Howard 17, or Premier, from a private breeder has been a very important variety for many years.

Only one blueberry variety, Rubel, is still being grown as a representative of berries introduced from the wild. At first only wild selections were planted and a dozen or more were named, but practically all these have disappeared from commercial plantings, although still to be found in some home gardens, or more rarely in a commercial field where the grower has not gotten around to taking them out. This is rather rapid development when we consider that blueberry culture started only about forty years ago, based first on wild selections, now almost completely shifted to hybrids of known parentage. Rubel has had qualities of production and behavior which are important to persist so long. However, some of the newer varieties are definitely superior, and Rubel will very likely bow out of the picture as the present plantings become old and less productive.

HOW A PLANT BREEDER WORKS. Perhaps it would be of interest to indicate how a plant breeder works, since there are various conceptions of this particular field of activity. Some may think of plant breeding as the application of genetics to plants, involving a very technical study of chromosomes. Certainly there is a large volume of genetic literature dealing with plants, with their chromosome numbers and behavior as affecting inheritance. Some of this material is extremely technical, and prospective breeders may be overwhelmed by its extent and character. However, we should consider plant breeding as touching both the fields of genetics and horticulture. Actually some plant breeders have had a relatively meager knowledge of genetics and still have produced superior varieties.

Many times breeders have simply had to take the best varieties they could find of a particular fruit, and those which contained specific characters wanted in so far as possible, and intercross them. Usually such crosses have been of some value and have yielded either superior selections, or types which had characters indicating value for further crossing. A major part of the breeding work with fruits has been the selection of superior seedlings, which has required horticultural, rather than genetic, proficiency. This is particularly true where one is breeding for disease resistance, hardiness, or other physiological characters, where extensive tests have to be set up and carried out before final selection can be made. Selecting simply for size, color, and flavor of fruit is reasonably easy. Once you have a plant of the type you want, it can be increased to an infinite number by asexual propagation. Of course you may find that it is especially susceptible to disease, or lacking in hardiness, but if you can eventually determine that all of the more or less intangible physiological characters, which cannot be seen, are satisfactory, then you may consider that you have accomplished your purpose.

There is no doubt that the raising of large numbers of seedlings from crosses between two good varieties is a good way to produce superior new varieties of small fruits, a shotgun method to a certain extent but effective in the long run. There is no doubt either that very large numbers will have to be raised, and that they will have to be sorted out and culled down by horticulturists who know the older varieties, so that they can determine whether or not these new ones are as good as the old ones, or possibly better. This is not to say that genetic experiments are of no value with the small fruits. It is simply to say that such genetic research is more difficult than it is with certain annual plants which have small chromosome numbers, and chromosomes which are fairly readily seen under the microscope. Up to the present time I believe most breeders have felt that they could make more progress with small fruits by the method suggested than by studying chromosomes and genetic ratios. This method of approach may lead just so far, and, from there on, progress may have to wait on more detailed genetic and physiological studies.

CHROMOSOMES AND GENES. Without attempting to give a detailed discussion, it might be worth while to explain very briefly what chromosomes are and how this knowledge may be used in improving plants. Briefly, chromosomes are very tiny, rod-shaped, or irregularly shaped, bits of dense material within the nucleus that is present in each cell of plant or animal. At certain stages in the development of a plant cell these chromosomes may be seen and counted if properly stained, and the number and character typical of the species determined. Presumably the genetic factors which determine the heredity of any living organism are carried in these chromosomes. The factors themselves, or rather the genes which control these factors, are so small that ordinarily they cannot be seen with the ordinary microscope.

By correlating the behavior of the chromosomes with the expression of certain genetic characters such as, for instance, color of flower, it has been possible to work out a rather detailed explanation of how genetic factors are distributed. All of this is based more or less on circumstantial evidence, but is logical and meaningful, so has come to be accepted as presumably the correct theory.

THE BASIC THEORY OF INHERITANCE. This theory is that each gene controls some one characteristic. For instance, Mendel, in his classic work with peas, found some with wrinkled and some with smooth seeds. Apparently in this case the character of the seed coat was controlled by one gene, and there were no in-betweens; that is, the seeds were either all wrinkled or all smooth. In the same way there were genes for dwarfness and tallness and, in his early work at least, there were no intermediates. The tall character was dominant and dwarfness recessive, and so when he crossed a tall and dwarf all of the seedlings were tall; but when he selfed that generation the seedlings were one quarter dwarf and three quarters tall.

As time went on more characteristics were studied, many of which were apparently governed by several different factors. As a matter of fact, with many plants, if you were to select a very large growing seedling and cross it with a very dwarf seedling, you would get many gradations in between. The theory is that these differences are due, not to one contrasting pair of factors, but to a number, each of which may add something to the expression of a particular character. It has been found also that certain genes may not have any visible character expression of their own, but modify a character primarily controlled by some other gene. There are many other rather complicated gene interrelationships.

With the small fruits, few genes have been found to govern simple pairs of contrasting visible characters. The offspring are usually intermediate with respect to most characters found in the parents. This means that, if one wants to produce larger berries, he must find a very large-fruited variety to start with, or preferably two large-fruited berries. When these are crossed, most of the progeny will be somewhat intermediate, but there will be some smaller, and possibly a few larger. The latter, if they have other good characters, might be selected for testing, or for further breeding to increase size still more.

INHERITANCE COMPLEX IN THE SMALL FRUITS. Presumably one of the reasons why evidence of simple contrasting characters is so uncommon in the berry crops is that many of them have very high chromosome numbers. For instance, the strawberry is a polyploid, and more specifically an octoploid; that is, it has eight sets of seven chromosomes in each cell, in contrast to the normal two sets. This results in complex genetic ratios in hybrid offspring. For instance if we are concerned with one particular unit character, then the pair of genes governing that character occur not in just one pair of chromosomes, but actually in four pairs, so when two plants are crossed there may be a number of combinations of dominant and recessive genes.

The chromosome number is high in the brambles also, ranging from well over one hundred to a minimum of about forty-eight. The lowbush blueberry, found in New England, is mostly diploid in nature—that is, each cell contains only one pair of each particular type of chromosome. The highbush, or cultivated blueberry, however, is tetraploid, having two pairs of each type.

The practical result of these high chromosome numbers in small fruits is that breeders have, to a large extent, avoided the genetic methods used with corn and other annual crops where particular characters are tied, by experimental evidence, to a particular pair of chromosomes; and where certain genes may be located rather specifically at one end of a particular pair of chromosomes, or at some other definite location in between certain other known genes. Geneticists studying chromosomes, and the theory of inheritance, have usually worked with annual plants which have relatively small chromosome numbers, their aim to increase knowledge in this field. The practical plant breeder uses all the scientific knowledge he can obtain but is concerned primarily with producing better varieties, and any genetic facts discovered might be considered somewhat as a bonus.

HOW TO MAKE CROSSES. The technic of making crosses between varieties of small fruits is fairly simple. The flowers are emasculated —that is, the stamens are cut off with scissors or pulled off with a fine pair of forceps before the flower opens. This work is most easily done on potted plants in the greenhouse, since insects can be kept

These paper bags cover rather large blueberry branches, each of which bear several flower clusters now ready for cross pollination.

under control there and so the individual flowers or shoots will not have to be bagged. If work is done out-of-doors it is customary to cover the emasculated flowers, or flowering shoots, with a bag of some type, cheesecloth or paper, in order to keep pollen-bearing insects away.

Usually flowers are pollinated two or three days after emasculation, although this will depend on the weather. It is possible to tell fairly easily, by examination of the stigma, whether or not the flower is ready to receive pollen. If it is ready, the stigma, or tip of the pistil, will be slightly enlarged and sticky. The pollen itself should be collected from flowers of the plant chosen to be the male parent before the anthers dehisce, or shed their pollen. If under a hand lens you can see pollen grains coming out from the sides of the anther where it splits apart, then it is pretty late for saving that pollen. That is, if you want to be sure that the pollen has not mixed in any way with that from another variety, with the help of visiting insects. The pollen may be dried in any dry place, at room temperature. This is sometimes accomplished by picking the entire flower and letting the pollen dry out, later using the flower with the drying stamens as a brush. In experiments involving large numbers of pollinations the pollen may be dried in a desiccator, and then applied with a camel's-hair brush. After the pollen has been applied the flowers or twigs are tagged with the names of the parents, and later the seed is harvested as it ripens. Incidentally, seed of the small fruits will germinate better if it is planted as soon as it is removed from the fruit and not permitted to dry out.

Pollination is the term given to the actual applying of the pollen to the stigmatic surface. Fertilization occurs if a pollen grain sends out a microscopic tube, which grows down through the pistil to the ovary, and a male nucleus unites with, or fertilizes, one of the ovules so that it can develop into a seed. In some cases, as when crossing different strawberry varieties, it is usually easy to get almost 100 per cent set. With some other fruits that may not be so easy. When it comes to crossing different species, such as, for instance, crossing the highbush blueberry with the rabbiteye, there may be no set at all, or there may be a fair set of fruit but the production of viable seeds almost if not quite zero. When making wide crosses, such as between species, at least some sterility is to be expected.

CHOOSING PARENTS. The choice of parents is very important if worth-while results are to be expected. Usually a breeder will have some particular objective, such as, for instance, resistance to a certain disease. He may have to look far and wide to find a species, or possibly a single plant, which is resistant to this particular disease. Perhaps the plant has very inferior fruit. However, by crossing with a type which produces good fruit but is susceptible to the disease, it may be possible to obtain a disease-resistant plant with perhaps fair fruit characters. By backcrossing that plant to others which have better fruit characters, it may be possible, in this or later generations, to improve greatly the quality of fruit and still maintain the resistance to disease.

MAKING SELECTIONS. Although it is easy enough to evaluate visible plant characters, eventually one must determine hardiness, disease resistance, soil adaptation, and other characters of a potential new variety. This means breeders customarily select very freely the first fruiting season, sometimes keeping as many as a hundred seedlings out of a thousand fruiting, although usually much less. These selections are allowed to fruit again the next year, and then they are culled much more severely. This gives a little more time to choose a few from among those that appear to be outstanding, and also permits a much better check on disease resistance and hardiness.

After the breeder has selected a very few out of the very many, he usually propagates these selections and then has them tested at experiment stations, or by co-operative arrangement with various growers. It is a problem to get a good test without people's becoming excited about a new variety and wanting to plant it before the breeder is sure that it is good enough. Some growers seem to feel that any selection made by a particular breeder is bound to be outstanding, and will rush to plant a large acreage before it is adequately tested. This is taking quite a chance, and the breeder should always have very careful tests made before releasing a new variety. However, if the variety appears to be resistant to some serious pest, which is causing distress to commercial growers, there may be a great deal of pressure to turn it loose.

The home gardener may wonder when it is safe to try out a new introduction. If it has been tested by a nearby experiment station or experimental farm and recommended for his area he need not hesitate. Unless he goes wild and tries everything he can find, probably little damage will be done if he does occasionally try a new variety which later turns out to be not quite as good as he expected it to be. Perhaps he will not get as much fruit, or as good fruit, as he would have obtained from something else, but on the other hand, he may find something outstanding. At any rate he is not jeopardizing his economic status, as the large grower would be, by plunging on a new and untried variety.

PRIVATE VERSUS PUBLIC BREEDERS. In the early days of horticultural activity in this country, all of the small fruits breeding was done by private individuals. More recently the U.S.D.A., various experiment stations, and other institutions supported by public funds have been very active in the breeding field. The question sometimes arises as to whether this is good business from the administrative standpoint, the feeling occasionally being that private enterprise could do the job just as well or better.

It is true that a few private breeders have done very well and have been very careful in their work. Frequently, however, the private individual is doing his breeding experiments just incidentally. He sees two varieties which he likes, makes a cross, grows a hundred or so seedlings, and if one of them looks outstanding, he does not have the time or the facilities to make extensive tests. Possibly he

The Atlantic blueberry, a product of the U.S.D.A. plant breeding project.

may not be very familiar with the many other varieties of the same kind of fruit that are being grown or have been grown in the past. If he finds an opportunity to sell his new variety to a nursery there is great temptation to cash in. The nurseryman may advertise it highly, banking on the originator's statements, which is fine if they stand up.

Contrasted to this, the experiment-station breeder usually has a large collection of already known varieties from which to select parents and with which to compare any selections he may make. He also has the advice of his colleagues, usually including pathologists, entomologists, soils men, and horticulturists, in evaluating certain characteristics of the new variety, which may be of extreme importance. The breeder at a publicly supported institution has no pecuniary interest in promoting the variety, except the urge to do a good job for the growers and the others in the state who are paying his salary through taxes. There is no extreme urge to get the variety out and cash in on it. This usually results in more adequate testing. Very commonly, varieties are sent from one experiment station to those in other states, where they will get a cold and unbiased evaluation in comparison with many other varieties.

The experiment stations, of course, if they really go into the business, are able to spend thousands of dollars in carrying on a long-term breeding experiment to accomplish some definite objective. I hasten to add that these thousands of dollars may very frequently be returned to the state in one year, by the extra income derived from a superior variety after it is once introduced.

This is not to discourage the private breeder at all, but simply to indicate that, in some ways, he may be working against odds, as compared to the experiment station breeder. This should be of some interest to the home gardener who, perhaps, has no method of evaluating a variety except by the description in the nursery catalog. It would seem to me that the fact that a particular variety has been named and introduced by an experiment station, for a particular purpose, is a pretty good indication that it has merit. In the past some varieties that were originated by private breeders, or were simply picked up as seedlings in the wild, have not lived up to their catalog descriptions. Occasionally they have.

PLANT BREEDING AS A HOBBY. What I have just said should not in any way discourage a home gardener who feels that he would like to raise some seedlings and determine for himself whether or not he can produce a superior type of plant. This is quite interesting and often rewarding. However, I would not suggest going into it with the idea of producing valuable varieties, and making a lot of money, unless one is prepared to spend years of study and effort, and a considerable amount of money, in building up a good collection of plant material to be used as parent stock, and later in testing seedlings over a period of several years.

Just as a garden hobby, the making of crosses, and the raising of seedlings, is something that could produce a lot of pleasure, and possibly quite a fair measure of reward. It often happens that a variety is particularly well adapted to the conditions under which it is grown and selected, and it might be very good for you but still not of general commercial importance. If it does do well for you, and possibly for your neighbors, there is no reason why you should not grow it in preference to the standard varieties. Of course there is always the possibility that it might be sufficiently good to make it worthy of sale.

If you do decide to go into this field as a hobby, I would suggest reading just as much as you can about the fruit you are going to work with, and also about the science of genetics, particularly as it applies to plant breeding. Actually you might never see a chromosome under the microscope, or work out a genetic ratio for yourself, but a knowledge of this field will certainly be helpful to you in planning your work, and in interpreting it as you go along. The chances are against your getting anything that is really worth while unless you raise very large numbers. However, with the small fruits, most of the seedlings you raise will produce good edible berries, which will certainly be acceptable on your own table. Much of this fruit from the seedlings may be just as good as that from standard varieties, and of course there is always that long shot of finding one that is actually better than anything else you can obtain.

CHAPTER 20

Year-Round Enjoyment

Fresh berries right out of the patch, prepared for immediate use at the dinner table, undoubtedly represent the ultimate so far as flavor and general desirability are concerned. Personally, if I couldn't eat the berries fresh I would be much less likely to bother to raise them. I wouldn't want to be without frozen berries, or strawberry jam, or blackberry jelly, but these delicacies can be purchased, or the berries to make them can usually be bought. What you buy may not be quite as good as what you "put up" yourself, but it is easier. But for fresh berries there just isn't any way to get exactly what you want that compares with growing them yourself. However any one type of berry is available for a relatively short period, sometimes less than a month. This may be extended by planting two or three varieties to cover the season from very early to very late but only a couple of weeks will be gained with strawberries and raspberries, a little longer with blueberries, and some two to three months with the blackberries, from earliest dewberries to latest Evergreen type.

The everbearing varieties of strawberries and raspberries present another method of extending the fresh berry season, but even with them there will be a period of about eight months when fresh berries will be only a memory and a hope of things to come. This applies to the central and northern parts of the country, as gardeners in the Far South, and in parts of California, will have a season somewhat longer, possibly all winter for strawberries. But where strawberries ripen all winter they are usually out of season in midsummer, so no gardener can normally have fresh berries the year around. This leads us to the problem of preserving berries for consumption during the rest of the year, for the gardener who grows his own berries is very likely to feel that it is really worth while to grow enough to take care also of his winter supply of frozen and preserved products.

HOME FREEZING. Of all the methods of preserving or holding berries for future use, probably freezing is the most satisfactory, and conversely the best fruits to freeze are the berry crops. The home freez-

Next to strawberries eaten one by one just as they are picked, for greatest eating pleasure come garden fresh berries dipped in confectioners' sugar, using the stem as a handle with which to dip and eat.

ing of various types of berries generally involves putting them in a freezer bag, or other vaporproof container, either with or without sugar in some form, and storing them in a low-temperature cabinet or locker. There is one possible exception—the rabbiteye blueberry. Some investigations have shown that blanching, of at least some varieties of this blueberry of the South, has been effective in eliminating gritty cells in the flesh and producing a better product. With the so-called cultivated blueberries of the Middle States, however, blanching is entirely unnecessary.

FREEZING STRAWBERRIES. More strawberries are frozen than any other berry, so let's begin our discussion of what and how to freeze with this fruit. In the first place we should have a variety which freezes well. There is a great deal of difference in varieties in this respect, and about the only way this can be determined is by actual freezing tests. Various experiment stations have conducted tests, and most of the standard varieties are known as being good, poor, or indifferent for freezing. Fortunately there are a number of multiple purpose varieties, which are good for freezing as well as for fresh use.

If you are growing a strawberry and do not know its name, you may easily find out its freezing qualities by trying it. At the worst you will have a product which is not very well colored, and the berries may have a poor texture when they thaw out, and perhaps not the best of flavor. However, any kind of strawberry can be frozen into an edible product, although the better ones are distinctly more desirable than the poor ones. Usually a medium-tart berry, with fairly high flavor and a firm texture, is desirable.

Berries for freezing should be picked when they are fully ripe but still firm; that is, they should be in prime edible condition. It would seem advisable to take out small or misshapen berries and use them fresh. After all, freezing involves labor and expense, and it seems reasonable to freeze only the better fruit, provided you have enough to make a choice. The berries should be capped and washed as promptly as possible after picking, discarding, of course, any that have a soft spot, indicating the beginning of decay.

FREEZE WITH SUGAR. For certain purposes the berries may be frozen whole, without any sugar. Some people like to have such berries for the children to eat just as they thaw out. However, the flavor is never as good, for berries frozen without sugar have a rather tart off-flavor just as soon as they thaw, and so must be eaten while practically frozen solid if they are not to lose their prime quality. Most of the strawberries frozen, both commercially and for home use, are packed with sugar, usually in the proportion of about four cups of berries to one cup of sugar, commonly spoken of as "four plus one" pack. The sugar has a definitely preserving effect in maintaining the delicate, natural fresh flavor of the fruit.

Large berries may be cut into two or three pieces so the sugar will better reach all parts of the fruit. Medium-sized and small berries may be left intact or cut, just as you wish. The berries are then mixed with dry sugar so that all of the berries, or parts of berries, are coated, placed in a container, and frozen as quickly as possible. Slightly more, or less, sugar may be used for the particular variety which you are freezing, if you prefer it that way, although the four plus one is more or less standard.

Containers for freezing should be moisture- and vaporproof, to prevent drying out, and should also prevent, to a very large extent, the entrance of oxygen, which will eventually cause an oxidized, off-flavor of the product. The containers may be polyethylene bags, paraffin-coated, cardboard boxes, plastic boxes, fruit jars (leave room for expansion), or possibly others. Cellophane was formerly used as a liner for cardboard cartons or boxes of various types, and was satisfactory, except that it sometimes cracked, under freezing conditions which made it brittle, and the juice might then leak out during the storage period. The question immediately occurs as to how juice could leak out when the berries are frozen solid. The fact is that when sugar is mixed with the berries, juice comes out, dissolves the sugar, and the result is a very thick syrup with a high concentration of sugar. Such a solution does not freeze at the freezing point of water, but may remain in a liquid or semiliquid condition to about zero degrees.

RASPBERRIES ARE EXCELLENT FOR FREEZING. Red raspberries make an excellent frozen product if handled in the same way as described for strawberries. There is quite a variation in sugar content of various kinds of raspberries, and it may be necessary to change the amount of sugar to match the particular variety you are freezing.

Purple raspberries also make a very fine product, although they are not as popular as the reds and are difficult to find, unless you raise them yourself. Most varieties are more acid and have a strong flavor as compared to the delicate, red raspberry flavor.

Black raspberries are considerably firmer than red varieties, which may indicate some change in methods. The fruit of strawberries and red raspberries is rather soft, and when mixed with sugar, enough juice comes out to dissolve most of the sugar and coat the berries with a very thick syrup. With black raspberries, especially if they are a bit on the dry side, or not quite fully ripe, there may not be enough juice to dissolve the sugar and provide the syrup coating. In that case they may be put into the container without sugar, and then covered with a syrup made of sugar and water. The usual method is to pour the sugar into cold water and heat while stirring, but without boiling, until the sugar is all dissolved. A 40 per cent syrup, which would be made from 3 cups water and 2 cups of sugar, should be quite satisfactory. Use as little syrup as possible and still cover the berries, so as not to have an excessively juicy product when thawed.

MOST BLACKBERRIES GOOD FOR FREEZING. The various blackberries, including the dewberries, make a very desirable product when frozen. The varieties with high quality, rather tender flesh, and relatively small seeds are superior for freezing, just as they are for use fresh. The dry-sugar method is usually preferred.

HOW TO FREEZE BLUEBERRIES. The syrup pack is much to be preferred to the dry-sugar pack for blueberries. There is not enough juice to dissolve the sugar, and the undissolved sugar in the package, if not in close contact with the berry itself, has no preservative effect. Blueberries packed with dry sugar are inclined to have a rather tough skin, after they have been frozen for two or three months. If frozen in syrup, they will retain good edible quality for a much longer time, and a flavor much more nearly like that of the fresh berries. Even a 30 per cent syrup will be satisfactory, although possibly a 40 per cent syrup would be a little better.

Many people have frozen blueberries without any sugar or syrup, and find them satisfactory for pies. However, after two or three months, enzyme action does cause noticeable changes in the berry, particularly in the skin, which may become quite tough and leathery. This soon reaches the point where the berries would be rather undesirable for eating, with cream, as a dessert fruit. When cooked up in a pie, even fairly tough-skinned frozen berries may be reasonably satisfactory. It would seem that the syrup pack, which is relatively easy to put up, would be desirable, so that the berries could be used for any purpose and would have maximum resemblance to the texture and flavor of fresh berries.

There is considerable difference in varieties of blueberries, probably more than there is with most other berries, in so far as their suitability for freezing is concerned. Some of the varieties remain in very good condition, for a long period of time while frozen. Others produce a rather inferior product. Perhaps I should say a relatively inferior product, as most of them can be made into an acceptably good blueberry pie, if properly handled by one who knows how to make good pies.

FREEZE CURRANTS FOR PROCESSING LATER. Since currants are used almost exclusively for the making of jelly, or sometimes combined with other fruits to make a conserve, there is no particular necessity of freezing them to maintain dessert flavor and quality. That is, if you are ready to make your jelly just when the currants are ripe. If not, it is quite feasible to freeze them and make jelly during the winter or whenever you want it. It might be stated at this point that the freezing of berries, for later jelly making, is something very much worth considering with all of the small fruits, as jelly freshly made is considerably better than that which has been on the shelf for several months. A fresh-flavored jelly, practically equal to that made from fresh berries, can be made from frozen berries.

In holding currants for the later making of jelly, it would seem advisable to freeze them with some sugar, or syrup, in order to maintain as nearly as possible the fresh flavor. It might be desirable to go one step further and squeeze out the juice and freeze it. This will somewhat reduce the volume which you will have to store in the freezer. However, one of the reasons for freezing berries for later jelly making is so you can make the jelly when you have more time, and freezing the currants whole would be considerably quicker than extracting the juice. It would be desirable, of course, before freezing the currants, to strip them from the stems. This will reduce the volume, permit the sugar to make closer contact with the berries, and eliminate the messy job of taking out the stems at a later date. Possibly the currants could be squeezed with the stems present, but the green stems sometimes impart a flavor which is not exactly desirable.

FREEZE GOOSEBERRIES DRY. Gooseberries also are used cooked almost entirely, and so the preservation of a fresh-fruit flavor is not quite so important. Gooseberries may be frozen very satisfactorily dry, without any sugar at all, and can be used later for gooseberry pie. The stems and the petals, which adhere to the fruit when picked, should be taken off before freezing, as the berries will be quite soft to work with after they thaw.

VARIOUS USES FOR FROZEN GRAPES. For various reasons grapes have not been frozen as extensively as most other fruits. However, certain varieties can be frozen for later use in salads or fruit cocktail. I have known people who have frozen Concord grapes, and find that their children very much enjoy eating them while they are still frozen. The freezing of grapes for later use in the making of juice, jellies, or conserves may be followed as previously outlined for some of the berries. The grapes should be removed from the stems before freezing. The addition of sugar will tend to prevent oxidized flavors, but it is possible to freeze grapes reasonably satisfactorily without the addition of sugar.

CRANBERRIES EASY TO FREEZE. Cranberries are the easiest fruit there is to freeze, as they are simply poured into a freezing container and put under low-temperature conditions. Sugar is not necessary, as the berries are to be used cooked, and if a slightly oxidized flavor does develop, it will be dispersed at the time of cooking.

USE YOUR FREEZING CABINET. Much has been said in the past about the rapidity of freezing, and for a while the success of the opera-

Surprise your friends sometime with a gift package of strawberries in an egg carton. Of course you'll have to pick out the big ones.

tion was thought to depend on freezing almost instantaneously. This had led some people to feel that they could not "quick freeze" in their own home freezers, but would have to have it done in a locker plant, or a regular commercial freezing plant. Freezing as rapidly as possible is important, but if you have a cabinet which runs from about 0 to 5 below, you can freeze berries very satisfactorily. The only caution is to not load it up too much all at once. By putting in a very large number of packages you will bring up the temperature in the box, and if you have distributed the warm packages over the other food that is already in the freezer you may cause slight thawing of the other products, which may slightly detract from their quality when you eventually use them.

We have an 11-cubic-foot freezer and think nothing of freezing a dozen packages at a time. If we put them in in the evening, they are quite solid by the next morning. For all practical purposes this is quick freezing, and more rapid freezing probably would not make the product appreciably better. Of course, packages to be frozen under these conditions should be spread out in a single layer, and preferably not touching each other, although that is not absolutely essential.

A good deal of the emphasis on extremely fast freezing came about because of attempts to freeze large quantities commercially. Even with a high refrigerating capacity, and a well-insulated room, if fairly large quantities of warm product are put in at one time it will take a long while for them to freeze to the center. In the meanwhile some deterioration may take place. Commercial freezing is now done very rapidly in an air blast or with the packages well spaced out in a warehouse, with ample opportunity for each small package to freeze on all sides. This does not mean that the larger institutional packs freeze slowly enough to affect the quality adversely, as the freezing will be completed within a few hours.

DETERIORATION DOES OCCUR. In spite of the preservative effect of freezing, deterioration of quality due to enzyme action undoubtedly begins almost immediately, although it is hardly noticeable for several weeks, or possibly several months. However, it does continue, and one should not count on keeping frozen berries indefinitely. I have known of cranberries being kept as long as ten years and still making an acceptable sauce, but I would not recommend it. It seems to me that the logical procedure is to freeze enough berries to last through the season, until the next crop comes, and not plan to carry them over from year to year. If you do have some packages remaining in the freezer or locker by the end of the season, do not throw them out. However, it would be desirable to use them up by making jelly, or some other processed product, or else plan to use them in the normal way rather promptly. Then put in the new crop with the idea that the old one will soon be out of the way.

It should be understood that frozen fruit left in the freezer too long, perhaps overlooked in some way, is not harmful to human health. If it tastes alright, and looks alright, by all means go ahead and use it.

Occasionally we find people who are afraid of eating fruit which has been thawed even slightly, and then refrozen. If the current should go off for a day or so, and the packages become somewhat thawed on the outside, it does not mean that they will be unfit to eat then or when they are refrozen. They may not look quite as good on the surface, and may not have quite as fresh a flavor, but certainly they would not be harmful. The modern freezer cabinet, if left tightly closed while the current is off, should keep the product in a satisfactorily frozen condition for at least two or three days. As long as ice crystals remain in frozen berries, especially if they are frozen with sugar, or a sugar syrup, there should be relatively little deterioration.

SOME BERRIES NOT WELL ADAPTED TO CANNING. Strawberries and the bramble fruits have never been considered as especially well adapted to canning, either home canning or commercial. If heated enough to sterilize them, strawberries tend to become rather soft and may lose a part of their color and flavor. They also tend to come to the top of the can or jar. This is also true with all the bramble fruits—raspberries, blackberries, and dewberries. When canned in a glass jar, eventually most of the berries will be found floating close to the top, and the bottom part of the jar will contain only liquid. The best solution to this problem, with raspberries and blackberries at least, is to process just as short a time as possible, and still effect sterilization. Then, by storing the jars on their sides and turning them occasionally, it is possible to get the berries to absorb enough of the liquid so that they will remain fairly well dispersed throughout the jar.

Canned berries almost invariably will have a considerable amount of juice with them, and if used in pies, this is not very desirable. Furthermore, the second cooking, in the preparation of a pie, will reduce the berry almost to a condition of juice and seeds, so that the identity of the berry is lost. In contrast with this, frozen berries are usually more nearly intact, if put into the pie just as they are thawing out. Many people use canned raspberries and blackberries as a dessert fruit, and they can be quite good for that, but frozen berries, of most varieties, if consumed just as they are thawed out, will usually have a better fresh-berry flavor, and perhaps a better texture.

BLUEBERRIES, CRANBERRIES, AND GOOSEBERRIES FOR CANNING. Canned blueberries for pies have been a standard product in many homes, and they do make very good pies. One family I know, blueberry growers on a large scale, by the way, canned large quantities of certain varieties and used them for dessert, covered with brown sugar. They were really excellent. However, blueberries also have a tendency to come to the top of the jar and to separate from the juice.

Gooseberries may be canned satisfactorily for pies, and do not seem to rise to the top of the jar as much as some of the other fruits.

Cranberries are well adapted to canning as a cranberry sauce, either as a whole sauce or jellied sauce that has had the seeds and skins strained out.

CANNING VERSUS FREEZING. Considering the whole field of small fruits, it would seem that the best method of preservation is probably freezing rather than canning. However, some may not have the facilities for freezing, or they may not have facilities for keeping the amount of berries that they would like to have. In this case it would seem logical to freeze those berries best adapted to that process, and can those which make a good canned product, such as cranberries, gooseberries, and blueberries.

SPREADS OF VARIOUS TYPES. Jams can be made from other fruits also, but most of us think first of berries when jam is mentioned. Although jam making is not a lost art, a smaller and smaller percentage of young homemakers do preserving of any kind at home, relying more and more on commercially processed spreads of various kinds. However, there is not a great deal of variation in jam and jelly-making methods, and it is hardly the function of this book to provide recipes, which can be found in dozens of cookbooks and pamphlets published by producers of fruit jars, pectin, or other ingredients, as well as by the Extension Service in forty-eight states. A concise set of directions for many different fruits will be found in U.S.D.A. Home and Garden Bulletin No. 56, "How to Make Jellies, Jams and Preserves at Home." The following remarks will be rather general and directed mostly to encouraging the home gardener to obtain full satisfaction from his efforts, which to my way of thinking would certainly include winter enjoyment of the fruits of his labors.

If there is anyone who doesn't like strawberry jam I have never met him, although I suppose that a person who is allergic to fresh strawberries might be allergic to strawberry jam. That is a bit of knowledge I do not have. Raspberry and blackberry jams are also very delicious. With the larger seeded blackberries, such as the Evergreen, using a machine which removes the seeds, or putting the fruit through a colander to take out the seeds, will permit a much smoother and more satisfying product to be made.

Blueberry jam has not been a very popular product because the flavor is so bland. However, putting cranberries with the blueberries will give a much better flavor and apparently a better keeping quality. The proportion will depend on the varieties used, especially their relative tartness, and personal likes and dislikes. Do a little experimenting and mix and sweeten to taste would be my suggestion. Rhubarb may also be used with blueberries to provide the needed acidity.

Several very delicious products may be made from grapes, particularly the Concord, or others of its type which have a rather strong flavor. Grape conserve has been one of my favorites, essentially a grape jam, not too sweet, with raisins, orange, and chopped nuts added.

Berry preserves, especially strawberry, have long been a stand-by in the American pantry; they are essentially similar to jam, except made with whole berries. The latter is probably a more useful product, especially where there are children's snacks to be prepared. Preserves were once used much more freely than now, as an added treat with the meat course.

IDEAL JELLY FRUITS. Berries are also ideal jelly fruits, although it may be necessary to add pectin to most of them, except the currant. The use of commercially bottled, or packaged, pectin is certainly very general, for jams as well as jellies, and usually results in a better flavored product, as it is not necessary to "cook down" the juice to such an extent. This gives a better yield from a given amount of fruit, and also prevents the loss of much of the aroma through long cooking. Fully ripe fruit, with its maximum flavor, may be used, rather than the slightly immature fruit which would be necessary to furnish enough natural pectin. With pectin added, the boiling can be done by the clock, one minute for the final boil, instead of the rather agonizing older method of watching the material drip off a spoon until it "sheets." A great deal of good jelly has been made using the sheet test, but I can testify that it is easy to over- or undercook.

Strawberry jelly can be made, although probably most people prefer strawberry jam. However, with raspberries and blackberries, jelly has one advantage over jam, in that it involves the elimination of the seeds which in these fruits may be rather large and objectionable.

It is dangerous to rate jellies from the various berry crops, because of the personal taste factor. However, my preference is for raspberry and blackberry jelly. Currants make an excellent, but tart, product often used with meats. Based on limited experience, my feeling is that the foregoing berries are easier to make into jelly with good texture and keeping quality than the following. With additional pectin, however, very tasty jellies may be made from grapes, strawberries, blueberries, cranberries, and elderberries, but the process is a bit tricky, and especially so without the added pectin.

Freshly made jelly, and jam also, has better flavor, texture, and appearance. If freezing facilities are available it is quite practical, and desirable if you are a jelly connoisseur, to hold the fruit as frozen berries, or frozen juice, and make fresh jelly from time to time. It will be necessary to make some record of the amount of sugar added at the time of freezing, as that will have to be considered in determining how much to add when the jelly is made.

UNCOOKED JAM. During recent years a cold or uncooked jam, or jellied fruit, made from fresh, or frozen, fruit and pectin, has become quite popular. Its specific advantage is its excellent fresh-fruit flavor. It must be stored in the refrigerator, or frozen if it is to be kept more than three or four weeks. Next to the fresh fruit itself this cold mix probably has the best true-fruit flavor of all the berry products.

FRUIT JUICES. Certain berries lend themselves very well to the production of fresh fruit juice for serving in cold drinks, either straight or mixed with some other juice. These fruit-juice drinks are so good that the commercial berry growers, and various research agencies, have been working for years trying to develop a product to compete with the synthetic bottled drinks. So far they have been successful from the standpoint of quality but not of price. The home gardener can have these delicious juices with his own efforts being the major cost. Raspberry juice is very delicious, but a little heavy with flavor and aroma. Diluting to taste, and possibly adding a little lemon juice, or a little cranberry juice, will improve the flavor. The same may be said for blackberry juice. These juices are probably best if frozen or canned at full strength, to be diluted later to make them go further and also to cut the flavor, which may be a trifle too strong. Any of them may be diluted with ginger ale or other carbonated beverages to give added zip.

Cranberry juice makes a very delightful drink and is manufactured commercially. As this is not a home-garden fruit to any extent, home gardeners may not have an opportunity to make juice out of their own cranberries. However, it is being mentioned here because of its possibilities as a diluter for some of the other berry juices. It has red color and acidity, which will be helpful in making a combination drink with most any of the other fruit juices. Most of the commercial cranberry juice on the market has already been diluted with water to the consistency desired for drinking straight. It is possible to obtain full-strength cranberry juice, which is very strong-flavored and should be diluted before drinking. If you are unable to obtain the straight juice, it will be fairly easy to make your own from fresh cranberries, at least sufficient to blend with other juices. It is also quite practical to blend the fresh fruit—that is, put enough cranberries in with the other berries that you are processing, before cooking, to give you the desired amount of acidity and flavor. The juice is then strained out, already blended.

GRAPE JUICE UNIVERSALLY LIKED. Grape juice is a very well-known product, although probably not a very large proportion of present-day homemakers have actually made the juice themselves. Most of the commercial juice is made from the Concord variety, which probably has the best, or most generally liked, flavor of any for this purpose. However, many other varieties may be used. Some work has been done in studying the blending of varieties in order to obtain new flavors and in order to utilize, for this purpose, those varieties which do not have a very distinctive flavor of their own. Grape juice and cranberry juice mix well, to produce a delicious combination.

Although our general conception of sweet, or unfermented, grape juice is one with a dark purplish color, several of the white varieties make juice that has excellent flavor. It will be clear, or slightly pinkish in color, but, after all, flavor and aroma are the things we look for when drinking fruit juices.

The making of wine from home-grown grapes or berries is usually based on individual recipes and varietal preferences. There is little I could add which would be very helpful.

CHAPTER 21

Could I Make a Few Dollars from Berries?

Many home gardeners have had the experience of producing more than they actually need—with vegetable crops as well as with berries. Once one has satisfied his own needs, and has taken care of members of the family who live nearby, and possibly one or two especially favored neighbors, there is the problem of what to do with the remainder. There is a rather elastic limit to the amount of berries that can be used and processed, so many gardeners may plan to process everything that they cannot eat fresh. However, in good crop years the amount may go beyond that limit, and then one must decide whether the surplus should be given away, allowed to spoil, or sold. If there are children in the family who could pick the berries and sell them, that is a natural way to dispose of the surplus and give the youngsters an interesting project. Regardless of that, the berries represent a value, and many feel it is better to sell them than to let them spoil.

GOING COMMERCIAL. Once you have had to dispose of an unexpected surplus, the next step is to plant a few more berries than you think you need, with the idea of selling some locally. After that you are in business, and whether you will expand and become a regular commercial grower or whether you will be primarily a home gardener, with a few extra berries to sell, will depend on your own inclinations and local conditions. Actually a number of commercial berry growers have started in just this way.

Berries as a part-time home garden project have the advantage of yielding a product of relatively high unit value. Profits are possible fairly quickly, certainly much more quickly than with tree fruits, and more quickly than from some other farm enterprises. A relatively small area is needed and also a modest investment of actual cash. There may be a fairly high investment of labor, which, of course is quite real, but if anything happens to the project it may be easier to lose the investment of labor than an actual outlay of cash. This is not to intimate that such loss is likely to occur, but, like all farming, berry growing is dependent on the weather.

There are three ways of making money from small fruits. One is to sell the plants; the second is to sell the fruit; and the third is to sell processed fruit such as jams, jellies, or canned fruit. Very often all three sources of income may be tapped.

SALE OF PLANTS. The selling of plants, particularly of new varieties, may develop into a fairly desirable small business. It takes a little time to work up a stock of new varieties, and hence established nurserymen, unless they are berry plant specialists, are not always ready to list them in their catalogs. They usually have many of the old standard varieties, which they feel they must stock, and sometimes they do not wish to take on a new variety until it has been thoroughly tested. However, if you have tried a new variety and it it does well for you, then there is no reason why you should not sell plants to your neighbors if they want them. It is quite true, also, that plants freshly dug and set out quickly are always a little more satisfactory than those which are shipped long distances and which may have been dug quite a while before.

With strawberries, it is often possible to work up a small demand for potted plants. The ordinary plants, as secured for commercial planting, are dug, bare root, from a one-year-old field and shipped in bundles of twenty-five. They are quite satisfactory for planting in early spring to produce a crop a year later. Potted plants, however, may be set out successfully during the summer, or even in the fall. This will permit a home gardener to set his strawberries where he has already grown and removed a crop of vegetables the same season. Potted plants because of the extra labor involved, and because the plants are actually superior and have a better chance of survival are more expensive. Some seed companies offer potted plants, and it should be possible to determine a fair price, based on quoted prices as seen against your actual cost of production.

It will be necessary, if you are going to sell plants as a regular thing, to purchase a nursery license. Some states have special requirements, so it would be advisable to get in touch with your state department of agriculture on this point if you are thinking of the plant business. In most states, an incidental sale, now and then to a neighbor, would probably not be considered as requiring a license.

PRODUCTION OF CERTIFIED PLANTS. In some states there are special provisions set up for qualified nurseries to grow and sell certified plants. Requirements may vary in different states, but the general purpose is to provide a superior quality of plant especially true to name and more nearly free of virus diseases and other pests. If these meet the rigid inspection requirements they may be sold as certified plants and usually bring a slightly higher price. If you expect to sell strawberry plants as a regular thing, it would be advisable to look into the requirements in your state and see what responsibilities you would be assuming in attempting to produce specially certified plants.

The production for sale of small-fruit plants, other than strawberries, will probably involve a little more effort. With raspberries and blackberries, of course, it is possible to dig sucker plants, or tip layers, which would be destroyed if not dug for plants. However, in order to produce any considerable number of plants it would be necessary to keep planting young, vigorous stock, as you will get more and better plants from a newly set row than from an old bearing row. There are various methods of encouraging an extra large number of suckers, or tip layers, but these fall in the realm of commercial nursery practice. If you decide to go that far, then some study should be made of propagation methods.

Selling plants will cease to be a part-time, home-garden project as soon as you decide to sell beyond your own neighborhood and acquaintances. That will mean advertising and shipping, delivering plants at the time when the consumer wants them and not just when it is convenient for you to thin the extra runners from your strawberry patch. That is when problems begin to multiply, and serious study should be given the whole proposition before crossing that particular barrier. Of course you might sell to some other nurseryman and let him worry about advertising and packing. Then you will be functioning as a wholesale nurseryman, supplying the retail nurserymen, and the retailers will expect your prices to be in line with those of other wholesalers.

SELLING SURPLUS FRUIT. Most home garden small fruits plantings, which spill over into the commercial field, are involved only in the selling of fruit. This may start when there is a particularly good crop, and a family-size planting actually produces more fruit than the family can use.

If you really expect to sell some berries, then it seems to me that it would be wise to plant enough to have a reasonable amount to sell. If you have just a little surplus each year, you may have difficulty in disposing of it, and you will also have calls for fruit when you have none to offer, which is always a bit irritating to the per-

For local sales berries may be displayed in single layer field trays to good advantage.

son who wants the fruit and to the home gardener who does not have it to sell.

It is hardly possible to suggest any definite size of planting for a project of this kind. It will depend on whether you are actually growing the fruit primarily for your own use and just want to be sure that you have enough, and so to do that provide for a definite but small surplus.

If you really want to make some extra money by raising small fruits, the matter of the most advantageous size of planting should be very thoroughly studied. There are many facts to consider. If you have to hire someone to plow the land, for instance, it will cost very little more to have an acre plowed and fitted than to have a half acre prepared, provided the land is available. If you have to put on a spray, it is not much more trouble to apply two tankfuls of material than it is one, provided you have the necessary equipment, and while you have everything ready and are prepared to do the work. There is more incentive to do some advertising if you have plenty of berries to sell, and there is more incentive for buyers to think of your place as a source of supply if they know that you have sufficient quantity so that they can count on obtaining the amount they desire.

If this is to be a self-contained enterprise and you are going to do all the work yourself, you will need power tools, at least for fitting the land before planting. This may involve anything from a small Rotavator to a larger tractor, plow, and harrow. If you are going to have to purchase and maintain power tools to do your work, you will certainly want to have a large enough enterprise to make efficient use of your equipment eventually defray the cost and make a profit. In other words, you will be functioning as a regular commercial grower.

SELLING BERRIES FROM THE FARM GARDEN. There are many people who raise berries in the home garden who are actually farmers by profession. They will have power tools and equipment that they use in their other types of farming, which could be used for producing berry crops. They are, therefore, in a better position to grow a small amount of berries, or a large amount as the case might be, than is a suburbanite who has a limited supply of land and no special equipment to start with.

A POSSIBLE 4-H PROJECT. However, the suburbanite, who probably works regular hours at some other business, can count on having a certain amount of time during evenings or weekends to devote to a small fruits enterprise. The farmer, on the other hand, often has regular chores, and lots of them, which can take practically all of his available time, if he permits them to do so. He will probably consider the berry project as just another crop in his farming operations, and will have to determine to his own satisfaction that time spent on the berry crops will be more profitable than the same time spent on his other farm projects. On the farm, and to a more limited extent in the suburbs, the presence of teen-age boys or girls who are interested in 4-H or Girl Scout projects will provide an added incentive for starting some kind of an enterprise of interest to them, and it might well be growing berries. Certainly some 4-H berry-growing projects have been quite successful.

HARVESTING PROBLEMS. One of the real problems with all berry crops is harvesting. Practically all berries are hand-picked, except cranberries, which, as stated before, are not really adapted to home garden culture. If there are children in the family who would like to earn a little money and who are not averse to garden work, then a part of the picker problem is solved.

A small strawberry patch, of one fourth of an acre, if it is in good condition, will require from two to four pickers working rather steadily to keep it picked as frequently as it should be. Just as soon as you decide to hire pickers, problems begin to increase. You will now be an employer of labor and will have to think about child labor laws, Social Security, and all such things.

One of the most difficult things may be to find people to do the picking and to determine a wage scale, or piecework rate, for picking, which will encourage them to want to work and which will return a satisfactory profit to you. Fortunately, most berry crops ripen during the summer vacation, and, fortunately also, youngsters make good pickers. If there are children in your neighborhood who might be interested in working, that will likely prove the most satisfactory source of pickers. However, you must be prepared to have your best pickers suddenly decide to quit to go to summer camp, or for some other reason. Transportation of pickers is always a problem unless they are available in your immediate neighborhood. The adequacy of harvesting labor will be a big factor in deciding how large an enterprise you want to attempt.

"PICK YOURSELF" AS A SOLUTION. One of the ways many berry growers, especially the smaller ones, have been solving the problem is a "Pick yourself" or a "U-pick" arrangement. With this setup, the owner can take care of everything himself, unless he has a rather large planting. Prospective customers are shown a row from which they may pick the berries at a given price. Arrangements must be made as to who furnishes the picking container, and a few other details. When a person has picked all he wants, he takes them to a check-out stand, where the berries are weighed, and he pays on the basis of so many pounds. Some operators furnish berry cups, as they figure the weight of a cup is about equal in value to the same weight of berries; so the customer can pay for the gross weight, including the cups, or he can pour them into his own container, and pay on a net weight basis.

The U-pick system saves a great deal of the effort involved in securing pickers, supervising, and paying them, but it provides almost as many additional problems. The people who purchase berries may never have picked before, and it may be difficult to keep them on the row to which they were assigned. Some may pick berries that are too green, but most of them will be more inclined to miss many ripe berries, especially the small ones, which should be removed from the plants. If one party goes over and skims off the cream, taking all the larger and more luscious berries, those who follow will want to have the fruit at lower cost, or will be dissatisfied. Usually the supervisor has to be quite firm, tell people how the berries are to be picked, and if they do not want to pick them that way, then request them to leave.

With bush berries, and particularly blueberries, there may be a problem of breakage of plants, especially where families with very small children come in to pick on a U-pick basis. Youngsters may want to climb up through the bushes, or break them down, as they play around their parents who are working. Paid pickers also may want to bring their children along, but they may have more of a feeling of responsibility for keeping them from causing damage.

If there is a good demand for fruit and the U-pick operation is not very large it may be necessary to make advance dates. If there are enough people already picking to take care of all the fruit which is ripe on a particular day, and if other customers come they should be offered the opportunity to be definitely assigned a row the following day, or the day after, or on some specific date. Anyone who comes two or three times and finds no room will probably be lost as a customer.

The pricing of berries from a U-pick operation must be worked out on the basis of value. People do not expect to pick their own berries and then pay as much for them as they would pay somewhere else for equivalent quality already picked. The operator will have to study his local conditions and prices rather thoroughly to work out a satisfactory price schedule.

While the U-pick system is still relatively new in some localities, it has been in operation in other places for a good many years. In general, it has seemed to work out fairly satisfactorily, as indicated by the fact that people who once start it usually go ahead with it year after year.

LOCAL SALES VS. SHIPPING. Another advantage of U-pick, as of all retail sales, is that the berries are taken by the buyer and presumably paid for when they are taken. This is in contrast to sending to a market, where the berries will have to be delivered, to a motor-freight station, or express office, or auction block, in which case there will be transportation charges and payments may be delayed. If the shipment is for a long distance, there may be arguments as to the condition of the fruit on arrival, and prices may sometimes be less than the grower was led to believe he might receive.

A question might be raised as to the advisability of securing as many pickers as possible and then handling the rest on a U-pick basis. This might be reasonably satisfactory if different fields are

These Latham raspberries were packed, by a roadside market operator, so the cavities left when they were pulled from the receptacles were all turned down. They brought a premium price.

involved, each to be handled in one way, but it does not seem that it would be desirable to mix the two methods of harvesting in the same field.

BERRY GROWING AS A 4-H PROJECT. Mention has already been made of the possibility of berry growing being used as a 4-H project. Actually such projects have been used in many different states, and for the most part have been quite satisfactory. This is due primarily to two reasons, one being that a fairly high return may be anticipated from a relatively small area, and the second that the returns will be received slightly more than a year after planting in the case of strawberries, and in two to three years in the case of the bush fruits; although with the latter a full return may not be received until the third or fourth year. There are 4-H Club leaders in many counties of the United States, and probably any of them would have information available concerning the formation and operation of a 4-H berry-producing project.

MARKETING BERRY PRODUCTS. The selling of home-processed berry products, rather than fresh fruit, or in addition to fresh fruit, is something that has been tried in many areas. In a few places it has been quite definitely successful and has sometimes developed into fairly large, semicommercial operations. Here again one must consider all of the problems involved very carefully before starting. There is not a great deal of help that can be given in a book of this kind, as local conditions will so very greatly affect the possibility of making a satisfactory profit.

One could get into the business of making berry products without growing the berries, provided he could find a satisfactory source of supply in the neighborhood. There is a question whether one could go into the open market, pay commercial prices for berries, and turn them into a profitable processed product in his own kitchen in competition with the large processing plants that have to work very efficiently and turn out products to sell at relatively low prices. If one is using his own berries, naturally the first thing to consider is whether the profit will be greater, considering labor and time involved, from processing and selling jams, jellies, juices, and other products than it would be from selling the fresh fruit.

One thing is self-evident, and that is that a very high quality must be maintained. Not only must quality be high, but the container must be attractive, and there must be a distinctive label which the customer will remember.

A home-processing project of this type often develops because a homemaker has a particularly good recipe for some berry product, or at least is particularly successful in preparing the product from a standard recipe. It usually develops much as selling fruit from the home garden enterprise develops—that is, because there is a little more than the family can use. Perhaps in order to salvage fresh berries from a large crop an unusual amount is processed. Then the question arises as to whether someone would purchase a part of the pack, which apparently will not be needed by the family.

There is a distinct borderline between selling locally, based on advertising by word of mouth, and personal delivery, and selling through the regular trade channels. When one goes beyond local sales there are problems of advertising, packing, and shipping, and, of course, state and federal requirements governing food-processing plants. If we insist that processing plants be thoroughly inspected and made to conform to sanitary regulations, it is quite logical to assume that you will also need to meet those requirements if you are processing berries for general sale in your own kitchen. Actually specific sanitary requirements have been worked out for large-scale operations, and they involve equipment which the home-owner may be without, and which may be quite expensive to purchase for a small-scale operation.

OUTLETS FOR PROCESSED BERRIES. I have known of a few home-processing businesses that were eventually successful in finding commercial outlets for their products, in addition to local sales to individuals. A high-class grocery store, or a department store with a grocery division, offers better outlets for home-processed foods than the ordinary grocery or chain store, where volume is so important and where the source of supply is already established. This means that the product must be an excellent one, or there will be little chance of any profitable store outlet.

A roadside market provides a natural outlet for both home-grown fresh berries and berry products. Whether a successful market could be built up on berries alone will depend on local conditions. Most roadside markets have a varied line of fruits and vegetables, and possibly other horticultural products, in order to attract sufficient business. This may mean purchasing many of the items, in addition to the ones produced on the farm. If the market is strictly a berry outlet, then it will operate for only a short period, which will permit maximum sales over a minimum period. It would hardly be profitable to keep such a market open throughout the year to sell only home processed berry products, unless this operation becomes quite large. There are other profitable outlets of course, such as restaurants and tearooms, especially those that cater to tourists, or to a high-class trade, which may be able to move quite a lot of berry products during the year.

Most people who have gone into this field and are making extra money from berries, either from the sale of plants, or fruit, or processed berries, have developed their enterprise gradually, so that they have been able to learn as they go. Such projects do not always seem to follow the commonly accepted rules of economics, because of local conditions and the individuals' personal problems. The best advice, or the best directions to follow, are those developed on the basis of experience as you go along, and that also applies, in a very real sense, to the whole home garden program.

Index

Acidifying blueberry soil, 266
Aluminum sulfate, 266
Ammonium sulfate for acidification, 75, 266
Anthracnose, in dewberries, 246
  in raspberries, 229
Antibiotics, 126
Aphids, 137, 208, 260

Bacterial diseases, 116
Barrel sprayer, 129
Berries, as a 4-H project, 358
  in the home orchard, 160
  in the landscape, 160
  in the vegetable garden, 159
Berry, definition of a, 8
  plants in the lawn, 167
  products, selling, 361
Biennial canes of brambles, 221
Biological control of insects, 145
Birds, damage by, 150
  difficult to control, 150
Blackberries, 234
  varieties, 237
Black raspberries, 213, 225
Black root rot of strawberry, 148, 205
Black rot of grapes, 320
Black vine weevil, 286
Blanching berries, 342
Bleeding of late pruned grapes, 317
Bloom on blueberry fruits, 280
Blueberries, in the landscape, 163, 272
  in the wild, 263
  prefer ammonium, 266
  under alkaline conditions, 276
Blueberry, 263
  breeding, 330

canker, 284
diseases, 283
fertilizers, 275
for florists' greens, 264, 282
fruiting habits, 277
maggots, 287
nutritional requirements, 265
soils, 267
stunt, 283
varieties, 268
Blueberry-cranberry jam, 350
Borers on blueberry, 287
Botanical names, 9
Botrytis blight on blueberry, 286
Bottom heat for cuttings, 308
Bramble fruits, 8
  are aggressive, 165
  in the landscape, 165
Brown aphids, 322
Bud nematode, 206
Bud weevil, 207
Burning over lowbush blueberries, 282

Calcium and its effects, 73
Cane blight of currant, 260
Cane renewal pruning, 312
Cankers, 120
Canning berries, 349
Carbohydrate-nitrogen relationship, 67
Catalogs, critical reading of, 24
Cells and their functions, 62
Certified plants, 203, 355
Chelates, 74, 192, 276
Chemicals for disease control, 125, 128

Chemical sprays, safety of, 146
Chemical weed killers, 107, 218, 226
Chewing insects, 136
Chlorophyll and its functions, 63
Choice of parents for breeding, 336
Chromosomes, 332, 334
Climate, for berries, 10
    for blueberries, 267
    for grapes, 298
Clone, 156
Cold storage of strawberry plants,
    184
Cold weather as affecting berries, 14
Commercial areas, 10
Commercial production, xi, 354
Compatibility of spray materials, 133
Compressed air sprayer, 130
Concord grape, importance of, 298
Contact poisons for insects, 140
Containers for freezing, 343
Cover crops, 45
Coville, Dr. F. V., 264
Cranberries, 263, 289
    not adapted to garden use, 289
Cranberries magazine, xiii
Crosses, technique of making, 334
Crown borer on strawberry, 208
Crown gall, 230, 260
Cultivar, 152
Cultivation, 40, 42, 44, 101
    avoid in bearing strawberries, 196
Cultural methods, 40
Currant, borer, 261
    fruit fly, 262
    sawfly, 261
    varieties of, 251
Currants, 249
    method of picking, 258
Cuttings, rooting blueberry, 272
Cyclamen mites, 148, 209

Darrow, Dr. George, 265
Day length, 21

Deepening of the soil, 36
Deer, damage by, 154
Deficiences, detection of, 113
Deficiency symptoms, 71, 113
Defoliating grapes, effect of, 317
Depth of rooting, 23
Designing the small fruits garden,
    156
Dewberries, 234
    grown without staking, 245
Dewberry, types, 235
    varieties, 238
Dioecious grapes, 300
Disease, identification, 118
    resistance, 121
Diseases, of blackberries and dew-
        berries, 246
    of blueberries, 283
    of currants, 259
    of gooseberries, 259
    of grapes, 320
    of raspberries, 228
    of strawberries, 203
    of the fruit, 121
Diseases cause damage, how, 119
Disease, symptoms, 113
    transmission by insects, 137
Dominant characters, 333
Double blossom disease, 246
Downy mildew of grape, 321
Drainage, 34, 220
    methods, 95
Dryland blueberry, 282
Dusters, 131
Dust mulch, 43

Eastern grapes, 299
Elderberry, 291
    culture, 293
Emasculation of flowers, 334
Espaliers, 257
Estate sprayers, 129
European corn borer, 232, 261
European grapes, 298

Everbearing strawberries, 176, 180, 199
Evergreen blueberry, 282

Fence out the birds, 152
Fertilizer, injury, 88, 112
    materials, 80
Fertilizers, 42, 61, 76, 78, 192
    band application of, 192
    for blackberries, 242
    for blueberries, 275
    for currants, 254
    for gooseberries, 254
    for grapes, 319
    for raspberries, 219
    for strawberries, 192
    methods of applying, 84
Fertilizing, at planting time, 170
    in the fall, 190
Flooding cranberries, 289
Foliar feeding, 83
Fragaria
    chiloensis, 176
    virginiana, 176
Freezing, blackberries, 344
    blueberries, 344
    cabinet, home, 346
    raspberries, 344
    strawberries, 342
    with syrup, 344
Freshness, 3
Fresh vs. processed berries, 341
Frost, hazard to strawberries, 191
    pockets, 17
Frosts, 17, 21
Fruit, juices, 352
    rots, 205
    spurs, 254
Fruiting habit, of blueberries, 277
    of grapes, 310
    of raspberries, 221
Functions of various elements, 70
Fungicides, 128
Fungus diseases, 116

Galls on blueberry, 284
Gaultheria shallon, 295
Geese as weeders, 109
Genes, 332
Genetic research, 332
Gibberellin, 60
Girdling, 65
Gooseberries, 249
    method of picking, 258
    varieties of, 252
Grafting grapes, 309, 323
Grape arbors, 162, 307
Grape berry moth, 323
Grape leaf hoppers, 322
Grape prunings, weigh, 312
Grape varieties, 301
Grapes, 297
    in the landscape, 306
    under glass, 319
    with small fruits, 7

Hand sprayers, 129
Hardiness, ratings, 15, 16
    zone map, 15
Hardpan, 95
Hardy grape varieties, 301
Hardy strawberries, 195
Harmless and beneficial insects, 139
Harvesting, blueberries, 279
    currants, 257
    gooseberries, 258
    problems, 358
    raspberries, 227
    strawberries, 197
Heat as affecting berries, 12
Heath family, 9
Heaving of soil, 195
Highbush blueberry, 264
Highbush cranberry, 290
Hill system, for raspberries, 224
    for strawberries, 186
Home freezing, 341
Hormones and berry growing, 59, 172

Hose sprayer, 130
Hot water treatment for nematodes, 149
How to pick berries, 197
How to pick blueberries, 280
Huckleberry, 263

Implements for soil working, 44
Improved varieties, 157
Indexed plants, 201
Inheritance, complex in small fruits, 334
  theory of, 333
Injury, caused by frost, 115
  by poor drainage, 115
Insect attractants, 144
Insecticides, 140, 143
Insect, injury, types of, 137
  parasites, 145
  pests, of blackberries, 247
    of blueberries, 286
    of currants, 260
    of dewberries, 247
    of gooseberries, 260
    of grapes, 322
    of raspberries, 231
    of strawberries, 206
  preferences for plants, 138
  repellents, 144
  varietal preferences, 138
Insects, and their control, 135
  classified by mouth parts, 135
  types of, 136
Iron chlorosis, 276
Irrigation, 12, 86, 88, 190, 220, 254, 277
  methods, 90

Jams, 350
Japanese beetle, 207, 323
Japanese wine berry, 227
Jellies, 351
Jelly from frozen berries, 345
June-bearing strawberries, 176

Knapsack sprayer, 129
Kniffin system, 315
Krilium, 47

Labrusca grapes, 299
Landscape use, 6
Late growth to be avoided, 82
Layering grapes, 309
Leaching of sandy soils, 30
Leaf curl of raspberries, 229
Leaf hoppers on blueberry, 287
Leaf roller on strawberry, 210
Leaf scorch, 204
Leaf spot, of blueberry, 286
  of currants and gooseberries, 260
  of raspberry, 231
  of strawberry, 204
Leaves, as mulching material, 53
  function of, 63
Length of day affects strawberries, 177
Life of frozen berries, 348
Lime, 76
Lingonberry, 290
Loam soil, 27
Local sales, 360
Lowbush blueberry, 282

Matted row system, 184, 199
Mendel, 333
Mice, damage by, 154
Micro-organisms as affecting fertility, 42
Mildew on strawberry, 204
Minor elements, 73
Mites, 147
Mixed fertilizers, 78
Moles, damage by, 154
Mosaic of raspberries, 228
Mulching, 43, 47, 189, 241
  advantages of, 48
  and weed control, 190
  blueberries, 274
  disadvantages of, 55

for winter protection, 194
materials, 49, 52, 195
strawberries, 194
to keep strawberries clean, 195
Mulch, removal of, on strawberries, 195
Mummy berry, 284
Muscadine grapes, 300
Mutations of disease organisms, 122, 327

Nematodes, 148
on strawberries, 205
Nitrogen and its effects, 72
Nitrogen deficiency under mulch, 49
Nutritive values, 6

Old world grapes, 297
Orange rust, 246
Organic gardening, 77
Organic matter, 37, 77
Organic vs. inorganic fertilizers, 76
Osmosis, 88
Outlets for processed berries, 363
Over fertilizing, 70, 84

Paper mulch, 51
Peat soils, 42
Pectin for jellies, 351
Periclinal chimera, 236
Permanency of strawberry bed, 187
Phosphorus and its effects, 72
Photosynthesis, 63
Phylloxera, 322
Pickers, 359
Picking methods, raspberry, 228
Pick yourself, 359
Plant diseases, 111
growth, xii
Plant breeders and small fruits, 324
Plant breeding, as a hobby, 339
methods, 331
Planting, 43
blueberries, 274
distances, 158

grapes, 309
methods, 169
raspberries, 217
strawberries, 183
with a trowel, 170
Plant spacing, 184
Poison baits, 144
Pollination, 335
Pollinizers, for blueberries, 271, 281
for grapes, 300
Polyethylene mulch, 51, 102
Portable irrigation systems, 90
Potassium and its effects, 72
Potted strawberry plants, 355
Powdery mildew of grape, 321
Power sprayers, 128
Pre-emergent weed killers, 106
Private plant breeders, 337
Processing, 4, 341
Profit from berries, 354
Propagation, of blackberries, 240
of black raspberries, 225
of blueberries, 272
of currants, 252
of elderberries, 293
of gooseberries, 253
of grapes, 307
of raspberries, 217
of strawberries, 181
Pruning, 56
at planting time, 169, 218
blackberries, 242
black raspberries, 226
blueberries, 277
currants, 255
dewberries, 244
gooseberries, 256
grapes, 310
muscadine grapes, 316
red raspberries, 221
vinifera grapes, 316
Purple raspberries, 213, 226

Quick freezing, 347

Rabbiteye blueberry, 281
Rabbits, damage by, 154
Raspberries, in the garden, 211
    kinds of, 211
Raspberry, cane borer, 231
    crown borer, 232, 247
    diseases, 228
    insects, 231
    planting systems, 218
    varieties, 214
Recessive characters, 333
Red berry mite, 248
Red fruited blueberry, 283
Red mites, 147, 209, 233, 248
Red-necked cane borer, 231, 247
Red raspberries, 212
Red stele, 177, 203
Re-frozen fruit, 348
Renovation of strawberry beds, 198
Resistance, to DDT, 142
    to pests, 325
Rest period, 267
Retaining the old strawberry bed,
    187
Ribes nigrum, 250
Ridging of wet soil, 34
Roadside market, 363
Roguing, 124
Root aphids, 322
Root knot nematode, 206
Root pruning, 168
Root rots, 120, 231
Roots, functions of, 66
Rose family, 9
Rubus
    idaeus, 212
    occidentalis, 212
    phoenicolasius, 227
    strigosus, 212
Runners, handling the, 186
Running out of varieties, 177

Salal, 295
Sale of plants, 355

Salmonberry, 296
Salt hay mulch, 52
Sambucus
    canadensis, 291
    coerulea, 293
Sandy soil, 29
Sanitary practices, 111, 123, 139
Sawdust, and soil acidity, 49
    as a mulch, 49
Saxifrage family, 9
Scale insects, 137, 248
Scarecrows, 151
Scoops for lowbush blueberry, 282
Scott, Dr. Don, 265
Seedless grapes, 299
Selection, 336
Selective weed killers, 105
Self-sterility in elderberry, 294
Selling surplus fruit, 356
Senescense of bramble canes, 111
Sex in the strawberry, 176
Shading, 14
Shallow cultivation for blueberries,
    274
Shrub border, berries in the, 7
Side dressing with fertilizer, 193
Sites for berries, 18
Slugs, damage by, 154
Small fruits defined, 7
Smog damage, 114
Soil, acidity, 36, 74, 192, 265
    affected by rainfall, 75
    aeration, 41
    conditioners, 47
    fumigants, 150
    improvements, 26
    insects, insecticides for, 142
    management for grapes, 318
    management for raspberries, 218
    preparation, 166
    sterilants, 104
Soil-borne diseases, 126
Soils, for different kinds of berries,
    28, 252

for small fruits, 26
too alkaline, 36
too heavy, 32
too light, 29
too rich, 33
too wet, 34
Space for small fruits, 2
Spittle bug, 208
Spraying, equipment, 128
vs. dusting, 127
Spray materials, safety of, 146
Sprays, methods of application, 132
Spreaders and stickers, 133
Spring vs. fall planting, 167, 217
Sprinkling, to prevent frost, 19, 191
to prevent heat damage, 13
Spur blight, 230
Spur pruning, 312
Standard gooseberries, 257
Starter solutions, 172
Stems, functions of, 65
Sterility, 336
Stomach poisons for insects, 140
Strawberries, in the landscape, 164
in the South, 167
treatment of, after harvest, 198
Strawberry, barrel, 187
breeding, 328
culture, 174
fall vs. spring planting of, 181
origin of the, 176
planters, 189
rash, 175
varieties of, for various regions,
178
variety descriptions of the, 179
vitamins in the, 6
weevils, 207
Strawberry-sick soil, 201
Straw mulch, 52
Streak of raspberries, 229
Suckers, red raspberry, 217
Sucking insects, 136
Sugar for frozen berries, 343

Sulfur for acidification, 192, 266
Summer pruning grapes, 317
Sunburn, 114
Symphylids, 148
Synthetic insecticides, 142
Syrup pack for blueberries, 344
Systemic diseases, 124

Tetraploid plants, 154
Thinning, of blueberry fruit buds,
277
of fruit, 67
out raspberry canes, 223
Thornless blackberries, 236, 325
Time for pruning grapes, 317
Tip layers, 225, 236
Top dressing with fertilizer, 193
Toxic injections by insects, 137
Trailing blackberries, 234
Training plants, 59
Transpiration, 65
Trellises, for blackberries, 242
for dewberries, 244
for grapes, 307, 315
for raspberries, 223

Uncooked jam, 352
U-pick system, 359
Upright blackberries, 234

Vaccinium
angustifolium, 263
ashei, 264
australe, 264
corymbosum, 264
lamarckii, 263
macrocarpon, 290
membranaceum, 264
ovatum, 264
pallidum, 264
parvifolium, 283
pennsylvanicum, 263
quadripetalum, 290
virgatum, 264
vitis-idaea, 290

Varietal differences, 23
Variety, importance of, 23, 175
  improvement of, 324
Verticillium root rot, 204
Verticillium wilt, 230
Viburnum americanum, 290
Vine family, 9
Vinifera grapes, 298
Virus disease complex, 202
Viruses, 116, 119, 201, 203, 228, 246,
      284, 321
Virus-free strawberry plants, 201
Virus resistant varieties, 202
Vitamins in berries, 6
Vitis
  labrusca, 299
  rotundifolia, 300
  vinifera, 298

Water, absorption, 88
  availability, 88
  content of plants, 64
  function of, in the plant, 86
  how to apply, 92
  requirement, measuring, 90
  requirements, 22
  source of, 93

  table, high, for blueberries, 267
Weed control, 40, 96, 98
  by chemicals, 104
  by fire, 109
  by mulching, 102
Weed killers, application methods
      for, 108
  injury by, 112
Weeds, as cover crops, 47
  bad or harmless, 98
  effect of, 96
  effect of fertilizers on, 103
  hoeing, 100
  pulling, 99
Western blackberry hybrids, 237
When to fertilize, 81
When to pick, 198
Where to buy plants, 24
White grubs, 206
White pine blister rust, 259
White, Miss Elizabeth, 264
Wine grapes, 297
Winter protection of raspberries, 227
Wonderberry, 295

Yellow leaves on blueberries, 276
Yield per plant, 158

A CATALOGUE OF SELECTED DOVER BOOKS
IN ALL FIELDS OF INTEREST

A CATALOGUE OF SELECTED DOVER BOOKS
IN ALL FIELDS OF INTEREST

THE NOTEBOOKS OF LEONARDO DA VINCI, edited by J.P. Richter. Extracts from manuscripts reveal great genius; on painting, sculpture, anatomy, sciences, geography, etc. Both Italian and English. 186 ms. pages reproduced, plus 500 additional drawings, including studies for Last Supper, Sforza monument, etc. 860pp. 7⅞ x 10¾.   USO 22572-0, 22573-9 Pa., Two vol. set $15.90

ART NOUVEAU DESIGNS IN COLOR, Alphonse Mucha, Maurice Verneuil, Georges Auriol. Full-color reproduction of Combinaisons ornamentales (c. 1900) by Art Nouveau masters. Floral, animal, geometric, interlacings, swashes — borders, frames, spots — all incredibly beautiful. 60 plates, hundreds of designs. 9⅜ x 8¹/₁₆ .   22885-1 Pa. $4.00

GRAPHIC WORKS OF ODILON REDON. All great fantastic lithographs, etchings, engravings, drawings, 209 in all. Monsters, Huysmans, still life work, etc. Introduction by Alfred Werner. 209pp. 9⅛ x 12¼.   21996-8 Pa. $6.00

EXOTIC FLORAL PATTERNS IN COLOR, E.-A. Seguy. Incredibly beautiful full-color pochoir work by great French designer of 20's. Complete Bouquets et frondaisons, Suggestions pour étoffes. Richness must be seen to be believed. 40 plates containing 120 patterns. 80pp. 9⅜ x 12¼.   23041-4 Pa. $6.00

SELECTED ETCHINGS OF JAMES A. McN. WHISTLER, James A. McN. Whistler. 149 outstanding etchings by the great American artist, including selections from the Thames set and two Venice sets, the complete French set, and many individual prints. Introduction and explanatory note on each print by Maria Naylor. 157pp. 9⅜ x 12¼.   23194-1 Pa. $5.00

VISUAL ILLUSIONS: THEIR CAUSES, CHARACTERISTICS, AND APPLICATIONS, Matthew Luckiesh. Thorough description, discussion; shape and size, color, motion; natural illusion. Uses in art and industry. 100 illustrations. 252pp.
21530-X Pa. $3.00

TEN BOOKS ON ARCHITECTURE, Vitruvius. The most important book ever written on architecture. Early Roman aesthetics, technology, classical orders, site selection, all other aspects. Stands behind everything since. Morgan translation. 331pp.
20645-9 Pa. $3.75

THE CODEX NUTTALL. A PICTURE MANUSCRIPT FROM ANCIENT MEXICO, as first edited by Zelia Nuttall. Only inexpensive edition, in full color, of a pre-Columbian Mexican (Mixtec) book. 88 color plates show kings, gods, heroes, temples, sacrifices. New explanatory, historical introduction by Arthur G. Miller 96pp. 11⅜ x 8½.   23168-2 Pa. $7.50

VISUAL ILLUSIONS: THEIR CAUSES, CHARACTERISTICS, AND APPLICATIONS, Matthew Luckiesh. Thorough description and discussion of optical illusion, geometric and perspective, particularly; size and shape distortions, illusions of color, of motion; natural illusions; use of illusion in art and magic, industry, etc. Most useful today with op art, also for classical art. Scores of effects illustrated. Introduction by William H. Ittleson. 100 illustrations. xxi + 252pp.

21530-X Paperbound $2.50

A HANDBOOK OF ANATOMY FOR ART STUDENTS, Arthur Thomson. Thorough, virtually exhaustive coverage of skeletal structure, musculature, etc. Full text, supplemented by anatomical diagrams and drawings and by photographs of undraped figures. Unique in its comparison of male and female forms, pointing out differences of contour, texture, form. 211 figures, 40 drawings, 86 photographs. xx + 459pp. 5⅜ x 8⅜.

21163-0 Paperbound $5.00

150 MASTERPIECES OF DRAWING, Selected by Anthony Toney. Full page reproductions of drawings from the early 16th to the end of the 18th century, all beautifully reproduced: Rembrandt, Michelangelo, Dürer, Fragonard, Urs, Graf, Wouwerman, many others. First-rate browsing book, model book for artists. xviii + 150pp. 8⅜ x 11¼.

21032-4 Paperbound **$4.00**

THE LATER WORK OF AUBREY BEARDSLEY, Aubrey Beardsley. Exotic, erotic, ironic masterpieces in full maturity: Comedy Ballet, Venus and Tannhauser, Pierrot, Lysistrata, Rape of the Lock, Savoy material, Ali Baba, Volpone, etc. This material revolutionized the art world, and is still powerful, fresh, brilliant. With *The Early Work,* all Beardsley's finest work. 174 plates, 2 in color. xiv + 176pp. 8⅛ x 11.

21817-1 Paperbound **$4.00**

DRAWINGS OF REMBRANDT, Rembrandt van Rijn. Complete reproduction of fabulously rare edition by Lippmann and Hofstede de Groot, completely reedited, updated, improved by Prof. Seymour Slive, Fogg Museum. Portraits, Biblical sketches, landscapes, Oriental types, nudes, episodes from classical mythology—All Rembrandt's fertile genius. Also selection of drawings by his pupils and followers. "Stunning volumes," *Saturday Review.* 550 illustrations. lxxviii + 552pp. 9⅛ x 12¼.

21485-0, 21486-9 Two volumes, Paperbound $12.00

THE DISASTERS OF WAR, Francisco Goya. One of the masterpieces of Western civilization—83 etchings that record Goya's shattering, bitter reaction to the Napoleonic war that swept through Spain after the insurrection of 1808 and to war in general. Reprint of the first edition, with three additional plates from Boston's Museum of Fine Arts. All plates facsimile size. Introduction by Philip Hofer, Fogg Museum. v + 97pp. 9⅜ x 8¼.

21872-4 Paperbound **$3.00**

GRAPHIC WORKS OF ODILON REDON. Largest collection of Redon's graphic works ever assembled: 172 lithographs, 28 etchings and engravings, 9 drawings. These include some of his most famous works. All the plates from *Odilon Redon: oeuvre graphique complet,* plus additional plates. New introduction and caption translations by Alfred Werner. 209 illustrations. xxvii + 209pp. 9⅛ x 12¼.

21966-8 Paperbound **$6.00**

SLEEPING BEAUTY, illustrated by Arthur Rackham. Perhaps the fullest, most delightful version ever, told by C.S. Evans. Rackham's best work. 49 illustrations. 110pp. 7⅞ x 10¾. 22756-1 Pa. $2.00

THE WONDERFUL WIZARD OF OZ, L. Frank Baum. Facsimile in full color of America's finest children's classic. Introduction by Martin Gardner. 143 illustrations by W.W. Denslow. 267pp. 20691-2 Pa. $3.50

GOOPS AND HOW TO BE THEM, Gelett Burgess. Classic tongue-in-cheek masquerading as etiquette book. 87 verses, 170 cartoons as Goops demonstrate virtues of table manners, neatness, courtesy, more. 88pp. 6½ x 9¼. 22233-0 Pa. $2.00

THE BROWNIES, THEIR BOOK, Palmer Cox. Small as mice, cunning as foxes, exuberant, mischievous, Brownies go to zoo, toy shop, seashore, circus, more. 24 verse adventures. 266 illustrations. 144pp. 6⅝ x 9¼. 21265-3 Pa. $2.50

BILLY WHISKERS: THE AUTOBIOGRAPHY OF A GOAT, Frances Trego Montgomery. Escapades of that rambunctious goat. Favorite from turn of the century America. 24 illustrations. 259pp. 22345-0 Pa. $2.75

THE ROCKET BOOK, Peter Newell. Fritz, janitor's kid, sets off rocket in basement of apartment house; an ingenious hole punched through every page traces course of rocket. 22 duotone drawings, verses. 48pp. 6⅞ x 8⅜. 22044-3 Pa. $1.50

CUT AND COLOR PAPER MASKS, Michael Grater. Clowns, animals, funny faces ... simply color them in, cut them out, and put them together, and you have 9 paper masks to play with and enjoy. Complete instructions. Assembled masks shown in full color on the covers. 32pp. 8¼ x 11. 23171-2 Pa. $1.50

THE TALE OF PETER RABBIT, Beatrix Potter. The inimitable Peter's terrifying adventure in Mr. McGregor's garden, with all 27 wonderful, full-color Potter illustrations. 55pp. 4¼ x 5½. USO 22827-4 Pa. $1.00

THE TALE OF MRS. TIGGY-WINKLE, Beatrix Potter. Your child will love this story about a very special hedgehog and all 27 wonderful, full-color Potter illustrations. 57pp. 4¼ x 5½. USO 20546-0 Pa. $1.00

THE TALE OF BENJAMIN BUNNY, Beatrix Potter. Peter Rabbit's cousin coaxes him back into Mr. McGregor's garden for a whole new set of adventures. A favorite with children. All 27 full-color illustrations. 59pp. 4¼ x 5½. USO 21102-9 Pa. $1.00

THE MERRY ADVENTURES OF ROBIN HOOD, Howard Pyle. Facsimile of original (1883) edition, finest modern version of English outlaw's adventures. 23 illustrations by Pyle. 296pp. 6½ x 9¼. 22043-5 Pa. $4.00

TWO LITTLE SAVAGES, Ernest Thompson Seton. Adventures of two boys who lived as Indians; explaining Indian ways, woodlore, pioneer methods. 293 illustrations. 286pp. 20985-7 Pa. $3.50

EAST O' THE SUN AND WEST O' THE MOON, George W. Dasent. Considered the best of all translations of these Norwegian folk tales, this collection has been enjoyed by generations of children (and folklorists too). Includes True and Untrue, Why the Sea is Salt, East O' the Sun and West O' the Moon, Why the Bear is Stumpy-Tailed, Boots and the Troll, The Cock and the Hen, Rich Peter the Pedlar, and 52 more. The only edition with all 59 tales. 77 illustrations by Erik Werenskiold and Theodor Kittelsen. xv + 418pp. 22521-6 Paperbound **$4.00**

GOOPS AND HOW TO BE THEM, Gelett Burgess. Classic of tongue-in-cheek humor, masquerading as etiquette book. 87 verses, twice as many cartoons, show mischievous Goops as they demonstrate to children virtues of table manners, neatness, courtesy, etc. Favorite for generations. viii + 88pp. 6½ x 9¼.
22233-0 Paperbound **$2.00**

ALICE'S ADVENTURES UNDER GROUND, Lewis Carroll. The first version, quite different from the final *Alice in Wonderland,* printed out by Carroll himself with his own illustrations. Complete facsimile of the "million dollar" manuscript Carroll gave to Alice Liddell in 1864. Introduction by Martin Gardner. viii + 96pp. Title and dedication pages in color. 21482-6 Paperbound **$1.50**

THE BROWNIES, THEIR BOOK, Palmer Cox. Small as mice, cunning as foxes, exuberant and full of mischief, the Brownies go to the zoo, toy shop, seashore, circus, etc., in 24 verse adventures and 266 illustrations. Long a favorite, since their first appearance in St. Nicholas Magazine. xi + 144pp. 6⅝ x 9¼.
21265-3 Paperbound **$2.50**

SONGS OF CHILDHOOD, Walter De La Mare. Published (under the pseudonym Walter Ramal) when De La Mare was only 29, this charming collection has long been a favorite children's book. A facsimile of the first edition in paper, the 47 poems capture the simplicity of the nursery rhyme and the ballad, including such lyrics as I Met Eve, Tartary, The Silver Penny. vii + 106pp. (USO) 21972-0 Paperbound **$2.00**

THE COMPLETE NONSENSE OF EDWARD LEAR, Edward Lear. The finest 19th-century humorist-cartoonist in full: all nonsense limericks, zany alphabets, Owl and Pussycat, songs, nonsense botany, and more than 500 illustrations by Lear himself. Edited by Holbrook Jackson. xxix + 287pp. (USO) 20167-8 Paperbound **$3.00**

BILLY WHISKERS: THE AUTOBIOGRAPHY OF A GOAT, Frances Trego Montgomery. A favorite of children since the early 20th century, here are the escapades of that rambunctious, irresistible and mischievous goat—Billy Whiskers. Much in the spirit of *Peck's Bad Boy,* this is a book that children never tire of reading or hearing. All the original familiar illustrations by W. H. Fry are included: 6 color plates, 18 black and white drawings. 159pp. 22345-0 Paperbound **$2.75**

MOTHER GOOSE MELODIES. Faithful republication of the fabulously rare Munroe and Francis "copyright 1833" Boston edition—the most important Mother Goose collection, usually referred to as the "original." Familiar rhymes plus many rare ones, with wonderful old woodcut illustrations. Edited by E. F. Bleiler. 128pp. 4½ x 6⅜. 22577-1 Paperbound **$1.50**

HOUDINI ON MAGIC, Harold Houdini. Edited by Walter Gibson, Morris N. Young. How he escaped; exposés of fake spiritualists; instructions for eye-catching tricks; other fascinating material by and about greatest magician. 155 illustrations. 280pp. 20384-0 Pa. $2.75

HANDBOOK OF THE NUTRITIONAL CONTENTS OF FOOD, U.S. Dept. of Agriculture. Largest, most detailed source of food nutrition information ever prepared. Two mammoth tables: one measuring nutrients in 100 grams of edible portion; the other, in edible portion of 1 pound as purchased. Originally titled Composition of Foods. 190pp. 9 x 12. 21342-0 Pa. $4.00

COMPLETE GUIDE TO HOME CANNING, PRESERVING AND FREEZING, U.S. Dept. of Agriculture. Seven basic manuals with full instructions for jams and jellies; pickles and relishes; canning fruits, vegetables, meat; freezing anything. Really good recipes, exact instructions for optimal results. Save a fortune in food. 156 illustrations. 214pp. 6⅛ x 9¼. 22911-4 Pa. $2.50

THE BREAD TRAY, Louis P. De Gouy. Nearly every bread the cook could buy or make: bread sticks of Italy, fruit breads of Greece, glazed rolls of Vienna, everything from corn pone to croissants. Over 500 recipes altogether. including buns, rolls, muffins, scones, and more. 463pp. 23000-7 Pa. $4.00

CREATIVE HAMBURGER COOKERY, Louis P. De Gouy. 182 unusual recipes for casseroles, meat loaves and hamburgers that turn inexpensive ground meat into memorable main dishes: Arizona chili burgers, burger tamale pie, burger stew, burger corn loaf, burger wine loaf, and more. 120pp. 23001-5 Pa. $1.75

LONG ISLAND SEAFOOD COOKBOOK, J. George Frederick and Jean Joyce. Probably the best American seafood cookbook. Hundreds of recipes. 40 gourmet sauces, 123 recipes using oysters alone! All varieties of fish and seafood amply represented. 324pp. 22677-8 Pa. $3.50

THE EPICUREAN: A COMPLETE TREATISE OF ANALYTICAL AND PRACTICAL STUDIES IN THE CULINARY ART, Charles Ranhofer. Great modern classic. 3,500 recipes from master chef of Delmonico's, turn-of-the-century America's best restaurant. Also explained, many techniques known only to professional chefs. 775 illustrations. 1183pp. 6⅝ x 10. 22680-8 Clothbd. $22.50

THE AMERICAN WINE COOK BOOK, Ted Hatch. Over 700 recipes: old favorites livened up with wine plus many more: Czech fish soup, quince soup, sauce Perigueux, shrimp shortcake, filets Stroganoff, cordon bleu goulash, jambonneau, wine fruit cake, more. 314pp. 22796-0 Pa. $2.50

DELICIOUS VEGETARIAN COOKING, Ivan Baker. Close to 500 delicious and varied recipes: soups, main course dishes (pea, bean, lentil, cheese, vegetable, pasta, and egg dishes), savories, stews, whole-wheat breads and cakes, more. 168pp. USO 22834-7 Pa. $2.00

CREATIVE LITHOGRAPHY AND HOW TO DO IT, Grant Arnold. Lithography as art form: working directly on stone, transfer of drawings, lithotint, mezzotint, color printing; also metal plates. Detailed, thorough. 27 illustrations. 214pp.
21208-4 Pa. $3.50

DESIGN MOTIFS OF ANCIENT MEXICO, Jorge Enciso. Vigorous, powerful ceramic stamp impressions — Maya, Aztec, Toltec, Olmec. Serpents, gods, priests, dancers, etc. 153pp. 6⅛ x 9¼.
20084-1 Pa. $2.50

AMERICAN INDIAN DESIGN AND DECORATION, Leroy Appleton. Full text, plus more than 700 precise drawings of Inca, Maya, Aztec, Pueblo, Plains, NW Coast basketry, sculpture, painting, pottery, sand paintings, metal, etc. 4 plates in color. 279pp. 8⅜ x 11¼.
22704-9 Pa.$5.00

CHINESE LATTICE DESIGNS, Daniel S. Dye. Incredibly beautiful geometric designs: circles, voluted, simple dissections, etc. Inexhaustible source of ideas, motifs. 1239 illustrations. 469pp. 6⅛ x 9¼.
23096-1 Pa. $5.00

JAPANESE DESIGN MOTIFS, Matsuya Co. Mon, or heraldic designs. Over 4000 typical, beautiful designs: birds, animals, flowers, swords, fans, geometric; all beautifully stylized. 213pp. 11⅜ x 8¼.
22874-6 Pa. $5.00

PERSPECTIVE, Jan Vredeman de Vries. 73 perspective plates from 1604 edition; buildings, townscapes, stairways, fantastic scenes. Remarkable for beauty, surrealistic atmosphere; real eye-catchers. Introduction by Adolf Placzek. 74pp. 11⅜ x 8¼.
20186-4 Pa. $3.00

EARLY AMERICAN DESIGN MOTIFS, Suzanne E. Chapman. 497 motifs, designs, from painting on wood, ceramics, appliqué, glassware, samplers, metal work, etc. Florals, landscapes, birds and animals, geometrics, letters, etc. Inexhaustible. Enlarged edition. 138pp. 8⅜ x 11¼.
22985-8 Pa. $3.50
23084-8 Clothbd. $7.95

VICTORIAN STENCILS FOR DESIGN AND DECORATION, edited by E.V. Gillon, Jr. 113 wonderful ornate Victorian pieces from German sources; florals, geometrics; borders, corner pieces; bird motifs, etc. 64pp. 9⅜ x 12¼.
21995-X Pa. $3.00

ART NOUVEAU: AN ANTHOLOGY OF DESIGN AND ILLUSTRATION FROM THE STUDIO, edited by E.V. Gillon, Jr. Graphic arts: book jackets, posters, engravings, illustrations, decorations; Crane, Beardsley, Bradley and many others. Inexhaustible. 92pp. 8⅛ x 11.
22388-4 Pa. $2.50

ORIGINAL ART DECO DESIGNS, William Rowe. First-rate, highly imaginative modern Art Deco frames, borders, compositions, alphabets, florals, insectals, Wurlitzer-types, etc. Much finest modern Art Deco. 80 plates, 8 in color. 8⅜ x 11¼.
22567-4 Pa. $3.50

HANDBOOK OF DESIGNS AND DEVICES, Clarence P. Hornung. Over 1800 basic geometric designs based on circle, triangle, square, scroll, cross, etc. Largest such collection in existence. 261pp.
20125-2 Pa. $2.75

150 MASTERPIECES OF DRAWING, edited by Anthony Toney. 150 plates, early 15th century to end of 18th century; Rembrandt, Michelangelo, Dürer, Fragonard, Watteau, Wouwerman, many others. 150pp. 8⅜ x 11¼.   21032-4 Pa. $4.00

THE GOLDEN AGE OF THE POSTER, Hayward and Blanche Cirker. 70 extraordinary posters in full colors, from Maîtres de l'Affiche, Mucha, Lautrec, Bradley, Cheret, Beardsley, many others. 9⅜ x 12¼.   22753-7 Pa. $5.95

SIMPLICISSIMUS, selection, translations and text by Stanley Appelbaum. 180 satirical drawings, 16 in full color, from the famous German weekly magazine in the years 1896 to 1926. 24 artists included: Grosz, Kley, Pascin, Kubin, Kollwitz, plus Heine, Thöny, Bruno Paul, others. 172pp. 8½ x 12¼.   23098-8 Pa. $5.00
23099-6 Clothbd. $10.00

THE EARLY WORK OF AUBREY BEARDSLEY, Aubrey Beardsley. 157 plates, 2 in color: Manon Lescaut, Madame Bovary, Morte d'Arthur, Salome, other. Introduction by H. Marillier. 175pp. 8½ x 11.   21816-3 Pa. $4.00

THE LATER WORK OF AUBREY BEARDSLEY, Aubrey Beardsley. Exotic masterpieces of full maturity: Venus and Tannhäuser, Lysistrata, Rape of the Lock, Volpone, Savoy material, etc. 174 plates, 2 in color. 176pp. 8½ x 11.   21817-1 Pa. $4.50

DRAWINGS OF WILLIAM BLAKE, William Blake. 92 plates from Book of Job, Divine Comedy, Paradise Lost, visionary heads, mythological figures, Laocoön, etc. Selection, introduction, commentary by Sir Geoffrey Keynes. 178pp. 8½ x 11.   22303-5 Pa. $4.00

LONDON: A PILGRIMAGE, Gustave Doré, Blanchard Jerrold. Squalor, riches, misery, beauty of mid-Victorian metropolis; 55 wonderful plates, 125 other illustrations, full social, cultural text by Jerrold. 191pp. of text. 8⅛ x 11.
22306-X Pa. $6.00

THE COMPLETE WOODCUTS OF ALBRECHT DÜRER, edited by Dr. W. Kurth. 346 in all: Old Testament, St. Jerome, Passion, Life of Virgin, Apocalypse, many others. Introduction by Campbell Dodgson. 285pp. 8½ x 12¼.   21097-9 Pa. $6.00

THE DISASTERS OF WAR, Francisco Goya. 83 etchings record horrors of Napoleonic wars in Spain and war in general. Reprint of 1st edition, plus 3 additional plates. Introduction by Philip Hofer. 97pp. 9⅜ x 8¼.   21872-4 Pa. $3.50

ENGRAVINGS OF HOGARTH, William Hogarth. 101 of Hogarth's greatest works: Rake's Progress, Harlot's Progress, Illustrations for Hudibras, Midnight Modern Conversation, Before and After, Beer Street and Gin Lane, many more. Full commentary. 256pp. 11 x 14.   22479-1 Pa. $7.95

PRIMITIVE ART, Franz Boas. Great anthropologist on ceramics, textiles, wood, stone, metal, etc.; patterns, technology, symbols, styles. All areas, but fullest on Northwest Coast Indians. 350 illustrations. 378pp.   20025-6 Pa. $3.75

CONSTRUCTION OF AMERICAN FURNITURE TREASURES, Lester Margon. 344 detail drawings, complete text on constructing exact reproductions of 38 early American masterpieces: Hepplewhite sideboard, Duncan Phyfe drop-leaf table, mantel clock, gate-leg dining table, Pa. German cupboard, more. 38 plates. 54 photographs. 168pp. 8⅜ x 11¼. 23056-2 Pa. $4.00

JEWELRY MAKING AND DESIGN, Augustus F. Rose, Antonio Cirino. Professional secrets revealed in thorough, practical guide: tools, materials, processes; rings, brooches, chains, cast pieces, enamelling, setting stones, etc. Do not confuse with skimpy introductions: beginner can use, professional can learn from it. Over 200 illustrations. 306pp. 21750-7 Pa. $3.00

METALWORK AND ENAMELLING, Herbert Maryon. Generally coneeded best all-around book. Countless trade secrets: materials, tools, soldering, filigree, setting, inlay, niello, repoussé, casting, polishing, etc. For beginner or expert. Author was foremost British expert. 330 illustrations. 335pp. 22702-2 Pa. $4.00

WEAVING WITH FOOT-POWER LOOMS, Edward F. Worst. Setting up a loom, beginning to weave, constructing equipment, using dyes, more, plus over 285 drafts of traditional patterns including Colonial and Swedish weaves. More than 200 other figures. For beginning and advanced. 275pp. 8¾ x 6⅜. 23064-3 Pa. $4.50

WEAVING A NAVAJO BLANKET, Gladys A. Reichard. Foremost anthropologist studied under Navajo women, reveals every step in process from wool, dyeing, spinning, setting up loom, designing, weaving. Much history, symbolism. With this book you could make one yourself. 97 illustrations. 222pp. 22992-0 Pa. $3.00

NATURAL DYES AND HOME DYEING, Rita J. Adrosko. Use natural ingredients: bark, flowers, leaves, lichens, insects etc. Over 135 specific recipes from historical sources for cotton, wool, other fabrics. Genuine premodern handicrafts. 12 illustrations. 160pp. 22688-3 Pa. $2.00

DRIED FLOWERS, Sarah Whitlock and Martha Rankin. Concise, clear, practical guide to dehydration, glycerinizing, pressing plant material, and more. Covers use of silica gel. 12 drawings. Originally titled "New Techniques with Dried Flowers." 32pp. 21802-3 Pa. $1.00

THOMAS NAST: CARTOONS AND ILLUSTRATIONS, with text by Thomas Nast St. Hill. Father of American political cartooning. Cartoons that destroyed Tweed Ring; inflation, free love, church and state; original Republican elephant and Democratic donkey; Santa Claus; more. 117 illustrations. 146pp. 9 x 12.
22983-1 Pa. $4.00
23067-8 Clothbd. $8.50

FREDERIC REMINGTON: 173 DRAWINGS AND ILLUSTRATIONS. Most famous of the Western artists, most responsible for our myths about the American West in its untamed days. Complete reprinting of *Drawings of Frederic Remington* (1897), plus other selections. 4 additional drawings in color on covers. 140pp. 9 x 12.
20714-5 Pa. $5.00

THE FITZWILLIAM VIRGINAL BOOK, edited by J. Fuller Maitland, W.B. Squire. Famous early 17th century collection of keyboard music, 300 works by Morley, Byrd, Bull, Gibbons, etc. Modern notation. Total of 938pp. 8⅜ x 11.
ECE 21068-5, 21069-3 Pa., Two vol. set $15.00

COMPLETE STRING QUARTETS, Wolfgang A. Mozart. Breitkopf and Härtel edition. All 23 string quartets plus alternate slow movement to K156. Study score. 277pp. 9⅜ x 12¼.
22372-8 Pa. $6.00

COMPLETE SONG CYCLES, Franz Schubert. Complete piano, vocal music of Die Schöne Müllerin, Die Winterreise, Schwanengesang. Also Drinker English singing translations. Breitkopf and Härtel edition. 217pp. 9⅜ x 12¼.
22649-2 Pa. $5.00

THE COMPLETE PRELUDES AND ETUDES FOR PIANOFORTE SOLO, Alexander Scriabin. All the preludes and etudes including many perfectly spun miniatures. Edited by K.N. Igumnov and Y.I. Mil'shteyn. 250pp. 9 x 12.
22919-X Pa. $6.00

TRISTAN UND ISOLDE, Richard Wagner. Full orchestral score with complete instrumentation. Do not confuse with piano reduction. Commentary by Felix Mottl, great Wagnerian conductor and scholar. Study score. 655pp. 8⅛ x 11.
22915-7 Pa. $11.95

FAVORITE SONGS OF THE NINETIES, ed. Robert Fremont. Full reproduction, including covers, of 88 favorites: Ta-Ra-Ra-Boom-De-Aye, The Band Played On, Bird in a Gilded Cage, Under the Bamboo Tree, After the Ball, etc. 401pp. 9 x 12.
EBE 21536-9 Pa. $6.95

SOUSA'S GREAT MARCHES IN PIANO TRANSCRIPTION: ORIGINAL SHEET MUSIC OF 23 WORKS, John Philip Sousa. Selected by Lester S. Levy. Playing edition includes: The Stars and Stripes Forever, The Thunderer, The Gladiator, King Cotton, Washington Post, much more. 24 illustrations. 111pp. 9 x 12.
USO 23132-1 Pa. $3.50

CLASSIC PIANO RAGS, selected with an introduction by Rudi Blesh. Best ragtime music (1897-1922) by Scott Joplin, James Scott, Joseph F. Lamb, Tom Turpin, 9 others. Printed from best original sheet music, plus covers. 364pp. 9 x 12.
EBE 20469-3 Pa. $7.50

ANALYSIS OF CHINESE CHARACTERS, C.D. Wilder, J.H. Ingram. 1000 most important characters analyzed according to primitives, phonetics, historical development. Traditional method offers mnemonic aid to beginner, intermediate student of Chinese, Japanese. 365pp.
23045-7 Pa. $4.00

MODERN CHINESE: A BASIC COURSE, Faculty of Peking University. Self study, classroom course in modern Mandarin. Records contain phonetics, vocabulary, sentences, lessons. 249 page book contains all recorded text, translations, grammar, vocabulary, exercises. Best course on market. 3 12" 33⅓ monaural records, book, album.
98832-5 Set $12.50

MODERN CHESS STRATEGY, Ludek Pachman. The use of the queen, the active king, exchanges, pawn play, the center, weak squares, etc. Section on rook alone worth price of the book. Stress on the moderns. Often considered the most important book on strategy. 314pp. 20290-9 Pa. $3.50

CHESS STRATEGY, Edward Lasker. One of half-dozen great theoretical works in chess, shows principles of action above and beyond moves. Acclaimed by Capablanca, Keres, etc. 282pp. USO 20528-2 Pa. $3.00

CHESS PRAXIS, THE PRAXIS OF MY SYSTEM, Aron Nimzovich. Founder of hyper-modern chess explains his profound, influential theories that have dominated much of 20th century chess. 109 illustrative games. 369pp. 20296-8 Pa. $3.50

HOW TO PLAY THE CHESS OPENINGS, Eugene Znosko-Borovsky. Clear, profound examinations of just what each opening is intended to do and how opponent can counter. Many sample games, questions and answers. 147pp. 22795-2 Pa. $2.00

THE ART OF CHESS COMBINATION, Eugene Znosko-Borovsky. Modern explanation of principles, varieties, techniques and ideas behind them, illustrated with many examples from great players. 212pp. 20583-5 Pa. $2.50

COMBINATIONS: THE HEART OF CHESS, Irving Chernev. Step-by-step explanation of intricacies of combinative play. 356 combinations by Tarrasch, Botvinnik, Keres, Steinitz, Anderssen, Morphy, Marshall, Capablanca, others, all annotated. 245 pp. 21744-2 Pa. $3.00

HOW TO PLAY CHESS ENDINGS, Eugene Znosko-Borovsky. Thorough instruction manual by fine teacher analyzes each piece individually; many common endgame situations. Examines games by Steinitz, Alekhine, Lasker, others. Emphasis on understanding. 288pp. 21170-3 Pa. $2.75

MORPHY'S GAMES OF CHESS, Philip W. Sergeant. Romantic history, 54 games of greatest player of all time against Anderssen, Bird, Paulsen, Harrwitz; 52 games at odds; 52 blindfold; 100 consultation, informal, other games. Analyses by Anderssen, Steinitz, Morphy himself. 352pp. 20386-7 Pa. $4.00

500 MASTER GAMES OF CHESS, S. Tartakower, J. du Mont. Vast collection of great chess games from 1798-1938, with much material nowhere else readily available. Fully annotated, arranged by opening for easier study. 665pp. 23208-5 Pa. $6.00

THE SOVIET SCHOOL OF CHESS, Alexander Kotov and M. Yudovich. Authoritative work on modern Russian chess. History, conceptual background. 128 fully annotated games (most unavailable elsewhere) by Botvinnik, Keres, Smyslov, Tal, Petrosian, Spassky, more. 390pp. 20026-4 Pa. $3.95

WONDERS AND CURIOSITIES OF CHESS, Irving Chernev. A lifetime's accumulation of such wonders and curiosities as the longest won game, shortest game, chess problem with mate in 1220 moves, and much more unusual material — 356 items in all, over 160 complete games. 146 diagrams. 203pp. 23007-4 Pa. $3.50

THE ART DECO STYLE, ed. by Theodore Menten. Furniture, jewelry, metalwork, ceramics, fabrics, lighting fixtures, interior decors, exteriors, graphics from pure French sources. Best sampling around. Over 400 photographs. 183pp. 8⅜ x 11¼.
22824-X Pa. $4.00

THE GENTLEMAN AND CABINET MAKER'S DIRECTOR, Thomas Chippendale. Full reprint, 1762 style book, most influential of all time; chairs, tables, sofas, mirrors, cabinets, etc. 200 plates, plus 24 photographs of surviving pieces. 249pp. 9⅞ x 12¾.
21601-2 Pa. $6.00

PINE FURNITURE OF EARLY NEW ENGLAND, Russell H. Kettell. Basic book. Thorough historical text, plus 200 illustrations of boxes, highboys, candlesticks, desks, etc. 477pp. 7⅞ x 10¾.
20145-7 Clothbd. $12.50

ORIENTAL RUGS, ANTIQUE AND MODERN, Walter A. Hawley. Persia, Turkey, Caucasus, Central Asia, China, other traditions. Best general survey of all aspects: styles and periods, manufacture, uses, symbols and their interpretation, and identification. 96 illustrations, 11 in color. 320pp. 6⅛ x 9¼.
22366-3 Pa. $5.00

DECORATIVE ANTIQUE IRONWORK, Henry R. d'Allemagne. Photographs of 4500 iron artifacts from world's finest collection, Rouen. Hinges, locks, candelabra, weapons, lighting devices, clocks, tools, from Roman times to mid-19th century. Nothing else comparable to it. 420pp. 9 x 12.
22082-6 Pa. $8.50

THE COMPLETE BOOK OF DOLL MAKING AND COLLECTING, Catherine Christopher. Instructions, patterns for dozens of dolls, from rag doll on up to elaborate, historically accurate figures. Mould faces, sew clothing, make doll houses, etc. Also collecting information. Many illustrations. 288pp. 6 x 9. 22066-4 Pa. $3.00

ANTIQUE PAPER DOLLS: 1915-1920, edited by Arnold Arnold. 7 antique cut-out dolls and 24 costumes from 1915-1920, selected by Arnold Arnold from his collection of rare children's books and entertainments, all in full color. 32pp. 9¼ x 12¼.
23176-3 Pa. $2.00

ANTIQUE PAPER DOLLS: THE EDWARDIAN ERA, Epinal. Full-color reproductions of two historic series of paper dolls that show clothing styles in 1908 and at the beginning of the First World War. 8 two-sided, stand-up dolls and 32 complete, two-sided costumes. Full instructions for assembling included. 32pp. 9¼ x 12¼.
23175-5 Pa. $2.00

A HISTORY OF COSTUME, Carl Köhler, Emma von Sichardt. Egypt, Babylon, Greece up through 19th century Europe; based on surviving pieces, art works, etc. Full text and 595 illustrations, including many clear, measured patterns for reproducing historic costume. Practical. 464pp.
21030-8 Pa. $4.00

EARLY AMERICAN LOCOMOTIVES, John H. White, Jr. Finest locomotive engravings from late 19th century: historical (1804-1874), main-line (after 1870), special, foreign, etc. 147 plates. 200pp. 11⅜ x 8¼.
22772-3 Pa. $3.50

MANUAL OF THE TREES OF NORTH AMERICA, Charles S. Sargent. The basic survey of every native tree and tree-like shrub, 717 species in all. Extremely full descriptions, information on habitat, growth, locales, economics, etc. Necessary to every serious tree lover. Over 100 finding keys. 783 illustrations. Total of 986pp. 20277-1, 20278-X Pa., Two vol. set $9.00

BIRDS OF THE NEW YORK AREA, John Bull. Indispensable guide to more than 400 species within a hundred-mile radius of Manhattan. Information on range, status, breeding, migration, distribution trends, etc. Foreword by Roger Tory Peterson. 17 drawings; maps. 540pp. 23222-0 Pa. $6.00

THE SEA-BEACH AT EBB-TIDE, Augusta Foote Arnold. Identify hundreds of marine plants and animals: algae, seaweeds, squids, crabs, corals, etc. Descriptions cover food, life cycle, size, shape, habitat. Over 600 drawings. 490pp. 21949-6 Pa. $5.00

THE MOTH BOOK, William J. Holland. Identify more than 2,000 moths of North America. General information, precise species descriptions. 623 illustrations plus 48 color plates show almost all species, full size. 1968 edition. Still the basic book. Total of 551pp. 6½ x 9¼. 21948-8 Pa. $6.00

HOW INDIANS USE WILD PLANTS FOR FOOD, MEDICINE & CRAFTS, Frances Densmore. Smithsonian, Bureau of American Ethnology report presents wealth of material on nearly 200 plants used by Chippewas of Minnesota and Wisconsin. 33 plates plus 122pp. of text. 6⅛ x 9¼. 23019-8 Pa. $2.50

OLD NEW YORK IN EARLY PHOTOGRAPHS, edited by Mary Black. Your only chance to see New York City as it was 1853-1906, through 196 wonderful photographs from N.Y. Historical Society. Great Blizzard, Lincoln's funeral procession, great buildings. 228pp. 9 x 12. 22907-6 Pa. $6.95

THE AMERICAN REVOLUTION, A PICTURE SOURCEBOOK, John Grafton. Wonderful Bicentennial picture source, with 411 illustrations (contemporary and 19th century) showing battles, personalities, maps, events, flags, posters, soldier's life, ships, etc. all captioned and explained. A wonderful browsing book, supplement to other historical reading. 160pp. 9 x 12. 23226-3 Pa. $4.00

PERSONAL NARRATIVE OF A PILGRIMAGE TO AL-MADINAH AND MECCAH, Richard Burton. Great travel classic by remarkably colorful personality. Burton, disguised as a Moroccan, visited sacred shrines of Islam, narrowly escaping death. Wonderful observations of Islamic life, customs, personalities. 47 illustrations. Total of 959pp. 21217-3, 21218-1 Pa., Two vol. set $10.00

INCIDENTS OF TRAVEL IN CENTRAL AMERICA, CHIAPAS, AND YUCATAN, John L. Stephens. Almost single-handed discovery of Maya culture; exploration of ruined cities, monuments, temples; customs of Indians. 115 drawings. 892pp. 22404-X, 22405-8 Pa., Two vol. set $9.00

AUSTRIAN COOKING AND BAKING, Gretel Beer. Authentic thick soups, wiener schnitzel, veal goulash, more, plus dumplings, puff pastries, nut cakes, sacher tortes, other great Austrian desserts. 224pp. USO 23220-4 Pa. $2.50

CHEESES OF THE WORLD, U.S.D.A. Dictionary of cheeses containing descriptions of over 400 varieties of cheese from common Cheddar to exotic Surati. Up to two pages are given to important cheeses like Camembert, Cottage, Edam, etc. 151pp. 22831-2 Pa. $1.50

TRITTON'S GUIDE TO BETTER WINE AND BEER MAKING FOR BEGINNERS, S.M. Tritton. All you need to know to make family-sized quantities of over 100 types of grape, fruit, herb, vegetable wines; plus beers, mead, cider, more. 11 illustrations. 157pp. USO 22528-3 Pa. $2.25

DECORATIVE LABELS FOR HOME CANNING, PRESERVING, AND OTHER HOUSEHOLD AND GIFT USES, Theodore Menten. 128 gummed, perforated labels, beautifully printed in 2 colors. 12 versions in traditional, Art Nouveau, Art Deco styles. Adhere to metal, glass, wood, most plastics. 24pp. 8¼ x 11. 23219-0 Pa. $2.00

FIVE ACRES AND INDEPENDENCE, Maurice G. Kains. Great back-to-the-land classic explains basics of self-sufficient farming: economics, plants, crops, animals, orchards, soils, land selection, host of other necessary things. Do not confuse with skimpy faddist literature; Kains was one of America's greatest agriculturalists. 95 illustrations. 397pp. 20974-1 Pa. $3.00

GROWING VEGETABLES IN THE HOME GARDEN, U.S. Dept. of Agriculture. Basic information on site, soil conditions, selection of vegetables, planting, cultivation, gathering. Up-to-date, concise, authoritative. Covers 60 vegetables. 30 illustrations. 123pp. 23167-4 Pa. $1.35

FRUITS FOR THE HOME GARDEN, Dr. U.P. Hedrick. A chapter covering each type of garden fruit, advice on plant care, soils, grafting, pruning, sprays, transplanting, and much more! Very full. 53 illustrations. 175pp. 22944-0 Pa. $2.50

GARDENING ON SANDY SOIL IN NORTH TEMPERATE AREAS, Christine Kelway. Is your soil too light, too sandy? Improve your soil, select plants that survive under such conditions. Both vegetables and flowers. 42 photos. 148pp. USO 23199-2 Pa. $2.50

THE FRAGRANT GARDEN: A BOOK ABOUT SWEET SCENTED FLOWERS AND LEAVES, Louise Beebe Wilder. Fullest, best book on growing plants for their fragrances. Descriptions of hundreds of plants, both well-known and overlooked. 407pp. 23071-6 Pa. **$4.00**

EASY GARDENING WITH DROUGHT-RESISTANT PLANTS, Arno and Irene Nehrling. Authoritative guide to gardening with plants that require a minimum of water: seashore, desert, and rock gardens; house plants; annuals and perennials; much more. 190 illustrations. 320pp. 23230-1 Pa. $3.50

THE RED FAIRY BOOK, Andrew Lang. Lang's color fairy books have long been children's favorites. This volume includes Rapunzel, Jack and the Bean-stalk and 35 other stories, familiar and unfamiliar. 4 plates, 93 illustrations x + 367pp.
21673-X Paperbound $3.00

THE BLUE FAIRY BOOK, Andrew Lang. Lang's tales come from all countries and all times. Here are 37 tales from Grimm, the Arabian Nights, Greek Mythology, and other fascinating sources. 8 plates, 130 illustrations. xi + 390pp.
21437-0 Paperbound $3.50

HOUSEHOLD STORIES BY THE BROTHERS GRIMM. Classic English-language edition of the well-known tales — Rumpelstiltskin, Snow White, Hansel and Gretel, The Twelve Brothers, Faithful John, Rapunzel, Tom Thumb (52 stories in all). Translated into simple, straightforward English by Lucy Crane. Ornamented with headpieces, vignettes, elaborate decorative initials and a dozen full-page illustrations by Walter Crane. x + 269pp.
21080-4 Paperbound $3.00

THE MERRY ADVENTURES OF ROBIN HOOD, Howard Pyle. The finest modern versions of the traditional ballads and tales about the great English outlaw. Howard Pyle's complete prose version, with every word, every illustration of the first edition. Do not confuse this facsimile of the original (1883) with modern editions that change text or illustrations. 23 plates plus many page decorations. xxii + 296pp.
22043-5 Paperbound $4.00

THE STORY OF KING ARTHUR AND HIS KNIGHTS, Howard Pyle. The finest children's version of the life of King Arthur; brilliantly retold by Pyle, with 48 of his most imaginative illustrations. xviii + 313pp. 6⅛ x 9¼.
21445-1 Paperbound $3.50

THE WONDERFUL WIZARD OF OZ, L. Frank Baum. America's finest children's book in facsimile of first edition with all Denslow illustrations in full color. The edition a child should have. Introduction by Martin Gardner. 23 color plates, scores of drawings. iv + 267pp.
20691-2 Paperbound $3.00

THE MARVELOUS LAND OF OZ, L. Frank Baum. The second Oz book, every bit as imaginative as the Wizard. The hero is a boy named Tip, but the Scarecrow and the Tin Woodman are back, as is the Oz magic. 16 color plates, 120 drawings by John R. Neill. 287pp.
20692-0 Paperbound $3.00

THE MAGICAL MONARCH OF MO, L. Frank Baum. Remarkable adventures in a land even stranger than Oz. The best of Baum's books not in the Oz series. 15 color plates and dozens of drawings by Frank Verbeck. xviii + 237pp.
21892-9 Paperbound $2.95

THE BAD CHILD'S BOOK OF BEASTS, MORE BEASTS FOR WORSE CHILDREN, A MORAL ALPHABET, Hilaire Belloc. Three complete humor classics in one volume. Be kind to the frog, and do not call him names . . . and 28 other whimsical animals. Familiar favorites and some not so well known. Illustrated by Basil Blackwell. 156pp.
(USO) 20749-8 Paperbound $2.00

JEWISH GREETING CARDS, Ed Sibbett, Jr. 16 cards to cut and color. Three say "Happy Chanukah," one "Happy New Year," others have no message, show stars of David, Torahs, wine cups, other traditional themes. 16 envelopes. 8¼ x 11.
23225-5 Pa. $2.00

AUBREY BEARDSLEY GREETING CARD BOOK, Aubrey Beardsley. Edited by Theodore Menten. 16 elegant yet inexpensive greeting cards let you combine your own sentiments with subtle Art Nouveau lines. 16 different Aubrey Beardsley designs that you can color or not, as you wish. 16 envelopes. 64pp. 8¼ x 11.
23173-9 Pa. $2.00

RECREATIONS IN THE THEORY OF NUMBERS, Albert Beiler. Number theory, an inexhaustible source of puzzles, recreations, for beginners and advanced. Divisors, perfect numbers. scales of notation, etc. 349pp. 21096-0 Pa. $4.00

AMUSEMENTS IN MATHEMATICS, Henry E. Dudeney. One of largest puzzle collections, based on algebra, arithmetic, permutations, probability, plane figure dissection, properties of numbers, by one of world's foremost puzzlists. Solutions. 450 illustrations. 258pp. 20473-1 Pa. $3.00

MATHEMATICS, MAGIC AND MYSTERY, Martin Gardner. Puzzle editor for Scientific American explains math behind: card tricks, stage mind reading, coin and match tricks, counting out games, geometric dissections. Probability, sets, theory of numbers, clearly explained. Plus more than 400 tricks, guaranteed to work. 135 illustrations. 176pp. 20335-2 Pa. $2.00

BEST MATHEMATICAL PUZZLES OF SAM LOYD, edited by Martin Gardner. Bizarre, original, whimsical puzzles by America's greatest puzzler. From fabulously rare Cyclopedia, including famous 14-15 puzzles, the Horse of a Different Color, 115 more. Elementary math. 150 illustrations. 167pp. 20498-7 Pa. $2.50

MATHEMATICAL PUZZLES FOR BEGINNERS AND ENTHUSIASTS, Geoffrey Mott-Smith. 189 puzzles from easy to difficult involving arithmetic, logic, algebra, properties of digits, probability. Explanation of math behind puzzles. 135 illustrations. 248pp. 20198-8 Pa. $2.75

BIG BOOK OF MAZES AND LABYRINTHS, Walter Shepherd. Classical, solid, and ripple mazes; short path and avoidance labyrinths; more — 50 mazes and labyrinths in all. 12 other figures. Full solutions. 112pp. 8⅛ x 11. 22951-3 Pa. $2.00

COIN GAMES AND PUZZLES, Maxey Brooke. 60 puzzles, games and stunts — from Japan, Korea, Africa and the ancient world, by Dudeney and the other great puzzlers, as well as Maxey Brooke's own creations. Full solutions. 67 illustrations. 94pp. 22893-2 Pa. $1.50

HAND SHADOWS TO BE THROWN UPON THE WALL, Henry Bursill. Wonderful Victorian novelty tells how to make flying birds, dog, goose, deer, and 14 others. 32pp. 6½ x 9¼. 21779-5 Pa. $1.25

EGYPTIAN MAGIC, E.A. Wallis Budge. Foremost Egyptologist, curator at British Museum, on charms, curses, amulets, doll magic, transformations, control of demons, deific appearances, feats of great magicians. Many texts cited. 19 illustrations. 234pp. USO 22681-6 Pa. $2.50

THE LEYDEN PAPYRUS: AN EGYPTIAN MAGICAL BOOK, edited by F. Ll. Griffith, Herbert Thompson. Egyptian sorcerer's manual contains scores of spells: sex magic of various sorts, occult information, evoking visions, removing evil magic, etc. Transliteration faces translation. 207pp. 22994-7 Pa. $2.50

THE MALLEUS MALEFICARUM OF KRAMER AND SPRENGER, translated, edited by Montague Summers. Full text of most important witchhunter's "Bible," used by both Catholics and Protestants. Theory of witches, manifestations, remedies, etc. Indispensable to serious student. 278pp. 6⅝ x 10. USO 22802-9 Pa. $3.95

LOST CONTINENTS, L. Sprague de Camp. Great science-fiction author, finest, fullest study: Atlantis, Lemuria, Mu, Hyperborea, etc. Lost Tribes, Irish in pre-Columbian America, root races; in history, literature, art, occultism. Necessary to everyone concerned with theme. 17 illustrations. 348pp. 22668-9 Pa. $3.50

THE COMPLETE BOOKS OF CHARLES FORT, Charles Fort. Book of the Damned, Lo!, Wild Talents, New Lands. Greatest compilation of data: celestial appearances, flying saucers, falls of frogs, strange disappearances, inexplicable data not recognized by science. Inexhaustible, painstakingly documented. Do not confuse with modern charlatanry. Introduction by Damon Knight. Total of 1126pp.
23094-5 Clothbd. $15.00

FADS AND FALLACIES IN THE NAME OF SCIENCE, Martin Gardner. Fair, witty appraisal of cranks and quacks of science: Atlantis, Lemuria, flat earth, Velikovsky, orgone energy, Bridey Murphy, medical fads, etc. 373pp. 20394-8 Pa. $3.50

HOAXES, Curtis D. MacDougall. Unbelievably rich account of great hoaxes: Locke's moon hoax, Shakespearean forgeries, Loch Ness monster, Disumbrationist school of art, dozens more; also psychology of hoaxing. 54 illustrations. 338pp. 20465-0 Pa. $3.50

THE GENTLE ART OF MAKING ENEMIES, James A.M. Whistler. Greatest wit of his day deflates Wilde, Ruskin, Swinburne; strikes back at inane critics, exhibitions. Highly readable classic of impressionist revolution by great painter. Introduction by Alfred Werner. 334pp. 21875-9 Pa. $4.00

THE BOOK OF TEA, Kakuzo Okakura. Minor classic of the Orient: entertaining, charming explanation, interpretation of traditional Japanese culture in terms of tea ceremony. Edited by E.F. Bleiler. Total of 94pp. 20070-1 Pa. $1.25

Prices subject to change without notice.
Available at your book dealer or write for free catalogue to Dept. GI, Dover Publications, Inc., 180 Varick St., N.Y., N.Y. 10014. Dover publishes more than 150 books each year on science, elementary and advanced mathematics, biology, music, art, literary history, social sciences and other areas.